This Life

ALSO BY MARTIN HÄGGLUND

Dying for Time: Proust, Woolf, Nabokov

Radical Atheism: Derrida and the Time of Life

Kronofobi: Essäer om tid och ändlighet

This Life

This Life

Why Mortality Makes Us Free

MARTIN HÄGGLUND

PROFILE BOOKS

First published in Great Britain in 2019 by
Profile Books Ltd
3 Holford Yard
Bevin Way
London
WC1X 9HD

www.profilebooks.com

First published in the United States of America in 2019 by
Pantheon Books, a division of Penguin Random House LLC

A portion of chapter 2 first appeared, in slightly different form, as 'Knausgaard's
Secular Confession' in *boundary 2* (*www.boundary2.org*) on 23 August, 2017

1 3 5 7 9 10 8 6 4 2

Printed and bound in Great Britain by
Clays Ltd, Elcograf S.p.A.

A CIP catalogue record for this book is available from the British Library.

ISBN 978 1 78816 300 2
Export edn 978 1 78816 386 6
eISBN 978 1 78283 579 0

For my friend
Niklas Brismar Pålsson
with whom all time is free time

If I were in heaven, Nelly, I should be extremely miserable. . . . I dreamt, once, that I was there. . . . Heaven did not seem to be my home; and I broke my heart with weeping to come back to earth; and the angels were so angry that they flung me out, into the middle of the heath on the top of Wuthering Heights, where I woke sobbing for joy.

—EMILY BRONTË, *Wuthering Heights*

Contents

This Life

Introduction

My family comes from northern Sweden. The house where my mother was born, and where I have spent every summer of my life, is on the Baltic Sea. The dramatic landscape—with its sweeping forests, ragged mountains, and tall cliff formations looming over the sea—is carved out by the descent of the ice from the last glacial period, twelve thousand years ago. The land is still rising, the retreat of the glaciers allowing further parts of the landscape to emerge. What used to be the sandy bottom of the sea when my mother was a child is now part of our garden. The rocks under my feet are a reminder of the geological time in which we are but a speck. Being there, the brevity of my life is made salient by the forms of time to which I am recalled. As I step into the house where my grandmother lives, I can see our family tree on the wall—fragile lines of farmers and rural workers reaching back into the sixteenth century. As I climb the mountains that rise out of the ocean, I can see the scale of glacial time, still forming the landscape in which we find ourselves.

To return to my family house is to be reminded of how my life is dependent on history: both the natural history of evolution and the social history of those who came before me. Who I can be and what I can do is not generated solely by me. My life is dependent on previous generations and on those who took care of me, with all of us in turn dependent on a history of the Earth that so easily could have been different and that might never have brought any of us into being.

Moreover, my life is historical in the sense that it is oriented toward a future that is not given. The worlds of which I am a part, the projects I sustain and that sustain me, can flourish and change in a dynamic way, but they can also break apart, atrophy, and die. The worlds that open up through my family and friends, the projects that shape my work and political commitments, carry the promise of my life but also the risk that my life will be shattered or fail to make sense. In a word, both my life and the projects in which I am engaged are *finite*.

To be finite means primarily two things: to be dependent on others and to live in relation to death. I am finite because I cannot maintain my life on my own and because I will die. Likewise, the projects to which I am devoted are finite because they live only through the efforts of those who are committed to them and will cease to be if they are abandoned.

The thought of my own death, and the death of everything I love, is utterly painful. I do not want to die, since I want to sustain my life and the life of what I love. At the same time, I do not want my life to be eternal. An eternal life is not only unattainable but also undesirable, since it would eliminate the care and passion that animate my life. This problem can be traced even within religious traditions that espouse faith in eternal life. An article in *U.S. Catholic* asks: "Heaven: Will It be Boring?" The article answers no, for in heaven souls are called "not to eternal rest but to eternal activity—eternal social concern."[1] Yet this answer only underlines the problem, since there is nothing to be concerned *about* in heaven. Concern presupposes that something *can* go wrong or *can* be lost; otherwise we would not care. An eternal activity—just as much as an eternal rest—is of concern to no one, since it cannot be stopped and does not have to be maintained by anyone. The problem is not that an eternal activity would be "boring" but that it would not be intelligible as my activity. Any activity of mine (including a boring activity) requires that I sustain it. In an eternal activity, there cannot be a person who is bored—or involved in any other way—since an eternal activity does not depend on being sustained by anyone.

Far from making my life meaningful, eternity would make it meaningless, since my actions would have no purpose. What I do and what I love can matter to me only because I understand myself as mortal. The understanding of myself as mortal does not have to be explicit and theoretical but is implicit in all my practical commitments and priorities. The question of what I ought to do with my life—a question that is at issue in everything I do—presupposes that I understand my time to be finite. For the question of how I should lead my life to be intelligible *as* a question, I have to believe that I will die. If I believed that my life would last forever, I could never take my life to be at stake and I would never be seized by the need to do anything with my time. I would not even be able to understand what it means to do something sooner rather than later in my life, since I would have no sense of a finite lifetime that gives urgency to any project or activity.

The sense of my own irreplaceable life, then, is inseparable from my sense that it will end. When I return to the same landscape every summer, part of what makes it so poignant is that I may never see it again. Moreover, I care for the preservation of the landscape because I am aware that even the duration of the natural environment is not guaranteed. Likewise, my devotion to the ones I love is inseparable from the sense that they cannot be taken for granted. My time with family and friends is precious because we have to make the most of it. Our time together is illuminated by the sense that it will not last forever and we need to take care of one another because our lives are fragile.

The sense of finitude—the sense of the ultimate fragility of everything we care about—is at the heart of what I call *secular faith*. To have secular faith is to be devoted to a life that will end, to be dedicated to projects that can fail or break down. Ranging from the concrete (how we approach funerals) to the general (what makes a life worth living), I will show how secular faith expresses itself in the ways we mourn our loved ones, make commitments, and care about a sustainable world. I call it *secular* faith because it is devoted to a form of life that is bounded by time. In accordance with the meaning of the Latin word *saecularis,* to have secular faith is to be dedicated to persons or projects that are *worldly* and *temporal*. Secular faith is the form of faith that we all sustain in caring for someone or something that is vulnerable to loss. We all care—for ourselves, for others, for the world in which we find ourselves—and care is inseparable from the risk of loss.

In contrast, the common denominator for what I call *religious* forms of faith is a devaluation of our finite lives as a lower form of being. All world religions (Hinduism, Buddhism, Judaism, Islam, and Christianity) hold that the highest form of existence or the most desirable form of life is eternal rather than finite. To be religious—or to adopt a religious perspective on life—is to regard our finitude as a lack, an illusion, or a fallen state of being. Moreover, such a religious perspective on life is not limited to institutionalized religion or to actual believers. Even many people who do not have religious faith still subscribe to the idea that our finitude is a restriction and that we suffer from a lack of eternal life.

From a religious perspective, our finitude is seen as a lamentable condition that ideally should be overcome. This is the premise with which I take issue. I seek to show that any life worth living must be finite and requires secular faith.

Secular faith is committed to persons and projects that may be lost: to make them *live on* for the future. Far from being resigned to death, a secular faith seeks to postpone death and improve the conditions of life. As we will see, living on should not be conflated with eternity. The commitment to living on does not express an aspiration to live forever but *to live longer* and *to live better,* not to overcome death but to extend the duration and improve the quality of a form of life.

The commitment to living on bears the sense of finitude within itself. However long the movement of living on may last—and however much the quality of living on may be improved—it can always end. Even when we fight for an ideal that extends far beyond our own lives—a political vision for the future, a sustainable legacy for generations to come—we are devoted to a form of life that may cease to be or never come to be. This sense of finitude is intrinsic to why it matters that anyone or anything lives on. If we seek to engender, prolong, or enhance the existence of something—to make it live on in a better way—we are animated by the sense that *it may be lost* if we fail to act. Without this risk of loss, our efforts and our fidelity to the project would not be required.

To have secular faith is to acknowledge that the object of our faith is *dependent* on the practice of faith. I call it secular *faith*, since the object of devotion does not exist independently of those who believe in its importance and who keep it alive through their fidelity. The object of secular faith—e.g., the life we are trying to lead, the institutions we are trying to build, the community we are trying to achieve—is *inseparable* from what we do and how we do it. Through the practice of secular faith, we bind ourselves to a normative ideal (a conception of who we ought to be as individuals and as a community). The ideal itself, however, depends on how we keep faith with our commitment and remains open to being challenged, transformed, or overturned. The object of religious faith, by contrast, is taken to be *independent* of the fidelity of finite beings. The object of religious faith—whether God or any other form of infinite being—is ultimately regarded as *separable* from the practice of faith, since it does not depend on any form of finite life.

The most fundamental example of finitude in our historical moment is the prospect that the Earth itself will be destroyed. If the Earth were destroyed, all life forms that matter to us would be extinguished. No one would live on and no aspect of our lives would be remembered.

Yet, from the standpoint of religious faith, such an end of life is only apparent. Even if all forms of living on are terminated, nothing essential is lost, since the essential is eternal rather than finite.

As William James observes in the conclusion to his classic work *The Varieties of Religious Experience*, the subordination of the finite to the eternal is the common denominator both for orthodox religions and for all forms of religious mysticism. "This world may indeed, as science assures us, some day burn up or freeze," James writes, but for those with religious faith "God's existence is the guarantee of an ideal order that shall be permanently preserved."[2] Accordingly, from a religious point of view, the end of the world is ultimately not a tragedy. On the contrary, many religious doctrines and religious visions look forward to the end of the world as the moment of salvation. This moment can either be imagined as the collective end of humankind when damnation and salvation are decided (as in Judaism, Christianity, and Islam) or as the end of an individual through absorption into a timeless state of being (as in Hinduism and Buddhism). In either case, our lives as finite beings are not seen as ends in themselves but rather as a means to reach the end of human history.

For the same reason, climate change and the possible destruction of the Earth cannot be seen as an *existential* threat from the standpoint of religious faith. To grasp the existential threat to yourself and to future generations, you have to believe not only that life is finite but also that everything valuable—everything that matters—depends on finite life. This is exactly what religious faith denies. If you have religious faith, you believe that all finite life can be terminated and yet what is truly valuable will still remain.

The Dalai Lama summed it up perfectly when asked how a Buddhist—for whom the finite world is an illusion and who seeks to be detached from everything that passes away—can be worried about our current ecological crisis. "A Buddhist would say it doesn't matter," the Dalai Lama replied.[3] This may seem surprising, since Buddhist ethics famously advocates a peaceful relation to nature and all living beings. Yet Buddhist ethics is not motivated by a concern for nature or living beings as ends in themselves. Rather, the motivation is to be released from karma, with the aim of being released from life altogether and helping others to reach the same end. The goal of Buddhism is not for anyone to live on—or for the Earth itself to live on—but to attain the state of nirvana, where nothing matters.

The Buddhist perspective is not an exception, but makes explicit what is implicit in any religious commitment to eternity. If you are aiming for eternal life, finite life does not matter *for its own sake* but serves as a vehicle to attain salvation.

Of course, even if you identify as religious you can still care intensely for the fate of our life on Earth. My point, however, is that if you care for our form of life *as an end in itself,* you are acting on the basis of secular faith, even if you claim to be religious. Religious faith can entail obedience to moral norms, but it cannot recognize that the ultimate purpose of what we do—the ultimate reason it matters how we treat one another and the Earth—is *our fragile life together.* From a religious perspective, the ultimate purpose of what we do is to serve God or attain salvation, rather than to care for our shared lives and the future generations for which we are responsible. As soon as we acknowledge that our finite lives—and the generations that may carry on our finite legacy—are ends in themselves, we make explicit that our faith is secular rather than religious.

Hence, our ecological crisis can be taken seriously only from the standpoint of secular faith. Only a secular faith can be committed to the flourishing of finite life—sustainable forms of life on Earth—as an end in itself. If the Earth itself is an object of care in our time of ecological crisis, it is because we have come to believe that it is a resource that can be exhausted, an ecosystem that can be damaged and destroyed. Whether we care about the Earth for its own sake or for the sake of species that depend on it, the awareness of its precarious existence is an intrinsic part of why we care about it. This is not to say that we care about the Earth *only* because it can be lost. If we care about the Earth it is rather because of the positive qualities we ascribe to it. However, an intrinsic part of why we care about the positive qualities of the Earth is that we believe they *can* be lost, either for us or in themselves.

The same holds for the ways in which we care about our own lives, the lives of those we love, or those for whom we are responsible. Caring about someone or something requires that we believe in its value, but it also requires that we believe that what is valued can cease to be. In order to care, we have to believe in the future not only as a chance but also as a risk. Only in the light of risk—only in the light of possible failure or loss—can we be committed to sustaining the life of what we value. Secular faith is not in itself *sufficient* to lead a responsible life—and it does not automatically make one improve the conditions of the world—but it is *necessary* for motivating ethical, political, and filial commitments.

Accordingly, I will seek to show that secular faith lies at the heart of the sense of responsibility. Let me take a basic example: the Golden Rule. To treat others as you would like to be treated is a fundamental principle in both secular and religious moral teachings. The Golden Rule, however, does not require any form of religious faith. On the contrary, a genuine care for others must be based on secular faith. *If* you follow the Golden Rule because you believe it is a divine command, you are motivated by obedience to God rather than by care for another person. Likewise, if you follow the Golden Rule because you believe it will yield a divine reward (e.g., the release from karma), you are acting not out of concern for the well-being of others but rather out of concern for your own salvation. If your care for another person is based on religious faith, you will cease to care about her if you lose your religious faith and thereby reveal that you never cared about her as an end in herself.

As with all the arguments in this book, I address here both religious and secular audiences. I invite the readers who identify as religious to ask themselves if their care for others is actually motivated by faith in a divine command or divine reward. Moreover, I encourage both religious and secular readers to recognize their commitment to finite life as the condition of responsibility. The Golden Rule does not depend on a religious sense of eternity. On the contrary, it depends on a secular sense of finitude.

To treat others as we ourselves would like to be treated requires that we recognize our shared finitude, since only finite beings can be in need of mutual care. An infinite being is never in need of anything and cannot care about how it is treated. The Golden Rule therefore demands that we recognize one another as finite and keep faith with one another as ends in ourselves. It is because I am finite that I am in need and that it can matter to me how I am treated. Likewise, it is because I recognize you as finite that I can understand that you are in need and that it matters how I treat you. If we do not recognize our shared vulnerability and finitude, the demand for mutuality is not intelligible and we cannot be compelled to care for one another as ends in ourselves.

Hence, I will present a vision of the emancipatory potential of recognizing our secular faith and our essential finitude. The emancipatory potential of secular faith is a *possibility* and far from being achieved in our current state of secularization, which should not be conflated with an emancipated form of secular life. Moreover, even in being achieved, secular life will always remain fragile, since it is sustained only through our commitments. The recognition of finitude does not provide any *guarantee* that we will care for one another in the right way. The recognition of our shared finitude is a necessary condition for the demand of mutual care to be intelligible, but this recognition is in no way sufficient for actual mutuality. Rather, our dependence on one another and the fragility of our lives call for us to develop *institutions* of social justice and material welfare. Our ability to treat others justly depends on how we have been treated and cared for in turn, all the way from our first experiences of parental love to the organization of the society in which we find ourselves. Only a secular perspective allows us to focus on these normative practices— our forms of upbringing, education, labor, political governance, and so on—as essentially matters of what *we* do, as practices for which *we* are responsible and that have to be sustained or questioned or revised by *us*, rather than being given by nature or supernatural decree.

For the same reason, secular faith is the condition of *freedom*. To be free, I argue, is not to be sovereign or liberated from all constraints. Rather, we are free because we are able to ask ourselves what we *ought* to do with our time. All forms of freedom—e.g., the freedom to act, the freedom to speak, the freedom to love—are intelligible *as* freedom only insofar as we are free to engage the question of what we should do with our time. If it were given what we should do, what we should say, and whom we should love—in short: *if it were given what we should do with our time*—we would not be free.

The ability to ask this question—the question of what we ought to do with our time—is the basic condition for what I call *spiritual freedom*. To lead a free, spiritual life (rather than a life determined merely by natural instincts), I must be responsible for what I do. This is not to say that I am free from natural and social constraints. I did not choose to be born with the limitations and abilities I happen to have. Moreover, I had no control over who took care of me, what they did *to* me and *for* me. My family—and the larger historical context into which I was born—shaped me before I could do anything about it. Likewise, social norms continue to inform who I can take myself to be and what I can do with my life. Without social norms—norms I did not invent on my own and that shape the world in which I find myself—I can have no understanding of who to be or what to do. Nevertheless, *I* am responsible for upholding, challenging, or transforming these norms. I am not merely causally determined by nature or norms but act *in light of* norms that I can challenge and transform.[4] This is what it means to have a spiritual life. Even at the price of my biological survival, my material well-being, or my social standing, I can give my life for a principle to which I hold myself or for a cause in which I believe.

My freedom therefore requires that I can ask myself what I *should* do with my time. Even when I am utterly absorbed in what I do, what I say, and what I love, the possibility of this question must be alive in me. Being engaged in my activities, I must run the risk of being bored—otherwise my engagement would be a matter of compulsive necessity. Being devoted to what I love, I must run the risk of losing it or giving it up—otherwise there would be nothing at stake in maintaining and actively relating to what I love. Most fundamentally, I must live in relation to my irrevocable death—otherwise I would believe that my time is infinite and there would be no urgency in dedicating my life to anything.

The condition of our freedom, then, is that we understand ourselves as finite. Only in light of the apprehension that we will die—that our lifetime is indefinite but finite—can we ask ourselves what we ought to do with our lives and put ourselves at stake in our activities. This is why all religious visions of eternity, as we shall see, ultimately are visions of *unfreedom*. In the consummation of eternity, there would be no question of what we should do with our lives. We would be absorbed in bliss forever and thereby deprived of any possible agency. Rather than having a free relation to what we do and what we love, we would be compelled by necessity to enjoy it.

II

This Life addresses both religious and secular audiences. I invite the religious (and the religiously inclined) to ask themselves if they actually have faith in eternity and if this faith is compatible with the care that animates their lives. Furthermore, I encourage both religious and secular readers to see why the finitude of our lives should not be regarded as a lack, a restriction, or a fallen condition. Instead of lamenting the absence of eternity, we should acknowledge the commitment to finite life as the condition for anything to be at stake and for anyone to lead a free life.

My critique of religious faith does not primarily appeal to scientific *knowledge* and my critique of religious values does not primarily appeal to scientific *facts*. Rather, I provide a new perspective on what we believe and what we value. In caring about anyone or anything, we are already practicing an *implicit* form of secular faith in what we do, since we are devoted to someone or something that is fragile. My aim is to make our secular faith *explicit* in our understanding of what we do and thereby open up emancipatory possibilities for transforming our practices of care as well as our communal life.

My argument challenges one of the most widely held assumptions about religion. According to many surveys, more than 50 percent of Americans hold that religious faith is necessary to live a moral, responsible life. The same assumption is part of a more general revival of political theology, among both prominent philosophers and the general public. The intellectual historian Peter E. Gordon has provided the most capacious definition of political theology, while tracing its resurgence in thinkers such as Charles Taylor, Jürgen Habermas, and José Casanova. In Gordon's account, political theology is defined by two theses. The first thesis postulates a *normative deficit:* secular life suffers from a lack of moral substance and cannot establish a viable ground for our political life together. The second thesis postulates a *religious plenitude:* to compensate for its normative deficit, secular life must turn to religion as the unique and privileged resource of moral-political instruction without which society cannot cohere. As Gordon shows, these two theses of political theology are remarkably persistent not only in the history of ideas but also in contemporary philosophy and sociology.[5]

Such political theology contributes to a pervasive negative narrative regarding the possibilities of secular life. In our secular age, faith in eternal life or eternal being is said to have declined. Yet there is a widespread notion that the lapse in religious faith is a great loss and that the hope for eternity expresses our deepest desire, even if it cannot be fulfilled. Secular life would then be characterized by both a *normative* and an *existential* deficit. Owing to secularization, we have supposedly lost both the moral foundation that is required to hold our society together and the redemptive hope that is needed to find meaning in our lives.

The most influential version of such a negative assessment of secular life was formulated by the sociologist Max Weber in the early twentieth century. Weber's famous claim that secular life suffers from a "disenchantment" of the world continues to serve as an alibi for political theology and to instill the sense that a society without religious faith is hopelessly lacking. According to Weber, disenchantment has three major implications.[6] First, disenchantment means that we no longer appeal to any "mysterious incalculable forces"—or any other forms of supernatural explanation—for what happens in the world. Rather, the form of reason becomes an instrumental reason, which assumes that "we can, in principle, control everything by means of calculation." Second, Weber takes disenchantment to mean that "the ultimate and most sublime values have retreated from public life," so that we are deprived of any form of "genuine community." Third, Weber laments that disenchantment entails that death is no longer "a meaningful phenomenon."

Weber holds that the human beings who lived in an enchanted world (his example is "Abraham, or some peasant of the past") had a "meaningful" relation to death because they supposedly died "fulfilled by life" and regarded themselves as belonging to an "organic cycle." When Abraham or the peasant of the past was on the verge of death, he could take himself to have had "enough" of life because it "had given to him what life had to offer" and "for him there remained no puzzles he might wish to solve." In contrast, the person whom Weber describes as disenchanted ("civilized man") cannot ever regard his life as completed, since he is committed to the possibility of progress ("the continuous enrichment of culture by ideas, knowledge, and problems") in which he wants to participate. Such a person will always be dissatisfied, Weber argues, since his life can never be completed: "what he seizes is always something provisional and not definitive, and therefore death for him is a meaningless occurrence." Rather than being seen as the meaningful conclusion of a life and as the ascent to eternity, death comes to be regarded as the meaningless interruption of a life. This leads Weber to the conclusion that the commitment to earthly progress makes our lives meaningless rather than meaningful: "Because death is meaningless, civilized life as such is meaningless; by its very progressiveness it gives death the imprint of meaninglessness."

Ever since Weber delivered his diagnosis in the early twentieth century, many thinkers have tried to offer a cure for the disenchantment and sense of meaninglessness that are supposedly inherent in secular life. My argument is, on the contrary, that the diagnosis itself is deeply misleading and should be called into question on every count.

The basic problem is that Weber fails to grasp the commitment to *freedom* that is a distinct historical achievement of modern, secular life. For Weber, all that remains when we subtract religious norms and values from our lives is an impoverished instrumental reason that disables any "ultimate value" or "genuine community." Yet the idea of an instrumental reason that operates on its own is unintelligible. We cannot reason instrumentally without a purpose for the sake of which we lead our lives, since nothing can count as a means except in light of a value that we hold to be an end in itself. If we had no defining purposes—if everything were reduced to instrumental means—it would be impossible to understand the *point* of doing anything. In contrast to religious faith, secular faith recognizes that the defining purposes of our lives depend on our commitments. The authority of our norms cannot be established by divine revelation or natural properties but must be instituted, upheld, and justified by our practices. If we do not appeal to mysterious forces or a supernatural authority, it does *not* mean (as Weber claims) that we believe everything can be mastered by calculation. On the contrary, to have secular faith is to acknowledge that we are essentially dependent on—and answerable to—other persons who cannot be mastered or controlled, since we are all free, finite beings.

By the same token, the norms in light of which we lead our lives can be called into question, contested, and revised. Far from being an impediment to "genuine community," the recognition that we are responsible for the form of our shared life is at the heart of the modern, secular commitment to *democracy*. Like other political theologians, however, Weber has no faith in democracy as an actual power of the people but believes that democracy must be subordinated to a charismatic leader (a *Führer*, as Weber designated the function fifteen years before Hitler's ascent to power). Without a leader who occupies the role of a religious authority, democracy supposedly will have no animating "soul," since for Weber there is no feature of secular life itself that can bind people together in genuine community.[7]

Hence, while Weber portrays himself as someone who offers a "value-neutral" diagnosis, his negative assessment of the possibilities of secular life betrays his religious presuppositions. By religious presuppositions I do not mean that Weber believes in God or eternity, but that he regards our finitude as a negative restriction and assumes that secular life necessarily suffers from a lack of meaning. Weber prides himself on having the courage to face the "emptiness" of life without religion—contrasting himself to those who "cannot bear the fate of the times" and flee into "the arms of the old churches"[8]—but his idea of secular life as empty or meaningless is itself a religious notion.

Thus, when Weber claims that the commitment to earthly progress makes our lives meaningless rather than meaningful, the authority to which he appeals is the devoutly religious author Leo Tolstoy. Weber's entire argument here exhibits a striking inability to understand the dynamic of leading a free, finite life. Weber apparently thinks that a fulfilling life should lead one to a sense of final satisfaction or completion, where one has had "enough" of life and can welcome death itself as "meaningful." This is a profoundly misguided view of what it means to be a person who is leading her life. Being a person is not a goal that can be achieved but a purpose that must be sustained.

For example, if I take my vocation to be sociology (as Weber did), I understand the significance of my life in light of my commitment to being a sociologist. Being a sociologist is not a project that can be completed but a purpose for the sake of which I lead my life and engage in what I do. If my life as a sociologist is satisfying, it does not mean that I have had enough of being a sociologist. On the contrary, it means that I am committed to sustaining my life as a sociologist. Even if I retire as a sociologist and focus on other activities, I am still committed to being a sociologist insofar as I identify with the work I have done (an identification that can include revising my views or conceding that the work of others has superseded my own). If I were truly done with being a sociologist—if I truly *had* had "enough"—it would mean that I renounced any form of care for the work I did and who I was as a sociologist. Even if I am done with being a sociologist, however, my life is not complete. As long as I lead my life, I have to be committed to one or several purposes—e.g., being retired, being a grandparent, being a citizen, being a friend—which define who I take myself to be. Leading my life is not a process that can end in final fulfillment, but an activity that I have to sustain for the sake of something that matters to me. Even if a defining purpose of my life breaks down, the breakdown matters to me because I am striving to have a purpose. The activity of leading my life—my striving to have a purpose—cannot even in principle be completed. If my life were complete, it would not be *my* life, since it would be over. In leading my life, I am not striving for an impossible *completion* of who I am but for the possible and fragile *coherence* of who I am trying to be: to hold together and be responsive to the commitments that define who I take myself to be. Leading a satisfying life is not to achieve a state of consummation but to be engaged in what I do and put myself at stake in activities that matter to me.

For the same reason, if I reach a point when I welcome death because I have had enough of myself altogether, it does *not* mean that my life is fulfilled and reveals its final meaning. On the contrary, if I have had "enough" of my life, it means that I am failing to lead a meaningful life. Death cannot be a meaningful completion of my life, since my life is not something that can "be" complete. My death is not something I can experience as the completion of anything, since it excludes my existence. As long as my life is mine—as long as I lead my life—the book of my life is still open, and it is neither possible nor desirable to be "done" with myself.

Contrary to what Weber holds, there is no correlation between leading a meaningful life and embracing death as the supposed completion of life. As long as our lives matter to us, we are committed to the continuation (rather than the completion) of our lives.

For the same reason, the commitment to the possibility of

progress—which entails that what we care about extends beyond and cannot be "completed" in our own lifetime—does not make our lives meaningless. On the contrary, part of the meaning of what we do is that it can have significance for future generations and make their lives better than ours.[9]

If we take the possibility of democratic progress seriously, we should therefore counter Weber's conservative nostalgia for a premodern, enchanted world. As the critic Bruce Robbins has argued in an insightful analysis of Weber, "the suggestion that 'genuine community' used to exist omits any consideration of those who were excluded from such community—the slaves and women of ancient Greece, to pick at random from a long series of examples. Opinion on the genuineness of community would depend on whose experience was consulted. If you asked landless laborers in the Middle Ages, such community might have seemed less unquestionably genuine."[10] Furthermore, if contemporary workers express greater discontent with their lives than did Weber's imagined peasant of the past, it is "a result of rising expectations rather than disenchantment— a product of democratic progress to be set against centuries of resignation by the poor to their inevitable social fate. No, there was no malaise back then. Why? Because people knew their places."[11] We can thus offer a quite different diagnosis of our predicament than the one proposed by Weber and his followers. The dissatisfactions of our current state of secularization are *not* due to the idea of progress. As Robbins emphasizes, the dissatisfactions are rather due to "the *failure* of progress," namely, our "failure to achieve a level of social justice that the premodern world did not even strive to achieve."[12]

The key to such an understanding of the promise of secular life can be found in the work of Karl Marx. Marx's thinking is often conflated with the totalitarian communist regimes of the twentieth century, but I will argue that he is the most important inheritor of the secular commitment to freedom and democracy. In contrast to Weber and other political theologians, Marx has no nostalgia for the premodern world. Rather, he makes clear that both capitalism and liberalism are historical conditions of possibility for the emancipation that he espouses. This is why Marx, in his critique of capitalism and liberalism, takes issue with these forms of life on their own terms. He seeks to show that capitalism and liberalism require their own overcoming by virtue of the secular commitment they bear within themselves to freedom and democracy.

At the time when Marx lived—and subsequently inspired by his writings—there was a growing secular recognition that *we are what we do* and that we can do things differently. We do not have to be subjected to the laws of religion or capital, but can transform our historical situation through collective action and create institutions for the free development of social individuals as an end in itself.

Thus, in the late nineteenth and early twentieth centuries—during the same decades when Weber lamented the supposed loss of "genuine community"—workers formed democratic socialist organizations that provided a sense of practical identity and solidarity, as well as ethical and political purpose. The workers' movements organized youth groups, choirs, book clubs, sports teams, and other communal activities. They pursued democracy on the ground by publishing daily newspapers and journals that provided a forum for ongoing, open debate about the stakes and goals of the movement. Workers of all stripes were offered further education, women came together to pursue their own emancipation, and there was a common cause in the shared effort to build a better society. The words of a German miner, aged thirty-three and with eight children, echo the testimony of many workers from this period. "The modern labor movement," he said in 1912, "enriches me and all my friends through the growing light of recognition. We understand that we are no longer the anvil but rather the hammer that forms the future of our children, and that feeling is worth more than gold."[13] This sense of spiritual freedom—that we can be the subjects *of* our history and not merely subject *to* our history—is at the core of Marx's notion of emancipation.

The growing international solidarity of the workers' movements was largely broken by the First World War, which erupted in 1914. By the time of the Russian Revolution in 1917, the material and social conditions for creating a new form of society were largely in ruins. As the great political thinker, feminist, and activist Rosa Luxemburg observed at the time, Russia was "an isolated land, exhausted by world war, strangled by imperialism, betrayed by the international proletariat."[14] Under such circumstances, it was virtually impossible to achieve an exemplary democratic socialism. As Luxemburg put it, the revolutionaries could not be expected "to perform miracles" but must be understood "within the limits of historical possibilities."[15] Yet, already during the first stages of the Russian Revolution, Luxemburg rightly warned against the dangers of making a virtue of necessity and losing hold of the commitment to democracy. It would be fatal, she maintained, if the revolutionaries were "to freeze into a complete theoretical system all the tactics forced upon them by these fatal circumstances" and "place into its storehouse as new discoveries all the distortions prescribed in Russia by necessity and compulsion—in the last analysis only by-products of the bankruptcy of international socialism in the present world war."[16]

By the time of Stalin and Mao, the bankruptcy would be in full force. No one who takes up Marx's ideas today should make any excuses for such totalitarian regimes, which failed to grasp the insights of Marx not only in practice but also in theory. To retrieve and develop Marx's insights in a new direction, we need instead to engage the fundamental question of freedom with which he is concerned.

The task is all the more important because the appeal to freedom in recent decades has been appropriated for agendas on the political right, where the idea of freedom serves to defend "the free market" and is largely reduced to a formal conception of individual liberty. In response, many thinkers on the political left have retreated from or even explicitly rejected the idea of freedom. This is a fatal mistake. Any emancipatory politics—as well as any critique of capitalism—requires a conception of freedom. Only in light of a commitment to freedom can we render anything intelligible *as* oppression, exploitation, or alienation. Moreover, only in light of a commitment to freedom can we give an account of what we are trying to achieve and why it matters.

Thus, we cannot understand Marx's critique of capitalism unless we understand the notion of freedom to which he is committed. Understanding this notion requires understanding why questions of economy and material conditions are inseparable from all spiritual questions of freedom. The economic organization of our society is not a mere instrumental *means* for the pursuit of individual ends. Rather, our shared economy is itself expressive of how we understand the relation between means and ends. Economic matters are not abstract but concern the most general and concrete questions of what we do with our time. As I will show in detail, how we organize our economy is intrinsic to how we live together and what we collectively *value*.

From his early to his late works, Marx's analyses of economic questions proceed from a philosophical grasp of what it means to be *living* and *free*. All living beings are finite, both in the sense that they are not self-sufficient and in the sense that they can die. Living beings must therefore draw on their environment to sustain themselves. A living being cannot simply exist but must *do something* to stay alive. The need of the living organism to sustain itself—the labor required to keep ourselves alive—minimally defines what Marx calls the realm of necessity. Because we are living beings, we must *work* to maintain ourselves. Yet, all the time we have is not necessarily required to ensure our biological survival and it is an open question for us what we should do with the surplus of time. This is why, for Marx, we also live in the realm of freedom. We are able to engage our life activity *as a free activity*, since we can ask ourselves what to do and if it is the right thing to do.

Moreover, through technological innovations (from simple tools to advanced machines) we can reduce the time we need to expend on securing our survival, by replacing large parts of our living labor with nonliving capacities for producing social goods. We can thereby decrease our realm of necessity (the time required to keep ourselves alive) and increase our realm of freedom (the time available for activities that we count as ends in themselves, which includes time for engaging the *question* of what matters to us and which activities we *should* count as ends in themselves).

The exercise of our spiritual freedom depends both on material conditions of production and social relations of recognition. Insofar as we spend our time working a job that is not fulfilling but merely serves as a means for our survival, our labor time is unfree, since we cannot affirm that what we do is an expression of who we are. Instead of being free to engage the question of what makes our life worth living—the question of what we *ought* to do with our time— our lives are mortgaged to a form of labor that is required for our survival. To live a free life, it is not enough that we have the *right* to freedom. We must have access to the material resources as well as the forms of education that allow us to pursue our freedom and to "own" the question of what to do with our time. What belongs to each one of us—what is irreducibly our own—is not property or goods but the time of our lives.

To be clear, the emphasis on my *own* life—or your *own* life—is not in opposition to sociality. As Marx underlines: "My *own* existence *is* social activity, and therefore that which I make of myself, I make of myself for society and with the awareness of myself as a social being."[17] Hence, to "own" your life is not to be independent but to be able to acknowledge your dependence. A good example is the experience of love. When you love someone—e.g., as a friend, as a parent, as a life partner—your dependence on the other is not a restriction that prevents you from being free. Rather, your dependence on the other belongs to the life you affirm as your own. Acting on behalf of the one you love is not an alien purpose but the expression of a commitment in which you can recognize yourself, since caring for the interests and the well-being of the other is part of your own understanding of who you are. Likewise, if the work you do is for the sake of something you believe in as an end in itself—as it is for me when I teach my classes or when I write this book—then even the difficult or exhausting demands of the work are not an external imposition on a prior freedom. On the contrary, the demands of my students and the difficulties of my writing are an intrinsic part of the form of life to which I am committed. Thus, even when it is hard to sustain my work I can recognize the challenges as ones to which I hold myself.

If you cannot see yourself in the purpose of your occupation, then your labor time is alienated, even if your job entails a high salary and great social prestige. This may seem like a small problem compared with the labor conditions of most of the people who produce the commodities that populate our world. There is certainly a harrowing difference between those who assemble our computers in factories or manufacture our clothes in sweatshops and those of us who turn on our computers or put on our clothes while forgetting the labor conditions under which they were produced. Yet from Marx's perspective these issues are all connected, since they concern how our shared economic life is organized and how it is inimical to our freedom. To be able to lead free lives and own what we do, we must be able to see ourselves both in the purpose of our occupation and in the social conditions of the labor that sustains our lives; to recognize our own commitment to freedom in the institutions on which we depend and to which we contribute. Such identification requires that all of us have the freedom to participate in possible transformations of the purpose of what we do—democratic transformations of the social institutions of labor—as well as the freedom to give up or call into question our supposed vocation in favor of different occupations.

In short, our freedom requires that we can own the question of what to do with our time. For Marx, political progress is measured by the degree to which it allows for such freedom. This is why all readings of Marx that posit a final resolution as the goal of politics— either in the form of a totalitarian state or a utopian life that would overcome finitude—betray the most important insights of his work. The goal is not to overcome finitude, but to transform qualitatively our ability to lead free lives. Even in their most ideal state our lives will have to reckon with the risks of finitude—the risks of losing what we love and losing our ability to do what we love—since these risks are intrinsic to freedom itself.

Moreover, there is no question of leaving the realm of necessity behind. How we *lead* our lives in the realm of freedom is inseparable from how we *live* our lives in the realm of necessity. As living beings, we will always have to do some form of work to maintain our lives, and labor is not in itself something bad. On the contrary, all forms of free activities—as in my examples of teaching and writing—are themselves forms of labor. An emancipated life is not a life that is free from work, but a life in which we pursue work on the basis of our own commitments. Even our socially necessary labor can be an expression of our freedom if it is shared for the sake of the common good. The aim, then, is to decrease the realm of necessity and increase the realm of freedom by making the relation between the two a democratic question. We will always have to work—for better or for worse—but what will count as necessary labor and what will count as free labor is a matter of our commitments and our social organization. For the same reason, the relation between necessity and freedom cannot be settled once and for all but must always be negotiated. There are no definitive political solutions in Marx but rather the clarification of a vital problem. What we need to negotiate—both individually and collectively—is how to cultivate the finite time that is the condition of our freedom.

We can thus understand why the advent of capitalism is a form of progress for Marx. Wage labor under capitalism is historically the first social form which in principle recognizes that each one of us "owns" the time of our lives and that our lifetime is inherently "valuable." Unlike slaves—who are systematically denied ownership of their time—we are "free" to sell our labor to someone who is willing to buy it. Moreover, wage labor is explicitly conceived as a *means* for us to achieve the *end* of leading a free life.

The promise of achieving freedom through wage labor is necessarily contradicted, however, by how we measure the *value* of our lives under capitalism. Marx's critique of the measure of value under capitalism is the most important argument in all of his work, but also the most misunderstood. Contrary to a widely held assumption— among both his followers on the Left and his critics on the Right—

Marx does *not* subscribe to a general labor theory of value, which holds that labor is the necessary source of all wealth. Rather, Marx argues that the production of wealth under capitalism entails a his- torically specific measure of value (socially necessary labor time), which contradicts the value of free time and must be overcome for the sake of our emancipation.

In developing Marx's critique of the capitalist measure of value, I argue that it calls for a *revaluation* of value. The revaluation in ques- tion requires not only a theoretical but also a practical transformation of the way we lead our lives. All the way from our social organization of labor and our technological production of goods to our forms of education, we need to pursue a revaluation that acknowledges our finite lifetime as the condition for anything to matter and for any- thing to be valuable. Marx himself has notoriously little to say about how we would be able to lead our lives beyond capitalism. Drawing on what Marx calls communism, however, I outline a new vision of *democratic socialism* that is committed to providing the material and spiritual conditions for each one of us to lead a free life, in mutual recognition of our dependence on one another. Through a critique of capitalism and liberalism on their own terms, I specify the gen- eral principles of democratic socialism and elaborate their concrete implications. What I call democratic socialism is neither an imposed blueprint nor an abstract utopia. Rather, I derive the principles of democratic socialism from the commitment to freedom and equality that we already avow.

The political project of democratic socialism requires secular faith. To have faith in the possibility of actualizing freedom is *not* to believe that it is guaranteed or that it can be secured. To have faith in the possibility of freedom is to have faith in something that will always be precarious and contestable, even in its fullest actualization.

The struggle for freedom is an act of secular faith because it is committed to a form of individual and collective life that is essen- tially finite. This commitment to a free, finite life is implicit in all forms of resistance to exploitation and alienation. The only ability that can be exploited or alienated—and the only one that can be liberated—is our ability to own the question of what to do with our time, since that ability is presupposed by all forms of freedom. The ability is certainly developmental and in need of cultural formation, but without faith in such an ability the idea of freedom is unintelligible. To be responsive to the exploitation or alienation of someone's life, you have to believe in the fragile possibility and the intrinsic value of her ability to own her time. The same secular faith is exhibited by anyone who takes up the struggle against her own oppression. To understand yourself as being exploited or alienated, you have to believe that you have a finite, precious time to live and that *your own life* is being taken away from you when that time is taken away from you.

Accordingly, the cultivation of secular faith is indispensable for progressive politics. The pursuit of emancipation requires that we are committed to improving the material and social conditions of freedom as an end in itself. This is why Marx emphasizes that the critique of religion must be accompanied by a critique of the existing forms of our life together. That those who are enslaved or live in poverty may need faith in God to carry on with their lives is not a reason to promote religious faith but a reason to abolish slavery and poverty.

The need for such a critical and emancipatory perspective is as pressing as ever. We live in an epoch when social inequality, climate change, and global injustice are intertwined with the resurgence of religious forms of authority that deny the ultimate importance of these matters. A dominant response is to retreat from a secular faith in the possibility of progress, in favor of asserting the necessity of a religious sense of "fullness" to sustain our moral and spiritual lives. This book seeks to combat all such forms of political theology. In contrast, I offer a secular vision of why *everything depends on what we do with our time together*. The decline of religious faith in eternity is not something to be lamented. Rather, it provides an opportunity to make explicit and strengthen our secular faith in *this life* as an end in itself.

III

The book is divided into two parts, which are devoted to the two concepts discussed throughout: secular faith and spiritual freedom.

The first part of the book pursues the stakes of the difference between secular and religious faith. What I call religious faith is any form of belief in an eternal being or an eternity beyond being, either in the form of a timeless repose (such as nirvana), a transcendent God, or an immanent, divine Nature. Religious faith is not a system of belief that I am trying to *disprove*, in the sense of demonstrating the nonexistence of eternity. What I am calling into question is the idea that eternity is *desirable*. The assumption that eternity is desirable is much more pervasive than any alleged certainty concerning its existence. Theological attempts to prove the existence of God are outdated for many contemporary religious believers, but the idea that eternity is worth being devoted to is indispensable for the defense of religious faith. There is no reason to have faith in eternity unless one believes that it offers a meaningful consolation for, alternative to, or escape from the loss of what we love.

In contrast, I seek to show that an eternal life would not fulfill our desire to live on. The commitment to living on—rather than to eternal life—lies at the heart of secular faith. My account of secular faith does not depend on the contrast to religious faith, since secular faith is intrinsic to any form of care. However, in our historical situation, the understanding of faith is still deeply entangled with religious ways of thinking. In order to transform our received notions of faith, these ways of thinking need to be engaged directly, which is why my arguments in the first half of the book emerge in explicit dialogue with religious writers. To engage their work is an opportunity to develop the understanding of secular faith and to defend it against the most serious objections. Thus, I elaborate my notion of secular faith through readings of both the Bible and Buddhist philosophy, as well as prominent religious writers ranging from Greek and Roman Stoics to Saint Augustine, Martin Luther, Dante Alighieri, Meister Eckhart, Baruch Spinoza, Søren Kierkegaard, Paul

Tillich, C. S. Lewis, and Charles Taylor. Precisely because they aim to transcend secular faith, these religious writers have a sharp eye for the perils of such faith and they describe its dynamic at length.

Chapter 1 develops my account of secular faith as a condition of intelligibility for any form of care. To make vivid the phenomenology of secular faith, I proceed from the most difficult and agonizing event: the death of the beloved. My aim is to show that secular faith lies at the heart of what matters, even for those who claim to have religious faith, such as Martin Luther when mourning the death of his daughter Magdalena and C. S. Lewis when mourning the death of his wife, Joy Davidman. Across different historical epochs, their accounts of grief testify to how their faith in God and eternity is incompatible with the secular faith that animates their commitment to the beloved. Only secular faith can do justice to the experience of love as well as mourning. This becomes salient when we are moved to acknowledge our deepest commitments, making explicit what is implicit in our passion and pain.

Chapter 2 elaborates the notion of secular faith through an analysis of time and eternity in Augustine's *Confessions*. In addition to being one of the most influential narratives of religious conversion, the *Confessions* is also recognized as the first major autobiography in the Western tradition and a profound philosophical treatise, especially in the way it addresses the question of time. Augustine here reveals that secular faith is at work in every aspect of our lives. Whether in bliss or in mourning, in joy or in pain, we *live on* after a past that has ceased to be and before a future that may not come to be. Indeed, all the activities that Augustine describes—from speaking and singing to loving, hoping, and remembering—depend for their meaning on the temporal experience of living on. Inversely, the eternal presence that Augustine holds out as the goal of religious aspiration would put an end to these activities. There cannot be any meaningful activities in eternity, since nothing can live on in a timeless presence and nothing can matter in an everlasting existence.

Thus, Augustine's own account gives us reasons to keep faith in temporal life and overcome faith in eternity. To pursue this perspective would be to write a secular—rather than a religious—confession. I read such a secular confession in Karl Ove Knausgaard's *My Struggle*, which can be seen as a contemporary response to Augustine. Knausgaard's painstaking attention to a secular life places us in the midst of everyday existence. Like Augustine, he explores the care that binds us to others and how the experience of time cuts through every moment. But while Augustine seeks to turn us toward eternity, Knausgaard turns us back toward our finite lives as the heart of everything that matters. The animating principle of his writing is one of *attachment* to finite life, which is all the more profound because it remains faithful to the ambivalence of any attachment. Devoted to secular life, we can be moved both to bliss and devastation, hope and despair, success and failure. Knausgaard, then, makes vivid what it means to keep faith in a life that is bound to die. This secular faith, I argue, opens the possibility for all passion and meaningful engagement.

Chapter 3 proceeds from a question that is bound to arise in response to my first two chapters. Why is secular faith—devoted to this world and invested in finite lives—*necessarily* at odds with religious faith in eternity? A defender of religious faith may object that the latter can make one more engaged in this life, rather than make one turn away from it. I take on this argument through the thinker who pursues it most profoundly, Søren Kierkegaard, in his classic work *Fear and Trembling*. For Kierkegaard, religious faith should not lead us out of this world but rather enable a more profound commitment to the life we live. Yet he is well aware of the conflict between the commitment to a temporal, finite being and the commitment to an eternal, infinite being. In *Fear and Trembling* this conflict is staged most dramatically as the meaning of God's command that Abraham sacrifice his son Isaac. Abraham's love for Isaac expresses a commitment to living on: he wants Isaac's life to flourish for its own sake and he also prizes Isaac as the only one who can let his own legacy survive. It is precisely this commitment to a unique life—the life of Isaac—that has to be renounced for the sake of eternity. To love Isaac is to be susceptible to an irreversible loss, since Isaac is a finite being, and therefore he has to be given up in advance, sacrificed for God. Nevertheless, Kierkegaard holds that the highest form of faith is one that can retain all the love for Isaac—all the love for the finite—while at the same time giving him up, trusting that God will restore everything that is lost. Such faith would allow one to be fully committed to the finite world, while at the same time being invulnerable to loss, since one would believe that everything is possible for God.

The effect of Abraham's religious faith, however, turns out to be an actual indifference to what happens. Abraham is able to kill Isaac because he believes that God will bring him back, so in the end it makes no difference (from the standpoint of his faith) whether Isaac is sacrificed. Likewise, the modern version of Abraham—the knight of faith—is ultimately revealed to be indifferent to the fate of the finite. The knight of faith is presented as someone who is utterly committed to finite life, but when his hopes in this life are shattered, "curiously enough, he is just the same." Precisely because his faith makes him immune to the experience of loss, he cannot care about the outcome of what actually happens.

I argue that the above problem is not limited to Kierkegaard's telling of the story, but reveals why care and responsibility cannot be based on religious faith. If you claim that your responsibility for Isaac is based on God's command, then you are committed to killing Isaac if that turns out to be the command. If you object that God would never command such a thing, you in fact profess faith in a standard of value independent of God, since you believe that it is wrong to kill Isaac regardless of what God commands. By the same token, you profess faith in the irreplaceable value of a finite life. *If* you believe that this value can be replaced—that Isaac will live on in eternity or be restored on earth—you will be indifferent to his fate in being put to death. Whether he lives or dies will ultimately make no difference to you, since everything that is lost will be returned.

In contrast, the care for Isaac is sustained by secular faith in the value of a life that *can* be irrevocably lost. Secular faith, I show, is the condition for any life-defining commitment and for anything to matter.

The second part of the book pursues the emancipatory possibilities of secular faith. Here I develop my concept of spiritual freedom, in relation to fundamental questions concerning the constitution of life, time, and value. Moreover, by engaging with Marx's critique of capitalism and religion in a new way, I draw together the threads of the book as a whole and make explicit their far-reaching implications for how we should lead our lives.

Chapter 4 presents my central philosophical arguments regarding why the finitude of life is a necessary condition for agency and freedom. My starting point is the fundamental activity of all living beings: the activity of self-maintenance. No form of life is intelligible *as living* unless it is engaged in the activity of keeping itself alive. It follows that all forms of life must be finite and must be dependent on a fragile material body. The activity of self-maintenance—e.g., eating, drinking, sleeping—would have no purpose if the living being were not subject to disintegration. For anything to be at stake in maintaining a life, it must be running the risk of death. Moreover, it is only through the activity of self-maintenance that there can be any time to live in the first place. The self-maintenance of a living being necessarily generates more lifetime than it needs to "spend" on keeping itself alive, which is why there is at least a minimal surplus of time for every living being. Even a simple plant does not have to expend all its time on securing the nourishment required for its survival. This surplus of time is even more evident in the lives of animals that have the capacity to engage in activities of self-enjoyment that are distinct from the activity of self-preservation—e.g., the singing of birds, the purring of cats, the playful interaction of dogs. Through such forms of self-enjoyment, many kinds of animals have a capacity to enjoy their surplus time as a form of "free" time. Yet, insofar as they cannot understand their time *as* free time—insofar as they cannot ask themselves what they *ought* to do with their time— even animals with highly refined capacities for self-enjoyment remain within the bounds of what I call "natural" freedom. In contrast, what I call spiritual freedom requires that the agent in question can ask herself how she *should* spend her time and be responsive to the risk that she is wasting her life. Without the relation to such a risk, we would not be able to lead a spiritual life, since we could never engage the question of what we ought to do with our time and what matters to us.

Chapter 5 turns to Marx in order to show how his critique of capitalism—as well as the possibility of emancipation—hinges on what we do with our surplus of time. The key is to grasp that questions of economy and value are at the heart of our spiritual freedom. How we organize our economy expresses what we take to be *worth* doing with our time and what we *prioritize* in our society. Under capitalism our collective priority is profit, since that priority is inscribed in how we measure and produce the capital wealth that sustains our lives. Without the growth of capital, we have no social wealth to distribute across society. For the same reason, we must prioritize doing what is *profitable*, even at the expense of doing what we actually believe needs to be done and what we actually believe would be meaningful to do. Marx offers a powerful account of the pernicious practical consequences that follow from the priority of profit: the alienation of our labor, the exploitation of our time, the commodification of our lives, the necessity of unemployment, and the inherent tendency toward destructive economic crises. I provide an analytical reconstruction of these arguments and their relevance for understanding the historical conditions under which we still live. Yet, understanding fully *why* the capitalist measure of value is contradictory—and why the priority of profit alienates us from our spiritual freedom—requires a level of analysis that Marx presupposes but never explicitly elucidates. This level of analysis concerns how any economy of spiritual life is intelligible in the first place: what it means to be someone for whom something can be taken *as* a cost, *as* a value, and who can relate to her life *as* an economy of time that reflects her priorities.

By taking on the deepest level of analysis, I unlock a new understanding of Marx's notion of value and defend it against the classical objections, as well as against the influential neoclassical revolution in economics. I demonstrate that the reigning theory of supply and demand presupposes the conception of value that is at the center of

Marx's analysis. Most importantly, I disclose the inherent contradiction in capitalism as a historical form of life and why it calls for a *revaluation* of value.

Chapter 6 elaborates what the revaluation of value demands of us in both theory and practice. For Marx—contrary to a persistent misconception—the overcoming of capitalism is not meant to abolish democracy but to make *actual* democracy possible. Under capitalism, we cannot actually negotiate the fundamental questions of what we collectively value, since the purpose of our economy is beyond the power of democratic deliberation. We can make decisions regarding the *distribution* of our social wealth, but the final purpose of the *production* of our wealth (profit) is already decided. If we are committed to achieving actual democracy, we must therefore be committed not only to the redistribution of wealth but also to the revaluation of the measure of value that shapes our production of wealth. Almost all forms of left-wing politics—from most kinds of Marxism to the social democratic welfare state and advocates for a universal basic income—restrict their critiques of capitalism to the mode of distribution, failing to interrogate the measure of value that informs the mode of production. All redistributive reforms, however, will be caught in contradictions that I explain and exemplify. The point is not that we should abandon redistributive reforms but that our reforms need to be reconceived—both strategically and substantially—as means toward the end of democratic socialism. The latter can be achieved only through a fundamental practical revaluation of the way we lead our lives together.

To present and answer the challenges of democratic socialism, I engage in an immanent critique of leading liberal thinkers of political economy: Mill, Rawls, Keynes, Hayek. The aim of democratic socialism is not to resolve the economic questions of our priorities once and for all, since those questions are intrinsic to our spiritual freedom. Rather, in elaborating the principles of democratic socialism, I give an account of how life under democratic socialism would allow us to "own" the question of what we ought to do with our finite time, both individually and collectively. For the same reason, I take issue with all forms of utopian Marxism that conflate the overcoming of capitalism with the overcoming of finitude. The most sophisticated example is the philosopher and sociologist Theodor W. Adorno, who has influenced a wide range of Marxism. I bring the chapter to a close by showing how Adorno conflates a secular promise of freedom (the liberation *of* finite life) with a religious promise of salvation (the liberation *from* finite life). In contrast, I develop the stakes of Marx's critique of religion and explain why we ought to be committed to freedom rather than salvation.

Finally, in my Conclusion to the book, I engage in depth with the political philosophy and political activism of Martin Luther King, Jr. Spanning over King's entire career, I show how his commitment to the actualization of freedom led him to an increasingly radical critique of capitalism. King's policy proposals center on the redistribution of wealth, but he also senses that there is a deeper problem of *value* under capitalism. Toward the end of his life he comes close to grasping the need for what I call a revaluation of value, which requires a movement toward democratic socialism. Moreover, by following King's trajectory, we can see how the stakes of secular faith and spiritual freedom come together in the pursuit of actual emancipation. By attending closely to King's political speeches and the concrete historical practices in which he participates, I seek to disclose that the faith which animates his political activism is better understood in terms of secular faith than in terms of the religious faith that he officially espouses.

The keys to my secular understanding of King's work are provided by a philosopher who was of crucial importance for both Marx and King: Georg Wilhelm Friedrich Hegel. Hegel's philosophy is an implicit presence throughout my entire book and explicitly addressed at length in the Conclusion. For the record, it should be noted that Hegel's work may be the most difficult to read in the entire history of philosophy and any interpretation of his work is bound to be controversial. The philosopher Michael Thompson has memorably charged Hegel with "a completely indefensible form of expression in writing" and the young Marx in a letter to his father speaks of "the grotesque craggy melody" of Hegel's texts.[18] I would nevertheless testify to the unparalleled logical precision of his thinking and the moments of devastating beauty in his philosophical prose. From Hegel, I have learned the most profound lessons regarding what it means to lead a spiritual life and why our freedom is possible only through our mutual recognition of one another as essentially social, historical, material, and finite living beings.[19] The depths of life are not revealed through faith in eternity. Rather, our spiritual commitments proceed from caring for what will be irrevocably lost and remaining faithful to what gives no final guarantee. Secular faith will always be precarious, but in its fragility it opens the possibility of our spiritual freedom.

PART I

Secular Faith

Faith

I

He never knew it would feel like this. She had entered his life, transformed his world, opened his body and mind. Yet, throughout it all, he had told himself that his devotion to her did not compromise his devotion to God. "I had warned myself," he recalls, "not to reckon on worldly happiness."[1] But it turns out that this is precisely what he did. He loved her, and because he loved her he is shattered by her death. For days and nights, he records "the mad words, the bitter resentment, the fluttering in the stomach, the nightmare unreality, the wallowed-in-tears."[2]

His pious friends tell him to take solace in God and in the words of Saint Paul: "Do not mourn like those who have no hope." He comes to understand, however, that "what St. Paul says can comfort only those who love God better than the dead."[3] His faith in God would direct him toward an eternal life. But in loving her and in mourning her death, he is not comforted by his faith in God and eternity. He does not want to repose in eternal peace; he wants her to come back and their life together to go on, in the time and space of their shared existence. "The earthly beloved," he writes, "incessantly triumphs over your mere idea of her. And you want her to; you want her with all her resistances, all her faults, all her unexpectedness. That is, in her foursquare and independent reality. And this, not any image or memory, is what we are to love still, after she is dead."[4]

The words belong to C. S. Lewis in his book *A Grief Observed*, written after the death of his wife, Joy Davidman. While Lewis was one of the most influential Christian writers of his time, *A Grief Observed* strikes a different tone. Rather than preach or instruct, Lewis seeks to describe what is happening to him in the experience of mourning, as he explores the pain and desperation of losing his beloved. What emerges through this account is not simply a crisis of faith, in the sense that the death of his wife makes him doubt the existence of God. What emerges is something deeper: an insight that his faith in God cannot offer any consolation for the loss of a loved one. If a mother is mourning the death of her child, Lewis writes, "she may still hope to 'glorify God and enjoy him forever,'" which may be "a comfort to the God-aimed, eternal spirit within her. But not to her motherhood. The specifically maternal happiness must be written off. Never, in any place or time, will she have her son on her knees, or bathe him, or tell him a story, or plan for his future, or see her grandchild."[5]

In contrast to his religious faith in eternity, Lewis describes a passionate commitment to a finite life. The mother who is mourning her child, or the lover who is mourning his beloved, is devoted to a relationship that requires time to be what it is. Love is not something that can take place in an instant. Rather, love expresses a commitment to caring for another person across time. The temporality of such love is not merely an unavoidable condition; it is intrinsic to the positive qualities of being with the beloved. In loving another, one cherishes a projected future, the repetition of acts, and the ongoing time of living together. It is the end of such a temporal life that one mourns when the beloved is lost. And as Lewis makes clear, the hope for eternity is not a consolation. Even if the hope for eternity were fulfilled, it would not bring back the life they shared together:

Suppose that the earthly lives she and I shared for a few years are in reality only the basis for, or prelude to, or earthly appearance of, two unimaginable, supercosmic, eternal somethings. Those somethings could be pictured as spheres or globes. Where the plane of Nature cuts through them—that is, in earthly life—they appear as two circles (circles are slices of spheres). Two circles that touched. But those two circles, above all the point at which they touched, are the very thing I am mourning for, homesick for, famished for. You tell me, "[S]he goes on." But my heart and body are crying out, come back, come back. Be a circle, touching my circle on the plane of Nature. But I know this is impossible. I know that the thing I want is exactly the thing I can never get. The old life, the jokes, the drinks, the arguments, the lovemaking, the tiny, heartbreaking commonplace. On any view whatever, to say, "H. is dead," is to say "All that is gone." It is a part of the past. And the past is the past and that is what time means, and time itself is one more name for death, and Heaven itself is a state where "the former things have passed away. . . ."

Unless, of course, you can literally believe all that stuff about family reunions "on the further shore," pictured in entirely earthly terms. But that is all unscriptural, all out of bad hymns and lithographs. There's not a word of it in the Bible.[6]

Lewis here vividly articulates how the attachment to the beloved is expressed through a commitment to *living on* with her. He cannot come to terms with the death of his wife because he wants their life together to continue, in the temporal rhythm and physical concreteness that gave their relationship its unique quality. Accordingly, he does not want them to be self-sufficient, timeless beings (what he describes as "two unimaginable, supercosmic, eternal somethings"). Rather, he wants them to be in need of each other, vulnerable and open to being transformed by the touch of the other. For the same reason, the promise of an eternal state of being cannot deliver what he desires. In the consummation of eternity—here described as a state of heaven where all "former things" have passed away in favor of eternity—there would be no time for their relationship to live on. Eternity would put an end to their time together and in such a state their love could not survive.

The commitment to his beloved that animates *A Grief Observed* is therefore at odds with Lewis's commitment to God. As a long-standing reader of Christian theology, he is well aware that he is not supposed to love mortal beings as ends in themselves but only as means toward the love of God. As he explains in *A Grief Observed:* "If you're approaching Him not as the goal but as a road, not as the end but as a means, you're not really approaching Him at all."[7] This is why Lewis emphasizes that the Bible does not support visions of an afterlife that project reunions with the people you have loved throughout your life. Such visions are not directed toward God as the End, but at most treat God as a means for retrieving the mortal beloved. The vision of an afterlife where Lewis's wife would welcome him is attached to living on with the beloved rather than to dwelling in the eternity of God.

Lewis thus illuminates my central distinction between *living on* (prolonging a temporal life) and being *eternal* (absorbed in a timeless existence). As he makes agonizingly clear, the former cannot be reconciled with the latter. In mourning his wife, Lewis loves her as an end in herself. He does not want anything beyond her; he wants her to return and their life as lovers to go on: "the jokes, the drinks, the arguments, the lovemaking, the tiny, heartbreaking commonplace." This desire is committed to sharing a life that requires time to be what it is. In wanting his beloved to come back, an eternal life is not only unattainable but also *undesirable*. He wants their relationship to live on, rather than to be absorbed in an eternal life.

One may ask here why the choice between living on and eternity has to be an either/or. Many popular conceptions of the afterlife assume that living on and being in eternity can be combined, allowing one to keep the positive qualities of life without the threat of losing them. Thus, in response to my argument, the prominent theologian Miroslav Volf has emphasized that Christian visions of eternity are better understood as visions of an *endless* rather than a *timeless* existence.[8] Volf concedes that a timeless life would be meaningless, since there can be no experiences and no events without time. Nevertheless, he maintains that it would be desirable to live forever. In such an eternity, there would still be time, but none of the changes in time would be experienced as a negative loss. Rather, all forms of change would be experienced as an ongoing part of the divine good. The afterlife would thus enable one to live on with the beloved, in an experience of eternity that is untouched by the prospect of tragic loss.

My argument, however, is that an endless life is just as meaningless as a timeless one. The risk of tragic loss—the loss of your own life and the loss of what you love—is not a prospect that can be eliminated but an intrinsic part of why it matters what you do with your life. If you and your beloved did not believe that your lives were finite, neither one of you could take your lives to be at stake and there would be no urgency to do anything with your time. You could never care for yourselves, for one another, or for the commitment that you share, since you would have no sense of fragility. By the same token, you could feel no need to make an effort on behalf of the relationship, since you would have no apprehension that the other person could leave you or that your relationship could break down. The moments of profound intimacy would not be experienced as precious, but as the given state of things. You would expect everything to be settled, rather than dependent on your engagement and attention, as well as on the unforeseeable responses of your beloved. This is why living on with your beloved is incompatible with being in eternity, even on the level of the imagination. As soon as you remove the sense of finitude and vulnerability, you remove the vitality of any possible love relationship.

The sense of finitude reverberates in every aspect of your life. In living on, you always remain vulnerable by virtue of leading a temporal life. Living on does not protect you against the regret of having done something irreversible, the pain of not being able to fulfill a given ambition, or the heartbreak of being left by the one you love. Indeed, your world can break down precisely because you live on after the death of everything you love. This "death" can be much more painful and fearful than the prospect of your own death, not least because it is a death that you have to survive.

Hence, as long as you are attached to someone or something that you can lose, you are susceptible to suffering. To attain a peaceful state of eternity you must be liberated from the risk of losing what you love. Were such liberation possible, however, nothing would matter to you. You literally *would not care.* There would be no urgency to do anything or maintain love for anyone, since nothing of value could be lost. You could not even be motivated to sustain a single activity, since it would not count as a loss for you if you did not engage in the activity.

The passion and pathos of living with your beloved are therefore incompatible with the security of an eternal life. The sense of something being unique and irreplaceable is inseparable from the sense that it *can* be lost. This relation to loss is inscribed in the very form of living on. To live on is never to repose in a timeless or endless presence. Rather, to live on is to remain after a past that has ceased to be and before an unpredictable future that may not come to be.

The precarious experience of time is not only a negative peril but also the positive possibility of coming into being, living on, and being motivated to act. The motivation to undertake any form of project—to sustain a commitment, to pursue a course of action— requires that the project be precarious: that it not be given as a fact but must be upheld by conviction and fidelity. You have to believe in the value of the project, but you also have to believe that the project may cease to be and needs to be sustained. Thus, when you love someone, that love exists only insofar as you sustain it. Your love is not given as a fact but is something that has to be achieved and— once achieved—has to be maintained and developed. This project requires that you believe in the value of the love, but it also requires that you believe that the love can be lost and solicits you to care.

II

The connection between caring and believing has a long philosophical lineage. With his characteristic lucidity, Aristotle makes clear that any form of care depends on belief. The beliefs that we hold should not be understood primarily as theoretical propositions but as practical commitments. Aristotle's argument proceeds by showing that even our most immediate emotions are intelligible only in terms of the beliefs to which we are committed. For example, if you fear death you believe in the value of your life but you also believe that your life is under threat. As Aristotle points out, "nobody will be afraid who believes nothing can happen to him."[9] This sense of precariousness is not limited to the prospect of your own death but extends to everything that matters to you. If you feel fear when your beloved is walking next to the edge of a cliff, it is both because you believe that the beloved is vulnerable and because you believe that his or her life is valuable. Without either of these beliefs—without your commitment to the beloved *as* valuable or *as* vulnerable—you would feel no fear, even if the other elements of the situation were the same.

Pursuing the implications of Aristotle's analysis, the Greek and Roman Stoics argue that all our passions are forms of belief. The beliefs do not have to be consciously held, but are forms of practical commitments that are evident in the passions themselves. If you suffer from envy, you believe in the value of what someone else possesses and are committed to attaining it. If you are seized by anger, you believe in the value of what someone else has damaged and are committed to retribution. If you are overcome by grief, you believe in the value of what you have lost and are committed to remembering it. If you are elated by joy, you believe in the value of what you receive and are committed to maintaining it.

The passions are forms of acknowledging your dependence on others and on events that exceed your control. If you are hopeful, you believe in the value of what is promised, and if you are fearful, you believe in the value of what is threatened. By the same token, you are vulnerable, since you cannot finally control what will happen. Your hopes may be shattered and your fears may come true.

The goal of Stoicism is to overcome such vulnerability and attain peace of mind. The Stoic is well aware that everything he has will be taken away, but he seeks to eliminate the passions that make him suffer from the loss.[10] Developing this argument, the early modern philosopher Spinoza advocates release from the "bondage" of the passions. Both the Stoics and Spinoza are eminently *religious* thinkers in my sense of the term. They seek to overcome secular faith—the commitment to a life that is finite and dependent on the fragile recognition of others—in favor of religious devotion to eternity. While Spinoza is deeply critical of religious superstition and pious submission to authority, he takes his own philosophical method to fulfill the deepest aim of religion—namely, to provide the path to "true salvation and blessedness," which "consists in true peace of mind."[11] In a characteristic passage, which draws on the Stoic analysis of the passions, Spinoza describes the path to such peace of mind:

> Strife will never arise on account of what is not loved, nor will there be sadness if it perishes, nor envy if it is possessed by another, nor fear, nor hatred—in a word, no disturbances of the mind. Indeed, all these happen only in the love of those things that can perish, as all the things we have just spoken of can do.
>
> But love toward the eternal and infinite feeds the mind with a joy entirely exempt from sadness. This is greatly to be desired, and to be sought with all our strength.[12]

The source of all "disturbances of the mind"—from sadness and fear to envy and hatred—is here identified as "the love of those things that can perish." The key to achieving peace of mind is to remove your love from those things that can perish and instead direct your love toward the eternal, which "feeds the mind with a joy entirely exempt from sadness." This joy is not itself a passion but rather the state of blessedness (*beatitudo*) that provides the "complete peace of mind," which Spinoza identifies with religious salvation.

For Spinoza, salvation is not achieved by a personal, immortal soul or through transportation to a transcendent afterlife. Rather, salvation is achieved by letting go of your passions and seeing yourself as part of what he calls God or Nature. The two terms are interchangeable for Spinoza, since both designate the eternal, immanent substance of everything that exists, in contrast to finite bodies that perish. As Spinoza makes clear, any given idea or affection of a finite body is susceptible to decomposition. Furthermore, as a finite body you can always suffer from being overpowered by external forces that are stronger than yourself and leave you shattered. Yet, by aligning yourself with the eternal substance of God or Nature, you will be able to bear all this with equanimity. You will neither be hopeful nor fearful, since you will not be guided by passionate love for something finite but rather by an intellectual, contemplative love of God's eternal nature. Accordingly, Spinoza asserts that we should strive toward pure contemplation as the highest good. While we cannot escape the fact that everything we are passionate about will be lost, we can eliminate the passion that makes the loss agonizing and achieve peace of mind by contemplating the world from the standpoint of eternity (*sub specie aeternitatis*).

Spinoza presents a clear version of what I call the religious aspiration to eternity. This aspiration is not limited to visions of a transcendent afterlife, but pertains just as well to an immanent ideal of attaining complete peace of mind. Indeed, I define as religious *any ideal of being absolved from the pain of loss.* While many religious ideals include pain and suffering as necessary steps on the way to salvation, the ultimate goal is to be absolved from vulnerability. I argue that such absolution is not only impossible to attain but also not a goal worthy of our striving, since it would remove the care that animates our lives. Whether the absolution is conceived as transcendent or immanent, it requires that we renounce our commitment to finite life. To achieve absolution we cannot love any mortal beings as ends in themselves but only as means toward the end of suffering. If we were absolved from suffering—viewing the world from the standpoint of eternity—we could no longer care about whether someone lives or dies, since nothing that happens could count as a loss for us. Being eternal is therefore *undesirable* and a standpoint of eternity is *unintelligible*, since it would remove any form of practical commitment that makes it possible to be engaged in the world.

My argument can helpfully be compared to that of a thinker who is often aligned with Spinoza, but who in fact comes close to grasping the dynamic of secular faith: Friedrich Nietzsche. Nietzsche's critique of religious faith should not be reduced to his famous saying "God is dead," meaning that belief in eternal life or eternal being has been discredited. Rather, Nietzsche's important argument is that the death of God should not be received as bad news. If one laments the absence of eternal life, one is still in the grip of the religious ideal, even though one does not believe that it can be realized. In contrast, Nietzsche pursues a *revaluation* of the value of an eternal life that would be free from suffering and loss. As Nietzsche emphasizes, it is pernicious to endorse the ideal of eternal life or eternal being, since it leads to a devaluation of the commitment to temporal, finite life. Suffering and loss are not merely necessary steps on the way to bliss or inescapable, unfortunate conditions; they are intrinsic parts of what makes life worth living.[13]

Yet there is a crucial difference between saying that "suffering is part of the life I desire" and saying that "I desire suffering." Nietzsche's deepest insights adhere to the first formulation, but he is continually tempted to embrace the second formulation and thereby loses hold of his own insight. For example, Nietzsche regularly advocates a love of fate (*amor fati*) that would be so "strong" that one does not resent anything that happens, no matter how much suffering it causes: "One wants nothing to be different, not forward, not backward, not in all eternity."[14] By the same token, however, one would no longer suffer, since to suffer is to be at odds with what happens, to struggle against it. Nietzsche's idealization of a "strength" of life or "embrace" of death leads him to deny the very condition of suffering that he seeks to affirm. Contrary to what Nietzsche tends to claim, affirming mortal life does *not* entail embracing death. To affirm mortal life is to oppose death, to resist and defer it as best as possible. But since mortal life is essentially linked to death, it is internally bound to what it opposes.

To keep faith in mortal life, then, is to remain vulnerable to a pain that no strength can finally master. Mortality is not only intrinsic to what makes life meaningful, but also makes life susceptible to lose meaning and become unbearable. The point is not to overcome this vulnerability but to recognize that it is an essential part of why our lives *matter* and why we care.

III

Secular faith is a condition of intelligibility for any form of care. For anything to be intelligible *as mattering*—for anything to be at stake—we have to believe in the irreplaceable value of someone or something that is finite. This secular faith—which the religious aspiration to eternity seeks to leave behind—is expressed by care for anyone or anything living on. Secular faith is a condition of possibility for commitment and engagement, but by the same token secular faith leaves us open to devastation and grief.

The most fundamental form of secular faith is the faith that life is worth living, which is intrinsic to all forms of care. In caring about our own lives and the lives of others, we necessarily believe that life is worth living. This is a matter of faith because we cannot *prove* that life is worth living despite all the suffering it entails. That life is worth living cannot be demonstrated through a logical deduction or rational calculation. Rather, the faith that life is worth living sustains us even when our lives seem to be unbearable or intolerable. Moreover, it is because we believe that life is worth living that our lives can appear *as* unbearable or intolerable in the first place. If we did not believe that life is worth living, we could not experience our lives either as fulfilling or as unbearable, since we would be indifferent to the quality of our lives and unmoved by anything that happens.

Even our most elementary ability to care depends on secular faith. Secular faith has three interrelated aspects, which are inseparable in the dynamic of care but can be distinguished analytically.

First, secular faith is an *existential commitment*. The faith that life is worth living is not caused by some vital force but is constituted by the commitment to a fragile form of life. The form of life to which we are committed is *normative*, since we lead our lives in light of a conception of who we *ought* to be and what we *ought* to do. Our existential commitment to a form of life is *not* reducible to a drive for self-preservation and is a condition for even the most altruistic deeds. If I give my life for another person, it is because I believe that her life is worth living and am committed to her sustenance. Similarly, if I sacrifice my life for a cause, it is because I believe in its importance and seek to help the cause be carried on in history. The existential commitment to a form of life is a condition for caring at all. If I did not have faith that life is worth living, I would never be compelled to fight for the memory of the past or for a better future.

Second, secular faith is a *necessary uncertainty*. In being committed to someone or something, I must have faith in the future and in those on whom I depend. I cannot be *certain* of what others will do, so I have to relate to them on the basis of faith. Faith provides the positive chance of having a relation to others—of trusting them—but it also opens the negative threat of being deceived or betrayed. The same holds for any relation to the future. I cannot be *certain* of what will happen, so I have to take the future on faith. Secular faith marks the possibility of having a future—of being committed—but for the same reason it entails the peril of having faith in a future that may shatter my hopes and wreck the cause to which I am devoted.

Third, the precariousness of secular faith is a *motivational force*. In keeping faith with a form of life—whether expressed through the commitment to a person, a project, or a principle—I have to believe that the object of faith is precarious. My commitment to the continued life of someone or something is inseparable from my sense that it cannot be taken for granted. There has to be a prospective risk of loss for anything to be at stake in sustaining a form of life. Without the exposure to loss, there would be no impetus to care for anything, since there would be no risk that could motivate the act of taking care. Part of what compels me to keep faith with a person, a project, or a principle is my apprehension that it *can* be lost or compromised and thereby requires my fidelity.

Secular faith animates *both* our relation to what we want to protect *and* our relation to what we aspire to achieve. In caring, we may be devoted not only to what we have and strive to maintain but also to what we do not have and strive to achieve. Even in the latter case, the threefold dynamic of secular faith is at work. Our faith in the future expresses an existential commitment. We are committed to pursuing one possibility rather than another. This commitment entails the necessary uncertainty of secular faith, since we run the risk of failure or loss in pursuing the possibility to which we are devoted. Furthermore, the risk of failure or loss is intrinsic to the motivational force of the commitment itself. In order to be motivated to act, we have to believe that the possibility is not given once and for all but requires that we sustain it through our engagement.

The risk of loss is thus an essential part of the dynamic of secular faith. Keeping faith with an existential commitment—to a political transformation, a filial relation, an artistic creation, and so on—can always leave us bereaved, since what we believe in may cease to be or never come to be. For this reason, one may think that the most desirable form of commitment would be to have faith in someone or something that will *always* be, that cannot ever be lost. This ideal of eternity—which can take many different forms—is the common denominator for what I call religious forms of faith.

I emphasize the adjective *religious* (rather than the noun *religion*), since the ideal I am targeting is not limited to specific forms of institutionalized religion. Moreover, my critique of religious faith is not restricted to beliefs concerning a supernatural God, a divine creation of the universe, or an otherworldly state of being. At least one of the major world religions (Buddhism) does not promote either a supernatural God or a cosmogony that seeks to explain why the universe exists. Furthermore, certain forms of Buddhism emphasize that the highest goal of aspiration—nirvana—is a way of being in the here and now, rather than an otherworldly state of being. In either case, however, to attain nirvana is to be "released" from the time and suffering of finitude. One who has attained nirvana does not suffer from the loss of anything, since he or she is detached from everything that is finite. For this reason, the Buddhist notion of nirvana—whether conceived as an immanent tranquillity of being in the world or as a transcendent peace beyond life—is a clear and consistent version of the religious ideal of eternity. Even according to religious teachings that do not advocate detachment, the commitment to secular projects must be subordinated—or serve as a step on the way—to eternity. "If souls please you, love them in God, because by themselves they are subject to change," as Augustine underlines in his *Confessions*. If one loves mortal beings and is committed to secular projects, one should not be attached to them as ends in themselves but rather love the eternal *through* them.

What I call religious faith, then, is characterized by the attempt to convert us from our secular faith, since this faith makes us vulnerable to irrevocable loss. To have religious faith is to *disown* our secular faith in a fragile form of life. Religious faith holds that our ultimate aim should be to transcend the finitude we share. As a consequence, *this life* is devalued and comes to be seen as a transitional state of being from which we ought to be saved. In contrast, I seek to show what it means to *own* our secular faith and to engage the transformative possibilities that are opened up by acknowledging our commitment to our only life.

IV

The stakes of my arguments can be elucidated in relation to Charles Taylor's seminal book *A Secular Age*. Taylor's philosophical and historical account of the rise of secularity is motivated by a question that is central to my account—namely, what are the conditions for faith today, in the period that Taylor calls a secular age? The established notion of secularity (from which Taylor departs) mainly refers to two phenomena. First, secularity designates the retreat of religion from the public sphere and the public use of reason. For example, deliberations in politics are justified with regard to a conception of the public good that does not depend on religious belief and scientific inquiry is encouraged even if it may threaten religious convictions. Religious dogma is no longer accepted as an authoritative reason in public life and rather becomes a matter of private belief. Second, secularity refers to a decline in religious belief itself, with more and more people living their lives without practicing religion.

One of Taylor's important contributions is that he articulates a third aspect of secularity. To live in a secular age changes the conditions of faith even for those who hold on to religious belief. As Taylor puts it:

> The change I want to define and trace is one which takes us from a society in which it was virtually impossible not to believe in God, to one in which faith, even for the staunchest believer, is one human possibility among others. I may find it inconceivable that I would abandon my faith, but there are others, including possibly some very close to me, whose way of living I cannot in all honesty just dismiss as depraved, or blind, or unworthy, who have no faith (at least in God, or the transcendent). Belief in God is no longer axiomatic. There are alternatives.[15]

Even though one may question Taylor's historical narrative (with its postulation of "a society in which it was virtually impossible not to believe in God"), he is making an insightful argument about the increasing pressures on religious belief. In previous historical periods, it was not impossible to be an atheist but it was very difficult to be an atheist *publicly* and in the United States today it is *still* difficult, at least if you are running for office. Living in a secular society puts pressure on this hegemony of religious belief, not only because a secular society may lead one to live close to and collaborate with those who do not share one's beliefs, but also because domains previously claimed by religion are shown to function and flourish without it. In a society where the public good is decided on without reference to the authority of religion—and where natural science provides explanations of the world that contradict religious claims—religious belief can no longer justify itself in the same way.

To be sure, there are many who deny that the conditions of belief have changed and reassert the authority of religion in politics, science, and other domains of public life. Such religious fundamentalism is the main target of the so-called New Atheists, who seek to debunk religious faith with scientific knowledge. Yet, a vast number of religious people do not regard their faith as competing with knowledge. While accepting the freedom of scientific inquiry and democratic pluralism, they hold that religious faith is crucial for the spiritual shape and profound meaning of life. An atheism that does not engage this sense of religion will fail to transform deep-seated notions about faith. Even many people who themselves do not have religious faith believe that it would be great and beneficial to have such faith. The latter attitude is what the philosopher Daniel Dennett has described as *believing in belief in God*. "Such a person doesn't believe in God but nevertheless thinks that believing in God would be a wonderful state of mind to be in, if only that could be arranged."[16] This belief in the existential value of religious faith (rather than in the truth of religious claims) is the main line of defense for religion in a secular age, after its authority to organize society or legislate over science has been conceded.

Taylor is an instructive example, since he explicitly defends religion in existential terms. Seeking to create a space of dialogue between atheism and religious faith, Taylor rightly emphasizes that we should not primarily regard the respective positions as "rival *theories*" about existence, but rather "focus attention on the different kinds of lived experience involved in understanding your life in one way or the other, on what it's like to live as a believer or an unbeliever."[17] Taylor's focal point here is the notion of "fullness" that animates a given life. With this term, he designates the conception of what a life realized to the full would mean. As Taylor explains:

> Every person, and every society, lives with or by some conception(s) of what human flourishing is: what constitutes a fulfilled

life? What makes life really worth living? What would we most admire people for? We can't help asking these and related questions in our lives. And our struggles to answer them define the view or views that we try to live by.[18]

Taylor is well aware that there are many conceptions of fullness—many visions of a life worth living—that do not depend on religious faith. Indeed, one of the hallmarks of a secular age is that commitments to social justice, the formation of communities, and ideals of a good life, are developed, fought for, and sustained without religious belief. Yet Taylor insists that secular notions of fullness ultimately cannot lead to a fulfilling life. Anyone who defines his or her life without reference to a religious sense of fullness will rather experience that something essential is missing, since human beings (according to Taylor) have "an ineradicable bent to respond to something beyond life," namely, "an irrepressible need" for an absolute "good beyond life."[19]

For Taylor, then, the religious distinguishes itself from other forms of orienting human life by referring to a fullness that is exempt from time and finitude (his main examples are the Christian idea of eternal life and the Buddhist notion of nirvana). From a religious perspective, the highest good is not the flourishing of finite lives. Rather, as Taylor argues, religious notions of the highest good appeal to an absolute fullness—or an absolute emptiness, as in Buddhism—which is held to be "independent of" and "beyond" the flourishing of finite life.[20] This is certainly not the only possible definition of a religious perspective on life; there are many others and their respective relevance depends on the context in which one intervenes. I focus on Taylor's definition because it is indispensable for the idea with which I take issue, namely, the idea that there is an essential human need for something called "religion" or "the religious," which a secular life will try in vain to fulfill. To defend such an idea, one cannot refer solely to the ability of religions to provide a sense of community, organize human life in accordance with a set of traditions, or motivate action based on ethical values. These are features that religious practices share with many other practices. We can build communities, cultivate ethical values, and foster political commitments without appealing to religious faith. There is, however, one thing that a secular form of life never will be able to promise: an *eternal* life or an *eternal* state of being. As we will see, the logic of Taylor's argument thus emerges most clearly when he defines the desire for religious fullness as a "desire for eternity." If one assumes that we have a fundamental desire for eternal life, then it follows that all secular forms of fullness—which are bound to forms of finite life—will be found lacking and inherently incapable of fulfilling our desire.

Taylor's main example is the experience of the death of the beloved. Drawing on the work of the French historian Philippe Ariès—as well as sociological studies of contemporary faith—Taylor emphasizes that the loss of loved ones is the experience that is hardest to bear in a secular age:

> It is significant that the salient feature of death today, the major drama around it, is this separation of loved ones. Ariès has shown that it was not always so. In the late medieval and early modern ages, the great issue was the judgment soon to be faced by the person dying. And before that, the dead were in a sense still in a sort of community with the living. So that Ariès distinguishes the periods under the titles: "la mort de nous" [our death], "la mort de moi" [my death], and "la mort de toi" [your death]. Just because Hell has faded, but love relationships are central to the meaning of our lives, we live with the greatest anguish *la mort de toi*.[21]

Again, one may question the details of the historical account given here. The experience of *your death* was certainly vivid and deeply painful long before the advent of the modern age, as any reading of literary history from Homer onward will testify. Nevertheless, the important point is that the pain and anguish of losing the beloved are allowed to emerge with greater force in an explicitly secular age. The question is whether a religious notion of eternity is capable of addressing the experience of mourning and offering consolation.

Taylor takes this for granted and laments the withdrawal of belief in eternal life. "There is a sense of void here, and of deep embarrassment," Taylor claims, and he adduces the lack of belief in eternity as an explanation for why "we very often feel awkward at a funeral; don't know what to say to the bereaved; are often tempted to avoid the issue if we can."[22] Moreover, he suggests that "even people who otherwise don't practice have recourse to religious funerals" because "here at least is a language which fits the need for eternity, even if you're not sure you believe all that."[23] The love for and resistance to letting go of the beloved would thus testify to a religious desire for eternity, since "love by its nature calls for eternity."[24]

To understand the stakes of the argument, it is worth pausing to consider how Taylor articulates the relation between time and eternity. Taylor reduces the notion of "secular time" to a mere succession of moments that have no intrinsic connection with one another. In contrast, all forms of "gathering time"—of holding on to the past and projecting into the future—are for Taylor expressions of our "irrepressible craving for eternity."[25] While Taylor acknowledges that our forms of gathering time cannot attain the absolute fullness of eternity, he holds that such fullness is the goal. According to Taylor, eternity should not be understood as a timeless state of being but rather as the gathering of time into an instant. "God's eternity," Taylor claims, "does not abolish time, but gathers it into an instant."[26]

Taylor's distinction has been made by many Christian thinkers, but it is specious. There is no intelligible difference between abolishing time and gathering time into an instant. If time is gathered into an instant there is no time, since the instant does not give way to the future and become past. Rather, everything is present and there is no time for anything to happen, since everything that can possibly happen is already contained in the eternal now. As Taylor himself underscores, in God's eternity "all times are present to him, and he holds them in his extended simultaneity. His now contains all time."[27] Such an eternal now cannot "gather" time but eliminates any sense of time. There is no analogy between the eternal presence of God and our attempts to hold on to the time of our lives. Far from gathering our experiences and allowing us to live on, an eternal now would deprive us of a past and a future. Our lifetime would be reduced to an instant and we would have no life to live.[28]

To distinguish between eternity and living on is therefore decisive. When we wish that the lives of those whom we love will last, we do not wish for them to be eternal but for their lives to continue. Likewise, when we "gather time" into a meaningful network of relations, we are not "craving for eternity." Taylor's argument is based on a conflation, which makes it seem as though we aspire to a religious form of eternity when we aspire to secular forms of living on. The secular experience of time *cannot* be reduced to a series of discrete moments. On the contrary, *any* experience of time depends on retaining the past and projecting into the future. This is the minimal form of living on, which is the condition for all forms of "gathering time." The form of living on makes it possible to bind the past to the future—to make our lives last and hold together beyond the moment—but it cannot even in principle reduce time to the simultaneity of an eternal present. On the contrary, to live on is to maintain the relation to a past that is no longer and the relation to a future that is not yet. The form of living on enables us to sustain a commitment—to safeguard what we love and bind together what matters to us—but it also marks the inherent fragility of the binding activity.

Furthermore, the fragility of any bond of love is an intrinsic part of *why it matters* that we keep faith with our love and bind our lives together. As is clear from Taylor's own account, love consists in sustaining a relation that can be lost and thereby expresses a commitment to living on rather than to eternity. "A deep love," Taylor points out, "already exists against the vicissitudes of life, tying together past and present in spite of the disruptions and dispersals of quarrels, distractions, misunderstandings, resentments."[29] To love one another is to be devoted to living on and flourishing together despite the forces that pull us apart. Indeed, the temporality of liv-

ing on is at work in the very experience of fulfillment. Even the greatest moments of happiness in love—gathering and deepening the
qualitative experience of a shared life—cannot be contained in an
instant, since the moment is bound up with a network of meaning
that extends to the memory of a shared past and anticipations of a
future together. As Taylor himself emphasizes: "The deepest, most
powerful kind of happiness, even in the moment, is plunged into a
sense of meaning," so that "when you look back on your life together,
those happy moments, those travels in the sun, were bathed in the
awareness of other years, other travels, which seemed to come alive
in the present one."[30]

In Taylor's own account, the experience of love cannot be reduced
to a simultaneous presence but opens onto a past and a future that
exceed any given moment. Yet Taylor persistently conflates the
desire to prolong our lives—to gather and preserve what we love—
with a supposed desire for eternity. Consider the following passage,
which symptomatically glosses the aspiration to live on as an aspiration for eternity:

> All joy strives for eternity, because it loses some of its sense if it
> doesn't last. . . . Even just holding in memory is akin to keeping
> the time alive; even more if you can write about it, capture it in
> art. Art aspires to a certain kind of eternity, to be able to speak to
> future ages. But there are also other lesser modes or substitutes for
> eternity. One can make the eternal be the clan, the tribe, the soci-
> ety, the way of life. And your love, and the children who come from
> it, have their place in the chain; as long as you have preserved, or
> better enhanced, that tribe or way of life, you've handed it on. In
> that way, the meaning continues.
>
> This just shows how joy strives for eternity, even if all that
> is available is a lesser form of it; and even if something is left out
> that matters to us highly individuated moderns, as the particular
> things that meant most to us are gradually lost in the general
> impact we've made. And of course, this eternity can't preserve

those who are really forgotten, or those who haven't left their
mark, or those who have been damned, excluded. There is no general resurrection in this "eternity" of grateful posterity.[31]

Taylor here assumes that when we strive to make something *last* we
are striving for *eternity*. But that is a mistaken inference. When we
strive to make something last we do not strive to make it eternal but
to make it last for a longer time and in a qualitative sense: to make
something live on *for the future*—for persons, projects, and generations that matter to us—rather than for eternity. Through memory
we can prolong precious periods of happiness, "keeping the time
alive"; through artistic creation and the rearing of children we can
make our legacy live on beyond our own death; through community
with others, political commitments, and the care for a sustainable
society we can extend a sense of purpose far beyond the duration of
our own lives. These endeavors are *not* oriented toward eternity but
express commitments to forms of living on, which have to reckon
with their own finitude. Memories are fallible and eventually erased,
artworks can fall into oblivion or wither away, and the very existence
of future generations is never guaranteed.

Following from his notion of a religious desire for fullness, Taylor
asserts that all these forms of living on are "lesser modes or substitutes for eternity." When we passionately strive to "keep the time
alive"—to sustain our lives or those of others—we supposedly seek
an eternal life, for which temporal life is merely a "substitute." Taylor thereby disregards that the desire for the continuation and flourishing of finite life does *not* entail a desire for eternity. If we seek to
prolong our own life, the life of another, or the life of our society, we
seek to transcend the limits of a particular time—to live on—but we
do not seek to transcend the condition of time altogether. Far from
fulfilling our desire to live on, eternity would deprive us of the life
we want to maintain.

For the same reason, an eternal life cannot remedy the loss I
mourn in the experience of *your death*, which Taylor highlights as the
central problem in our secular age. Indeed, the religious notions of

eternity that Taylor invokes as a supposed remedy (Buddhist nirvana and Christian eternal life) do not even pretend to offer the return of the beloved. Rather than supporting the attachment to a mortal beloved, the prerequisite for entering nirvana is the *detachment* from everything that is subject to loss. Similarly, the point of dwelling in heaven is not to adore and pursue one's life with the earthly beloved, but to turn one's adoration toward God. "In the resurrection they neither marry nor are given in marriage," as Jesus reminds us (Matt. 22:30).

Thus, the religious language of eternity—which according to Taylor should resonate with depth and reassurance at funerals—does not actually capture what we long for and express what we feel when we are in mourning. Taylor himself testifies to the difficulty of finding "a ceremony for death which will speak to our strongest feelings," but he never considers that this may be due to the assumption that what we need is a religious ceremony. Certainly, the secular funerals that I have attended in recent years—painfully mourning the loss of loved ones—have not been marked by the embarrassment and awkwardness that Taylor ascribes to funeral ceremonies in the absence of religious faith. Rather, these funerals have provided a space for profoundly felt expressions of secular faith in the irreplaceable value of a finite life—faith in the value of its past, faith in the importance of carrying it with us in the future—as well as devastation at the loss of this life.

V

Burying the dead can be seen as a fundamental form of secular faith. Through the act of burial—here understood as any form of honoring the deceased—we acknowledge both the irrevocable loss of a life and our continued fidelity to this life. We express our commitment to remembering and honoring the dead, avowing our responsibility for those who no longer exist. The dead can *live on* only in and through us: to the extent that we acknowledge them through our actions and as part of who we take ourselves to be. It is because the dead cannot be brought back to life—because they are irredeemably dead—that we are responsible for them. The very pain of loss can therefore be experienced as a form of fidelity in mourning. My love for you means that I *ought* to be utterly bereaved in the face of your death. This sense of responsibility is intelligible only from the standpoint of secular faith, since it is devoted to a life that is recognized as mortal and places demands on us precisely because it is mortal.

A religious faith in eternity cannot add anything to the dignity and pathos of mourning; it can only subtract from the mourning by diminishing the sense of loss. This is not to say that avowedly religious people do not mourn. But insofar as they do mourn, their mourning is animated by a secular faith in the irreplaceable value of a finite life rather than by a religious faith in eternity. If you truly believed in the existence of eternity—and in the superior value of eternal life—there would be no reason to mourn the loss of a finite life. Thus, Buddhism teaches that a fully enlightened person is beyond the pain of mourning and loss, having extinguished the desire to hold on to any life that is passing away. The same logic is articulated by the founding figures of Christianity. Saint Augustine forcefully argues against mourning the loss of mortal lives and upon the death of his mother—when he cannot hold back his tears—he condemns his weeping as an act of sin. Martin Luther in his turn declares, upon the death of his daughter Magdalena in 1542, that "I rejoice in the spirit, but sorrow in the flesh," emphasizing to the congregation after her funeral that "we Christians ought not to mourn."[32]

The one who takes his or her religious faith seriously will thus experience how it clashes with the secular faith that animates the experience of mourning. This is clear in the case of Luther. Despite declaring that the death of his daughter makes him rejoice in spirit, Luther movingly testifies to how "the flesh will not submit; parting grieves us beyond all measure."[33] Writing to his friend Justus Jonas, Luther confesses that although he and his wife should be grateful to God for Magdalena's death, they are unable to feel such gratitude in their hearts:

I and my wife should joyfully give thanks for such a felicitous departure and blessed end by which Magdalena escaped the power of the flesh. Yet the force of our natural love is so great that we are unable to do this without crying and grieving in our hearts, or even without experiencing death ourselves. For the features, the words and the movements of the living and dying daughter remain deeply engraved in our hearts. Even the death of Christ . . . is unable to take this all away as it should.[34]

Luther here confesses his secular faith in the value of a finite, irreplaceable life: his living and dying daughter, her singular features, words, and movements, which continue to haunt him and his wife with a poignancy that the promise of eternal life cannot redeem. The force of their "natural love" is at odds with the force of religious faith and Luther himself records how the former is stronger than the latter. Three years later, writing to Andreas Osiander in 1545, Luther maintains that "it may appear strange, but I am still mourning the death . . . and I am not able to forget her. Yet I know surely that she is in heaven, that she has eternal life there."[35]

The same conflict is rendered in greater depth and detail by Lewis in *A Grief Observed,* written in a secular age that allows even the devout believer more freedom to express his faith in the irreplaceable value of a finite life. Precisely because Lewis is more expressive, the clash between the secular faith that animates mourning and the religious standpoint becomes all the more palpable. From the standpoint of his religious faith, Lewis makes clear that he has no reason to feel bereaved after the death of his wife. Rather, her death should recall him to the devotion to God, which has priority over the devotion to any mortal beloved:

There's no practical problem before me at all. I know the two great commandments, and I'd better get on with them. Indeed, her death has ended the practical problem. While she was alive I could, in practice, have put her before God; that is, could have done what she wanted instead of what He wanted; if there'd been

a conflict. What's left is not a problem about anything I could
do. It's all about weights of feelings and motives and that sort of
thing. It's a problem I'm setting myself.[36]

Yet Lewis—like Luther—is not able to take this lesson to heart.
While he professes to believe in the superior value of devoting oneself to God or merging with Him in mystical union, the "weights
of feelings and motives" in *A Grief Observed* continue to testify to
his preference for being with his beloved. Indeed, the remarkable
passages that outline such a preference—which I analyzed at the
beginning—reverberate until the very end of the book, when Lewis
recalls a conversation he had with Joy Davidman on her deathbed:

> Once very near the end I said, "If you can—if it is allowed—
> come to me when I too am on my deathbed." "Allowed!" she said.
> "Heaven would have a job to hold me; and as for Hell, I'd break it
> into bits." She knew she was speaking a kind of mythological lan-
> guage, with even an element of comedy in it. There was a twinkle
> as well as a tear in her eye. But there was no myth and no joke
> about the will, deeper than any feeling, that flashed through her.[37]

Her will is the will to hold on to a mortal beloved, even in opposition to the supposed will of God or the harmony of heaven. This
passionate commitment—this resistance to letting go—is also what
animates Lewis's mourning for her and his dedication to what they
had together. From the perspective of such love, the source of suffering is not only the pain of separation but also the prospect *that
he could cease to suffer*, that he could reach a state where he would no
longer feel the pain of having lost her and the desire to have her back.
"This fate," writes Lewis in mourning, "would seem to me the worst
of all, to reach a state in which my years of love and marriage should
appear in retrospect a charming episode—like a holiday—that had
briefly interrupted my interminable life. . . . Thus she would die to
me a second time; a worse bereavement than the first. Anything but
that."[38]

Hence, it is all the more striking that the scene Lewis presents on the final page—as the religious resolution—marks the breaking of the will that binds him and his wife together. In direct contrast to the deathbed scene above, the last lines of the book celebrate her pious renunciation of the will to be with him: "She said not to me but to the chaplain, 'I am at peace with God.' She smiled, but not at me. *Poi si tornò all' eterna fontana.*"[39] The line that Lewis leaves in Italian—as the very last sentence of the book—is a quotation from the final canto of Dante's *Paradiso* and reads in translation: "Then she turned toward the eternal fountain." Dante's beloved Beatrice, after having guided him in the ascent to heaven, here turns away from him toward the glory of God. Beatrice thus achieves the state of *beatitude*—the complete bliss of contemplating the radiance of God—which according to Dante is the ultimate fulfillment of desire. "As that light strikes us," Dante emphasizes, we are transformed in such a way that "we cannot (this would be impossible) consent to turn and seek some other face."[40] Thus, even though Beatrice is the love of Dante's life (and vice versa), the supposed fulfillment of their desire is a state of being in which they no longer even care to turn toward one another. There is no Dante in Beatrice's beatitude and no Beatrice in Dante's beatitude. By analogy, there is no C. S. Lewis for Joy Davidman in heaven and no Joy Davidman for C. S. Lewis. Even their own individual identities can no longer be said to exist, since they are unable to do anything except be absorbed by the radiance of God. This religious consummation does not fulfill the wishes that animated their love and their lives; it rather obliterates them, as they are literally lost in the rapture of God.[41]

The religious faith that embraces the prospect of eternity is thus directly at odds with the secular faith that sustains the commitment to a shared, finite life. The state of being that is *the worst* from the standpoint of the one who is mourning—namely, a state of being in which one would not even care about the absence of the beloved—is presented as *the best* from the religious standpoint.

One may object here that many religious people nevertheless seem to find consolation in the hope that they will reunite with their loved ones in the afterlife and that there is no reason to deprive them of this consolation. Certainly, if the prospect of an afterlife helps others to cope with the experience of devastating loss it should be respected as such. Notice, however, that this argument itself is based on a secular commitment, since it is motivated by the care for how people can find a consolation that will enable them to go on living. The argument thereby reduces religious faith in eternity to a means toward the end of sustaining temporal lives. Furthermore, the hope that one will reunite with the beloved and live on together is a hope for something that the notion of eternity does not actually promise to fulfill, as we saw with Luther and Lewis. If the supposed consolation of religion breaks down even for these stalwart believers, there is reason to think that many religious people suffer the same fate and that they can benefit from having access to alternative ways of articulating what they are going through in the experience of mourning.

To provide an understanding of why religious consolations do not address the problem of death—and why we need other ways of expressing what we mourn, love, hope for, and believe in—is one of the aims of this book. In contrast to Taylor, I do not think that the reason many secular people still rely on religious funerals is that the latter speak to our "need for eternity." Rather, it is because secular forms of acknowledging mourning in communal ways are still underdeveloped. This situation is already changing, with the ongoing development of secular funerals, as well as secular ways of understanding the process of mourning and forms of grief counseling or collective support that do not depend on religious belief. While the available versions of such understanding and support can be improved in many ways, what is needed in order to develop them further is not religious faith or a religious vocabulary. On the contrary, if we want to achieve more richly articulated and meaningful forms of acknowledging the mourning of loved ones ("a ceremony for death which will speak to our strongest feelings," as Taylor puts it), we need a language that expresses our faith in the value of finite lives and our commitment to keeping the memory of the dead.

To get a sense of how secular faith is at work—and yet how far we are from achieving a language that expresses it in the public life of the United States—let us consider a contemporary, deeply tragic instance of mortality: the shootings at the Sandy Hook Elementary School in Newtown, Connecticut. On December 14, 2012, twenty children and six adult staff members were killed. The news of this mass murder was met with profound grief across the country, leading to intense efforts to change gun laws and restrict the use of assault weapons. I will not pretend that I can do justice to these important efforts here, or to the grief of those who lost their loved ones. What I want to highlight is that the efforts to increase gun control—as well as the grief over the lost lives—express a secular faith in the irreplaceable value of the lives that were brought to an end. If this secular faith were removed, there would be no inclination to mourn, since nothing irreplaceable would have been lost. Moreover, there would be no motivation to prevent similar events from happening, since there would be no risk against which to offer protection.

Nevertheless, the religious faith that is supposed to provide consolation is predicated on a denial or relativization of the irreplaceable loss. Thus, at a memorial service for the victims in Newtown, President Barack Obama delivered the following sermon: " 'Let the little children come to me,' Jesus said, 'and do not hinder them. For such belongs to the kingdom of Heaven.' God has called them all home." This religious faith—if one were to believe in it—would fundamentally alter the response to the shootings in Newtown. The children who were killed would not be irreplaceable, but rather transferable to a higher existence. Furthermore, the killings themselves would ultimately not be a tragedy but a transitional stage on the way toward God calling the children "home" to heaven. To be sure, this particular belief—that the slaying of children in the end amounts to God calling them home to heaven—may seem offensive even to many who take themselves to be endorsing religious faith. But one should then bear in mind that a similar relativization of death is entailed by any religious faith in redemption. A secular consolation does *not* have to redeem death. On the contrary, it can admit that there is an irredeemable loss at the heart of what happened. A secular consolation can thus focus on the social commitments that sustain our mourning, recognizing the love that is intrinsic to grief, extending it to care for others, and motivating us to try to prevent similar tragedies from taking place (e.g., in the case of Newtown: through stricter gun laws, better mental-health care, greater social justice). For there to be anything distinctive about a religious consolation, however, it has to offer something else and claim that—from a metaphysical point of view—the deaths in question are not really final.

For the same reason, any religious consolation diminishes the significance of death and lessens the gravity of our responsibility for mortal life. In a remarkable passage in *A Grief Observed*, Lewis makes precisely this point:

> It is hard to have patience with people who say, "There is no death" or "Death doesn't matter." There is death. And whatever is matters. And whatever happens has consequences, and it and they are irrevocable and irreversible. You might as well say that birth doesn't matter.[42]

In speaking out of his experience of mourning, Lewis here articulates a profound faith: not faith in a transcendent God, or in a life exempt from death, but faith in the irreplaceable value of a life that is bound to death. If what happens *matters* and our actions have *consequences*, it is because they are irreversible and cannot be undone. If they could be undone, what we say and do would not have the significance that it does. The sense that something matters thus emerges from a secular faith, which sustains the commitment to a finite and fragile form of life. The risk of death is not the "cause" of care, in the sense that it would explain why one cares about one thing rather than another. The risk of death, however, is an intrinsic part of the reasons one has to care about anything and to take responsibility for what happens. Without the risk of irrevocable loss, what happens would have no meaningful consequences and there would be nothing at stake in keeping faith with the ones we love.

2

Love

I

More than sixteen hundred years ago, Saint Augustine explored the experience of time through a simple exercise. You can still try it today. Choose a song that you love and learn it by heart. Keep practicing until you remember every part of the song and every shift in the melody. As you sing it, you will know how much of the song has passed since the beginning and how much of it remains until the end. Yet—in holding the song together—you will find that it is already slipping away. There is never a moment in which the song is present to you. You can sing it only by retaining the notes that have passed away, while anticipating the notes still to come. Even each individual tone is never present—it begins to recede as soon as it sounds and you have to hold on to it to hear anything at all.

This experience of time is, according to Augustine, at work in every moment of our lives. You may think that you are present here today. But in everything you do, you are divided between the past and the future. As you get up in the morning, part of the day is already gone and what remains of the day is still to come. Even if you wake up at dawn and focus only on the first hour of the day, you will never be able to seize it as a present moment. "An hour," Augustine writes, "is itself made of fleeting moments. Whatever part of the hour has flown away is past. What remains of the hour is future."[1]

You may then try to forget about the hour and direct all your attention to the present moment, concentrating on what you are experiencing *right now*. Yet, as you grasp the present moment, it is already ceasing to be. As Augustine observes, "if the present were always present and did not go by into the past, it would not be time at all, but eternity."[2] Even the most immediate experience is marked by this temporality. There is never a presence that reposes in itself. Rather, every moment of time is disappearing. This is not to say that the experience of time is an illusion. On the contrary, it is at work in everything you do. Any experience requires that you hold on to a past that is no longer and project yourself into a future that is not yet.

In one of his sermons, Augustine describes the experience of time as follows:

> Do not our years fail every day? Do they ever stand still? The years that have come exist no longer; those that are still to come have no existence yet. The years that have passed have already slipped away, and the years in our future will slip away in their turn. The same is true even of a single day. Take today: we are talking now, at this moment, but the earlier hours have slipped away, and the hours ahead have not yet arrived. When they have arrived, they too will slip away. . . .[3]

As in many of his sermons, Augustine dramatizes the experience of time by calling attention to his own act of speaking in the present: *today, at this moment, now*. He thereby invites his audience to feel concretely how the moment—*now, when I address these words to you*—is vanishing even when it is being apprehended. "I seek for the present," he emphasizes, "but nothing stands still. What I have said is now gone; what I am going to say has not yet come. What I have done is no longer present; what I am going to do has not yet arrived."[4]

Wherever you go, then, there is never a still point where you can come to rest. Augustine captures this insight through his beautiful renditions of the Latin verb *tendere:* to stretch and to strive, to strain toward something or reach out for someone. In everything you do, there is an element of stretching and striving. Even when you are at rest, you have to stretch out the period of rest, striving to maintain yourself in repose. This is ultimately because every activity is temporal. The activity in which you are engaged—including the activity of resting—cannot be reduced to a single moment but has to be sustained over time. In stretching out your period of rest, you are holding on to the state you are in and reaching out toward a continuation. As in the case of singing your beloved melody, even the simple act of resting requires that you hold on to the state you are in and project yourself into a continuation.

Hence, Augustine describes the *form* of the experience of time as a *distentio*, which both holds you together and pulls you apart. The experience of time is always distended, since you must retain the past and project into a future that exceeds your grasp. By the same token, there is no guarantee that you can sustain what you love. Happiness consists in having and holding (*habere et tenere*) what you love. But since both you and the beloved are temporal, your having and holding will always tremble with the anticipation of mourning. The moments you stretch out to keep in memory may be taken away, and the possibilities you strain toward in hope may never arrive.

The result is a life in which opportunity and danger are inseparable. The light of bliss—even when it floods your life—is always attended by the shadow of loss. "Either loss of what we love and have gained," Augustine explains, "or failure to gain what we love and have hoped for."[5] This is the condition of *secular* life. Augustine uses the Latin word *saecularis* to evoke how we are bounded by time, through our commitments to a shared world and history, as well as to generations before and beyond us. The historical world in which we find ourselves is the *saeculum*, and this world (*hoc saeculum*) depends on generations across time.

In a remarkable move, Augustine emphasizes that living in this world is always a matter of *faith*—not religious faith in eternity but secular faith in what is temporal and exposes you to risk. This is the faith I explore and defend in this book. While Augustine holds that we long to transcend the condition of secular faith in favor of religious revelation, the present chapter will draw on Augustine's own insights to show that secular faith animates and sustains our deepest commitments. Secular faith—rather than religious belief—is the source of our passion for the world and our care for one another.

A good place to start is our relation to and dependence on other persons. As Augustine points out in his treatise *Faith in Things Unseen*, you can never know for certain that another person loves you or harbors good will toward you. You may see that he performs good deeds or proves himself to be a source of support in difficult times. But these acts provide no guarantee that you can trust him. "It certainly is possible," Augustine reminds us, "for a man to deceive by feigning kindness and by cloaking malice. He may not even plan to do harm—still, by expecting some advantage from you, he simulates love because he does not possess it."[6] Accordingly, you can never *see* or be *certain* of his goodwill toward you. Rather, in trusting him, you have to *believe* in what you cannot see. Of course, this does not mean that you should blindly trust and believe in other people. But it does mean that—even when you do everything you can to know as much as possible—there is an irreducible element of faith and trust in giving yourself over to another person. Even in the most intimate relation, you have to believe in something that is never certain—namely that the other person loves you. This moment of uncertainty cannot be eliminated, since "out of your heart you believe in a heart that is not yours."[7]

Augustine proceeds to demonstrate how secular faith is at work throughout all aspects of our lives, ranging from friendship to marriage and parenthood, as well as social and communal life at large. "If this faith in human affairs is removed," Augustine asks, "who will not mark how great will be their disorder and what dreadful confusion will follow?" He continues:

For, who will be cherished by anyone in mutual charity, since love itself is invisible, if what I do not see I ought not to believe? Friendship, then, will wholly perish, since it rests upon nothing more than mutual love. What of this will one be able to receive from another, if it shall be believed that nothing of it can be shown? Furthermore, when friendship perishes, neither the bonds of marriage nor of relationship and affinity will be retained in the mind, because in these, also, there surely is a friendly spirit of harmony. Then a husband and wife will not be able to have mutual affection, since they do not believe that there is any love, inasmuch as love cannot be seen. Nor will they desire to have children, for they do not believe that the children will return their love. And, if children should be born and grow up, the parents themselves will love their own much less, and they will not see love for themselves in their children's hearts because love is invisible. . . . Therefore, when we do not believe what we cannot see, concord will perish and human society itself will not stand firm.[8]

Augustine here provides an account of what I call the *necessary uncertainty* of secular faith. Since you depend on others to live on and to flourish, you have to keep faith in your friends, your partner, or your children. While such faith may be maintained in a "spirit of harmony," it is always haunted by the possibility of being broken, since each trusted one is mutable and may overturn your expectations—for better or for worse.

Moreover, the uncertainty of secular faith is a necessary condition not only for your relation to others but also for your own experience of yourself. As Augustine emphasizes, all temporal experience involves an element of believing (*credere*), which is intrinsic to understanding (*intelligere*).[9] Augustine does not develop this remark, but following his analysis of time we can unpack the argument. Since the past is *no longer* it cannot be an object of certainty but requires that you trust your memory or other people's accounts of what has happened. And since the future is *not yet* it has to be taken on faith. This secular faith exposes you to an uncertainty that is an irreducible part of your experience. Given that you cannot ever repose in a present moment—always relying on memories of the past and expectations of the future—you are dependent on what is beyond your control.

The necessary uncertainty of secular faith is the source of both positive chance and negative risk. It gives access to your past and opens the promise of your future, but keeping faith in this promise may leave you shattered by what happens. Likewise, faith makes it possible to trust and love another person. But by placing trust in another, you may find yourself betrayed or left behind. These vulnerabilities testify to the *existential commitment* that is inherent in secular faith. It is because you are committed to sustaining your life—or the life of someone for whom you care—that the promise of your future may be broken. And it is because you are committed to living on with your beloved, affirming your life together, that you are vulnerable to the grief of parting. These commitments express what Augustine calls *cupiditas,* which is the love of a world that is temporal (*amor mundi* or *amor saeculi*). You are seized by *cupiditas* when you love someone for her own sake or when you are devoted to the flourishing of a shared, secular world as an end in itself.

Even when a secular love is maintained in the best possible way, it remains dangerous, since you are attached to someone or something that cannot be secured. The one whom you love can die and the world you seek to maintain can fall apart. Augustine recognizes that this exposure to loss is an essential part of why we care. Because everything we do and everything we love can come to an end, we are bound to care (*curare*) and be concerned. What we do and what we love are not given facts but something that must be sustained, so there is always a question of whether to hold on or let go, uphold or abandon what we do. This finitude—our finitude and the finitude of what we love—is internal to the *motivational force* of secular faith. Part of what compels us to keep faith with what we love is our apprehension that the relation can be lost and thereby requires our fidelity.

To make the dynamic of secular faith concrete, let me begin with the example of my writing the book you are now reading. In undertaking this project, the necessary uncertainty of secular faith is a condition for my relation to a future in which you will read what I write. I cannot be certain that my words will ever reach you, and if they do arrive I cannot be certain of how you will receive them. I can only trust that you will understand what I mean to say. Furthermore, as I write these words, the necessary uncertainty is a condition even for my own experience. I cannot be certain of what will happen to me before I get to the end of this sentence; I can only take it on faith that I will be able to remember the thread of my argument, that my heart will keep beating, and that there will be a continuous supply of oxygen to my brain. If this matters to me, it is because I have an existential commitment to the project of leading my life. In writing this book, I am not only concerned to survive long enough to finish the book and take part in its reception; I am also committed to a philosophical project that can succeed or fail. The project inspires me to carry on and to regard it as important that the book be understood. Yet, in holding myself to a standard of success, I leave myself open to failure. The book may be rejected or misunderstood, and it may not even live up to my own conception of what the book ought to be. This possibility of failure is intrinsic to the motivational force that sustains my commitment to writing the book. The motivational force depends on my belief in the significance of what I have to say, but it also depends on *my belief that I can fail*. The belief that I can fail is part of what motivates me to try to succeed, to keep my attention on what I am doing, to improve my arguments and formulations.

The dynamic of secular faith does not come to an end when I have attained what I strive for. The threefold dynamic continues to be at work in the very fulfillment of living, working, and loving. Returning to my example of a love relationship, let us assume an ideal scenario in which I love you and you love me and we are blissfully happy together. Even in this consummation of love, the dynamic of secular faith is at work. In loving you, I cannot know how our relationship will transform me—how it may open new depths in my life or shatter my conception of who I am. Part of what it means that I love you is that you are not identical to me and that I cannot control what you will do to me. This exposure to what I cannot know gives me the possibility of trusting you and remaining open to the unexpected, but it also leaves me open to agony and grief. This is the necessary uncertainty of our love. For the same reason, our happiness together depends on keeping faith with one another. Nothing can *prove* that being together is the best thing we can do with our lives; we have to *believe* that it is and act on the basis of that faith. This is the existential commitment of our love. Moreover, to sustain our commitment we have to believe not only in the value of our love but also in its precariousness. We have to believe that our love can fail: that it is not given once and for all, but that we must care for it. This risk of failure is intrinsic to the motivational force of our love.

My examples so far have focused either on individual aspirations or on intimate relationships of love. The dynamic of secular faith, however, is also expressed in collective endeavors. For example, if we are engaged in a project of creating greater social justice, we share an existential commitment to a set of principles and a form of practice that the principles demand. We believe in certain values and in the importance of upholding them through contestation and struggle. This existential commitment is subject to the necessary uncertainty of secular faith. We cannot be certain that our collective project will hold together and the consequences of our actions are not given in advance. This necessary uncertainty puts the project at risk—it may not succeed and it may fall apart through internal dissent or external conflict. Yet the risk is also part of the motivational force that sustains our commitment to the project. We devote ourselves to social justice because it is *not* given as a fact but requires our efforts for its continued existence. This dynamic of faith does not come to an end when we have achieved the social justice for which we strive, since social justice is a form of life that always has to be sustained. To be committed to social justice is to be committed to a project that lasts for as long as there are social relations.

The dynamic of secular faith thus accounts for the possibility of ongoing commitments—whether to individual aspirations, love relations, or collective endeavors. These are *secular* forms of faith because they are devoted to projects that are bound by time.

What is the difference, then, between secular and religious forms of faith? In his book *Dynamics of Faith,* the modern theologian Paul Tillich provides a distinction that is illuminating for my argument. Tillich defines faith as having "an ultimate concern."[10] You have faith (an ultimate concern) if you are devoted to someone or something as an end in itself, being willing—if the situation so requires—to sacrifice other interests and passions for the sake of what you believe in or hold to be most valuable. In this sense, both secular and religious persons have faith. The crucial difference, however, is that the ultimate concern of the religious is a state of being that would eliminate all concern. While religious faith is exposed to doubt and uncertainty, its goal is to reach a state in which "the element of distance is overcome and with it uncertainty, doubt, courage and risk."[11] The aim of religious striving is to attain a complete security, where one no longer has to rely on an uncertain faith and can let go of all concern. "There is no faith," Tillich emphasizes, "in the quiet vision of God. But there is infinite concern about the possibility of reaching such a quiet vision."[12] Following the same logic, Augustine maintains that faith is only provisional and will be replaced by certainty in the presence of God.[13] When we attain salvation we shall know rather than believe and possess rather than hope. Salvation will put an end to all care (*finis curae*). To be saved in the religious sense is no longer to care.

We can thus describe religious and secular faith as two different motivational structures. If I am motivated by *religious* faith, the goal of my striving is to rest in peace. I may never achieve such peace, but *if* my desire were fulfilled I would be free from all care. My ultimate concern is to have no concern.

In contrast, if I am motivated by *secular* faith, being concerned is part of what I strive for. Even if my desire were absolutely fulfilled— even if I lived in the midst of an achieved social justice, blissfully happy with my beloved, and with my work flourishing—I would still be concerned, since everything I care about must be sustained over time and will be lost. Moreover, the risk of loss is part of why I care, why it matters to me what happens, and why I am compelled to remain faithful.

II

From Augustine's religious perspective, secular faith is based on the most deplorable and misguided form of love. *Cupiditas*—the love of a finite being or a finite form of life as an end in itself—is for Augustine the "wrong" kind of love, since it makes us dependent on what we can lose. While this kind of love may inspire fidelity, it may just as well lead to destructive emotions. Being devoted to a political cause, we may feel rage or despair if the cause is defeated. Likewise, in loving another human being we may become vengeful or crushed if we are abandoned by the one we love. Our fidelity and love may turn into fear and hate, feeding aggression against what we perceive as threatening. This is why Augustine condemns *cupiditas* as the root of all evil and all sin. In loving what we can lose, we are liable both to be hurt and to hurt others.[14]

Augustine here identifies a problem that was most deeply understood by the Greek and Roman Stoics, with whom we began to acquaint ourselves in the previous chapter. The Stoics argued that the deepest cause of our vulnerability is not the fact that our bodies are frail, that accidents may befall us, or that other people may betray us. Rather, what makes us vulnerable is our *belief* that these things matter and define who we are. By attaching ourselves to things we cannot finally control—e.g., the fate of our loved ones or our political community—we risk being shattered by what happens. We become *dependent* on what we can lose and thereby open to grievances or grief.

In contrast, the aim of Stoicism is to make us *independent* of everything that may upset us. This requires that we stop believing in the value of anything that can make us suffer. If something is taken away from us, we will not feel bereaved because we are not attached to anything that can be lost. And if someone violates us, we will not be angry or retaliate because we are not attached to any part of ourselves that is vulnerable to harm. Through the practice of detachment, we will maintain peace of mind regardless of what happens. The goal of Stoicism is literally apathy (*apatheia*): the freedom from all passions, since passions hold us hostage to a world that is beyond our control.

Such a Stoic solution is rejected as an illusion by Augustine.[15] As he emphasizes, we cannot transform ourselves into self-sufficient and independent beings. We are essentially dependent and passionate creatures. We cannot retreat into a state free from need and desire, since we have to reach outside ourselves for support to sustain our own existence.

The solution, then, cannot be to extinguish our desire or withdraw our love. The decisive factor is rather *who* or *what* we love. "Love," Augustine advises, "but be careful what you love."[16] If you love someone who is finite, you will come to grief. At best, such love is interrupted by death or separation. At worst, it leads to violent upheavals and painful betrayals. According to Augustine, you should therefore convert your love for finite beings (*cupiditas*) into a love of God's eternal presence (*caritas*). When you love yourself or extend your love to others, you should not be attached to their finite existence but love God *through* them. This is the meaning of the Christian imperative to love your neighbor as yourself. As Augustine explains, the imperative does *not* mean that you should love your neighbor for his or her own sake. On the contrary, it means that you should *neither* love yourself *nor* your neighbors in their own right. Neither your own self nor your neighbors have any value in themselves, but only by belonging to the eternity of God.

Hence, Augustine underlines that you should not enjoy (*frui*) anything in this life as an end in itself. Rather, you should use (*uti*) what you love as a means for devotion to the eternity of God.[17] If you have a friend, a spouse, or a child, you should not love them for their own sake: you should use them as a means for the end of loving God. Through this conversion of your love, you will no longer depend on other finite beings but only on God. If your friend becomes your enemy, you can still love him and forgive even his most atrocious deeds, since you are not attached to his particular existence or his particular deeds but are using him as an occasion to love God. Similarly, if your spouse betrays you, you will not be angry or devastated, since you love God *through* her and this love cannot be affected by anything she does. Finally, if your child dies you will not mourn, since you only love your child insofar as he or she already belongs to the eternity of God.

Augustine and the Stoics present different methods for achieving the same religious goal: to be absolved from loss, attaining peace of mind. The difference is that Augustine does not think such a religious fulfillment can be achieved in this life. As long as we are part of a historical world, we can be misled to love this life for its own sake and we must continually be concerned about our salvation, which depends on the grace of God.

Salvation itself, however, is understood as the end of all care. Salvation would be to attain a state where all striving has come to an end, all action has come to rest, and all desire has been stilled. Augustine takes it for granted that we all strive toward such peace, whether we know it or not. Even those of us who devote ourselves to a life in this world are actually longing to repose in the peace—the *quies*—of God's eternal being. "Our heart is restless till it finds rest in Thee," as Augustine famously remarks in his *Confessions*.[18]

The ultimate aim of our lives would thus be to rest in peace. This assumption is the common denominator for all religious ideals of eternity. They would have us think that fulfillment—the highest state of being—consists in being liberated from care. Even though one always has to take care, the religious goal is to be free from all concern. Our attachments to finite life are thus devalued as restrictions that prevent us from attaining salvation. As long as we are attached to a finite life—including our own—we can never be relieved from concern. Depending on what happens, we may be moved to pain or enjoyment, hope or despair. For the one who embraces a religious ideal of eternity, such vulnerability may be recognized as a necessary evil on the way to salvation. But it cannot be seen as part of the good itself.

The most instructive example is the Buddhist notion of nirvana. To attain nirvana is emphatically described as being invulnerable. In nirvana, you are untouched by any concerns and safe from all possible harm. You do not worry about anything, since you have attained a state of perfect rest and absolute permanence. In Buddhism, such a state is the only one that counts as truly "satisfactory." All other forms of experience are deemed to be fundamentally "unsatisfactory." The key term here is *dukkha*, which is often rendered as "suffering" but more exactly translated as "unsatisfactoriness." The Buddhist claim is that all experiences of finite life—including our most extraordinary experiences of well-being and bliss—are unsatisfactory, since they are impermanent. Even when they last for a long time, we can lose them at any moment. This is why Buddhism advocates detachment from everything that is impermanent. To be attached to finite life is to put yourself at risk, to expose yourself to being hurt by what happens. In contrast, Buddhism holds that you should detach yourself and aspire to rest in the peace of nirvana.[19]

By subscribing to the value of absolute permanence, Buddhism devalues everything that is impermanent. The mere fact that something is not eternal is enough for it to be unsatisfactory and unworthy of our devotion. However, when one removes everything that is impermanent—when one removes everything that comes into being and passes away—one is literally left with nothing. In nirvana, there is no death but also no birth, no unrest but also no activity, no aging but also no growth, no distress but also no passion. Nothing can ever disturb the peace, which also means that nothing can ever happen.

The apparent paradox of nirvana haunts all religious conceptions of eternity. Absolute fullness is inseparable from absolute emptiness and absolute presence is inseparable from absolute absence. My argument is that we should reject the idea that such a state of being is a goal worth striving for. A religious redemption from loss—whether through an immanent detachment or a transcendent eternity—is not a solution to any of our problems. Rather than making our dreams come true, it would obliterate who we are. To be invulnerable to grief is not to be consummated; it is to be deprived of the capacity to care. And to rest in peace is not to be fulfilled: it is to be dead.

This is a therapeutic argument. I am asking us to let go of a way of thinking that leads to a dead end, to recognize that the peace of eternity only resides in the grave. Rather than try to become invulnerable, we should learn to see that vulnerability is part of the good that we seek. Thereby we can learn to see that our finitude—and the finitude of what we love—is not in itself a restriction. Our bonds to finite life are not only what constrain us but also what sustain us, opening us to the world and to others. This therapy will not exempt you from the risks of being committed to a finite life. You cannot bear life on your own, and those on whom you depend can end up shattering your life. Moreover, since your own powers are finite they may become depleted and make life unbearable. These are real dangers. But they are not reasons to try to transcend finitude altogether. They are reasons to take our mutual dependence seriously and develop better ways of living together.

The recognition of mutual dependence requires secular faith. It requires that you keep faith with others even though there are no guarantees. And it requires that you keep faith with what you love even though it makes you vulnerable to loss. This is difficult. All the dangers Augustine identified in loving what can be lost are actual possibilities. Your love may lead to anger when there is harm, grief when there is death, despair when hope is crushed. But the same vulnerability is also what makes you receptive to the world, to yourself, and to others. You cannot shut down your sense of uncertainty and risk without also shutting down your capacity to feel joy, connection, and love. Only by acknowledging the importance of something beyond your control—that is: only through vulnerability—can you be moved by what happens. The precious quality of joy is inseparable from a sense of its precariousness, and the value of connecting to another person would not be felt without the risk of disconnection.

Vulnerability, then, is not only passive exposure but also a condition for any form of active commitment. To be committed to something is to be vulnerable to success and failure. If you are committed to doing something, you are putting yourself at risk, since you will experience it as a failure if you are *not* able to do it. Yet it is only by taking that risk—of being committed—that you can enjoy and appreciate what you do. Similarly, if you are committed to someone, you are open to the wonder of receiving another person in your life, but you are also exposed to the danger of betrayal and loss. You cannot protect yourself against what happens through a solemn equanimity. Rather, you will experience what happens in terms of bliss and pain, success and failure, possibility and peril.

Augustine himself is sensitive to how deep such commitments can be. In book 4 of his *Confessions*, he recalls a friendship that lit up his time as a teacher of rhetoric in Tagaste. Augustine's account of this friendship is so radiant that many scholars have wondered if the two young men were lovers. Augustine here speaks of a bliss that illuminated his life as never before. The friendship was "sweet to me beyond all the sweetnesses of life that I had experienced," and "my soul could not endure to be without him."[20] Because of this intense attachment and receptivity, Augustine also becomes more vulnerable to the rhythms of time. He "longs with impatience" when his friend is absent and is seized by joy when he returns. Time spent together is an elevation to new heights, time apart an aching absence.

The experience of love thus brings a sharper focus to Augustine's life, but it also makes him more deeply dependent on another. This predicament is expressed most poignantly in a line that Augustine invokes from the Roman poet Horace: "He was half my soul." On the one hand, this means that Augustine had become so intimate with his friend that he shared the very substance of his being. On the other hand, it means that Augustine could be separated from himself—torn apart in the very substance of his being—if he were to lose his friend. And this is exactly what happened. After less than a year of their passionate relationship, his friend died, leaving Augustine haunted and bereaved:

> My heart was darkened over with sorrow, and whatever I looked at was death. My own country was a torment to me, my own home was a strange unhappiness. All those things that we had done and said together became, now that he was gone, sheer torture to me. My eyes looked for him everywhere and could not find him. And as to the places where we used to meet, I hated all of them for not

containing him; nor were they able to say to me now, "Look, he will soon come," as they used to say when he was alive and away from me. I had become a great riddle to myself and I used to ask my soul why it was sad and why it disquieted me so sorely. And my soul did not know what to answer. If I said, "Trust in God," it very rightly did not obey me, because the man whom I had lost, my dearest friend, was more real and better than the fantastic god in whom my soul was asked to trust.[21]

Augustine here keeps faith with his love for his friend, even though it makes him suffer from the pain of loss and run the risk of despair. This is an act of secular faith because it is devoted to someone who is finite and affirms a vulnerability that is also the source of love. "The reason why that grief penetrated me so easily and so deeply," Augustine recalls, "was that I had poured out my soul like water onto sand by loving a man who was bound to die."[22] The Christian Augustine deplores this expenditure of love. He should have invested his love in the eternity of God rather than binding it to a life that could be lost. Yet Augustine's own account of his experience testifies to a secular faith that remains legible in the *Confessions*. Given the fidelity to his friend, Augustine holds that an irreplaceable life has been lost and he refuses to be consoled by the thought of God, since his beloved friend "was more real and better than the fantastic god in whom my soul was asked to trust."[23]

Augustine's official narrative maintains that the God he refused was not the true Christian God he discovered later in his life. But Augustine's writing also tells another story. The reason he refused to seek comfort in God was not because he had an inadequate understanding of divine eternity, but because he loved his friend—and the life they shared together—as an end in itself. He wanted their lives to *go on*, rather than ascend to eternity. As Augustine himself makes clear, such secular love is incompatible with a religious love of eternity. A religious love of eternity treats the mortal beloved as a means and must be careful not to love him in his own right. As Augustine explains in the first book of his *Confessions*, "My sin was in this—that

I looked for pleasures, exaltations, truths not in God Himself but in His creatures (myself and the rest), and so I fell straight into sorrows, confusions, and mistakes."[24]

Accordingly, Augustine implores his soul not to be "foolish" by trying to hold on to what passes away. Unless the soul turns toward the eternity of God "it is fixed to sorrows," since all things that are temporal will cease to be.[25] With remarkable precision, Augustine locates the risk of mourning not only in passionate love but also in the basic enjoyment of his physical senses. Merely to enjoy the light that illuminates the world is for Augustine a dangerous temptation, since it makes him dependent on something that is transient. "That corporeal light," he explains, "is a tempting and dangerous sweetness."[26] Enjoying the light of the day leads him to want more light and to suffer when it is absent. Because he loves the light that makes the world visible, "if suddenly the light is withdrawn, I seek for it with longing. And if it is absent for long, my mind grows sad."[27] Similarly, when Augustine recites and is moved by a song, he warns himself against becoming attached to the sounds and words that vanish in time. "Do no let my soul attach itself to these words with the glue of love [*glutine amore*] through the sensations of the body. For all these things move along a path toward nonexistence. They tear the soul apart with contagious desires."[28]

The attachment to a song or a melody is here a small-scale version of the attachment to a life that is torn apart by time (*distentio*). Instead of pursuing the passions of such a life, Augustine urges his soul to turn toward God's eternal Word as "the place of peace that is imperturbable."[29] This turn toward eternity is the movement of his religious conversion.

III

As Augustine is well aware, even the most religiously devout person must live in a secular world, in being part of history and dependent on social relations. The decisive aspect of religious conversion, however, is that the secular world is treated as a means and not as an end in itself. If you go to church for the sake of experiencing the warmth of the community—with friends, family, and other members of the congregation—Augustine would reproach you for using the religious ritual as a means for the secular end of maintaining and celebrating social bonds. Augustine even worries that the use of music in Mass will make the congregation take too much pleasure in their bodily sensations and interactions, enjoying an experience that is temporal rather than contemplating the eternity of God. While Augustine acknowledges "the great utility of music in worship," it should only serve as a means and not be enjoyed as a source of pleasure in itself. Thus, "When it happens to me that the music moves me more than the subject of the song, I confess myself to commit a sin deserving punishment."[30]

Augustine's aim is to convert the passion of a secular experience that is bound by time into a passion for the eternity of God. He wants to persuade us that it would be better to enjoy the stillness of eternity than to suffer from the drama of living on in time, torn between the past and the future.

Yet Augustine's own account gives us good reasons to reject his appraisal of eternity. The attraction of eternity is supposed to be that "there you will lose nothing."[31] But if you can lose nothing in eternity, it is because there is literally nothing left to lose. Nothing that happens can matter anymore, and it is no accident that the "activities" offered in heaven turn out to be remarkably monotonous. "All our activity will consist in singing 'Amen' and 'Alleluia,'" Augustine explains in one of his sermons, and "we shall praise God not just for one day, but just as these days have no end in time, our praise does not cease."[32] Leaving aside the question of whether one could sing or praise something forever, the real questions are why one would want to and how any significant aspect of who we are could survive the transformation to timeless rapture. Being absorbed in eternity, there would be nothing left for you or me to do, since nothing could begin or end. As far as I am concerned, I would be dead.

That eternity would entail the death of the self can be seen in Augustine's own *Confessions*. Augustine provides a profound account of how the life of the self depends on the sense of time. The impossibility of reposing in a timeless presence—which Augustine laments as a fallen condition—is the possibility of living a life that is open to change and still has a future. Indeed, only someone who is subject to time can have a future at all. This future is never guaranteed, but if you close it down you close down any possibility of leading a life.

The condition of time is what allows anything to come into being. But it is also what destines everything to pass away. As Augustine reminds us, all the moments of our lives "pass away and no one can follow them with his bodily senses. Nor can anyone grasp them tight even when they are present."[33] Because the movement of time makes everything disappear, we are altogether dependent on memory and anticipation. Even sense perception is a matter of retaining what happens and relating it to what may come. Any given moment of our life is passing away, so we must hold on to it through memory—and open ourselves to the future through anticipation—to experience anything at all.

Moreover, Augustine makes clear that the distention of time reaches all the way into the deepest recesses of his soul. Even in his most devoted contemplations and engaged activities, he is torn by time, revealing his soul to be a *distentio animi*. In pursuing anything, he must stretch himself from the past toward the future and—in so doing—he runs the risk of breaking apart. This is why Augustine places such a profound emphasis on the power of memory. Without memory he could not hold himself together over time and not maintain his identity for even a moment. While the power of memory is fragile and exceeds his grasp, it gives him the chance of leading a life. "I cannot comprehend the power of my memory," he writes, "since I cannot even call myself myself apart from it."[34]

When Augustine turns to investigate his memory, he is therefore investigating the very condition of his existence. The power of memory may give continuity to his life, but it also reminds him of everything that is discontinuous with his current sense of self. While memory opens an interior space where he can resuscitate who he has been ("there I meet myself and recall myself"), it also reminds him of everything that is "hidden away, scattered, and neglected."[35] Moreover, Augustine is acutely aware of how even the most steadfast memory is susceptible to change, wear down, and be erased.

Nevertheless, Augustine confesses that "amazement grips me" when considering how memory can retain events of his life, allowing them to live on even though they have ceased to be.[36] This is a distinctly *secular* sense of wonder. The object of his amazement is not a timeless eternity but the power of memory that belongs to a finite being. Indeed, Augustine openly avows that he could not live without it: "So great is the power of memory, so great is the force of life in a human being whose life is mortal."[37]

In contrast, for the religious Augustine, memory is at best a means for ascending to God. "You are my true life," he says in turning toward God, "I will transcend even this my power which is called memory. I will rise beyond it to move toward you."[38] Thus, while Augustine pursues a remarkable secular investigation of the depths of memory, his religious aim is not to remember but to forget the self. As he explicitly asserts: "God must be loved in such a way that, if at all possible, we would forget ourselves."[39]

The same contrast between secular insights and religious piety can be traced in Augustine's explorations of love. Just as Augustine's philosophical work on memory speaks to a secular understanding of the self, the poetic and erotic qualities of his writing in the *Confessions* radiate beyond their purported religious aims. Even God is famously addressed as though He were a mortal beloved, tenderly invoked as "my beauty," "most beautiful one," "my life," "my light," "my sweetness." Furthermore, in expressing his longing for God, Augustine speaks the language of a lover in the grip of fervent physical desire for his beloved:

> Late have I loved you, beauty so old and so new: late have I loved you. . . . You called and cried out loud and shattered my deafness. You were radiant and resplendent, you put to flight my blindness. You were fragrant, and I drew in my breath and now I pant for you.

I tasted you and I hunger and thirst for you. You touched me, and
I burn for your peace.[40]

The moving quality of this passage is intimately bound up with a
sense of timing, evoking an event he could not have expected but
which transformed his life. "Late have I loved you" renders an experience of something that happened before it was *too late*, as a matter of
great fortune and precious circumstance. But the phrase also recalls
that it *could* have been too late. This sense of peril persists in the deep
dependence on another that Augustine expresses, with hunger and
thirst making the fulfillment of his love a matter of life and death. As
such, Augustine's words could go to the heart of a secular experience
of love. In secular love—where both lover and beloved are finite—
the precariousness of time is part of what makes the love valuable
and important. Everything that is given may be taken away and without this risk there would be nothing at stake in being devoted. Your
love can animate and illuminate, but your receptivity to the beloved
also leaves you vulnerable to someone who is beyond your control.

From Augustine's religious perspective, however, the experience
of vulnerability is only a means toward the end of union with God.
As long as he is still searching for his salvation, he must endure desire
and remain at the mercy of what happens. But the goal is to attain
a state of being (reposing in the absolute presence of God) where
desire has come to an end and nothing can shatter him ever again. He
may "burn" with desire for the peace of God, but if this desire were
fulfilled every flame of passion would be extinguished.

Augustine's own writing thus allows us to see that a religious
consummation of love would spell the death of erotic life. Augustine
wants to convince us that this is a good thing. By dramatizing the
risks of erotic passion, he wants to make us feel that being in the
grip of desire is a lack that needs to be filled, a sickness that needs
to be cured. He thus refuses to see what the power of his own erotic
language reveals. The risk of being shattered is not a weakness to be
overcome but remains in the fulfillment of love itself. The possibility

of being touched is *inseparable* from the peril of being wounded and the exposure to loss is *part of* the experience of rapture.

Augustine's blindness may be willful, since the vision is difficult and painful. To see that what you love is finite—and to see that the finitude of what you love is part of why you love it—is hard. It can really hurt, and there is no way to lose the pain except by losing the love itself. Yet the bond between love and grief is what I am asking us to see. To pursue this vision would be to write a secular—as distinct from a religious—confession. Such a confession would take up Augustine's explorations of how the identity of the self depends on the fragile operations of memory and how the experience of time cuts through every moment. Like Augustine in his *Confessions* it would declare: "See, my life is distended" (*Ecce distentio est vita mea*).[41] But unlike in Augustine, the distention of time would not be regarded as a fallen state from which we need to be redeemed by a religious revelation of eternity. Rather, the distention of time would be seen and felt as the opening of life itself. The task would be to "own" the fact that this is the only life we have—for better and for worse—rather than seeking to leave this life behind. While Augustine denounces the "glue of care" (*curae glutino*) that binds us to the world, a secular confession would maintain that it is only through finite bonds that we can seize our lives and become who we are.

IV

I turn here to the secular confession at work in Karl Ove Knausgaard's *My Struggle*. First published in Norwegian and now the subject of wide international acclaim, *My Struggle* can be read as a contemporary response to Augustine. Ranging over 3,600 pages, the six volumes of *My Struggle* are framed by Knausgaard's resolution to tell the truth about his life in detail. He places himself under the obligation to account for his life as it is actually lived, writing only about things he has experienced while confessing to *how* he experienced them—no matter how quotidian, painful, or intimate the details may be. The power of his project does not draw on a life of great adventures or on confessing scandalous thoughts and deeds. Rather, it stems from an extraordinary level of attention devoted to an ordinary life.

As readers, we get to follow the narrator and protagonist Karl Ove (avowedly identical to the author) in the midst of everyday life. At the time of writing *My Struggle*, he is in his early forties, absorbed and overwhelmed by being married with three young children. While this domestic life keeps getting in the way of his writing, he makes it a centerpiece of the story itself. We spend many pages going grocery shopping, pushing baby prams in the city, and attending to daily exchanges with his children—all rendered with a fidelity to everyday life that neither idealizes nor deprecates the experiences in question. We become attuned to the weight of waking up too early while trying to meet the demands of family life, the sinking feeling of facing an apartment in chaotic disorder, and the numbness that follows from an endless array of tasks. Yet the same attunement also yields the radiant moments of everyday life. Precisely because Knausgaard perseveres in exploring his mundane existence, he loosens the hold of habit and makes us see the world anew.

The same holds for those moments when Knausgaard shifts focus from his present life and descends into his past, excavating the world of being twenty-five, or eighteen, or twelve, or seven. His achievement is not simply an act of remembering but of reliving: inhabiting the way the world was given at a time, letting the constraints and the promises, the mistakes and the fortunes, reverberate with the same force they had when first experienced. The impact of falling in love at the age of seven, or despairing over the future at the age of twelve, is here revived with the same depth as the pain of losing a parent or the bliss of having a child in adult life.

As a result, Knausgaard enables the reader to turn back to his or her own life with a more profound attention and concern. This effect is one described not only by prominent critics but also by the large number of general readers who have been captivated by Knausgaard's work. When *My Struggle* was released in Norway (selling more than half a million copies in a country of less than five million people), readers testified to how Knausgaard—in opening up his life through writing—had opened their own lives to them. The same testimony can be found among many of his readers in the United States and elsewhere. The transformative effect of Knausgaard's writing does not depend on sharing his cultural background or personal circumstances. You are a potential addressee of his work by virtue of being a time-bound, practically committed agent who can be moved to explore and deepen your commitment to the life you are leading. Knausgaard's writing can give you new access to your own life *not* necessarily because you identify with his experiences but because *My Struggle* exemplifies a devotion to life as it is lived—a devotion that you can take up and practice in relation to your own existence.

The key here is the sustained act of attention that characterizes Knausgaard's writing. When he dedicates twenty pages to exchanges over breakfast with his daughters on a rainy Wednesday morning—or seeks to pry open every sensation and emotion that resonated in his twelve-year-old self on the way home from swim practice one particular winter night—he is not simply imposing his life on us. He is teaching us (and himself) how we can remember what we tend to forget. By describing the quotidian in painstaking detail, he opens our eyes to how much is going on even during days when nothing seems to happen. And by resuscitating his former selves, he sensitizes us to all the vanished moments that remain inscribed in us—triggering memories that can open painful wounds but also bring us back to life.

The appeal of Knausgaard's writing is not that it forces you to see *his* life with *your* eyes. Rather, his writing enables you to see *your* life with *his* eyes—with the level of attention he bestows on a life. Thereby you can come to recognize the myriad ways in which you are indeed alive, even when you seem dead to yourself or lost in the mundane events of everyday existence. As you take care of the tasks at hand, what you see bears the weight of your love and your evasions, the history of who you have been and may turn out to be.

Evenings that no one else can remember live in you, when the snow touched your face or the rain caught you unprepared, when you were all alone and yet marked by all the others who have made you who you are. There are things you cannot leave behind or wish you could retrieve. And there is hope you cannot extinguish—whether buried or insistent, broken or confident, the one never excluding the other.

Such a distended life is what Knausgaard's prose allows you to recognize as your own. Stretching toward the past and straining toward the future, an entire world emerges through you. You did not make this world, you were made by it, and now you sustain it. This is your life. There is nothing else. But what there is—and what you do—binds you to the world in ways that are deeper than you can ever disentangle.

The struggle is how to make this life your own. That is the starting point for Knausgaard's project. When *My Struggle* begins, he finds himself detached from the life he is living. He endures what he has to do, but he has withdrawn from being truly involved in what happens. At a remove from his existence, he feels as though he has nothing to lose, and by the same token his life appears to be meaningless. "The life around me was not meaningful. I always longed to be away from it," he writes. "So the life I led was not my own. I tried to make it mine, this was my struggle."[42]

The struggle to make life his own is *not* a quest to become independent or self-sufficient. His life is not his own in the sense that he would be able spontaneously to decide who he is or what he is going to do. On the contrary, there is a keen awareness in Knausgaard of how we belong to a world we did not create and depend on others who exceed our control. To own your life is not to free yourself from this dependence. Rather, your existence is inseparable from the ways you are engaged in and committed to being in the world. For example, you may find yourself (as Knausgaard does at the beginning of *My Struggle*) married with children and overcome by a sense that you cannot make it work. You are trying to succeed—trying to be there for your loved ones—but keep failing and feel yourself disintegrating in the process.

To disown your life in this situation is to settle for mere perseverance, going through the motions while numbing yourself and dreaming of being somewhere else. Knausgaard is attuned to this

temptation, and he himself repeatedly disowns his life. Yet the struggle he engages in through his writing is to own his life. He actively
seeks to identify himself with what he is doing and acknowledge what
he loves. This is an ongoing struggle. To *own* what you do and what
you love is to put yourself at stake, to recognize in practice that your
life depends on the fate of your commitments. To own your life is
not to own *what* you love (it is not your possession) but to own *that*
you love what you love. This is the condition for anything to matter
to you—for anything to have meaning—but it also puts your life at
risk. If you own what you do, you are bound to be deeply affected by
how it is received. Precisely because you are engaged in a meaningful
activity—precisely because you are doing something that matters to
you—you are susceptible to the experience of failure. Likewise, if
you own *that* you love what you love, you make yourself vulnerable
to what happens. Your dreams may come true or your hopes may be
shattered. Because you have something that matters to you, you have
something to lose.

To own your life, then, is not to have it as your sovereign property. On the contrary, to own your life is to expose yourself. Only
someone who owns his life—only someone who makes his life depend
on what he does and what he loves—can have the experience of it
being taken away from him.

Hence the temptation to disown your life: to bury your hopes
before they fail to come true, to withdraw your love before it makes
you suffer. These are paths of detachment, where you can come to
seek protection from the pain of failure or loss by divesting yourself in advance. There are certainly situations where such strategies
make sense and *some* degree of detachment is necessary to endure our
lives—otherwise anything could break us. But as a principle detachment is a dead end: it can lead to nothing but the destitution of
meaning or a nihilistic rejection of the world.

The animating principle of Knausgaard's writing is rather one of
attachment, which is all the more profound because it remains faithful
to the ambivalence of any attachment. The credo of his work, I will
show, is a phrase that recurs throughout *My Struggle* and is difficult to

translate. "Det gjelder å feste blikket," Knausgaard writes in Norwegian. The phrase could be rendered as "one must focus the gaze" or "what matters is to focus the gaze." But the Norwegian verb that we would then translate as *to focus* (*å feste*) literally means "to attach," and the phrase is clearly a personal injunction rather than a simple statement. So a better translation would be: attach yourself to what you see, focus your gaze by attaching yourself to what you see. This is the imperative of *My Struggle*.

The imperative can be understood in three different senses. The three senses are intertwined, but it is useful to distinguish them to see different aspects of Knausgaard's writing. The first sense of the imperative is to focus your gaze on the life you are actually living. This explains why Knausgaard can devote more pages to apparently trivial activities than to transformative life events. If he is going to focus his gaze on the life he is actually living, he cannot just capture the moments of trauma or bliss that glow in the dark (birth, death, love, mourning); he must also capture the stretches of time out of which they emerge and the things he does on days he would not remember: setting the table, cleaning the house, flipping through books, taking a walk on a gray afternoon, staring out the window. Knausgaard has an extraordinary ability to open up and dilate such moments, making even dull experiences come alive with the sensory, perceptual, and reflective richness of being in the world.

Yet it is not enough to focus your gaze on what you do; you must also acknowledge the ways in which you are attached to what you see. This is the second sense of the imperative. Accordingly, Knausgaard seeks to render the waves of boredom and elation, ambition and frustration, intense joy and absentminded occupation that form the rhythms of his days. Above all, he tries to focus his gaze on what means the most to him. Here too it is a matter of acknowledging how he is attached to what he sees, even at the cost of confessing painful ambivalence. We learn of the absorbing love affair that brought him and his wife together, but also of the fears, the petty grievances, the daily resentments, and the storming conflicts that almost tear them apart. In focusing his gaze on his children, there can be an exceptional tenderness in attending to their unique personalities and the daily dramas of their vulnerable, growing selves. But there are also detailed, excruciating accounts of how he loses sight of who they are and what they need—of parental love clouded by anger, exhaustion, or resignation.

Knausgaard's writing could here be described as a form of mindfulness, but one must then separate mindfulness from Buddhist meditation, with which it is often associated. According to Buddhism, you should focus your inner gaze and attend to your attachments with the aim of *detaching* yourself from the struggles they entail. By paying attention to the thoughts and feelings that arise in your consciousness, you are supposed to learn to disengage from them—to *not* identify with what you think and feel. The goal is to attain a state of pure consciousness, where there is perfect serenity because you have ceased to care. Thus, while certain meditation techniques can be adapted for the secular purpose of reengaging with the world—helping you recover from negative experiences or simply increasing your concentration and energy—the religious aim of Buddhism is quite different. On a secular understanding, meditative detachment is a relative and temporary means employed for the sake of being able to better engage the struggles that follow from being attached to life. In Buddhism, on the contrary, absolute detachment is an end in itself. Since all attachments entail suffering, only absolute detachment can bring about the elimination of suffering that Buddhism holds out as your salvation. What ultimately matters is not who you are or what you do; what ultimately matters is that you attain a state of consciousness where everything ceases to matter—so that you can rest in peace.

The aim of Knausgaard's mindfulness is the opposite. By attending to the struggles that emerge from his attachments, he seeks to identify more deeply with them: to become *more attached* to the life he is living. This is the third sense of his imperative. You must attach yourself to what you see—even at the cost of suffering—because without attachment there is no meaning: nothing to care for and no one who binds you to the world. To counter such nihilism is the animating ambition of Knausgaard's secular confession. "Indifference is one of the seven deadly sins, actually the greatest of them all, because it is the only one that sins against life," he writes at the end of the second volume. And in the final, sixth volume he presses home the stakes of being able to focus your gaze, attaching yourself to what you see:

> I know what it means to see something without attaching yourself to it. Everything is there, houses, trees, cars, people, sky, earth, but something is missing nonetheless, because it does not mean anything that they are there. They could just as well be something else, or nothing at all. It is the meaningless world which appears like that. It is possible to live in the meaningless world too, it is just a matter of enduring, and that one will do if one must. The world can be beautiful . . . but it does not make any difference to you, it does not affect you. You have not attached yourself to what you see, you do not belong to the world and can, if push comes to shove, just as well leave it.[43]

This is the position of someone who has disowned his life. What renders the world meaningless—or meaningful—is not an objective feature of what there is but proceeds from the degree of your attachment to what you see. This does not imply that you are free to decide the meaning of the world. But it does entail that any meaningful engagement depends on your attachment to others and to being in the world. Your capacity to attach is not simply up to you—it can be enabled or disabled by what happens to you—but whether and how you attach makes all the difference in the world.

The difficulty of owning such a life is an integral part of Knausgaard's writing. He struggles with the temptation to disown his life and dwells on the many ways in which we may come to give up on our existence. The quotidian way is the slow death of a gradually increasing indifference, but prominent in his work is also the reckless renunciation of obligation at the depths of alcoholism, the short-circuiting of emotion at the heart of depression, and the ultimate self-destruction of suicide. Knausgaard explores these forms of dis-owning one's life without having recourse to moralizing judgment. Yet, in and through his explorations, he recalls us to the fact that it is only by owning our lives—as essentially being in the world—that we have a chance at a meaningful existence. This is the secular conversion at work in Knausgaard's confessions. By focusing his gaze on his life and attaching himself to what he sees, he turns us around: not toward eternity but toward our finite lives as the site where everything is at stake. Like all conversions, this is not one that can be achieved once and for all: it is a continuous struggle to own our lives. But unlike a religious conversion, a secular conversion does not aim to bring the struggle to an end. Rather, to own our lives is to acknowledge that struggle belongs to the very life we want to lead. If we want our lives to matter, we want to have something that we can lose.

It is thus instructive to compare Knausgaard's and Augustine's confessions. Augustine initiated the genre of confessional autobi-ography with a move that was particularly radical in his religious context. Before Augustine, texts devoted to the lives of holy men (hagiographies) were all written in the third person, with the saint himself withdrawing from the world, leaving someone else to recount his path to transcendence. In contrast, Augustine tells the story of his own life, confessing his doubts, his carnal desires, and his sins. Rather than hide behind a third-person standpoint, he owns the first-person standpoint like no one before. We learn about his aging body, his psychological dramas, and even his nocturnal emissions. "In my memory," Augustine confesses, "there still live images of the past acts that are fixed there by my sexual habit. These images attack me . . . in sleep they not only are pleasurable but even elicit consent and are very like the act itself."[44]

To expose himself in such detail may seem risky for an aspiring theological authority, but for Augustine it is part of a strategy. He exhibits his finite life to inspire a sense of how shameful and inad-equate it is by comparison with the eternity of God. This is what Augustine calls "making truth" (*veritatem facere*). To make truth is not only to tell the truth—to confess what one has done—but also to make truth come into being in oneself by relinquishing the sinful attachment to life in this world and instead turn toward God. Augustine's explicit motivation for writing his *Confessions* is to enable such making of truth in himself and in others. "Why then do I put before you in order the story of so many things?" he asks in addressing God. "Not, certainly, so that you may come to know them through me, but to stir up my own and my readers' devotion toward you."[45]

Yet Augustine's vivid account of the life he is supposed to leave behind also opens the possibility of a secular inheritance of his work, where making truth is not a matter of devoting oneself to God but of remaining faithful to a finite life. The great writer Jean-Jacques Rousseau was the first to take up this possibility (in his own epochal *Confessions* from 1769), but Knausgaard pushes it further. Unlike Rousseau, Knausgaard does not claim to be exceptional, and he does not hold out the promise of a timeless presence. He is the subject of an ordinary life that will irrevocably end and yet he devotes more attention to its minute details than would have been thinkable for either Augustine or Rousseau. The one obligation he recognizes as the writer of *My Struggle* is to be true to this life.

Nevertheless, Knausgaard himself is liable to devalue his life from a religious perspective. At one point in the final volume, he is reading the church fathers (of whom Augustine is the most prominent) and comes to feel that his own experiences are impoverished in contrast to their mystical ecstasies. Knausgaard now maintains that his own search for meaning is pathetic compared to "the devotion of the mystics" and condemns himself as "one of the world's many soulless and banal human beings."[46] This is in line with the sense of shame Augustine hoped to inspire. From a religious point of view, a finite life without redemption is indeed soulless and banal. This view is inherited even by many who do not have religious faith—regarding their lives as futile because they lack a sense of the eternal—and Knausgaard is tempted by it in a number of the essayistic reflections that pervade *My Struggle*. He repeatedly claims that art aspires to retrieve a sense of the holy, while lamenting that we can no longer attain it. "The longing and melancholia that Romantic art expresses is a longing for this," he writes with reference to a religious sense of the holy, "and a mourning of its loss. At least that is how I interpret my own attraction to the Romantic in art."[47] According to this conception, art would strive to open a world that is "holy" in the sense of being untouched by time and finitude, a world where everything is present in itself but which we cannot enter because we are "fallen"— incapable of living in "the indifference of the divine" and "the all extinguishing light of the good."[48]

Since these religious ideas are so familiar—and supposedly profound—they are likely to be taken as a guide to Knausgaard's work. Yet that would be a mistake. Throughout *My Struggle* (and particularly in the final volume) there are numerous statements or small essays that appear to present the philosophy of the book. Many of them are in conflict with one another or internally contradictory and to take them at face value would be to miss almost everything that is important in them. Knausgaard is a tremendous essayist, but his particular talent is to allow his essays to emerge *as part of the narrative*. The theoretical reflections exist on the same plane as the practical actions; they reflect how someone thinks and feels at a particular time rather than expressing the perspective of someone who is outside the narrative and in control of its meaning.

To understand the philosophical poetics of *My Struggle*, then, we must attend to what happens in the narrative alongside the many and often contradictory statements of intent. The view that our secular lives are soulless and banal—that we need to be saved from our time-bound existence—belongs to the tendency to disown his life. While this tendency persists throughout *My Struggle*, the very writing of the book goes in the opposite direction. Far from regarding his life as soulless or banal, the writer of *My Struggle* depends on the faith that there is enormous significance and depth in the experiences of a finite life, worthy of being explored down to the most subtle nuances and emotional reverberations. The aim is to attach himself more deeply to his life, rather than transcend it. From this perspective, it is Augustine's mystical ecstasies that are soulless and banal, since they seek to leave the world behind in favor of an eternal presence where nothing happens. What is profound in Augustine is not the ascent to heaven but the descent into time and memory. It is the latter, descending movement that Knausgaard follows in his practice as a writer.

The key issue here is time. By using the first person like no one before, Augustine dramatizes what it means to be torn apart by time. Even his abstract philosophical speculations in the *Confessions* are marked by his concrete existence as he is longing and languishing, seized by hope or fear, elated by an insight or frustrated by an impasse. Accordingly, when Augustine pursues his philosophical analysis of time-consciousness in the *Confessions*, he also makes his readers feel how the problem of time is an intimate, personal concern. The investigation of time is itself a temporal activity and Augustine foregrounds the effort to articulate his own arguments, as an ongoing line of thought that at any moment may be broken. Likewise, when Augustine analyzes the work of memory, he does so by descending into "the caves and caverns" of his own memory, exposing the ways in which the integrity of his self is breached by a past he cannot fully recover.[49] Moreover, as Augustine is writing his *Confessions*, he is still vulnerable to change and this drama becomes a part of the book itself. Intensifying the sense of his own vanishing presence, Augustine even highlights the fleeting time in which he composes his text: "Consider what I am now, at this moment [*in ipso tempore*], as I set down my confessions."[50]

The same turn toward his own passing presence is pursued by Knausgaard in *My Struggle*. "Today is February 27, 2008. The time is 11:43 p.m." we read early in the first volume, as he records the night when he begins to work on the book.[51] A couple of pages later we learn that six days have passed for Knausgaard at the time of writing, as we find him at his desk again: "It is now a few minutes past eight o'clock in the morning. It is March 4, 2008. I am sitting in my office, surrounded by books from floor to ceiling, listening to the Swedish band Dungen while thinking about what I have written and where it is leading."[52] These explicit marks of time recur throughout *My*

Struggle, returning with a particular frequency in the final volume, when he is trying to complete the book. "I am sitting all alone as I am writing this. It is June 12, 2011, the time is 6:17 a.m., in the room above me the children are asleep, at the other end of the house Linda is asleep, outside the window, a few yards out in the garden, angular sunrays descend on the apple tree. The foliage is filled with light and shadow."[53]

These apparently simple observations encapsulate the poetics of *My Struggle*. Knausgaard's writing develops a careful attention to the time and place where he finds himself. The fundamental form of such attention is the turn toward what is happening at this very moment—trying to capture life as it unfolds *right now*. The aim is to slow down the experience of temporality, to dilate moments of time and linger in their qualities. This movement does not yield a stable presence but, on the contrary, a stronger sense of how the present moment is ceasing to be and has to be held in memory, as it opens onto a future that exceeds it. By instilling this sense of transience, Knausgaard seeks to awaken his own attention and the attention of his readers. He wants to counteract habit: to prevent himself from taking his life for granted and see the world anew. This attempt to break with habit—to deepen the sensation of being alive, to make moments of time more vivid—is necessarily intertwined with a sense of finitude. It is because his life is finite that he cannot take it for granted and his desire to linger in a moment is animated by the awareness that it is passing away. Indeed, the sense of transience is an essential part of the radiance of the moment itself. Seeing the world anew is inseparable from the sense that the world you see anew is finite. It has not always been, it will not always be, and therefore it must be seized before it vanishes.

The moments of rapture, then, are always marked by their own finitude. For example, in the third volume Knausgaard gives an extraordinary account of his first love, at the age of seven. This is his earliest recorded experience of how the world can light up because of his attachment to what he sees. "Inside me," he writes, "there suddenly existed a new sky under whose vaults even the most familiar of thoughts and actions appeared new."[54] This new sky is Anne Lisbet, with her thick, light-blue jacket, white cap, and dark, fierce eyes. One afternoon, as they play together in the forest, they pretend that he is a sailor who returns to her after a long separation. They run toward each other and, as she embraces him, his world is transformed:

> My heart was racing, for I was not only standing at the bottom of a forest with the sky far above me, I was also standing at the bottom of myself and looking up into something light and open and happy. Her hair smelled of apples. Through the material of her thick padded jacket I could feel her body. Her cold, smooth face against mine, almost glowing.[55]

This experience of standing at the bottom of himself is the experience of being attached to what he sees, bound to the world through the love for another. As autumn turns to winter, his love for Anne Lisbet makes him absorb every shifting nuance of what happens:

> When the snow began to fall we wandered around searching for suitable places to jump from, slide down, or dig holes in. Her hot, red cheeks then, the gentle but distinct smell of snow that changed so much according to the temperature, but that was everywhere around us nevertheless; all the possibilities that existed. One time the mist hung between the trees, the air was thick with drizzle and we were wearing waterproof clothing that was so frictionless on the snow that we could slide down it like seals. We climbed to the top of the slope, I lay on my front, Anne Lisbet sat astride me, Solveig astride Geir, and we slid down on our stomachs all the way to the bottom. It was the best day I had ever experienced. We did it again and again. The feeling of her legs clamped round my back, the way she held my shoulders, the howls of delight she gave when we picked up speed, the fantastic somersaults when we reached the

bottom, rolling around with our legs and arms entwined. All while the mist hung motionless amid the wet, dark green spruce trees, and the drizzle in the air lay like a thin film of skin on our faces.[56]

The sense of possibility that is felt here ("all the possibilities that existed") pervades every moment of bliss in *My Struggle*. The moments are not self-contained or timeless. On the contrary, their excitement resides in a sense of futurity, opening up ways of feeling and acting that were not possible before. By the same token, the moments are fragile. His love for Anne Lisbet makes him receptive and elated, but also torn by a sense of imminent loss. "The most contradictory feelings coursed through me. One moment I was on the verge of tears, the next my chest was bursting with happiness."[57] This pain of bliss will recur in all the moments of happiness in *My Struggle*. The more attached he is to what he sees, the more vulnerable he is to bereavement. But this agony is also part of what enlivens and deepens his experience. If he could not lose his proximity to Anne Lisbet, he would have no sense of the miracle of being close to her. There would be no urgency to absorb the situation, to enhance his attention to what happens, to strive to retain what he is feeling, since nothing of value could be lost.

Knausgaard's writing is at its most powerful when it strains to capture this relation between attachment and loss, receptivity and vulnerability. The second time he falls in love, at the age of sixteen, winter is on the verge of turning into spring and the upheaval takes place in him as much as in the landscape around him:

Few things are harder to imagine than that a cold, snowbound landscape, so marrow chillingly quiet and lifeless, will, within mere months, be green and lush and warm, quivering with all manner of life, from birds warbling and flying through the trees to swarms of insects hanging in scattered clusters in the air. Nothing in the winter landscape presages the scent of sun-warmed weather and moss, trees bursting with sap and thawed lakes ready for spring and summer, nothing presages the feeling of freedom that can come over you when the only white that can be seen is the clouds gliding across the blue sky above the blue water of the rivers gently flowing down to the sea, the perfect, smooth, cool surface, broken now and then by rocks, rapids, and bathing bodies. It is not there, it does not exist, everything is white and still, and if the silence is broken it is by a cold wind or a lone crow caw-cawing. But it is coming. . . . it is coming. . . . One evening in March the snow turns to rain, and the piles of snow collapse. One morning in April there are buds on the trees, and there is a trace of green in the yellow grass. Daffodils appear, white and blue anemones too. Then the warm air stands like a pillar among the trees on the slopes. On sunny inclines buds have burst, here and there cherry trees are in blossom. If you are sixteen years old all of this makes an impression, all of this leaves its mark, for this is the first spring you know is spring, with all your senses you know this is spring, and it is the last, for all coming springs pale in comparison with your first. If, moreover, you are in love, well, then . . . then it is merely a question of holding on. Holding on to all the happiness, all the beauty, all the future that resides in everything. I walked home from school, I noticed a snowdrift that had melted over the pavement, it was as if I had been stabbed in the heart. I saw boxes of fruit under an awning outside a shop, not far away a crow hopped off, I turned my head to the sky, it was so beautiful. I walked through the residential area, a rain shower burst, tears filled my eyes.[58]

This is an apparently romantic account of vitality, where the overflowing emergence of spring mirrors the upsurge of love. The barren, frozen landscape is flooded with glowing colors and released by animated movement, pulsating both in nature and in the teenager who finds himself attached to what he sees. Yet the sense of vitality is inseparable from a sense of finitude. The life that emerges has not always been (it is coming to be) and will not always be. The experience of beauty is therefore a stab in the heart, and he is seized by the desire to hold on to everything that will not last: "Holding on to all the happiness, all the beauty, all the future that resides in everything." Seized by this desire, he has the sense of seeing beauty for both the first and the last time. Seeing the beautiful for the last time, his experience can be all the more radiant, all the more intense, because he is on the verge of losing what he loves. The sense of finitude, however, is already at work in his experience of beholding something as beautiful for the first time. The colors of the world are alight and at the same time they already bear their future fading within themselves. Indeed, the anticipated fading of the colors *is part of what makes them glow.* When he is seized by the colors of the world, the sense that they will fade is part of what makes the colors absorbing, part of what compels him to pay attention to their qualities and linger over their beauty.

The distention of time—how every moment trembles on the verge of the past and the future—thus appears in the light of secular passion. Distention is not only the negative condition of loss but also the positive condition of wonder. Only someone who is torn open by time can be moved and affected. Only someone who is finite can sense the miracle of being alive.

V

Knausgaard's great predecessor is the modern writer who explored the experience of time more deeply than any other: Marcel Proust. Knausgaard recalls that he not only read Proust's *In Search of Lost Time* "but virtually imbibed it,"[59] and *My Struggle* bears the imprint of many passages from Proust. The influence is already visible in the basic form of the project. *In Search of Lost Time* devotes seven volumes, stretching over more than three thousand pages, to a man recollecting his life. *My Struggle* apparently follows the same model, devoting six volumes, also stretching over more than three thousand pages, to a man recollecting his life. While Knausgaard transforms the Proustian project in an important way—to which I will return—it is illuminating to dwell on what he learns from Proust.

The protagonist, Marcel, is himself in the process of learning throughout *In Search of Lost Time*. From early childhood he wants to become a writer, but he is plagued by doubts about his talent and not until the end does he discover what the subject of his book should be, namely, his own life. Rather than a transcendent topic of writing, which has always left Marcel's imagination blank, it is "this life, the memories of its times of sadness, its times of joy"[60] that he comes to see as the basis for his book. "The greatness of true art," he declares, "lies in rediscovering, grasping hold of, and making us recognize . . . this reality which we run a real risk of dying without having known, and which is quite simply our life."[61]

Accordingly, Marcel emphasizes that his work will be devoted to "the thing that ought to be most precious to us," namely, "our true life, our reality as we have felt it."[62] This is why he can dwell on the experience of falling asleep for more than thirty pages, or seek to distill every nuance of an erotic touch, a flickering memory, an awakening sensation. Through the power of his prose, he wants to sharpen our perception and refine our senses. The aim is not to transport us to another life but to make us genuinely experience the life we are already living. And as Marcel understands, to achieve this aim we must transform our relation to time. If habit tends to deaden and dull our experience, it is because it reduces the impact of time on our senses. Even though every day is different and there is no guarantee that there will be another one, habit makes us feel as though our life has been all the same and will continue indefinitely. Thus, when we get used to seeing something we love, we tend no longer to notice its details or marvel at its existence. Likewise, when we get used to living with someone we love, we run the risk of taking him or her for granted and no longer appreciating the unique qualities of the beloved.

The key to breaking habit is to recall that we can lose what we love. Far from devaluing life, the dimension of loss is part of what makes it emerge as valuable. We may *know* that we are going to die, but the role of art is to make us *feel* what that means and thereby intensify the commitment to our life. Accordingly, when Marcel comes to narrate his own life, he is all the more attentive to the impact and nuances of his past experiences. Even many events that were unremarkable or unhappy return with a luminous quality in his memory, since they appear as irreplaceable in the light of loss. The value of a past experience may thus be enhanced when it is infused with the pathos of being lost, just as the value of a current experience may be enhanced by the sense that it will be lost.

Yet Marcel pursues his insight only in relation to a distant past and not in relation to his ongoing life as he is writing. *In Search of Lost Time* ends with the revelation that leads Marcel to become an author and to write the book we have been reading. Nevertheless, we never learn under what circumstances Marcel is writing the seven volumes, how much time it takes, and what he is struggling with as he is trying to complete the book. To be clear, *In Search of Lost Time* is not Proust's autobiography. It does not tell the story of Proust's life but is the autobiography of the fictional character Marcel, who within the frame of the novel writes the story of his life. We know that Proust worked on *In Search of Lost Time* for more than thirteen years and was unable to finish the book before his death, struggling to enter revisions in the galley proofs up until the end. Within the frame of the novel, however, we do not get to witness an analogous struggle on the part of Marcel as the supposed author of the pages we are reading. We have no sense of what his daily life is like as he is writing, or what happens to him during the years it takes to compose his autobiography. All his efforts are devoted to giving meaning and significance to his past, not to his ongoing life.

This is the structure that Knausgaard transforms. Within the frame of *My Struggle*, the current life of the narrator, Karl Ove, is itself part of the story and we are even told exactly how long it takes for him to write the six volumes. He begins to work on the first volume at 11:43 p.m. on February 27, 2008, and he completes the last volume at 7:07 a.m. on September 2, 2011. To be sure, the beginning and end of the narration cannot be dated with such complete precision, but what is important is the ambition to situate his writing as part of an ongoing life. We learn in detail about how his work on the book is interrupted by childcare, practical worries, relationship troubles, and personal anxiety. All these things belong to the subject matter of the book itself. The struggle is not only to recover the past, but also to grasp hold of and engage with the life that continues.

Knausgaard thereby reveals a difficulty that Proust tends to conceal. If you focus only on the distant past (as Marcel does), it is relatively easy to gain a new appreciation of your life, since you can transform the past into an object of contemplation that no longer makes any direct demands on your engagement. You can dwell on details you previously overlooked, absorb the impact of events you did not understand at the time, and even feel a surge of nostalgia for things you did not enjoy when you first experienced them. Indeed, the sense that all these things are irrevocably gone can make them appear more precious than they actually were. Your nostalgia, then, can come to shelter you from the demands of a life that still has to be lived. It is telling that *In Search of Lost Time* ends with Marcel withdrawing from the world to write his book. His life is effectively over and the only thing that remains for him is to tell his story. Of course, Marcel still has to live, but we are supposed to forget about this in favor of an immersion in the past. The few times we catch a glimpse of him in the act of narration, it is the image of someone who has reduced his engagements to a minimum and apparently places no value on his current life: "I, the strange human who, while he waits for death to release him, lives behind closed shutters, knows nothing of the world, sits motionless as an owl, and like that bird can only see things at all clearly in the darkness."[63]

In contrast, the structure of *My Struggle* looks like a deliberate inversion of the one that shapes *In Search of Lost Time*. While Marcel's book ends with him becoming an author through the decision to write the story of his life, Karl Ove's book *begins* with him already being an author who decides to write the story of his life and *ends* with the declaration that he is no longer an author after the completion of his book. "I will enjoy, really enjoy, the thought that I am no longer an author," are the last words of *My Struggle*, followed by a separate page with two sole sentences that address his wife and children: "For Linda, Vanja, Heidi, and John. I love you."[64] Where

Marcel ends by retreating from life into literature, Karl Ove ends by retreating from literature and turning toward life. This is not a strict opposition, since Marcel retreats into literature to understand and appreciate life, while literature is an essential part of Karl Ove's ability to understand and appreciate life. Nevertheless, the way he transforms the ending of *In Search of Lost Time* indicates the challenge Karl Ove poses to himself. The retreat into writing is supposed to lead back into his actual life and not out of it. He explicitly wants to change and become a better person in his daily existence. In addition to recovering the past, his task in *My Struggle* is to keep faith with what he is seeing and living *now*—not years later when he is looking back on it.

Moreover, he has to confront the difficulty of appreciating his life and sustaining his deepest attachments. Loving his wife and children is not something that can be accomplished once and for all; it is an act of devotion that has to be sustained every day and one that can always fail, with joy giving way to tedium, loving care compromised by indifference or frustration, and the sense of wonder lost in deadening habit. The aim of *My Struggle* is not to purify one from the other, but to confront the daily, interminable battle between them. This is why we find the narrator in the midst of life, rather than at a remove from life as in the case of Marcel. Karl Ove is never at rest, and even when he retreats to the writing desk he is caught up in the practical engagements of everyday life. The engagements may be painful or passionate, tedious or elevating, but the point is to make them all glow in their concreteness.

Thus, at different intervals in telling the story of his life, Karl Ove moves from recounting the past to depicting himself at the time of writing. Within the space of a sentence, we can pass from a young Karl Ove in action to his older self recollecting the events several decades later. The first time this happens is early in the first volume, when we learn about his current life situation on the evening in February when he begins to work on the book. After an immersive description of one night when he was eight years old, Knausgaard looks up from his desk and speaks to us *in ipso tempore*—at the very moment of writing:

As I sit here writing this, I recognize that more than thirty years have passed. In the window before me I can vaguely make out the reflection of my face. Apart from one eye, which is glistening, and the area immediately beneath, which dimly reflects a little light, the whole of the left side is in shadow. Two deep furrows divide my forehead, one deep furrow intersects each cheek, all of them as if filled with darkness, and with the eyes staring and serious, and the corners of the mouth drooping, it is impossible not to consider this face gloomy.

What has engraved itself in my face?

Today is February 27, 2008. The time is 11:43 p.m. I who am writing, Karl Ove Knausgaard, was born in December 1968, and I am accordingly, at this moment, 39 years old. I have three children, Vanja, Heidi, and John, and I am married for the second time, to Linda Boström Knausgaard. All four are asleep in the rooms around me, in an apartment in Malmö, where we have now lived for a year and a half. Apart from some parents of the children at Vanja and Heidi's nursery we do not know anyone here. This is not a loss, at any rate not for me, I don't get anything out of socializing anyway. I never say what I really think, what I really mean, but always more or less agree with whomever I am talking to at the time, pretend that what they say is of interest to me, except when I am drinking, in which case more often than not I go too far the other way, and wake up to the fear of having overstepped the mark. This has become more pronounced over the years and can now last for weeks. When I drink I also have blackouts and completely lose control of my actions, which are generally desperate and stupid, but also on occasion desperate and dangerous. That is why I no longer drink. I do not want anyone to get close to me, I do not want anyone to see me, and this is the way things have developed: no one gets close and no one sees me. This is what must

have engraved itself in my face, this is what must have made it so
stiff and masklike and almost impossible to associate with myself
whenever I happen to catch a glimpse of it in a shopwindow.[65]

This is not only the night when he begins to write the book; it also
marks the degree zero of his project. The man who looks at himself
here is someone who can barely recognize himself. He has withdrawn
from the world, but by the same token he has disowned his life and
lost hold of himself. The writing of *My Struggle* is an attempt to
reverse this process, to turn him back toward his own life. He who
never says what he really thinks and really means will now do so for
thousands of pages. And he who does not want anyone to see him,
who does not want anyone to get close to him, will now expose himself and make his life visible for anyone to see. This is not to say that
he has a hidden kernel of identity that is independent of others and
ready to be revealed at will. On the contrary, the difficulty of owning his life is that he is inseparable from the way he is acting in the
world. Even withdrawing from others is a form of being with them,
and seeking to leave the world behind is itself a way of being in it.
To own his life is to acknowledge this dependence, to recognize—for
better and for worse—that he is attached to what he sees.

The project of owning his life, then, begins with a literal self-
reflection. He sees his face in the dark window and has to grapple
with what has happened to him. In a way, all of *My Struggle* can be
seen as an attempt to answer the question he asks here: "What has
engraved itself in my face?" He descends into the past to recover his
life, but also to be able to engage the present and the future.

Consequently, he has to confront what Proust calls "embodied
time" (*temps incorporé*). Embodied time designates how we carry the
past with us, even when we are not aware of it or in control of how
it affects us. This embodied time is for Proust the very condition of
writing an autobiography. Because the past is inscribed in our bodies,
we have the chance of reconnecting to our former selves, recalling
not only *what* we did but also *how* it felt and thereby retrieving a
genuine sense of our lives. For the same reason, however, our con-

nection to the past is tenuous. We may never gain access to many of the experiences that are stored in us and—even when we do—the meaning of the past is never given in itself but refracted through our current sense of self and our projections of the future. Moreover, if our memories are embodied it means that they can be damaged or effaced by what happens to the body. The duration of the past is not secured by an immaterial soul, but depends on the retention of time in a frail and material body.

Thus, when Marcel discovers the importance of embodied time, he is haunted by an awareness of all the factors that may eradicate the memories that are retained in his body: "I felt the present object of my thought very clearly within myself . . . but also that, along with my body, it might be annihilated at any moment."[66] The discovery of embodied time inspires him to write *In Search of Lost Time,* but it also marks the precariousness of his project. At the end of the last volume, on the verge of beginning to write, Marcel worries about how brain damage or various accidents may prevent him from composing his autobiography. And indeed, before starting to work on his book, Marcel falls down a staircase and suffers from a memory loss that heightens his anxiety over not being able to write. "I asked myself not only, 'Is there still enough time?' but also 'Am I still in a sufficiently fit condition?' "[67] In pursuing the implications of embodied time, Marcel is thus finally led to the dead body, which underlines the finitude of the lived time to which he is devoted. "After death," he writes on one of the last pages, "time leaves the body, and the memories—so indifferent, so pale now—are effaced from her who no longer exists and soon will be from him whom at present they still torture, but in whom they will eventually die, when the desire of a living body is no longer there to support them."[68]

While the problem of the dead body appears only at the end of Proust's novel, it is foregrounded from the beginning of *My Struggle.* Like Proust, Knausgaard wants to evoke the depths of time in our lives; how we go far beyond our physical location in space by bearing the past with us and projecting ourselves into a future. It is this distention of time that allows us to have a history and a lived experience. Yet in Knausgaard there is a strong parallel awareness of how the dimension of lived time—with its hopes and fears, hidden riches and emotional upheavals—depends on a material body that will remain after the distended life has expired.

Thus, with a remarkable incision, the first sentences in the first volume of *My Struggle* force us to witness the very transition from a living to a dead body:

> For the heart, life is simple: it beats for as long as it can. Then it stops. Sooner or later, one day, this pounding action ceases of its own accord and the blood begins to run toward the lowest point of the body, where it gathers in a small pool, visible from the outside as a dark, soft patch on ever whitening skin, as the temperature sinks, the limbs stiffen and the intestines drain. . . . The enormous hordes of bacteria that begin to spread through the body's innards cannot be halted. Had they tried only a few hours earlier they would have met with immediate resistance, but now everything around them is still, as they delve deeper and deeper into the moist darkness. They advance on the Havers Channels, the Crypts of Lieberkühn, the Isles of Langerhans. They proceed to Bowman's Capsule in the Renes, Clark's Column in the Spinalis, the black substance in the Mesencephalon. And they arrive at the heart. As yet, it is intact, but deprived of the activity for which its whole construction has been designed, there is something strangely desolate about it, like a production plant that workers have been forced to flee in haste, one may imagine, the stationary vehicles shining yellow against the darkness of the forest, the huts deserted, a line of fully loaded cable-buckets stretching up the hillside.
>
> The moment life departs the body, the body belongs to the dead. Lamps, suitcases, carpets, door handles, windows. Fields, marshes, streams, mountains, clouds, the sky. None of these is alien to us. We are constantly surrounded by objects and phenomena from the realm of the nonliving. Nonetheless, there are few things that arouse in us greater distaste than to see a human being

caught up in it, at least if we are to judge by the efforts we make to keep corpses out of sight. In larger hospitals they are not only hidden away in discrete, inaccessible rooms, even the pathways there are concealed, with their own elevators and basement corridors, and should you stumble upon one of them, the dead bodies being wheeled by are always covered. When they have to be transported from the hospital it is through a dedicated exit, into vehicles with tinted glass; in the church grounds there is a separate, windowless room for them; during the funeral ceremony they lie in closed coffins until they are lowered in the ground or cremated in the oven.[69]

For a novel that is so devoted to the first-person standpoint, it is striking to begin with a view of life that only can be given from a third-person standpoint. No one can experience the moment of death that Knausgaard describes. We can infer it when we observe another body at the moment of death, but when it happens to ourselves we are gone. And yet we belong to this body that is not under our command. We are altogether dependent on our body—cannot exist without it—but our body is not dependent on us. After we are gone it can remain as an object in the world, indifferent to our absence. Presumably, this is why the dead body is so uncanny and tends to be hidden away. The dead body reminds us that we are not only *in* the world but also *of* the world, made of materials that will degrade and decompose.

The materialist reminder runs throughout *My Struggle*. Specifically, Knausgaard employs a bifocal vision, where every existential phenomenon is seen both in its own right and as dependent on a physiological machinery. The paradigmatic example is the heart, which is the major and apparently conventional metaphor in *My Struggle*. The heart in Knausgaard is explicitly a metaphor for the living principle of his existence, expressed most forcefully in the intuitive experience of love. "The heart is never mistaken," is the phrase he employs repeatedly, to explain his life-changing decisions. The heart in this sense designates his deepest and most intimate sense of self. At the same time, the heart is treated not metaphorically but literally. As in the opening paragraph quoted above, Knausgaard repeatedly lays bare the heart as a physical mechanism that is utterly indifferent to his sense of self. The heart beats and then it stops beating, whether he wills it or not. The dissection of his heart becomes not only an intimate confession but also an exploration of his own biological-material constitution, as though he were opening his heart in both a romantic and a surgical sense.

Knausgaard thus pushes the notion of embodied time to a stark conclusion. Looking at pictures of himself as an infant, he asks:

> Is this creature [his infant self] the same person as the one sitting here in Malmö writing? And will the forty-year-old creature who is sitting in Malmö writing this one overcast September day—in a room filled with the drone of the traffic outside and the autumn wind howling through the old-fashioned ventilation system—be the same as the gray, hunched geriatric who forty years from now might be sitting dribbling and trembling in an old people's home somewhere in the Swedish woods? Not to mention the corpse that at some point will be laid out on a bench in the morgue. Still known as Karl Ove.[70]

Both the tenuous connections and the ultimate fragility of embodied time are here underscored, as he makes vivid the radical changes of his body across a lifetime. In composing his autobiography, Karl Ove has to reckon with physical decomposition and is haunted by the absolute termination of his life that will have taken place when his body is transformed into a corpse.

Thus, Knausgaard persistently reminds us of the automatic functions of our bodies, the decaying matter that we are made of, and the geological time that dwarfs the span of our existence. Yet this materialist perspective does not serve to diminish the importance of our lives. The fact that the duration of your existence is but a speck on the scale of geological time does not mean that it is insignificant.

Likewise, the fact that your first-person standpoint—the unique experience of your life—depends on a set of physical properties does not mean that it is an illusion. It only means that your life is finite.

Such finitude does not devalue your life, but is an essential part of why it can matter and take on significance, against the backdrop of its possible dissolution. "Death," Knausgaard writes in the final volume, "is the background against which life appears. If death had not existed, we would not have known what life is."[71] Death is the background against which life can light up as something cherished and irreplaceable, but it is also the background that can extinguish all light: "Death makes life meaningless, because everything we have ever striven for ceases when life does, and it makes life meaningful, too, because its presence makes the little we have of it indispensable, every moment precious."[72]

Death is here understood as an existential category but it also opens onto the organic death of the body. Indeed, to confront the corpse—in its material existence—as the fate of everyone we love is a challenge Knausgaard repeatedly poses to himself and to his reader. As we have seen, the first volume of *My Struggle* begins by depicting the moment of death in bacterial detail. The final paragraph of the same volume returns to the corpse, as Karl Ove visits the morgue to see the body of his deceased father one last time:

> Now I saw his lifeless state. That there was no longer any differ-
> ence between what once had been my father and the table he was
> lying on, or the floor on which the table stood, or the wall socket
> beneath the window, or the cable running to the lamp beside him.
> For humans are merely one form among many, which the world
> produces over and over again, not only in everything that lives
> but also in everything that does not live, drawn in sand, stone,
> and water. And death, which I had always regarded as the most
> important dignity in life, dark, compelling, was no more than a
> pipe that springs a leak, a branch that cracks in the wind, a jacket
> that slips off a clothes hanger and falls to the floor.[73]

A body has stopped breathing and thereby ceased to function as a living being, instead becoming an object among other objects in the world. "Dad was no longer breathing," we read a bit earlier. "That was what had happened to him, the connection with the air had been broken, now it pushed against him like any other object, a log, a gasoline can, a sofa."[74] To see the living body thus reduced to its dead counterpart is to see that nature is indifferent to our interests and desires, leaving the body to wither away when we can no longer draw on the world to sustain ourselves. "He no longer poached air, because that is what you do when you breathe, you trespass, again and again you trespass on the world."[75] This ability to interact with the world—and project yourself into a future—is precisely what is lost in death. No longer "poaching" the air but simply subject to its physical pressure, the individual body decomposes and is incorporated into a cycle of matter in transformation.

There are two traditional ways of addressing this material death and the anxiety it may provoke. The first is to argue that we have an immortal soul that is separate from the decomposing matter of our bodies. Even though our bodies perish, we do not really die but ascend to a higher existence, independent of any body or endowed with an incorruptible body. The second strategy is to argue that we are continuous with matter and therefore have no reason to fear death. Because the matter of our bodies is transformed into something else, nothing substantial is actually lost but only takes on another form. This is, for example, the Stoic view of death. "Yes, you will cease to be what you are, but become something else of which the universe then has need," as the Roman Stoic Epictetus holds in an influential argument.[76]

While these two perspectives are apparently opposed, they are united in their denial that death entails the loss of a life we should try to hold on to. In the first case, we are told to detach from the life that is lost in favor of an immortal soul. In the second case, we are told to detach from the life that is lost in favor of the continuation of matter. Both perspectives thus deny the tragedy of death. Only a secular faith—which remains committed to a life that irrevocably is lost in death—can counter these two forms of denial. Indeed, only a secular faith can account for why death is a tragic loss at all. The sense of tragic loss depends on keeping faith in the irreplaceable value of a life that is gone forever. Nature does not care whether we live or die, but that makes it all the more imperative that we care and remember what has been taken away.

VI

Precisely in and through a materialist vision of death, Knausgaard's writing is devoted to secular faith. In forcing us to look at the dead body, he makes vivid what separates the dead from the living. For the living, time is distended: we recall a past and project ourselves into a future. This is the time of our lives, the time that Knausgaard is dedicated to exploring. The dead no longer see anything or feel anything, no longer recall a past and project a future. Our fidelity to the person who has died requires that we acknowledge this absolute loss of life. When faced with a dead body, we can remember that this body belonged to someone who lost everything in death. In mourning the death of another, we recognize that her own standpoint on her life is absolutely gone. Only by acknowledging the absolute loss of her own first-personal life can we remain faithful to the memory of a person who is irreplaceable. Moreover, only by anticipating our own death—only by running ahead into the risk of losing everything— can we bring our own finite life into focus.

The remarkable thing with Knausgaard's writing is how the experience of mortality is allowed to be the source of both fear and love, terror and beauty. The anxiety before death is not something that can or should be overcome. Rather, it is an expression of love for a life that will cease to be.

Likewise, being bound to a mortal body can indeed be a source of terror. You may be crippled by injuries or ravaged by brain chemistry, and in the end all the living spirit you gather will dissipate in dead matter. Yet, being bound to a body that is beyond your control is also the condition for being touched and moved, the chance of being receptive to the vanishing beauty of the world.

Even in the most serene moments of bliss, Karl Ove is thus aware of mortality. The precious existence of those he loves is inseparable from their precarious material conditions:

> I looked at Linda, she sat with her head against the seat, with her eyes closed. Vanja's face was covered by hair, she lay like a tussock in her lap.
>
> I leaned forward a little and looked at Heidi, who gazed back at me uninterestedly.
>
> I loved them. They were my crew.
>
> My family.
>
> As pure biomass it was not very remarkable. Heidi weighed perhaps ten kilos, Vanja perhaps twelve, and if one added my and Linda's weight we reached perhaps one hundred ninety kilos. That was considerably less than the weight of a horse, I would think, and about as much as a well-built male gorilla. If we lay close together our physical range was not much to brag about either, any given sea lion would be more voluminous. However, regarding what cannot be measured, which is the only important thing when it comes to families, regarding thoughts, dreams and emotions, the inner life, this group was explosive. Dispersed over time, which is the relevant dimension for understanding a family, it would cover an almost infinite surface. I once met my grandmother's mother, which meant that Vanja and Heidi belonged to the fifth genera-tion, and fate permitting they could in turn experience three gen-erations. Thus, our little heap of meat covered eight generations, or two hundred years, with all that entails of shifting cultural and social conditions, not to mention how many people it included. A whole little world was being transported at full speed along the highway on this late spring afternoon.[77]

The gentle happiness here is all the more radiant because of the bifocal vision. On the one hand, the tender evocation of an intimate love, in which each member of the family is seen as an origin of the world, with "thoughts, dreams, and emotions" that distend beyond anything that can be measured. On the other hand, the reminder that this entire world depends on a limited "biomass" with a determinate weight and height, here even described as a "heap of meat" that is being "transported" along the highway. Remarkably, the latter perspective does not serve to denigrate the value of the lives that are interwoven. They can be lost forever if the car meets a fatal accident on the highway, transforming their biomass into a heap of dead meat. Yet the risk is not held out as a morbid fantasy, but as a reminder of how their lives are a treasure that cannot be taken for granted. Anticipating death in the midst of life is a way of focusing his gaze on the ones he loves, attaching himself to what he sees, making their unique existence vivid.

The love that radiates here is the love of a life that is secular in Augustine's sense: bound by time, marked by history, dependent on generations that have come before and may come after. Throughout *My Struggle* this temporal dimension is shown to hold the key to the passions of our lives. The distention of time marks every moment, but it can be stretched out in different ways and discloses the depths of who we are. Thus, Knausgaard explores the sedimentation and resuscitation of events in an individual body, the crystallization of a moment through memory and anticipation, the texture of time in a love relationship, intervals of pleasure and pain, the dead time of trauma, and the elation of bliss.

These are all forms of embodied time, through which we distend our lives beyond our physical location in space. At the same time, we are necessarily bound to a physical body. The wager of *My Struggle* is to hold these two perspectives together. We are spirit but also matter and the former depends on the latter. We can compose our lives—give them form and meaning—but in the end we will disappear in a meaningless process of decomposition. Knausgaard makes us confront such decomposition, while keeping faith in the value of finite existence. He turns us back to our lives to see both form and formlessness, integration and disintegration.

My Struggle thus moves in the opposite direction from the book whose title it takes over. Knausgaard's Norwegian title *Min Kamp* is a direct translation of *Mein Kampf,* the title of Adolf Hitler's autobiography. This may seem like a gratuitous provocation, but the choice of title is motivated in the final volume, where Knausgaard devotes more than four hundred pages to *Mein Kampf* and its context. Knausgaard gives a detailed account of the crisis of the times, as well as the complications of Hitler's childhood and early adulthood, while showing how *Mein Kampf* systematically subordinates Hitler's life story to ideology. The grittiness of everyday life is veiled by euphemism, the complexity of persons reduced to a typology of characters, and everything that is failure or suffering integrated in a narrative of gradual purification. Most importantly, all ambivalence, all doubts and hesitations, are dissolved in a discourse of certainty.

In a remarkable move, Knausgaard here shows how Hitler excludes a second-person mode of address. In *Mein Kampf,* there is an I, a *we,* and a *they,* but there is no *you* that would allow for an intimate relation. Hitler does not allow himself to be seen in any form of frailty, and he does not obligate himself to anyone else in his or her frailty. He merges himself with a strong, idealized *we* and projects all weakness onto an external *they.* Hitler's way of narrating his life is thus bound up with his larger ideological scheme for making sense of the world. In Hitler's universe, there is a pure, good "we" that is in peril of being corrupted by "them": the impure and evil others who most prominently are figured as the Jews. To the extent that *we* are in trouble—to the extent that our lives are unresolved or difficult—it is because of *them,* because of their corrupting influence. If only *they* (the evil forces) could be eliminated, *we* would be saved.

Nazi ideology is thus another version—a particularly sinister version—of the religious longing for purity. Knausgaard acknowledges and reckons with such longing for purity, but his writing is an active resistance to any temptation of purification. Indeed, *My Struggle* is devoted to the very imperfection that *Mein Kampf* sets out to erase. Nothing will save us, since irresolution, difficulty, and frailty are essential parts of the lives we care about. And no one can offer us a final salvation, since everyone who enters our lives is themselves finite. To own our lives is to acknowledge this essential finitude, as both the chance of being together and the risk of breaking apart. This is why *My Struggle*—which apparently is so devoted to the *I*—ultimately turns out to be dependent on *you*. In turning toward you, Karl Ove exposes himself in his dependence on a world that is beyond his control. But he also trains you to see and to acknowledge your own dependence and the dependence of others. This recognition of finitude does not offer any guarantees that we will lead a responsible life and take better care of one another. But without the recognition of finitude, the questions of responsibility and care could not even take hold of us. To turn toward *you*—to focus our gaze on another and attach ourselves to what we see—is the deepest movement of secular confession. We are turned back to our lives, not as something that is our property but as a form of existence that is altogether finite and altogether dependent on others. This is not the end of responsibility; it is the beginning.

3

Responsibility

I

He is born against all reasonable expectations. At the time, his mother is ninety-one and his father one hundred years old. No one else believes they can have a child. And yet he is born.

His father thinks the birth is a divine miracle, a fulfillment of the promise given to him by God. Through the son, the father shall establish a new people that will flourish and keep the memory of his name. "I will bless you and make your name great," God has promised him, "and in you all the families of the Earth shall be blessed."[1]

The father's future—as well as the future of his people—depends on the continued life of his son. All their hopes rest on this child. And yet the father is ready to kill the child, kill his son with his own hands, when God commands him to do so. Without raising any objections, the father rises early in the morning and takes his son with him. After traveling for three days, they arrive at the mountain where the sacrifice will take place. The father draws the knife and is ready to kill his son—ready to give everything away—but then God intervenes to stop him, as a reward for his obedience. "Now I know that you fear God," he is told, "since you have not withheld your son, your only son, from me."[2] As a reward for his obedience, the future that the father has been willing to give up—the future of his son and the future of generation after generation on earth—is given back to him in abundance. "Because you have done this thing and have not withheld your son," God explains, "I will bless you and I will multiply your descendants as the stars of the heaven and as the sand on the seashore."[3]

The story of Abraham's devotion to God—and the sacrifice of his beloved son Isaac—is both one of the most enigmatic and most poignant episodes in the Bible. Sparsely told as an existential drama of religious faith, it continues to provoke passionate responses and troubled questions. These questions are all the more pressing because Abraham is regarded as the "father of faith" in all three major monotheistic religions (Judaism, Christianity, Islam). How we understand Abraham's sacrifice of Isaac is therefore a central part of how we understand religious faith. The moral of the story may seem clear—man should subordinate his will to the command of God—but how we should respond to it remains an open question. Is Abraham a model of true faith because he obeys God even when doing so requires the sacrifice of what is dearest to him? Or does he exemplify a dangerous fanaticism that does not stop at anything in following what it takes to be the command of God?

While these questions have been debated for centuries, no one has pursued them with the philosophical depth and literary imagination of a young Danish philosopher in 1843. During a stay in Berlin, Søren Kierkegaard set out to bring the story of Abraham and Isaac back to life for a contemporary audience. The resulting work is *Fear and Trembling*, a book that more than any other has made Kierkegaard live on as an author and thinker. Professional philosophers as well as lay readers, religious believers as well as atheists, keep returning to *Fear and Trembling* as a profound exploration of what it means *to have faith*. This is a question that occupied Kierkegaard throughout all his works, but *Fear and Trembling* remains the book that attracts the most readers and inspires the most intense discussions. Kierkegaard himself seems to have predicted this response from posterity. "O, some day after I am dead," he writes in a journal entry from 1849, "*Fear and Trembling* alone will be enough to immortalize my name as an author. Then it will be read and translated into foreign languages. People will practically shudder at the frightful emotion in the book."[4]

Yet, as with the original Abraham story, it is far from clear how we should respond to the frightful emotion of *Fear and Trembling*. Kierkegaard himself regarded *Fear and Trembling* as part of his life-long project to demonstrate how demanding it is to have religious— and especially Christian—faith. In Kierkegaard's nineteenth-century Denmark, the majority of the population identified as Christian and the official religion of the state was Christianity. According to Kierkegaard, however, Christian faith had been reduced to a nominal belief and a social identity, as though it were enough to profess belief in God, be a member of the church, and attend service on Sundays in order to be a Christian. In contrast, Kierkegaard emphasizes how true Christianity requires that your entire existence be transformed by your faith. Christian faith is not reducible to *what* you believe but depends on *how* you believe. Merely to think or say that you believe in God is not sufficient; your faith in God has to change how you act, feel, and respond to what happens in your life.

Kierkegaard can thus be seen to revive the classical theological distinction between living and dead faith. The distinction is first formulated in the Letter of James, further articulated by Thomas Aquinas in his *Summa Theologica,* and most powerfully developed by Martin Luther in his catechetical writings. A living faith is one on which you are prepared to act, and it shapes how you are affected by what happens to you. At its strongest, it is the faith on which you are ready to stake your life. "Such faith which ventures everything on what it has heard concerning God, be it life or death, constitutes a Christian man," as Luther maintains.[5] A dead faith, by contrast, is one that does not make any real difference for how you live: something you claim to believe even though such faith is not manifested by your actions and even though you would never make your life depend on it.

In *Fear and Trembling,* Kierkegaard invokes Abraham's sacrifice of

Isaac as the most challenging example of what it means to have a living religious faith. To underline the challenge, Kierkegaard evokes Abraham's wholehearted and life-defining love for Isaac. Isaac is "the most precious" in his life and Abraham embraces him "with a love that is inadequately described by saying he faithfully fulfilled the father's duty to love the son."[6] Furthermore, Kierkegaard emphasizes that Abraham really *does* sacrifice Isaac. Even though Abraham in the end does not have to go through with the actual killing, the biblical story makes clear that he has completed the sacrifice of Isaac in his heart. Indeed, Abraham is rewarded precisely because God sees that he has given up Isaac ("you have not withheld your son, your only son, from me").

Thus, rather than allow the reader to conclude that the sacrifice of Isaac was only a hypothetical test, *Fear and Trembling* emphasizes that Abraham had to be resolved to kill his beloved son. Moreover, Abraham had to sustain his resolution for several days, in the concrete presence of the one he was going to sacrifice. With his characteristically precise imagination, Kierkegaard recalls the weight of these actions: "We forget that Abraham only rode an ass, which trudges along the road, that he had a journey of three days, that he needed some time to chop the firewood, to bind Isaac, and to sharpen the knife."[7]

By telling the story of Abraham's sacrifice, Kierkegaard wants the reader to imagine him- or herself in the same situation. His narrative strategy is to make you engage with the story from a first-person standpoint: to ask yourself what *you* would have done. Imagine that you have waited your whole life for the birth of your son, whom you love with all your heart, and now you are commanded to kill him. Imagine further that you have to make this sacrifice, not for any reason in the world and not to save anyone else, but only for the sake of your commitment to God. Imagine finally that you are able to make this sacrifice with an unshakable trust in God. The greatness of Abraham, according to *Fear and Trembling*, is that he is not paralyzed by "the anxiety, the distress, the paradox" of having to kill Isaac and instead ventures everything on his faith in God.

Kierkegaard holds that anyone who has a living religious faith must be ready to make such a sacrifice: to give up the finite (Isaac) for the eternal (God). To prove your religious commitment, you must be able to renounce your secular devotion to any form of *living on*—including the living on of your most beloved child—by virtue of your complete faith in the eternal. At the same time, Kierkegaard recognizes that the question of faith precedes any religious commitment and is a general feature of human existence. To approach *Fear and Trembling*, then, we first need to understand how Kierkegaard identifies faith as an issue that is always at stake in our lives. While his ultimate aim is to defend a version of religious faith, his own work provides profound insights into the dynamic of secular faith that he seeks to overcome.

II

A good place to start is the general definition of faith in Kierkegaard's *Concluding Unscientific Postscript:* "Without risk, no faith. Faith is the contradiction between the infinite passion of inwardness and the objective uncertainty."[8] This may seem like a difficult definition, but by unpacking Kierkegaard's terminology we can see how it makes sense.

Kierkegaard's notion of "objective uncertainty" refers to how all knowledge is subject to time. While we can develop methods for better understanding what happened in the past, it is always possible that new evidence may come to challenge what we thought we knew, or that new questions present the given evidence in a different light. Thus, no matter how subjectively certain we may be about what has happened, there is an element of objective uncertainty in our knowledge, since our account of the past cannot ever be definitive and may be refuted. Likewise, we may develop better methods for predicting what will happen, but the future remains objectively uncertain, since we cannot *know* what has not yet taken place.

These forms of uncertainty mark our experience of the present itself, which is already becoming past and becoming related to the future. A moment is never a still point of certainty but always passing away (*Forbigaaende*) and opening itself to what may come (*Tilkommende*). This is why life—in Kierkegaard's most famous phrase—can only be understood backwards but must be lived forwards. We have to act in view of the future, but we cannot know the consequences of our actions, since these consequences are given only in retrospect. Moreover, as Kierkegaard emphasizes, *your own self* is inseparable from this temporality. You are not a stable essence but always *existing* temporally; you are not a given being but always in a process of *becoming* that may transform your sense of who you are.

Because of the objective uncertainty, faith is a necessary condition of experience. Neither the past nor the future can be known and have to be taken on faith. This temporal condition—what I call the *necessary uncertainty* of secular faith—binds faith to risk from the beginning. Given that your relation to the past and the future depends on faith, you may be deceived by what you think is certain, mistaken about what you take for granted, and shattered by what you never expected. Your vulnerability to these risks is due to the *existential commitment* of secular faith. Because you are existentially committed to someone or something, you can feel the pain of being deceived, mistaken, or shattered. Moreover, temporal finitude is intrinsic to why an existential commitment matters in the first place. It is because something can be lost—and because such loss would have irreversible consequences—that there is anything at stake in being faithful. Continued fidelity to someone or something is inseparable from the apprehension of loss. This risk of loss is the *motivational force* of secular faith. The risk of loss is an essential part of keeping faith, at the same time as it makes all fidelity precarious, something that must be continually achieved.

The three aspects of secular faith—necessary uncertainty, existential commitment, motivational force—can be illuminated in and by Kierkegaard's own texts. Existential commitment is the aspect of secular faith that most occupies Kierkegaard. He understands that our lives can matter to us only if we are existentially committed to what we do. "Passion" and "appropriation" are two of Kierkegaard's favorite words to describe such a commitment. For an activity to matter in an existential sense, it is not enough that you learn to do it correctly: you have to be *passionate* about doing it right and *appropriate* the activity as your own by putting yourself at stake in it.

Passion and appropriation are a matter of "inwardness" because they can be given only from a first-person standpoint. I can study what you do from a third-person standpoint, but whether or not you are existentially committed to what you do—whether you have actually put yourself at stake in what you are doing—can be decided only from your first-person standpoint. Moreover, even from your first-person standpoint, your commitment is not decided once and for all but is something that must be sustained. Kierkegaard describes this capacity for passionate appropriation as "infinite," not because it is indestructible but because it consists in its own activity and defines what matters in your life. Your infinite passion is your capacity to be wholeheartedly devoted to your life as a finite being.

For the same reason, your infinite passion exposes you to loss. Even if you sustain your devotion—even if you keep faith with what you love—the object of your faith and devotion can itself be taken away from you. For example, if you dedicate your life to music or athletics, your body may break in such a way that you can no longer pursue the activity that made your life meaningful. Likewise, when you love another person he or she can leave you behind, and when you are devoted to a political project it can disintegrate despite your best efforts. This is why there is no faith without risk. To recall Kierkegaard's definition, the infinite passion of inwardness (your devotion to someone or something) is always at odds with the objective uncertainty (the temporal finitude that may take away your object of devotion).

Accordingly, the more you devote yourself to something—the more you allow a given passion to define who you are—the more you put yourself in peril. By committing yourself to a person, a political struggle, or a way of life, you become dependent on something whose continued existence is objectively uncertain. Yet Kierkegaard maintains that it is only through such an existential commitment that you can become a self. Biologically we may be described as human beings, but who we are—our "self" in Kierkegaard's existential sense—is defined by *what* we are committed to as well as *how* we sustain those commitments. This is why our self can live in more than a biological sense, but also why it can "die" before our biological death. If you fail to sustain a life-defining commitment—or have to give it up because it has become unsustainable—you suffer an existential "death" of your self, even though your life continues.

Kierkegaard can thus be seen to have a deep grasp of the dynamic of secular faith. An instructive example is his account of marriage. By marriage, Kierkegaard does not mean the legal procedure consecrated by a wedding, but the existential act of committing to another person for life. Such a life-defining commitment is *eternal* in a secular sense. To say that I will be committed to you forever is not to say that we will live forever or that our love can never end. Rather, it is to promise that I will sustain my love for you every day of my life. As Kierkegaard puts it: "The person who by marriage binds another person's life to his own, who by marriage makes a commitment that no time will dissolve and every day will require to be fulfilled, from that person a resolution is required."[9] While the resolution is eternal in the sense of being binding for my whole life, it is by the same token temporal, since it can exist only through a continuous devotion. Accordingly, in the covenant of marriage "eternity is not finished with time, but the covenant is eternity's beginning in time." Moreover, "the eternal resolution" of marriage "*must remain with the wedded pair in the union of love through time,* and there is to be celebration at its remembrance and power in its recollection and hope in its promise" (emphasis added).[10]

The resolution of marriage is not a religious devotion to a timeless eternity but a secular devotion to living on in time. The very joy of the resolution—its celebration of the continued love—must rely on the precarious remembrance of the past and the uncertain promise of the future. The resolution does not secure my future; it only decides what is at stake for me in the future. In making the life-defining commitment of marriage, I acknowledge that *who I am* and *what matters to me* is defined by my love for you. By the same token, who I am and what matters to me is dependent on what happens to us, exposed to a future that exceeds my control. Kierkegaard emphasizes that this risk is not external but *internal* to the resolution itself. "The person who is ignorant of the danger, who excludes the danger and does not include an actual conception of it in the resolution," he writes, "that person is not resolved."[11]

To be resolved is thus to reckon with finitude. In sustaining my commitment to you, I must continually forgo other possible ways of living my life. Without this finitude—where the commitment to one future closes down other possible futures—my commitment would be meaningless and automatic, since there would be no alternatives. There would be nothing at stake in wedding my life to you, since I could not do otherwise. Furthermore, my resolute commitment must always reckon with the finitude that is inherent in the marriage itself. Our love may break under the strain of conflicts, be drained of vitality because the other is taken for granted, or slowly languish in habitual patterns. This finitude is what calls for a resolution in the first place. As Kierkegaard reminds us, love "perishes in adversity if no resolution holds it firm, it perishes in prosperity if no resolution holds it firm, it degenerates in the everyday if no resolution encourages it."[12] Finally, even the most resolute and life-defining commitment is finite because we can literally die. Even if we remain faithful to our love for as long as we live, our lives will come to an end. We can only be married until death do us part, leaving one of us to mourn the other.

Kierkegaard's radical argument is that finitude in all these senses is vital for any meaningful commitment. Even if it were possible to have a life of guaranteed happiness, "the dangers of the life of resolution"[13] are still preferable, since they are the conditions for a life worth living. For anything to matter—for anything to be at stake—the chance of happiness and flourishing must be shadowed by the risk of loss. Thus, in a striking passage, Kierkegaard recommends that "the bridal couple, before going to the house where the wedding reception is held, go to the house of sorrow, that is, to the earnest consideration from which one does not obtain the bridal veil but the resolution."[14] This relation between resolution and finitude runs throughout Kierkegaard's work. As he argues in his remarkable text "At a Graveside," the thought that everything ends with death—that all is over when we die—is not a reason to devalue life. On the contrary, the thought of death is the source of any "earnest" engagement with life and makes the given time all the more precious. "The earnest understanding," Kierkegaard writes, "is that if death is night then life is day, that if no work can be done at night then work can be done during the day; and the terse but impelling cry of earnestness, like death's terse cry, is: This very day."[15]

Kierkegaard's own insights can thus be employed against the religious ideal of being absolved from the pain of loss. A Stoic life of tranquil apathy or a Buddhist life of peaceful detachment is meaningless for Kierkegaard. He does not want to be free from passions; he wants to be passionately engaged and wholeheartedly committed. Moreover, Kierkegaard understands that such passion is inseparable from vulnerability. In passionately identifying myself with a project—a political cause, a romantic relationship, a creative ambition—I risk my own life and identity, which may be shattered if the project fails. Far from being a reason for detachment, the risk is for Kierkegaard part of what makes the project meaningful and a matter of earnest engagement. Without the anticipation of loss, one could never be resolved to make the most of the time that is given.

Nevertheless, Kierkegaard himself ultimately subscribes to a version of the religious ideal of being absolved from the pain of loss. This absolution does not take place through detachment but rather through faith in God's power to redeem anything that is lost. Religious faith would thus enable you to be wholeheartedly committed and live with the danger of loss, without being defeated by any actual loss. "It is true that he who expects something in particular may be disappointed," Kierkegaard writes in one of his edifying religious discourses, "but this does not happen to the believer."[16] Rather, even faced with the most terrible loss, the religious believer asserts:

> There is an expectation that the whole world cannot take from me;
> it is the expectation of faith, and this is victory. I am not deceived,
> since I did not believe that the world would keep the promise it
> seemed to be making to me; my expectation was not in the world
> but in God. This expectation is not deceived; even in this moment
> I sense its victory more gloriously and more joyfully than all the
> pain of loss. If I were to lose this expectation, then everything
> would be lost. Now I have still conquered, conquered through my
> expectation, and my expectation is victory.[17]

This is the blueprint for Abraham's religious faith in *Fear and Trembling*. As long as Abraham keeps his faith in God, he is insulated from the actual experience of losing what he loves. For Kierkegaard, this is the deepest virtue of religious faith. *As long as you keep religious faith, you cannot be defeated by loss.* If you lose your religious faith, then everything is lost, but as long as you keep it you are safe. Abraham is the supreme example, since he keeps faith in God's promise regardless of what happens in the world. God has promised that Isaac will live a flourishing life, so Abraham keeps faith in this promise even when God's own command and his own action (killing Isaac) apparently undermine the promise. Thus, Abraham can maintain his love for Isaac and take the greatest risks—including the risk of sacrificing his own son—without ever being shattered. Even if Abraham has to kill Isaac, he believes that God will bring Isaac back to life, and as long as he keeps this expectation he cannot be defeated.

In contrast, secular faith necessarily remains vulnerable. *As long as you keep secular faith, you can be defeated by loss.* Affirming your life-defining commitment as a parent—and loving your child wholeheartedly—does not protect you from the pain of conflict, the bereavement of broken hopes, or the possible devastation of losing your child. On the contrary, it is because you are keeping faith with your child—and holding on to your life-defining commitment as a parent—that you are all the more vulnerable to these experiences.

Such vulnerability is the condition for any form of responsiveness to—and responsibility for—what happens to the one you love.

In being devoted to someone who is finite, I have to be responsive to what befalls him or her, even if the events are adverse to my own hopes and desires. I am committed to fight for him or her to live on and flourish, but also bound to recognize if and when there is defeat. If I am Abraham and maintain my secular faith, I believe that Isaac's life is priceless—I am devoted to his well-being as an end in itself—but I also believe that his life can be lost. Indeed, *it is only by acknowledging and being responsive to Isaac's finitude that I can care for him.*

As we will see, it is precisely the capacity to care for Isaac—to be responsive and responsible with regard to his fate—that Abraham has to sacrifice for the sake of his religious faith. In Kierkegaard's account, Abraham has a life-defining commitment to being a father. Abraham does not only have a sense of duty in caring for his son; he loves Isaac wholeheartedly and with such devotion that "there would not be many a father in the realms and lands of the king who would dare to maintain that he loved in this way."[18] Furthermore, Isaac is for Abraham the promise of his own future and of a blessed future for his people. It is through Isaac that Abraham makes sense of his life and it is only through Isaac that his legacy can survive. Thus, in having faith that Isaac will be born and live on, Abraham puts his own life at stake. His love for Isaac dramatizes—as Kierkegaard is keen to explore—an existential experience that goes beyond the particular details of biblical mythology. While most prospective parents do not have to face the unlikely odds of trying to have a child when they are as old as Abraham, any aspiring parent can feel the gravity of his situation. Regardless of the age of the parents, nothing can guarantee that a child will be born and nothing can secure his or her life after birth.

To commit oneself to becoming a parent (in this case a father) is thus a particularly poignant experience of objective uncertainty. I cannot know if I will become a father and—if I do—I cannot know what it will be like until I am already in the situation. I can certainly acquire knowledge about what it means to be a father from a third-person standpoint and benefit from learning about the experiences of others. But no amount of information or knowledge is sufficient to prepare me for the first-person experience of becoming a father. Rather, I have to commit myself in advance of the experience and thereby make *a leap of faith* into the unknown.

The leap is risky because I cannot know who I will turn out to be as a father, or who my child will turn out to be, or what will happen to my child. Furthermore, this objective uncertainty is an ongoing part of being a father. As long as I have a child, I am bound to a future that exceeds my control. To be a father in more than a biological sense—to make fatherhood an integral part of my identity, to care about my child in an active and passionate sense—requires that I sustain an existential, life-defining commitment to my child. This is why parenthood can be such a transformative event, reorienting my deepest relation to the world, making life more palpable and more meaningful. Yet the same existential commitment that makes me receptive to wonder and joy also makes me vulnerable to what happens. Even if my child causes me great grief, and even if a rational calculation would compute that I would be better off not being a parent, I cannot give up the commitment except by giving up my own sense of who I am.

The vulnerability to grief is a common denominator for all forms of secular faith, which are devoted to something or someone who is finite. In keeping faith with my child, I am bound to what Kierkegaard calls "external" factors, since I am devoted to someone whose fate exceeds my control. I can love and care for my child, but my love and care cannot secure the future of my child. The same holds for all forms of secular faith, which are committed to persons or projects that can live on and flourish but also come to an end. Even if my internal resolve is intact and I keep my faith, I can still suffer from an irrevocable loss because of circumstances that are external to my will.

Hence, in secular faith I can lose my object of devotion even if I keep faith. In contrast, Kierkegaard advocates a religious faith that cannot ever lose its object of devotion as long as it keeps faith.

The decisive difference concerns the relation to the future. As Kierkegaard emphasizes, there is a trembling of anxiety in every relation to the future, since we cannot know what will happen and may lose what we want to keep. The more we are devoted to something, the more powerful the anxiety, since our own being is at stake. Thus, if I am a father, the prospect of losing my son is anxiety producing, both because I care about him in his own right and because I would be devastated if I lost him. To live with such anxiety—which is intrinsic to any form of secular faith—is according to Kierkegaard to live "in despair." As he makes clear in *The Sickness unto Death*, being in despair is not limited to an experience of existential breakdown. Rather, even the greatest bliss is for Kierkegaard a matter of despair, insofar as "deep, deep within the most secret hiding place of happiness there dwells also anxiety, which is despair."[19] Being in despair, then, encompasses everyone who does not have religious faith. Anyone who lives with any form of anxiety—"an unrest, an inner strife, a disharmony, an anxiety about an unknown something or a something he does not even dare to try to know, an anxiety about some possibility in existence or an anxiety about himself"[20]—is in despair. Only those who have religious faith are free from despair. Religious faith is a state in which "despair is completely rooted out," "a state in which there is no despair at all" by virtue of complete faith in God.[21]

Kierkegaard emphasizes, however, that such freedom from despair cannot be achieved through naive optimism or simple trust that everything will work out. On the contrary, the religious believer must confront the fact that "every anxiety for which he feels alarm can come upon him at the very next instant," including "horror, perdition, and annihilation."[22] The true test of religious faith does not take place when things are going well, but "when the world commences its drastic ordeal, when the storms of life crush youth's exuberant expectancy, when existence, which seemed so affectionate and gentle, changes into a pitiless proprietor who demands everything back."[23] The task is to confront the worst possible scenario—to face what Kierkegaard calls "the anxiety of the possible," the possibility that you will lose everything that matters to you in the world—and still maintain your religious faith. "Only someone who passes through the anxiety of the possible," Kierkegaard writes, "is cultivated to have

no anxiety."[24] If you lose your religious faith when the worst happens
to you—when your trust in the world is shattered—you reveal that
you never actually had religious faith. The decisive moment is when
"a person is brought to his extremity, when, humanly speaking, there
is no possibility. Then the question is whether he will believe that for
God everything is possible, that is, whether he will *believe*."[25]

When God commands the sacrifice of Isaac, Abraham is brought
to such an extremity. Humanly speaking, there is no possibility left
for him if he kills Isaac. Following God's previous command, Abraham has already abandoned his native land and the promise of estab-
lishing a new community is altogether dependent on the existence
of his son. If Abraham kills Isaac, he will shatter the very possibility
of making sense of his life and his actions. He will have uprooted
his family for nothing, annulled the birth of his beloved son, and
extinguished the future of his people. When he returns from the
killing, his own wife will not be able to understand or recognize him:
how can he have done this to their son, to her, to everything they
had together? Moreover, Abraham will not even be able to recognize
himself. Being a father is a life-defining commitment for Abraham,
which means that it gives him an identity across time. Even if other
things change, he can still recognize himself through his devotion to
Isaac and his commitment to their future. In killing Isaac, however,
he will do what is unthinkable for himself as a father and undercut
any chance of recognizing himself in his deed.

Nevertheless, Abraham is able to face the prospect of killing Isaac
without despair, since he believes that for God everything is possible.
In Kierkegaard's account, Abraham can even go through with the
killing of Isaac and still maintain his "trusting expectation" that his
life will be saved. Even though Abraham cannot know how it will
be possible, he has faith that God will enable him to go on and to
flourish even if his entire world is devastated. This is why Abraham
is celebrated as a hero of religious faith in *Fear and Trembling*. The
benefit of religious faith is supposed to be that it saves you from all
forms of despair and enables you to go on with your life regardless of
what happens. As Kierkegaard explains in *The Sickness unto Death*, "the

believer has the ever infallible antidote for despair—possibility—
because for God everything is possible at every moment."[26]

To prove that you have such faith, however, there has to be a way
of *testing* it. It is easy enough to claim that you believe everything
is possible for God, but the vital test is to prove that you believe it
through how you act and how you respond. In *The Sickness unto Death*,
Kierkegaard describes the test as follows:

> Imagine that someone with a capacity to imagine terrifying
> nightmares has pictured to himself some horror or other that is
> absolutely unbearable. Then it happens to him, this very hor-
> ror happens to him. Humanly speaking, his collapse is altogether
> certain. . . . At this point, then, salvation is, humanly speaking,
> utterly impossible; but for God everything is possible! This is the
> battle of *faith*. . . . The *believer* sees and understands his downfall,
> humanly speaking (in what has happened to him, or in what he
> has ventured), but he believes. For this reason he does not col-
> lapse. He leaves it entirely to God how he is to be helped, but he
> believes that for God everything is possible. To *believe* his downfall
> is impossible. To understand that humanly it is his downfall and
> nevertheless to believe in possibility is to believe. So God helps
> him also—perhaps by allowing him to avoid the horror, perhaps
> through the horror itself. . . .[27]

While this passage does not explicitly invoke the example of Abraham, it illuminates the test of religious faith that is at the center
of *Fear and Trembling*. If Abraham kills Isaac, his collapse and downfall are—humanly speaking—altogether certain. There will be no
possible support from his loved ones and no possible way to make
sense of his life, since his own action will have made him unrecog-
nizable to himself. In short, his life will be "absolutely unbearable"
and "humanly speaking, utterly impossible." When Abraham raises
the knife to kill Isaac, he understands all this—he understands that
"humanly it is his downfall"—and yet he believes that God will make
it possible for him to go on with his life. Even in full *knowledge* that he

is killing Isaac, Abraham keeps *faith* that God will give him a "new Isaac" or "restore to life the one sacrificed."[28] Abraham does not believe that Isaac will be given back to him as a matter of *fact*, and he does not know *how* it will happen. Rather, Abraham renounces all forms of calculation and "leaves it entirely to God how he is to be helped."

III

The example of Abraham may seem extreme, but the formal features it exhibits are necessary for the test of religious faith that Kierkegaard envisages throughout his work. As long as you are supported by your family, your friends, or your community, what enables you to go on with your life may be a secular rather than a religious faith. To test if your religious faith is living or dead—to test if you actually trust in God or merely say that you do—you need a scenario in which you do not rely on anything other than faith in God. This is why the Danish words for "test" and "trial," *prøve* and *prøvelse*, are consistently used to describe Abraham's sacrifice in *Fear and Trembling*. A living religious faith must be able to overcome even the most extreme loss without recourse to anything other than faith in God. If you have faith in God, no circumstance can bring you to despair. If you have faith in God, you cannot be broken.

We can thus further specify the difference between secular and religious faith. My secular faith that life is worth living may carry me through devastating experiences, but it is essentially fragile, since I cannot sustain it on my own. My secular faith—my ability to hope for the future—relies on others who recognize me, as well as on my own ability to recognize myself. Even if I am all alone, my own sense of myself is inseparable from how I have been received by others and how they have given me resources to live on. Thus, if my son dies, I may be able to go on with my life despite the terrible grief, but at every step of the way I will depend on the world of which I am a part. If I can recollect my love for my son—if I can recognize myself as a loving father who inadvertently lost his son—I may be able to work through the grief and renew my commitment to the future. The pain will never entirely go away, but the memories of what we shared together may give me sustenance. If I am fortunate enough, the experience of having loved will enable me to love again. However, if there is no one to console me, no one to hold and comfort me, no one who gives me hope for a viable future, I may succumb to despair. Moreover, if I utterly betrayed or even killed my son—if I sacrificed him for no justifiable reason—I will have destroyed my own sense of myself, my own ability to love, and will be bound to despair. There will be no way to go on, since my world will have collapsed and my identity will be irreversibly broken.

The risk of such despair is built into any life-defining commitment. To have a life-defining commitment is to acknowledge that I am not self-sufficient but essentially a relational being. My identity is not given but relies on forms of recognition that must be upheld or transformed and that remain fragile at their core. My life-defining commitments give me a world and an identity, but they also underline my finitude and the risk that my world can break down.

In secular faith, the risk of despair is not only a negative threat but also intrinsic to my positive identity and engagement. The risk of despair—the anticipation that my world *can* break down—recalls me to what matters in my life and why it remains important what I do. My very life is at stake in my finite relations.

For Kierkegaard, by contrast, religious faith is supposed to annul the risk of despair. If you have religious faith, you believe that you can lose everything and still be saved, since for God everything is possible.

Religious faith thus requires a double movement, whereby you renounce trust in the world in favor of trust in God. Rather than rely on finite relations, you place your faith in God. The first movement of religious faith is what Kierkegaard calls infinite resignation, which plays a central role in *Fear and Trembling* but is most fully elaborated in the *Concluding Unscientific Postscript*. Infinite resignation does not mean that you give up hope, but that you renounce all forms of hope that depend on a finite world. Instead you maintain that the highest good is an "eternal happiness" beyond the finite. The task is to make eternal happiness into your absolute *telos:* the goal or end for which you strive. At the same time, you can never achieve eternal happiness as long as you are finite, so the striving for the absolute goal becomes a task that cannot be finished in this life. Rather, the striving for eternal happiness is expressed through the renunciation of all finite goals as inadequate.

In accordance with his emphasis on a living religious faith, Kierkegaard underscores that such renunciation cannot be merely theoretical but must be enacted in practice. To make the movement of infinite resignation you must demonstrate to yourself that you are willing to give up everything that is finite for the sake of eternal happiness. "If to him an eternal happiness is his highest good," Kierkegaard writes in the *Postscript*, "this means that in his acting the finite elements are once and for all reduced to what must be surrendered in relation to the eternal happiness."[29] And again: "If there is something he is not willing to give up for its sake, then he is not relating himself to an eternal happiness."[30]

To make the movement of infinite resignation, however, is not to leave the finite behind. Rather, it is to live in the finite while being literally insensitive to the fate of the finite. As Kierkegaard puts it, "when the individual has the absolute orientation toward the absolute *telos,* everything is changed, the roots are cut. He lives in the finite, but he does not have his life in it. . . . Just as the dentist loosens the gum tissue and cuts the nerve and lets the tooth remain, so also is his life in finitude loosened, and the task is to have the tooth not grow fast again."[31] Kierkegaard is here talking about an inward transformation. When the individual severs the nerves that make him sensitive to the finite, his outward life may still appear to be the same. He can pursue finite goals and maintain his worldly relations, but through the movement of resignation his bonds to them are loosened in such a way that he is ready to renounce them if that is required.

Nevertheless, just as the tooth may grow fast again, the threads that bind the individual to the world may reassert themselves. He continues to live in the finite and therefore runs the risk of devoting himself to a finite goal or a finite being as an end in itself. This is why Kierkegaard stresses that the movement of resignation cannot be made once and for all but constantly has to be undertaken anew, to ensure that one never treats anyone or anything finite as absolute (an end in itself) but only as relative:

> The individual is certainly in the finite (and the difficulty is indeed to preserve the absolute choice in the finite), but just as he took away the vital power of the finite in the moment of resignation, so the task is to repeat this. Suppose the world offers the individual everything. Perhaps he accepts it, but he says: Oh, well, but this "Oh, well" signifies the absolute respect for the absolute *telos*. Suppose the world takes everything away from him; he may wince, but he says: Oh, well—and this "Oh, well" signifies the absolute respect for the absolute *telos*.[32]

Kierkegaard here describes how you can remove your dependence on external factors by continually making the movement of resignation. Regardless of what happens in the external world—regardless of whether everything is given to you or everything is taken away from you—your response should be the same ("Oh, well"). Through the movement of resignation, you free yourself from "the vital power of the finite" by not allowing anything that happens to confirm or shatter your hope. You still live in the finite, but you do not have your life—your heart—in it. Your hope is invested in an eternal happiness and this hope cannot be refuted by anything that happens in or to the finite.

Hence, for all his insights into the dynamic of marriage, Kierkegaard holds that it must be subordinated to the absolute goal of eternal happiness. "Do not forget that marriage is not the absolute *telos*, and therefore what is absolutely true of the absolute is only imperfectly true of marriage."[33] If I stake my happiness on marriage, the fate of my commitment is not only up to me; it also depends on how you receive what I do. Being committed in marriage entails that

I cannot sovereignly decide the meaning of my actions or the terms of my commitment. I have to be responsive to what you say and do, which includes the risk that you may end our marriage. Indeed, even if I devote myself completely to you, there is no guarantee that you will remain faithful. "Deep within every person's soul," Kierkegaard reminds us, "there is a secret anxiety that even the one in whom he has the most faith could also become unfaithful to him."[34] As he emphasizes: "No merely human love can completely drive out this anxiety, which can very well remain hidden and undetected in the friendly security of a happy life-relationship, but which at times can inexplicably stir deep within and which, when the storms of life begin, is immediately at hand."[35] In contrast, God "remains faithful, every day of your life, whatever happens to you; he remains faithful to you in death; he meets you again in the hereafter as a trustworthy friend."[36] The demanding task is to keep faith in God. As long as you have "given yourself completely to him, had your whole life in him," he will never let you down, since "he himself eternally guarantees" his own fidelity.[37]

For Kierkegaard, devotion in marriage must therefore be subordinated to—or renounced in favor of—a religious devotion to God as the highest good and to eternal happiness as one's own highest good. He explains the move through the following contrast:

> In erotic love, the individual is still involved with another human being and can hear that person's yes or no. In every enthusiasm-inspired project, the individual still has something external, but in relation to eternal happiness the individual has only himself to deal with in inwardness.[38]

Even if I commit myself to you in the most wholehearted way, you may negate my will and defeat my hope by saying no. Likewise, even if I devote myself to the project of our marriage with my utmost enthusiasm—being willing to do anything to sustain it—there is still something external to my will, since the project may fail despite my best efforts and most fervent hopes. However, as long as I keep eternal happiness as my absolute *telos,* my hope is safe from any possible defeat. Unlike in marriage, where I have to deal with another person who may be resistant to my will or leave me behind, "in relation to eternal happiness the individual has only himself to deal with in inwardness."

Moreover, the inwardness of religious faith disarms the real risks of objective uncertainty. A marriage is objectively uncertain in the sense that it can actually break and leave me shattered. Eternal happiness, however, is objectively uncertain in the sense that it can neither be proved nor disproved. As long as I keep faith in eternal happiness, it cannot be taken away from me, since the only criterion for its existence is my own faith that it will be given to me. No external criteria can refute my hope for eternal happiness, and nothing external to my own will can force me to give it up. Eternal happiness cannot be given to me by the finite, but for the same reason it cannot be taken away from me by the finite. It has nothing to do with anything in the external world, but is entirely a matter of my inward relation to my absolute *telos.*

The mistake of monasticism, according to Kierkegaard, is to think that such a movement of infinite resignation requires one to withdraw from the world. He gives monasticism credit for recognizing that devotion to God as the highest good—and to eternal happiness as one's own highest good—requires the renunciation of one's family and secular aspirations. But for Kierkegaard it is deeply misleading to think that the inward resolution to renounce the finite needs to be expressed in outward behavior. Nothing is accomplished by merely withdrawing to a monastery, since a monastery belongs as much to the world and to finite life as any other place on earth. Anyone who makes the movement of infinite resignation should become "a stranger in the world of finitude," but he should "not define his difference from *worldliness* by foreign dress (this is a contradiction, since with that he defines himself in a worldly way)."[39] What matters is not outward manifestation—whether I wear a monk's robe or secular clothes—but inward transformation. Indeed, withdrawing to a monastery may deceive me into thinking that I have already accomplished infinite resignation, though I have not even begun to make the movement. Rather than devote myself to God and to the pursuit of my eternal happiness, I may be enjoying the camaraderie with the other monks, the rousing emotions of our communal singing, and the sense of self-control I attain through the spiritual exercises.

Moreover, for Kierkegaard, the need to withdraw to a monastery testifies to a religious faith that is lacking in strength, since it needs the external support of a pious environment. The one who can truly make the movement of infinite resignation should be able to do it while remaining in the midst of the temptations of worldly joy. For example, a husband who is making the movement of infinite resignation should be able to stay with his wife and children, apparently as devoted as ever to them, even though at every moment he is renouncing his care for them and is ready to give them up. Kierkegaard even recommends such an arrangement as a good exercise for strengthening one's internal power of renunciation: "The person who relates himself to the absolute *telos* may very well live in the relative ends just in order to practice the absolute relation in renunciation."[40]

We can thus begin to understand why Kierkegaard treats the sacrifice of Isaac as paradigmatic for what it means to have a living religious faith. Even if you do not receive an explicit command from God to sacrifice your son, the absolute *telos* of eternal happiness requires that you subordinate and ultimately surrender any finite object of your love. This movement of infinite resignation is at the core of what Kierkegaard calls Religiousness A. Religiousness A is not one religion among others, but the genus of which all specific forms of religious devotion (including Christianity) are the species. As Kierkegaard puts it: "infinite resignation is the last stage before faith, so that anyone who has not made this movement does not have faith, for only in infinite resignation do I become conscious of my eternal validity, and only then can one speak of grasping existence by virtue of faith."[41] The infinite resignation of Religiousness A is thus the common denominator for all forms of religious faith worthy of the name. The reason is simple. If you are not willing to sacrifice the finite for the eternal, your living faith—the faith that is revealed by how you actually respond to what happens—is secular rather than religious. You may profess that you believe in God and eternity, but as long as you are not ready to renounce the finite your supposed religious faith is dead, a matter of mere words. Or as Kierkegaard emphasizes: "If it does not *absolutely* transform his existence for him, then the individual is not relating himself to an eternal happiness; if there is something he is not willing to give up for its sake, then he is not relating himself to an eternal happiness."[42]

Nevertheless, in *Fear and Trembling* Kierkegaard acknowledges that the movement of infinite resignation leaves something to be desired. In making the movement of infinite resignation, I have to give up any particular hope I have for my finite life, teaching myself to say "Oh, well" even if my beloved son dies. According to *Fear and Trembling*, there is "peace and rest"[43] in this movement of infinite resignation, which "reconciles one to existence,"[44] but the peace and rest are bought at the price of having to renounce the beloved in this life. If I am Abraham and only able to make the movement of infinite resignation, I will go ahead and sacrifice Isaac—renounce him as an end in himself—but I will give up my hopes for Isaac in this life.

The "true" Abraham, however, makes a second movement simultaneously with the movement of infinite resignation: the movement of faith. This movement holds that everything is possible for God, even if it seems impossible or absurd from a human perspective.[45] Thus, even in sacrificing Isaac, Abraham keeps faith in God's promise that Isaac will live a flourishing life. By virtue of his religious faith, Abraham can renounce his son while at the same time believing that he will get him back. Indeed, Kierkegaard emphasizes that even in killing Isaac, "Abraham had faith specifically for this life—faith that he would grow old in this country, be honored among the people, blessed by posterity, and unforgettable in Isaac."[46] Likewise, Kierkegaard's modern version of Abraham—the knight of faith—is presented as someone who is utterly committed to finite life. Unlike his counterpart the knight of infinite resignation, who can make only the first movement of renunciation, the knight of faith can make the double movement through which he fully expects to receive the finite even after having given it up. Whereas the knight of infinite resignation becomes "a stranger and an alien"[47] in the world of finitude, the knight of faith is described as "the only happy man, the heir to the finite,"[48] since he has "this security that makes him delight in finitude as if it were the surest thing of all."[49]

These descriptions of the knight of faith have led many Kierkegaard scholars to claim that he has found a way to combine devotion to God with devotion to finite life.[50] Yet the double movement of religious faith actually denies the experience of finitude by precluding the experience of irrevocable loss. To say that Abraham embraces finite life is a hollow claim, since his religious faith insulates him from ever acknowledging the finitude of the finite. Regardless of what happens to Isaac, Abraham has faith that his son will emerge unscathed, which deprives him of the capacity to care for Isaac. He can even kill Isaac without thinking that this act compromises his love for his son and without worrying about what it will do to Isaac. Kierkegaard underscores this point through a scenario in which Isaac actually dies and Abraham still keeps faith:

> Let us go further. We let Isaac actually be sacrificed. Abraham had faith. He did not have faith that he would be blessed in a future life but that he would be blessed here in the world. God could give him a new Isaac, could restore to life the one sacrificed. He had faith by virtue of the absurd, for all human calculation ceased long ago.[51]

Through his faith in God, Abraham can thus retain his hopes for his beloved son in this life, even when he is literally destroying Isaac's life. To construe this double movement of religious faith as a genuine commitment to finite life is fatally misleading. In practice, the one who makes the double movement of religious faith is even more brutally indifferent to the fate of the finite than the one who performs the single movement of infinite resignation. The knight of infinite resignation kills Isaac, but at least he recognizes the loss of Isaac. The knight of faith also kills Isaac, but through the double movement of religious faith *he does not recognize the actual loss of Isaac* because he is fully confident that he will get him back even though he has taken his life. He can stand there with Isaac's severed head in his hand and still believe that he will live happily ever after with his son.

The brutal effects of such faith are evident from Kierkegaard's own text. Early on in *Fear and Trembling*, we are presented with four alternative stories of the sacrifice of Isaac, in which the fathers fail to live up to the supposed greatness of the "true" Abraham who is a knight of faith. What all the Abrahams have in common is that they love Isaac and nevertheless follow God's command to sacrifice him. Unlike the true Abraham, however, the failed Abrahams cannot overcome the conflict between their love for Isaac and their obedience to God. The first Abraham is resigned to sacrificing Isaac, but he tries to explain to Isaac why he will kill him. When Isaac cannot understand him (and how could he understand why his father would kill him?), Abraham instead pretends to be a madman who wants to kill Isaac out of his own desire, so as to spare Isaac the anguish of having been sentenced to death by God himself. The second Abraham does exactly what the true Abraham does—he travels for three days to Mount Moriah, where he is ready to sacrifice Isaac—but after the event he loses all his joy in the world, since he cannot "forget that God had ordered him to do this."[52] The third Abraham also does exactly what the true Abraham does, but is then seized by remorse because he has been willing to sacrifice his son. The fourth Abraham, finally, also sacrifices Isaac but as he draws the knife he cannot suppress how dreadful it is to kill Isaac. His left hand is "clenched in despair" and a "shudder" goes through his whole body.[53]

The true Abraham, by contrast, is not torn between his love for Isaac and his obedience to God. He does not try to explain anything to Isaac or to protect him from the terror of the ordeal. Furthermore, he loses none of his happiness in the world and feels no remorse because of the sacrifice, but is immediately ready to "rally to finitude and its joy"[54] when Isaac is given back to him. Finally, as he draws the knife to kill Isaac, his hand is not clenched in despair and no shudder passes through his body:

He did not doubt, he did not look in anguish to the left and to the right, he did not challenge heaven with his prayers. He knew it was God the Almighty who tested him; he knew it was the hardest sacrifice that could be demanded of him; but he knew also that no sacrifice is too severe when God demands it—and he drew the knife.[55]

This steadfastness of the true Abraham is held up as exemplary of religious faith and celebrated as the greatest virtue of all. But it is easy to see that the consequence of Abraham's religious faith is that he is utterly reckless with regard to Isaac. Abraham *loves* Isaac with all his heart, but because of his religious faith Abraham is deprived of the ability to *care* for Isaac, in the sense of being responsive to what happens to him. He does not try to protect Isaac, feels no remorse for sacrificing him, and does not tremble when he draws the knife to kill him, since he has complete faith that Isaac will be restored no matter what happens to him.

Abraham's brutality is a direct effect of giving up secular faith through the double movement of religious faith. Only by maintaining my secular faith as a father can I be responsive to Isaac's fate. To be responsive I have to be devoted to his well-being, but I also have to believe that his well-being is fragile and that his life can be lost. The precariousness of Isaac's life is an intrinsic part of why I care for him, and in caring for him I am therefore beholden to external factors.

In contrast, the double movement of religious faith aims to remove the dependence on external factors, so that my love for Isaac can become an entirely internal affair. In the first movement of infinite resignation, I give up my care for Isaac's fate in the external world. Whether I express my infinite resignation by actually killing Isaac or by spiritually renouncing my care for what happens to him (saying "Oh, well," whether he lives or dies), the principle is the same. By demonstrating to myself that I can sacrifice any concern for external outcomes—any concern for the worldly fate of what I love—I deprive the finite of its power over me. This in turn paves the way for the second movement of faith, which holds that I will receive Isaac even though I have renounced or killed him. The second movement depends on faith in a God for whom everything is possible, but it could never be sustained without a continuous movement of infinite resignation. To keep my faith that I will get Isaac regardless of what happens, I have to keep renouncing my care for what actually happens (e.g., that I am killing him).

Accordingly, Kierkegaard emphasizes that the double movement of religious faith must be made simultaneously. At every moment in his sacrifice of Isaac, Abraham has to make both the movement of infinite resignation and the movement of faith. Only through such a double movement can he kill Isaac while at the same time maintaining that he loves him. As long as he makes the double movement, he can never experience the devastating loss of Isaac, since at every moment he renews his faith that his son will be given back to him. This is how Abraham's love of Isaac becomes an entirely internal affair, where any concern for Isaac in his own right is eliminated. By virtue of his religious faith, Abraham is no longer responsive to what actually befalls Isaac, or to how he may be feeling, except insofar as it aligns with Abraham's own hopes. The impact of any negative outcome is immediately renounced in favor of the faith that he will receive exactly what he wants, since God can do anything that is needed to arrange it. That is how Abraham sacrifices his care for Isaac. Because Abraham believes that he ultimately cannot lose his son, he can take Isaac's life.

IV

The same carelessness is evident in the modern knight of faith, even if it is less immediately apparent and portrayed as an affirmation of finite life. The modern knight of faith walks the streets of Copenhagen rather than the path to Mount Moriah and seems to belong "entirely to the world."[56] He "finds pleasure in everything, takes part in everything, and every time one sees him participating in something particular, he does it with an assiduousness that marks the worldly man who is attached to such things."[57] For those readers

who think that a genuine attachment to finite life can be combined
with a living religious faith, he is the true hero of *Fear and Trembling*.

Yet, as soon as we observe how the knight makes the double movement of religious faith, we can see that he continually renounces any
actual attachment to the world and any actual experience of finitude.
Fear and Trembling makes this clear through a parable of how the
knight falls in love with a princess. As Kierkegaard explains, when
he is here talking about romantic love he is using it as an example of
the dynamics of any wholehearted commitment, demonstrating how
one should respond to it if one is a knight of faith. The parable is
meant to show how the double movement of religious faith works in
practice, but it also reveals what motivates the movement in the first
place and how it is a defense mechanism against the threat of loss.

On Kierkegaard's own account, the knight is wholeheartedly committed to the beloved *before* he begins to make the double movement
of religious faith. Indeed, "this love is the entire substance of his
life"[58] and he is willing to embrace it:

> He is not cowardly; he is not afraid to let the love steal into his
> most secret, his most remote thoughts, to let it twist and entwine
> itself intricately around every ligament of his consciousness—if
> his love comes to grief, he will never be able to wrench himself out
> of it. He feels a blissful delight in letting love palpitate in every
> nerve, and yet his soul is as solemn as the soul of one who has
> drunk the poisoned cup and feels the juice penetrate every drop of
> blood—for this is the moment of crisis. Having totally absorbed
> this love and immersed himself in it, he does not lack the courage
> to attempt and to risk everything. He examines the conditions of
> his life, he convenes the swift thoughts that obey his every hint,
> like well-trained doves, he flourishes his staff, and they scatter
> in all directions. But now when they all come back, all of them
> like messengers of grief, and explain that it is an impossibility, he
> becomes very quiet, he dismisses them, he becomes solitary, and
> then he undertakes the movement.[59]

The vivid phenomenological description goes to the heart of what it means to be committed to another finite being, with both the excitement and the trembling registered in the most precise Kierkegaardian prose. The wholehearted commitment is rendered literally as letting the love palpitate in every nerve, flow through every drop of blood, steal into his most secret and remote thoughts, entwine itself around every ligament of his consciousness. Moreover, the wholehearted commitment is explicitly a risky venture: something that requires courage and puts the lover's life at stake. To absorb and immerse himself in the "blissful delight" of love is inseparable from having a lethal poison spread through his body.

The moment of falling in love is "the moment of crisis," which is to say the moment that requires a decision. If he allows the blissful poison of love to continue soaring through his body, he will be bound to a finite being who can transform and illuminate his life but who may also shatter his existence. This is why his thoughts—which fly out as doves of hope—all come back as messengers of grief. The princess is not unattainable (we later learn that the knight can receive her love and live with her day after day), but their relationship is an "impossibility" if he demands to be sheltered from the pain of loss. On the contrary, his wholehearted commitment must entail that his own life be at risk in his love for her: "If his love comes to grief, he will never be able to wrench himself out of it."

If the knight here decided to remain wholeheartedly committed, he would have the courage of *secular* faith. The anticipation of loss—the doves of hope that come back as messengers of grief—would make him all the more resolved to be with the beloved and make the most of their time together. Instead, the knight begins to make the movement of *religious* faith in order to protect himself against the threat of loss that his thoughts have anticipated: "When they all come back, all of them like messengers of grief, and explain that it is an impossibility, he becomes very quiet, he dismisses them, he becomes solitary, *and then he undertakes the movement*" (emphasis added).

The first step is the movement of infinite resignation, through which the knight "renounces the love that is the substance of his life."[60] Before the princess can be taken away from him or leave him, he voluntarily gives her up, to free himself of his dependence on her. "He has grasped the deep secret that even in loving another person one ought to be sufficient to oneself. He is no longer finitely concerned about what the princess does, and precisely this proves that he has made the movement infinitely."[61] By virtue of this movement of infinite resignation, the princess can no longer hurt him. "What the princess does cannot disturb him; it is only the lower natures who have the law for their actions in someone else,"[62] whereas "the one who has resigned infinitely is sufficient to himself."[63] To avoid the pain of losing his beloved against his will, the knight thus prefers the pain of giving her up in advance. Rather than being at the mercy of his beloved, he actively renounces her, since the latter move allows him to remain in control: "By my own strength I can give up the princess, and I will not sulk about it but find joy and peace and rest in my pain."[64]

Yet, while the knight is reconciled to giving up the object of his love (the princess), he does not want to give up the love itself (the activity of loving). Instead, he wants to find a way of loving that will insure him against ever losing the object of his love. Thus, he tells himself that he never really loved the princess in her own right. Rather, his love was "the expression of an eternal love" and should be endowed with "a religious character" through which it is "transfigured into a love of the eternal being" and is given "an eternal form that no actuality can take away from him."[65] The love of the eternal being (God) cannot be fulfilled in this life, but by the same token it cannot be refuted in this life and allows the lover to pursue his love unimpeded by any external circumstances. Accordingly, the knight explains that "every time some finitude will take power over me, I starve myself into submission until I make the movement, for my eternal consciousness is my love for God, and for me that is the highest of all. . . . what I gain thereby is my eternal consciousness in blessed harmony with my love for the eternal being."[66]

If the knight does not go further than to renounce the finite for the eternal, he remains a knight of infinite resignation. What distinguishes the knight of faith, however, is that he makes another movement at the same time as he makes the movement of infinite resignation:

> Now let us meet the knight of faith on the occasion previously mentioned [falling in love with the princess]. He does exactly the same as the other knight did: he infinitely renounces the love that is the substance of his life, he is reconciled in pain. But then the marvel happens; he makes one more movement even more wonderful than all the others, for he says: Nevertheless I have faith that I will get her—that is, by virtue of the absurd, by virtue of the fact that for God all things are possible. The absurd does not belong to the differences that lie within the proper domain of the understanding. It is not identical with the improbable, the unexpected, the unforeseen. The moment the knight executed the act of resignation, he was convinced of the impossibility, humanly speaking; that was the conclusion of the understanding, and he had sufficient energy to think it. But in the infinite sense it was possible, that is, by relinquishing it, but this having, after all, is also a giving up. Nevertheless, to the understanding this having is no absurdity, for the understanding continues to be right in maintaining that in the finite world where it dominates this having was and continues to be an impossibility. The knight of faith realizes this just as clearly; consequently, he can be saved only by the absurd, and this he grasps by faith. Consequently, he acknowledges the impossibility, and in the very same moment he believes the absurd.[67]

Both of the knights want to "have" the object of their love without ever losing it. Both of them also understand that such having (absolute possession) is impossible in a finite world. That is why both of them renounce the woman they love. Because her presence cannot be guaranteed—because she may abandon them—they give her up in advance. The real object of their love, they tell themselves, is not any finite woman but an eternal God who will never leave them as long as they remain faithful to Him.

The knight of resignation accepts that such devotion to God entails the sacrifice of his loved ones (e.g., his wife and son), but he is reconciled to the pain because he renounces them in favor of the eternal being of God. The knight of faith does the same, but at the same time he believes that he will get his loved ones back precisely by renouncing—or even killing—them. This faith is absurd and, as Kierkegaard emphasizes, defies any possible understanding. There is absolutely no reason to think that you will receive the very thing you are renouncing and that the son you are killing will come back to live happily with you. For Kierkegaard, however, the absurdity is the point, since it underlines that the movement of religious faith requires that you relinquish any concern for external probabilities in favor of internal conviction. "By virtue of the absurd to get everything, to get one's desire totally and completely"[68]—that is how *Fear and Trembling* glosses the religious faith that defies any finite understanding. Rather than "find rest in the pain of resignation," the knight of faith can "find joy by virtue of the absurd" and "live happily every moment,"[69] since "he has this security [faith in the absurd] that makes him delight in finitude as if it were the surest thing of all."[70]

By the same token, however, the knight of faith does not have any real sense of finitude, since he takes the sting out of every loss and removes any lethal force from experience. He may claim that he is wholeheartedly committed to his wife and son, but he only dares to love them by renouncing his care for their fate in the world. Regardless of what happens to them, he maintains his internal conviction regarding *what will happen,* and as long as he keeps this faith he lives happily every moment. Any devastating outcome (even the killing of his own son) is immediately transformed into the renewal of hopeful expectation, since "he drains the deep sadness of life in infinite resignation, he knows the blessedness of infinity," and "is continually making the movement of infinity, but he does it with such precision and assurance that he continually gets finitude out of it, and no one ever suspects anything else."[71]

Those readers who want to see an affirmation of finitude in Kierkegaard have certainly not suspected anything else. But when we pay attention to the movements of the knight of faith it is clear that he does not actually care about the fate of the finite, even though he apparently is fully immersed in finite life. On his way home in the evening, with a spring in his step and seemingly taking pleasure in everything he sees, the knight of faith is looking forward to a special hot meal of "roast lamb's head with vegetables"[72] that his wife will have prepared for him. If he meets someone along the way he will talk "about this delicacy with a passion befitting a restaurant operator," and "to see him eat would be the envy of the elite and an inspiration to the common man, for his appetite is keener than Esau's."[73] Yet, if there turns out to be no dinner, "curiously enough, he is just the same" (*besynderligt nok—han er aldeles den Samme*).[74] Even though he is fully invested in the prospect of eating the delicious meal, it makes no difference to him if it does not appear.

The mundane example is important, since the knight is supposed to make the double movement of religious faith at every moment of his life, regardless of whether it concerns the existence of a beloved son or the apparently trivial existence of a delicious meal. Indeed, the knight of faith "is convinced that God is concerned with the smallest things."[75] Even when there is no roast lamb's head with vegetables, he keeps faith that he will get the dinner, just as Abraham keeps faith that he will get Isaac even when there is no sacrificial lamb and he has to kill Isaac himself. This may seem absurd, but the point is again that it looks that way only to someone who accepts the authority of the external world over the internal conviction of religious faith. The knight of faith is rather full of confident hope (of having dinner with his wife or a flourishing future with his son) while being unmoved by any refutation of his hope. If there is no dinner and he turns out to have killed Isaac *curiously enough, he is just the same.* Nothing can disturb his state of hopeful expectation, since he renews it at every moment through the double movement: renouncing his care for any given negative outcome (there is no dinner, Isaac is dead) while relaunching his faith that everything will be given to him by God, for whom everything is possible. Thus, "with the freedom from care of a reckless good-for-nothing, he lets things take care of themselves," since "he does not do even the slightest thing except by virtue of the absurd."[76]

The knight of faith thereby demonstrates what it would mean to be free from despair. While Kierkegaard promotes the elimination of despair as a desirable achievement of religious faith, his own account reveals why it is undesirable and why it would undermine the capacity to care. Recall that Kierkegaard defines despair as encompassing all forms of anxiety, ranging from the smallest worry to the most severe existential breakdown. Recall further that he defines religious faith as the complete eradication of despair. To have religious faith is not merely to sustain hope but to eliminate the very possibility of being in despair. "Not to be in despair must signify the destroyed possibility of being able to be in despair," Kierkegaard explains in *The Sickness unto Death*. "If a person is truly not to be in despair, he must at every moment destroy the possibility."[77] This elimination of despair is achieved anew at every moment through the double movement of religious faith. As long as the knight maintains his religious faith, he is not anxious about anything that may happen in the future and he cannot be brought to despair even if the worst happens to him.

For the same reason, however, the knight of faith is not actually at stake in any of his commitments. If I am at stake in my commitments, then I must run the risk of despair if I betray my commitments or if everything to which I am committed breaks down. The risk of despair is not a possibility that can be eliminated but *a necessary boundary condition for any life-defining commitment*. If I have a life-defining commitment, there are things I cannot do and a world I cannot lose on pain of losing myself. The knight of faith believes, on the contrary, that he will be able to go on with his life even if everything is taken away from him, and at every moment he overcomes any form of anxiety. It is therefore no accident that he turns out to be utterly insensitive and irresponsible with regard to what happens. In destroying his ability to be in despair, he is also destroying his ability to care about anyone or anything that is finite.

Fear and Trembling acknowledges that such faith may seem to be not only "absurd" but also "frightening," "terrible," and "dreadful." Yet these characterizations are not meant to repudiate religious faith but to make it appear even more awe-inspiring and sublime. Like many of Kierkegaard's books, *Fear and Trembling* is signed by a pseudonymous author—in this case Johannes de Silentio—who narrates the story and speaks directly to the reader. Johannes admits that he himself does not have religious faith and often finds himself "shattered" or "paralyzed" when thinking of Abraham. But this does not prevent Johannes from regarding Abraham as "the greatest of all" and from chastising himself for falling short of the religious faith that is required to sacrifice Isaac. If such faith seems absurd or terrible, it is because one fails to trust fully in God and still has a secular commitment to Isaac as a finite being who can be irrevocably lost. From the perspective of religious faith there is, on the contrary, nothing absurd or frightening about sacrificing your child if God demands it. As Kierkegaard himself explains in his later papers: "When the believer has faith, the absurd is not the absurd—faith transforms it. . . . Therefore, rightly understood, there is nothing at all frightening in the category of the absurd."[78]

Hence, in the writings that Kierkegaard signs with his own name (rather than with a pseudonym such as Johannes de Silentio) he can be seen to promote the double movement of religious faith even more emphatically than in *Fear and Trembling*. For example, in his *Christian Discourses*, Kierkegaard elaborates at length why the true religious believer should not have a care in the world, since he or she fully expects that God will provide for everything. Commenting on Jesus's Sermon on the Mount ("Do not worry about your life, what you will eat or drink"), Kierkegaard argues that a true Christian does not worry about any bodily or material needs, since he has faith that God will provide the daily bread that is needed.[79]

To renounce your care for bodily and material needs is of course deeply difficult, but the difficulty of the challenge makes it all the more valuable for Kierkegaard as a test of religious faith. Unlike the lilies and the birds (who supposedly live without care), a human being has many reasons to worry, so in order to be a true Christian he must continually sacrifice his cares for the sake of faith. Even if the Christian is poor and does not receive any bread in the literal sense, he does not worry about what to eat insofar as he is really a Christian. He may be poor in a worldly sense, but he is "without the care of poverty"[80] and therefore rich in a religious sense. He treats everything (including his own poverty) as a gift from God and trusts that God gives everything that is needed. Even at the moment of starving to death from not receiving any actual bread, the Christian does not worry about his life. Instead "he believes that, just as he will certainly receive the daily bread as long as he has to live here on earth, he will some day live blessed in the hereafter" and such "an eternal life" is "certainly beyond all comparison with food and drink."[81]

Those who claim to be Christian but still care about the fate of their finite lives, Kierkegaard chastises for lacking a living religious faith. If you are poor and cannot renounce the care for poverty, if you are dying and cannot renounce the care for your life, if you are a loving parent and cannot renounce the care for your child, then you are not a Christian. You may claim that you trust in God, but if you cannot prove it through your actions and through how you respond to what happens, then your religious faith is dead: something you claim to believe even though it does not actually shape how you think and feel. A living religious faith is rather achieved through a double movement, where you renounce the cares that follow from being finite and instead place your trust in God. Even though you are starving, you believe that you will be nourished, even though you are dying, you believe that you will live forever, and even though you are killing your son, you believe that he will be given back to you.

While Kierkegaard underlines that such religious faith cannot be attained once and for all—it has to be achieved anew at every moment—he holds that it is the best and most desirable way of living. "I know a way out of your difficulty, which will give you full assurance of victory," Kierkegaard maintains in one of his edifying religious discourses. "Act in the conviction that even if the opposite of what you wish results from your action, you will nevertheless have conquered."[82] This is, of course, exactly the logic of Abraham's sacrifice of Isaac in *Fear and Trembling*. Abraham passes the most difficult test of religious faith, since he is able to sacrifice his care and put his life in the hands of God even when it entails risking everything that matters to him. Even in killing Isaac, Abraham keeps faith that his beloved son will be given back to him by God.

Thus, while Kierkegaard promotes a living religious faith as the highest of all, his own texts reveal why such faith must be completely *irresponsible* with regard to any other concern. Having religious faith means *not being responsive* to anything that calls your faith into question, even if it is the cry of your child as you are taking his life.

The consequence of Kierkegaard's argument may seem extreme, but it makes explicit something that is implicit in all religious ideals of being absolved from the pain of loss. Being responsive to Isaac's fate requires that you are devoted to a life that can be lost. Only by loving Isaac for his own sake—while recognizing that his life is essentially fragile—can you care for him. And yet it is precisely such care that religious ideals of absolution demand that you give up. To achieve absolution you cannot love finite beings—including your own children—as ends in themselves, since all such love makes you vulnerable to loss. This is why Buddhists and Stoics, as well as religious mystics across many different traditions, preach detachment as the path to salvation. For example, the widely influential Christian mystic Meister Eckhart emphasizes that "the man who is in absolute detachment is carried away into eternity where nothing temporal affects him," since "true detachment means a mind as little moved by what happens, by joy and sorrow, honor and disgrace, as a broad mountain by a gentle breeze."[83] The practice of detachment is a movement of infinite resignation, which requires that you sacrifice your care for the finite in favor of the eternal. In order to be unmoved by what happens, you cannot be responsive to Isaac's fate. On the contrary, you must remain as insensitive as a mountain.

Even though Kierkegaard (unlike Meister Eckhart) does not want to be immobile and untouchable, the effect of his religious faith turns out to be the same. While Kierkegaard does not stop with detachment, his religious faith still demands the sacrifice of any care for Isaac in his own right. Thus, in *Fear and Trembling* he recalls the stern declaration by Jesus in the Gospel of Luke: "If anyone comes to me and does not hate his own father and mother and wife and children and brothers and sisters, yes, and even his own life, he cannot be my disciple" (Luke 14:26). On Kierkegaard's reading, Jesus here expresses how God demands an absolute love, for the sake of which all other loves must be renounced. That you should "hate" the ones you love does not mean that you should dislike them—in which case it would be easy to renounce them—but that you should sacrifice them for the love of God. Or as Jesus himself explains in the Gospel of Matthew: "Anyone who loves their father or mother more than me is not worthy of me; anyone who loves their son or daughter more than me is not worthy of me" (Matt. 10:37). According to the same logic, Abraham proves himself to be "worthy" by demonstrating in the most concrete way—through his readiness to sacrifice Isaac— that he loves God more than his son. This is the movement of infinite resignation, whereby Abraham gives up the finite for the sake of the eternal. And yet through the second movement—the movement of faith—Abraham is convinced that Isaac will be given back to him. In renouncing his care for Isaac, Abraham is at the same time ready to receive Isaac anew as a gift from God. The price of such faith, however, is that Abraham is completely insensitive to what befalls Isaac. Even if he turns out to have killed Isaac, Abraham is just the same.

V

The theological stakes are high, since the relation between Abraham and Isaac in the Old Testament is supposed to prefigure the relation between God and Jesus in the New Testament. The parallels between the two stories are striking and well established in the Christian exegetical tradition. A father (Abraham/God) sacrifices his beloved son (Isaac/Jesus). In the Binding of Isaac, the son is taken to Mount Moriah, where his father raises a knife to kill him. This prefigures the Crucifixion of Jesus, where the son is nailed to the cross on Golgotha and slowly dies in agony. In both stories the sacrifice is rewarded and praised as a holy act. Because Abraham was ready to kill Isaac, God blesses his descendants; because Jesus died on the cross, mankind is said to be redeemed from sin.

Yet the story of Abraham that has been handed down to us may conceal an earlier version. As scholars of the Hebrew text have shown, there are strong indications that in the original version Abraham chooses to protect Isaac's life in defiance of the divine command. In the official version (Gen. 22), Abraham is ready to kill Isaac when "an angel of the Lord" stays his hand. The angel relays a message from God, who explains that Abraham has passed the test and therefore can dispense with the actual killing of Isaac. In a second speech, the angel further explains that Abraham will be rewarded for his obedience. Because he has completed the sacrifice of Isaac in his heart—showing that he is willing to kill even his beloved son for the sake of following a divine command—Abraham is allowed to keep Isaac as a gift from God. There are good textual grounds, however, for regarding the angelic speeches as a later insertion. Both in terms of style and structure, they diverge in striking ways from the rest of the text. Most importantly, if one removes the angelic speeches one will find a consistent narrative where Abraham *disobeys* God's command. The angelic speeches would thus have been inserted to cover up Abraham's disobedience. As Omri Boehm has argued in a careful textual study: "A later redactor interpolated the figure of the angel, thereby shifting responsibility for interrupting the test from Abraham to the angel."[84]

While these philological arguments were not available to Kierkegaard, he does imagine a scenario where Abraham disobeys God and chooses not to sacrifice Isaac. "If Abraham had doubted as he stood there on Mount Moriah," we read in *Fear and Trembling*, "then he would have witnessed neither to his faith nor to God's grace but would have witnessed to how appalling it is to go to Mount Moriah."[85] For Kierkegaard, this is the worst possible scenario. Kierkegaard's entire argument depends on the assumption that Abraham showed complete devotion to God and had total trust in His promise. Otherwise Mount Moriah would not be the sublime site of religious faith that Kierkegaard celebrates but rather "a place of terror, for it was here that Abraham doubted."[86] In Kierkegaard's account, then, it is not the killing of Isaac that would make Mount Moriah a place of terror. From Kierkegaard's religious perspective, the terrible scenario is not that Abraham would murder his son but that he would lose his trust in God and not follow His command.

Yet what Kierkegaard laments as "doubt" with regard to religious faith can just as well be read as an affirmation of secular faith. If Abraham disobeys God, it is because he is committed to Isaac as an end in himself. Moreover, it is because he believes that Isaac can actually and irrevocably die. This is the core of secular faith: what you love is worth fighting for *even though it is finite* and calls for your care *because it is finite*. In contrast, the double movement of religious faith makes Abraham completely irresponsible with regard to Isaac's finitude. Because Abraham believes that God can restore anything that is lost, he can sacrifice the care for his son. Indeed, because Abraham believes that God will return Isaac to him, he can kill Isaac without even thinking or feeling that he is compromising his fatherly love.

The ability to sacrifice his beloved son is displayed even more emphatically by God in relation to Jesus. Through the Incarnation, the eternal and immutable God becomes a finite human being: Jesus of Nazareth. He is born, he lives, and he dies. While Jesus claims to be the Son of God, he is recognizably human in being seized by doubts and hopes, insecurities and joys, longing and despair. Most dramatically, his last days lead up to an utterly painful and humiliating death. Persecuted by the authorities, he hides outside the city and cannot sleep at night. His disciples betray him and he himself vacillates in fear. He is arrested, beaten, ridiculed, and tortured.

Finally, he is put to death in the most debasing way. A crucifixion in Roman times was the lowest and most quotidian way of being executed. Many times a day criminals were left to die hanging from a cross. That this should be the fate of the Messiah—the Son of God himself—was incomprehensible and shattering for those who had placed their trust in him. Rather than establish the Kingdom of God on earth, Jesus died alone and helpless on the cross.

On its own, the story of Jesus's death is a wrenching story of abandonment. His disciples desert him and his own father leaves him to die on the cross. Yet the Crucifixion of Jesus is the most celebrated sacrifice in human history. On churches all across the world, the cross is held forth not as a sign of injustice and torture but as a sign of redemption. Indeed, the sacrifice of Jesus is held to be the key to our salvation. "For God so loved the world, that he gave his only son, that whoever believes in him shall not perish but have eternal life" (John 3:16). Why would this be the case? Why would salvation and eternal life require the sacrifice of a beloved son? As Jesus explains, we should follow his example and sacrifice our lives for God. "For whoever wants to save their life will lose it, but whoever loses their life for me will save it" (Luke 9:24). As long as we are devoted to our lives—including the lives of those we love—we can suffer from loss. By trying to protect your own life or the life of your son, you are all the more vulnerable with regard to what may happen, since "whoever wants to save their life will lose it." However, if you renounce your care for what you love and put your trust in God, every loss will be redeemed, since "whoever loses their life for [God] will save it."

Even faced with the death of what you love, you can renew your faith in divine salvation, as long as you renounce your care for the death that has actually taken place. This is the double movement of religious faith and the Christian understanding of the Crucifixion is a paradigmatic example. To look at Jesus on the cross and see an image of salvation rather than irrevocable loss, you must make the double movement. Through the movement of infinite resignation you renounce your care for the finite Jesus who died on the cross, while maintaining—through the movement of faith—that God redeems the loss. Following an established religious logic, giving up the attachment to mortal life is a step on the way to overcoming death. Jesus's sacrifice—allowing himself to be crucified and then being resurrected in a movement of heavenly ascent—is supposed to show that we can be liberated from mortal life. "For if we have been united with him in a death like his," Saint Paul maintains, "we shall certainly be united with him in a resurrection like his" (Rom. 6:5). The suffering of Jesus is thus taken seriously, but only as a necessary step on the way to salvation. The temporal finitude of Jesus is only an intermediary stage on the way back to the timeless infinity of God. Even though God became mortal, was humiliated and died on the cross, he is just the same. Nothing has impaired him and nothing has been lost.

To affirm such a double movement, you must sacrifice or repress the fate of the mortal beloved. Just as Abraham in *Fear and Trembling* can leave Isaac for dead by virtue of his living religious faith, the Christian can leave Jesus for dead by virtue of belief in the Resurrection. While Christ returns to God—with whom he has always been united in the eternal Trinity—the finite Jesus, the one who can suffer and be moved by the passions, must be discarded and left behind. Thus, in both the Gospels of Matthew and Mark, Jesus's last words express a sense of utter abandonment: *Eli, Eli, lama sabachthani?* ("My God, my God, why have you forsaken me?"). After repeating this cry, Jesus gives up his last breath and dies. While his death is held to be an expression of God's pure love, it remains a brutal sacrifice for anyone who cares to see. God's love (*agape*) is boundless and constant, but for the same reason it is unmoved by anything that happens. God does not love anything more than anything else. He loves those who kill his son as much as he loves the son himself. Since it is God's nature to love, he loves everything regardless of any factors that are external to himself. In theological terms, his love is entirely spontaneous and "unmotivated," since it has nothing to do with the qualities or the fate of what he loves. Regardless of who the beloved is and regardless of what happens to the beloved, God is just the same.

What the Crucifixion reveals, then, is the emptiness of divine love. The reason God has abandoned his son is that he could never care about him in the first place. It makes no difference to God that his beloved son is tortured and put to death. Curiously enough, he is eternally just the same.

Yet the emptiness and meaninglessness of divine love should not lead us to despair. Rather, it should recall us to finitude as the condition for any sense of responsibility and love. Only someone who is finite—only someone who understands what loss means—can care for the beloved. Only someone who is finite can allow the world to matter and only someone who is finite can take responsibility for anyone else.

The death of Jesus thus leaves itself open to being read in the light of secular passion. On such a reading, Jesus has to be finite—not in order to redeem us from death but in order to be someone who can love and be loved. Recall here the extraordinary sequence in the Gospel of John, when Jesus on the cross says "I thirst," is given to drink, then says "It is consummated" and dies, with a soldier subsequently thrusting a lance into his side, water and blood pouring out.[87] The Christian move is to distinguish this body that is subject to need, dissolution, and decomposition from the "glorious" body of resurrection that is exempt from death. Yet the moment of consummation—of fulfillment of Scripture—is here the moment when the body of the beloved is shown to be a body of flesh and blood. If this body is "resurrected," it is not because it ascends to heaven or is transformed into an incorruptible body, but because it is commemorated by those who love him, compelled to remember him precisely because he died and thereby allowing him to live on, in a process of communion that itself is subject to dissolution and death.

Everything thus depends on how we apprehend the death of Jesus. Rather than celebrate his death as a pathway to heaven, we should recognize that Jesus died, as every beloved has always died, with no afterlife apart from those who cared to remember him. To behold the death of Jesus in this way is to acknowledge that every life, even the life of the most beloved, ends in death. The death of the beloved is irrevocable—it is a loss that cannot be recuperated—since there is no life other than this life. From a Christian perspective, this is the most devastating scenario. "If there is no resurrection of the dead," Paul writes in his First Letter to the Corinthians, "and if Christ has not been raised, then our proclamation has been in vain and your faith has been in vain" (1 Cor. 15:13–14). Indeed, Paul emphasizes that "if for this life only we have hoped in Christ, we are of all people most to be pitied" (1 Cor. 15:19). If there is no life other than this life—a life that ends in death—then life is vain and futile, according to Paul. All that is left is to "eat and drink, for tomorrow we die" (1 Cor. 15:32).

Yet Paul's conclusion is the wrong one. That life ends in death does not entail that our long-term commitments are futile, leaving us only with the physical pleasures of eating and drinking in the time that remains. On the contrary, the peril of death is an intrinsic part of why it matters what we do and why it matters that we devote ourselves to someone or something living on beyond ourselves. We have to take care of one another because we can die, we have to fight for what we believe in because it lives only through our sustained effort, and we have to be concerned with what will be passed on to coming generations because the future is not certain. This is the double movement of secular faith. You run ahead into the risk of irrevocable death—you acknowledge that everything will be lost—and yet you are resolved to make the most of the time that is given. You see that even the most beloved will die—that he actually can perish, that his life irrevocably can come apart—and yet you maintain your love for him. You see that death is utter darkness and yet you seek to maintain the light that will be extinguished.

Every time you care for someone who may be lost or leave you behind, every time you devote yourself to a cause whose fate is uncertain, you perform an act of secular faith. Through your passion, you apprehend that death is constitutive of life and yet you do not renounce your commitment to living on. You do not give in to death but seek to prolong the life of what you love. You see that death is senseless and yet you seek to make sense of life.

Only through such a movement of secular faith can you be responsive to Isaac's fate. In *Fear and Trembling*, Abraham closes his eyes to Isaac's suffering by virtue of religious faith. With calm resolve he takes time to chop the firewood, bind Isaac, and sharpen the knife without a tremble passing through his body. While Kierkegaard wants us to behold this scene as a tremendous example of piety, we can see that it is a disaster and that the dream of a God for whom everything is possible is a nightmare. Through the double movement of religious faith, Abraham infinitely renounces his care for what actually happens, to make room for his faith that God can restore anything that is lost. Likewise, Christian faith transforms the vision of Jesus's suffering: infinitely renouncing the care for actual bodily injury, for actual death, in favor of the belief that suffering is a path to salvation. But insofar as you maintain your secular faith, you can see that there is no life after death and that torture is not redemptive. You can still see Isaac's suffering and respond to his impending death. You can see that his life is fragile—that he can die once and for all—but that does not diminish your love for him. On the contrary, the finitude you share is an essential part of why you love and care for him with all your heart. You would never take his life, even if God commanded you, because you understand that death does not make sense and does not redeem anyone.

The story of Abraham and Isaac thus reveals, with utmost clarity, that the sense of responsibility cannot be based on divine command. In *The Brothers Karamazov*, Dostoyevsky famously claimed that if God does not exist, then everything is permitted. But *Fear and Trembling* shows that the truth is the other way around. If there is a God for whom everything is possible, then anything can be permitted, even the killing of your own child for no reason other than God's command. This is the truth that Kierkegaard forces you to confront. If you hold that your responsibility for Isaac is based on God's command, then you are committed to killing Isaac if that turns out to be the command. Moreover, if you make the double movement of religious faith, you will not even be able to apprehend how Isaac is calling out for your care. If you believe that he can be resurrected—that he will live on in eternity or be restored on earth—you will fail to see his fate in being put to death. Whether Isaac lives or dies ultimately makes no difference to you, since you believe that everything you lose will be returned.

The faith that makes you responsive to Isaac's fate is therefore secular rather than religious. If you care for Isaac and seek to shelter him from death, your living faith—the faith that actually informs how you act and respond—is a secular faith, even if you claim to be religious. It is a secular faith because you are devoted to the living on of a finite beloved. You are committed to sustain a life that may be lost, to fight for a cause that may be shattered, and you would never give them up for a religious promise of redemption.

If you object that God would never command the killing of Isaac, you profess faith in a standard of value independent of God, since you believe that it is wrong to sacrifice Isaac regardless of what God commands. Moreover, you profess secular faith in the irreplaceable value of a finite life. God has nothing to teach you about moral responsibility, since he cannot even understand a moral problem. He cannot understand what it means to lose someone irrevocably and thus cannot understand what it means to care for someone as irreplaceable. He is not constrained by anything, but for the same reason he is not committed to anything. Indeed, God is completely irresponsible because he is not bound by anything other than himself. Only someone who is committed—only someone who is bound by something other than herself—can be responsible. Only someone who is committed can care. And only someone who is finite can be committed.

PART II

Spiritual Freedom

4

Natural and Spiritual Freedom

I

One late summer afternoon, I am sitting on top of a mountain in northern Sweden. The ocean below me is calm and stretches toward an open horizon. There is no other human being in sight and barely a sound can be heard. Only a solitary seagull is gliding on the wind. Like so many times before, I find it mesmerizing to follow a seagull as it hovers in the air and lingers over the landscape. For as long as I can remember, seagulls have been a part of my life. Every summer morning at our family house I wake up to their shrill vocals as they ascend over the mountains or descend into the sea. When we return from fishing they accompany us, waiting for their part of the daily catch. In the evenings, I often stand on the beach just to watch their line of flight. Even in foreign cities, the sight or sound of a seagull feels like a message from home and brings back a flood of memories. Yet I have never encountered a seagull the way it happens this afternoon. As the seagull stretches its wings and turns toward an adjacent mountain, I try to imagine how the wind may feel and how the landscape may appear *for the seagull.*

Of course, I will never know what it is like to be a seagull. Nevertheless, inhabiting the question of what it means to be a seagull leads me to the notion of *freedom* at the heart of this book. In trying to apprehend a life that is so different from my own, I am reminded that I am both a *natural* being (in what I take myself to share with the seagull) and a *spiritual* being (in how I take myself to be different from the seagull).

Let me begin with what the seagull and I have in common. We are both living beings. As such there is always something at stake for us in our activities. We must do something—acquire nourishment, adapt to our environment—to sustain our lives. Likewise, both of us are capable of self-movement and self-determination. The seagull walks or flies of its own accord and no one except the seagull can determine how long it will linger in the air before diving into the ocean to catch a fish or settling down on a mountain to rest. Furthermore, both the seagull and I are responsive to a distinction between *appearance* and *essence*, between *how we take things* and *what they turn out to be*. If the seagull dives for a fish that it takes to be edible and it turns out to be inedible, the seagull will respond by discarding the fish. This is not simply a response to stimuli but a response to stimuli in terms of what counts *as* food for the seagull. The seagull is not merely an object in the world but an agent for which things appear *as* nourishing or damaging, appealing or threatening.[1]

The agency is especially clear if we compare the seagull with the mountain on which it lands. The mountain is not alive. The mountain was there long before the seagull or I existed—and it can be there long after we are gone—but the mountain does not care. Whether the sun is shining or the rain is pouring down, whether there are earthquakes that rip it apart or centuries of stability that leave it intact, the mountain does not care. Nothing that happens *to* the mountain will ever make a difference *for* the mountain, since it has no self-relation. For the same reason, the mountain has no capacity for self-movement and self-determination. Because nothing is at stake for the mountain, it cannot do anything and cannot relate to anything *as* anything. The mountain has no purpose for itself and only acquires one for a living being that makes use of it in some way (as when the seagull lands on the mountain to rest).

The seagull, by contrast, relates to the environment through its own sentience and responds to what happens in light of its own ends. For example, certain kinds of predators show up for the seagull *as* something to avoid and certain kinds of fish show up *as* something to catch. These forms of purposive activity can become much more advanced in highly developed animals, but they are all forms of what I call *natural freedom*. Natural freedom provides a freedom of self-movement, but only in light of imperatives that are treated as given and ends that cannot be called into question by the agent itself. As distinct from natural freedom, *spiritual freedom* requires the ability to ask which imperatives to follow in light of our ends, as well as the ability to call into question, challenge, and transform our ends themselves.

Philosophers often account for the difference between human beings and other animals in terms of a difference between norm-governed behavior and instinct-determined behavior. As human beings, we are socialized into a normative understanding of who to be—e.g., man or woman, black or white, working-class or aristocrat—and we act in light of those social norms. In contrast, the behavior of all other animals is supposedly hardwired by their natural instincts. This way of describing the difference, however, is misleading for at least two reasons. First, an instinct is already expressive of a norm, since it specifies something that the animal *ought* to do and that it can *fail* to do (e.g., the seagull instinctually understands that it ought to eat fish and it can fail to find any fish to eat). Second, many animals can be socialized into forms of behavior that are not hardwired by their natural instincts. For example, there are cats that behave like dogs because they have been raised by huskies, and there are huskies that behave like cats because they have been raised by them. Such behavior is clearly not hardwired by the nature of cats or dogs but acquired through a specific way in which they are raised.

The difference between human beings and other animals, then, cannot simply be explained by the difference between instincts and norms. Rather, the decisive difference is the difference between natural and spiritual freedom. Even when a cat behaves like a husky, she does not call into question the husky way of life but treats it as the given framework for her actions. She is able to learn the husky norms but not able to understand them *as* norms that could be otherwise. The cat cannot understand her norms as something for which she is answerable and which can be challenged by others, since she cannot hold herself responsible for the principles that govern her actions. The cat is responsive to success and failure in her pursuits, but whether the norms that govern her pursuits are valid—whether she *ought* to behave like a cat or a husky—is not at issue for her.

For human beings, by contrast, the validity of norms is always implicitly and potentially explicitly at issue. We act in light of a normative understanding of ourselves—of who we should be and what we should do—but we can also challenge and change our self-understanding. We are not merely governed by norms but answerable to one another for what we do and why we do it. Even when we are socialized into an identity as though it were a natural necessity—as when we are taken to belong naturally to a certain gender, race, or class—there remains the possibility of transforming, contesting, or critically overturning our understanding of who we are. Who we can be—as well as what we can do—is inseparable from how we acknowledge and treat one another. *How* we can change our self-understanding therefore depends on the social practices and institutions that shape the ability to lead our lives. Moreover, any ability to lead our lives can be impaired or lost by damages to our physical and psychological constitution. Yet as long as we have a self-relation—as long as we lead our lives in any way at all—the question of who we *ought* to be is alive for us, since it is at work in all our activities. In engaging the question "what should I do?" we are also engaging the question "who should I be?" and there is no final answer to that question. This is our spiritual freedom.

The difference between natural and spiritual freedom is not a matter of metaphysical substance, but a difference in the practical self-relation exhibited by human beings and other animals. Many kinds of animals exhibit forms of mourning, play, courage, deliberation, suffering, and joy. They may even in some cases (as studies of primates have shown) be able to experience a conflict of choice when certain instincts or loyalties are at odds with one another. Yet no other species we have encountered is capable of transforming its understanding of what it means to be that species. Changes in the environment can cause animal species—or certain members of species—to change patterns in their behavior, but the principles in light of which they act remain the same for as long as the species exist.

In contrast, the understanding of what it means to be human—as manifested in the actual behavior of human beings—varies dramatically across history and across the world at any given moment of history. The difference between a monk who renounces filial bonds for an ascetic life in a monastery and a father who devotes his life to taking care of his children is not merely an individual difference in behavior. Rather, the two forms of life express radically different understandings of what it means to be human. The two men may not only have different degrees of courage, but *what counts as courage* for them is radically different. They may not only experience different degrees of grief and joy, but *what counts as grief and joy* for them is radically different. Even the experience of suffering is never merely a brute fact for us as human beings, but an experience we understand and respond to in light of what matters to us. Such mattering is not reducible to our biological-physiological constitution, but depends on our commitments. We are certainly subject to biological constraints—and we cannot even in principle transcend all such constraints—but we can (and do) change our relation to these constraints. There is no natural way for us to be and no species requirements that can exhaustively determine the principles in light of which we act. Rather, what we do and who we take ourselves to be is inseparable from a historical-normative framework that must be upheld by us and may be transformed by us.

Let me be clear about the status of my argument. I am not asserting that only human beings are spiritually free. It is possible that we may discover other species that are spiritually free or that we may create artificial forms of life that are capable of spiritual freedom.

That is an empirical question, which I do not seek to answer. My aim is not to decide which species are spiritually free, but *to clarify the conditions of spiritual freedom.* Whether certain other animals are spiritually free—or whether we can come to engineer living beings who are spiritually free—is a separate and subordinate question, which in itself presupposes an answer to the question of what it means to be a free, spiritual being.

Two clarifications are here in order. First, the distinction between natural and spiritual freedom is not a hierarchical distinction. That we are spiritually free does not make us inherently better than other animals, but it does mean that we are free in a qualitatively different sense. Because we can call into question the purposes of our own actions, we can hold ourselves to principles of justice, but we can also engage in forms of cruelty that go far beyond anything observed in other species. Second, the distinction between natural and spiritual freedom does not legitimize the exploitation of other animals. Many contemporary thinkers are critical of any distinction between humans and other animals, since they fear that such a distinction will serve to justify sexism or racism, as well as buttress the mistreatment of other species and the willful extraction of natural resources. Yet such "posthumanism" rests on a conflation of historical facts and philosophical arguments. As a matter of historical fact, it is true that a human/animal distinction often has been employed to classify certain genders or races as "subhuman" and to legitimize ruthless exploitation of the nonhuman world. The critique of such politics is well taken, as is the reminder that we too are animals and dependent on the fate of our environment. However, it does *not* follow from these facts that *any* distinction between humans and other animals is illegitimate or politically pernicious. On the contrary, the pathos of posthumanist politics itself tacitly relies on a distinction between natural and spiritual freedom. When posthumanist thinkers take us to task for being sexist, racist, or too centered on our own species, they must assume that we are capable of calling into question the guiding principles of our actions. Otherwise it would make no sense to criticize our principles and enjoin us to adopt different ideals.

Likewise, it is clear that no posthumanist thinker seriously believes that other animals are spiritually free. If they were, we should criticize not only humans but also other animals for being sexist and too centered on the well-being of their own species.

To deny the distinction between natural and spiritual freedom is therefore an act of bad faith. Any political struggle for a better treatment of other animals—or for a more respectful relation to the natural environment—requires spiritual freedom. We have to be able to renounce our prior commitments and hold ourselves to a new ideal. No one is inclined to place the same demands on other animals, because we implicitly understand the distinction between natural and spiritual freedom. It would be absurd to reproach the seagull for eating fish, but it can make sense for me to stop eating other animals, since I am capable of transforming my relation to the norms that structure my world. For a naturally free being like the seagull, there is a normative "ought" that guides its actions (e.g., to eat fish in order to survive) but it cannot call into question the norm—the ought—itself. Natural freedom has a *single ought* structure, since the agent cannot question its guiding principles and ask itself what it should do. Spiritual freedom, by contrast, is characterized by a *double ought* structure. As a spiritually free being, I can ask myself what I should do, since I am answerable not only for my actions but also for the normative principles that guide my actions. There are not only demands concerning what I ought to do; there is also the question *if I ought to do what I supposedly ought to do.*

To be clear, our spiritual freedom does *not* entail that we can question all the norms of our lives at once, and we are *not* free to invent our principles out of nothing. Rather, our spiritual freedom should be understood in terms of the philosophical model that is known as Neurath's boat. "We are like sailors who have to rebuild their ship on the open sea, without ever being able to dismantle it in dry dock," we learn from the famous argument by the philosopher of science Otto Neurath. "Where a beam is taken away a new one must at once be put there, and for this the rest of the ship is used as support. By using the old beams and driftwood, the ship can be shaped entirely anew, but only by gradual reconstruction." Neurath presented his boat as a model for the acquisition and transformation of scientific knowledge, but his boat analogy can help us to grasp the conditions for any form of spiritual freedom.[2] In leading my life, I cannot retreat to an unshakable foundation or a view from nowhere. I find myself in Neurath's boat, which is out on the open sea from the beginning and until the end. Who I can be—how my boat is built—depends on socially shared norms, which I am bound to uphold, challenge, or transform through what I do. I can alter or replace parts of the boat, as long as enough of the other parts remain in place and keep myself afloat. I can even undertake major renovations, but my life depends on maintaining some form of integrity. Even if I try to wreck the boat—or try to refrain from repairing the boat so that it will sink—I have to sustain that decision with integrity for it to be *my* decision; *I* have to try to wreck the boat and try to give up my life.

I can ask myself what I am doing with my life and transform the commitments that define who I am. Yet all such transformations are possible only from the practical standpoint of trying to lead my life, just as all renovations of the boat are possible only from a practical standpoint that is trying to maintain the integrity of the boat. Even when I question who I am—even when I tear planks from the bottom of the boat—the questioning itself only makes sense because I am committed to having integrity as a person. To grasp anything as part of my life—as something that *I* do or experience—is *not* a theoretical observation of myself but a practical activity of spiritual self-maintenance in which I am always engaged.

The activity of spiritual self-maintenance should not be conflated with self-preservation and it is not necessarily conservative, since it is the condition of possibility for all forms of self-transformation. For anything I do to be intelligible as *my* action—and for anything that happens to be intelligible as something that *I* experience—I have to grasp it as part of *my* life. Moreover, since my life always runs the risk of falling apart, I must always sustain or renew my life in practice. The form of my self-consciousness is not primarily an explicit reflection regarding who I am, but the implicit activity of spiritual self-maintenance that is built into everything I do and everything I experience. The integrity of my life cannot be established once and for all but is inherently fragile. Indeed, the fragility of integrity—the risk of breaking apart and sinking to the bottom of the sea—is a necessary part of why it matters to maintain any form of integrity in the first place.

For the same reason, my self-consciousness cannot place me outside of my life. Even in my most explicit forms of self-reflection, I cannot be detached. On the contrary, my self-consciousness only exists in and through the practical activity of sustaining my life, which means that there is no contemplative self to which I can withdraw. Even the project of retreating into passivity is still a project that requires my engagement—a project to which I have to hold myself—and by the same token a project that I can transform or call into question. This practical activity of leading my life is the minimal form of my self-consciousness and the condition of my spiritual freedom.

II

The distinction between natural and spiritual freedom proceeds from the secular notion of *life* that underlies all my arguments in this book. From a religious perspective, a life that ends in death is meaningless and without purpose. For life to have meaning and purpose, it must ultimately be grounded or absorbed in something that is infinite—something that will never die. My argument is, on the contrary, that any purpose of life depends on the prospect of death. This is *not* to say that death is the purpose of life. Death is not a purpose, not a completion or fulfillment of anything, but rather the irrevocable loss of life. The point, however, is that nothing can be at stake in life—that no purpose can matter—without running the risk of death. Life can matter only in light of death.

Our individual and collective efforts to sustain life bear witness to our relation to death. It is a central feature of our spiritual life that we remember the dead, just as it is a central feature of our spiritual life that we seek to be remembered after our death. This importance of memory—of recollection—is inseparable from the risk of forgetting. Our fidelity to past generations is animated by the sense that they live on only insofar as we sustain their memory, just as we will live on only insofar as future generations sustain the memory of us. This form of living on should not be conflated with a religious notion of eternal life. If we are compelled to keep the memory of the dead—if we make ourselves responsible for keeping them alive in us—it is because we recognize that they are dead. Likewise, if we are concerned that we will be remembered after we are gone, it is because we recognize that we will be dead. Without the prospect of death—without the prospect that our lives will be lost forever—there would be no purpose in maintaining either natural or spiritual life. Life cannot make sense *as life* without death. Only a finite life can make sense *as a life*. This is the argument that I will deepen in this chapter, in showing how finitude is the condition of possibility for both any form of natural life and any form of spiritual life.

The starting point for my argument is the concept of life as characterized by self-maintenance. A living being cannot simply exist but must sustain and reproduce itself through its own activity. The concept of self-maintenance underlies all definitions of living organisms and living systems as self-organizing. To be alive is necessarily to have a self-relation, and any self-relation consists in the *activity* of self-maintenance. Nonliving entities do not have any form of self-relation because they are not *doing* anything to maintain their own existence. A stone simply lies on the ground for an indefinite amount of time. Whether the stone is moved or broken has nothing to do with an activity of its own. This is the categorical distinction between the nonliving and the living. Entities that exist without the activity of self-maintenance are intelligible neither as living nor as dead but *as nonliving*. In contrast, an entity is intelligible *as living* if its existence depends on its own activity of maintaining itself. If the activity of self-maintenance ceases, the entity is no longer intelligible as living but *as dead*.

Philosophically considered, the concept of life must be distinguished from specific biological forms of life. To assume that life depends on specific forms of biology is question begging. We cannot define life merely by listing the traits we encounter in various species of life, since this begs the question of what makes it possible to identify these species as species of *life* in the first place. Current biological notions of life confirm the concept of life as self-maintenance, but they do not exhaust all possible forms of life. The concept of life is *formal* in the sense that it is not specific to a certain substance or substrate. We may be able to engineer forms of life that rely on an artificial substrate, and we may discover species of life (e.g., on other planets) that do not exhibit the carbon base of our currently known forms of life.

The philosophical question is what makes any life *intelligible* as a life. Identifying a material substance or a set of material properties is not by itself sufficient to make something intelligible as living. Rather, an entity is intelligible as living only insofar as it exhibits the purposive activity of self-maintenance. If E.T. lands in your living room, you can make sense of him as a living being, even though he is made of a material that you have never seen before. Likewise, if you land on another planet, whether the entities you encounter are living or not depends on the *activity* they exhibit rather than on the material of which they are made.

Which kinds of material substrates are compatible with living activity is an empirical question that cannot be settled in advance. The philosophical task is rather to deduce the necessary features of life from the formal characteristic of self-maintenance. What is at stake is the very idea of life—all the way from the most elementary forms of natural life to the most elevated forms of spiritual life.[3]

The first feature we can deduce is that life must be inherently finite. The purposive activity of self-maintenance presupposes that the life of the living being depends on the activity, which is to say that the living being would disintegrate and die if it were not maintaining itself. Without this prospect of death, the purpose of self-maintenance would be unintelligible. *Living* activity is intelligible only for someone or something that has *to keep itself alive* in relation to an immanent possibility of death. If life could not be lost, there would be no vital interest in the activity of self-maintenance.

The second feature we can deduce is that life must be dependent on a *fragile* material body. Life cannot be reduced to a specific material substrate, but it requires *some form* of material body that is in need of self-maintenance. The material body of a life must be fragile, in the sense that it must run the risk of disintegrating or ceasing to function. If the living being were not dependent on a fragile material body, there would be neither a subject nor an object of self-maintenance. To be alive is necessarily to be engaged in the activity of sustaining a material body that may cease to be animated.

The third feature we can deduce is that there must be an asymmetrical relation of dependence between the living and the nonliving. Any form of animation necessarily has a relation to the inanimate (the prospect of its own death), but the inverse argument does not hold. Inanimate matter does not need any form of animation in order to exist. While the living cannot exist without a relation to nonliving matter, nonliving matter *can* exist without any relation to the living. This is why it is intelligible that a material universe can exist before there are any living beings and why it is intelligible that a material universe can remain after all forms of life are extinguished. The very existence of life is a fragile and destructible phenomenon.

The concept of life as self-maintaining must therefore be distinguished from any idea of life as self-sufficient. The form of self-maintenance is not a form of sovereignty but a form of finitude. The reason a living being must maintain and reproduce itself is that it is *not* self-sufficient but susceptible to disintegration and death.

These features of the concept of life make any life intelligible *as a life*. To be alive is *a formally distinctive way of being an entity*, which is characterized by the self-maintaining activity of a fragile material being. The concept of life has two genera, which I call natural life and spiritual life. In keeping with the concept of life itself, the genera of life are defined not in terms of material substances or material properties but in terms of two different forms of life-activities. The genera of natural and spiritual life are *two formally distinctive ways of being a living being,* which are characterized by natural and spiritual freedom respectively.[4]

The genus of natural life comprises all species that exhibit the traits of natural freedom. Any species that is engaged in the purposive activity of self-maintenance—while being unable to call into question the purpose of the activity itself—belongs to the genus of natural life. The genus of natural life thereby encompasses all known species of life except for human beings, all the way from plants to the most advanced primates. While these forms of life are vastly different, they all belong to the genus of natural life insofar as they remain within the bounds of natural freedom. Any forms of life that we would be able to engineer—and any forms of life that we would discover on other planets—would also formally belong to the genus of natural life, insofar as the life-activities of these species were restricted to a form of natural freedom.

The first trait of natural freedom is the activity of self-reproduction. Any form of natural life is acting for the sake of self-preservation or the preservation of the species and thereby exhibits a fundamental form of self-determination. The continuous reproduction of the individual organism across a lifetime, as well as its possible replication or procreation in the form of other individuals, are expressions of the natural freedom of self-determination. The capacity for self-determination can vary greatly among different species of natural life. There is a vast difference between a plant that can replicate merely by disseminating its seeds, or an insect that necessarily dies in the act of copulation, and an animal that can survive its own act of procreation to live on with its descendants. The latter has a greater capacity for self-determination, since it can care for its own progeny and recognize itself in a generational chain, rather than being immediately subsumed by the reproduction of the species. Yet all these forms of life remain within the bounds of natural freedom, insofar as they cannot call into question the purpose of procreation and cannot transform the given ends of generational life.

The second trait of natural freedom is the ability of a living being to bear a negative self-relation. When faced with adversity, a liv-

ing being does not passively submit to what happens but engages
in some form of active resistance in accordance with its own self-
determination. Even in disease or other forms of internal rupture, a
living being is not simply negated but maintains itself in the negative experience of suffering. A stone, by contrast, cannot suffer from
anything, since it has no self-relation and no ability to bear the negative within itself. The latter ability is a minimal condition for the
natural freedom of self-determination. The ability to bear a negative
self-relation makes it possible for a living being to *strive* to be itself,
even when the striving entails great difficulty and pain. Moreover,
the striving to be itself is intrinsic to any form of life. A living being
always has to continue striving, not because it is incomplete or necessarily lacking anything, but because it has to keep itself alive. There
is no final goal or completion of life, since life can come to an end only
in death. Even in its fullest actuality, a living being must continue
to strive to be alive, since life is essentially a temporal activity. The
relation to the negative cannot be eliminated, since a living being is
subject to constant alteration and has to maintain itself as it changes
across time. The relation to the negative is therefore internal to the
living being itself and part of its positive constitution.[5]

The third trait of natural freedom is the relation to a surplus
of time. The striving self-maintenance of a living being necessarily generates more lifetime than is required to secure the means of
survival, so there is at least a minimal amount of "free time" for
every living being. The capacity to engage with free time is of course
something that varies greatly among different species of natural life.
Even a simple plant generates free time *in itself*, since it does not
necessarily have to devote all its time to absorbing the light, water,
and other forms of nourishment that are needed for its sustenance.
If you remove a plant from any form of nourishment, it can still
survive for a period of time, which is why the plant is a source of
surplus. A plant, however, does not have the capacity to use its free
time *for itself*, insofar as there is no activity that is distinct from the
activity of self-preservation in the life of plants. In contrast, animals
that can play games, explore new aspects of their environment, or be

absorbed in purring, have a capacity for *self-enjoyment* that is distinct from self-preservation.[6] Through this capacity, they are able not only to generate free time *in themselves* but also to enjoy their free time *for themselves*. In the free time of self-enjoyment, animals exceed the realm of necessity that is defined by self-preservation and open the realm of freedom. Yet even animals with highly refined capacities for self-enjoyment remain within the bounds of natural freedom, insofar as they cannot ask themselves how they *should* spend their time and thereby cannot relate to their time *as free*.

III

The genus of spiritual life comprises all species that *do* have the capacity to ask themselves how they should spend their time. The only known species of spiritual life is human being, but in principle there is nothing that precludes the possibility of discovering or engineering other species of spiritual life. Whether other species of spiritual life *in fact* can be discovered or engineered is again an empirical question that is not within the purview of my argument. My aim is rather to establish the formal traits of spiritual freedom, which are required for any possible spiritual life and thereby define the genus.

The traits of spiritual freedom are higher forms of the traits of natural freedom. To avoid any form of supernaturalism, an account of the traits of spiritual freedom must render intelligible how they can have evolved from the traits of natural freedom, which in turn have emerged from nonliving matter. At the same time, it is important to emphasize that the purposive structures of natural freedom are qualitatively transformed in spiritual freedom. By virtue of spiritual freedom, I am a *person* and not merely a living being.

The first trait of spiritual freedom is that the purposes of life are treated as *normative* rather than as natural. As a spiritual being, I am acting not simply for the sake of preserving my life or the life of my species but for the sake of *who I take myself to be*. Who I take myself to be is a practical identity because it requires that I keep faith with a commitment. For example, if I have a life-defining commitment to a political cause, I take my life to be worth living because I am a political activist. My practical identity gives me a standard of integrity (a norm) in relation to which I understand myself as succeeding or failing to be myself. Many inclinations that I may otherwise have acted upon will be ruled out because they are not compatible with the integrity of my life as a political activist. My practical identity makes certain things show up as worthwhile and important, while others appear as distractions or temptations. My practical identity informs both how I lead my life and how I respond to what happens in my life. What it means to have a certain practical identity—e.g., what it means to be a political activist—is not only up to me but depends on socially shared norms. I can transform the norms through my practice, but in doing so I am always answerable to others and held to account for myself. In light of my practical identity, I am not just subject *to* my desires and aspirations but the subject *of* my desires and aspirations. In *living* my life I am also *leading* my life.

The notion of practical identity was pioneered by the philosopher Christine Korsgaard in her groundbreaking work on agency. The notion of practical identity, however, is not by itself sufficient to account for the formal unity that is required for personhood and for leading a life. As Korsgaard herself points out with characteristic rigor, there is a "missing principle" in her account of agency.[7] There must be a principle of unity—of coherence—that makes it possible for a person to have several practical identities and adjudicate conflicts between them. For example, the demands of my practical identity as a political activist may become incompatible with my practical identity as a father and how I respond to the conflict is a question of which practical identity I prioritize.

The order of priority among a person's practical identities is what I call her "existential identity." A person's existential identity consists in how she prioritizes her practical identities and responds to conflicts between their respective demands. My existential identity—what it means to be "Martin"—is not an additional practical identity, but the constitutive practical activity of striving to hold together an order of priority between my practical identities. In terms of Neurath's boat, my practical identities are different planks and my existential identity is the boat that holds the planks together in a fragile form. To be someone and do something, I cannot merely have a number of practical identities. There must be a principle of unity—being Martin—that renders my practical identities intelligible *as mine* and gives them an order of priority in *my life*. Without a principle of unity, I could not even experience a conflict or a contradiction between two of my practical identities, since I would not be able to understand that both practical identities are *mine*.

Moreover, without an order of priority among my practical identities, I could have no sense of *what* matters in my life and *when* it matters. What it means to be Martin is inseparable from the relative priority of my practical identities. This order of priority is my existential identity. The form of the boat as a whole (my existential identity) establishes the relative importance of the different planks (my practical identities). If a plank that is fundamental to the construction were to break, I would be in crisis. My existential identity does not designate the *completion* of who I am but the fragile *coherence* of who I am trying to be. Being Martin is not a final identity but consists in striving to be Martin, striving to maintain or transform the relations of priority among my practical identities in the form of an existential identity. I can be only one person, but what it means to be that person—what it means to be Martin—is never established once and for all. My existential identity is itself at issue in my life. If my being a political activist has priority over my being a father, my existential identity is different than if my priority is the reverse. The order of priority that defines me can change, but without the question of priority being at stake—without my existential identity being at stake—I would not be able to lead a life and experience a conflict among my practical identities in the first place.

The second trait of spiritual freedom is the ability of a person to bear a negative self-relation. The negative self-relation may be expressed as a crisis of existential identity—a conflict or breakdown in the relation *among* my different practical identities—but it also lives *within* any given practical identity. Korsgaard suggests that living up to a practical identity is what makes someone "a person at all," since a person who betrays her own integrity is "for all practical purposes dead or worse than dead."[8] Yet this cannot be right. If I ceased to be a person when I failed to live up to my practical identity, the experience of failure would be unintelligible. The motivational force of the dreaded prospect to which Korsgaard herself calls attention—"I couldn't live with myself if I did that"[9]—stems from my anticipation that I will have to live with myself even if I betray my own integrity. Betraying my integrity may in some cases be a fate worse than death, but it is *not* the same as death. If it were, I would not have to experience the pain of failure, since I would be dead. When I experience the pain of failing to be myself it is rather because *I am still alive and trying to lead my life.* This is my ability to bear a negative self-relation. Because my identity is practical (a matter of what I do), it can fail or break down. Even the established order of priority among my practical identities—my existential identity—can break down. Planks that hold my boat together can break or fall apart, leaving me shipwrecked. The breakdown of my established integrity, however, is not the end of my life as a person. If I experience the disintegration of the boat, I have not yet drowned and am still trying to hold it together. Being a failed person is still being a person.

The activity of trying to be myself—trying to maintain or rebuild the boat, trying to be answerable for what I do and what I have done—is the minimal form of my personhood. As long as I lead my life in any way at all, I am trying to have integrity, even if I fail. Being a person is not necessarily to succeed in living up to the demands of my practical identities but consists in *trying* to maintain or to change my practical identities. Likewise, being a person is not necessarily to succeed in sustaining an existential identity but consists in *trying* to sustain or to transform my existential identity. When I fail to be the person I am trying to be—when I am shipwrecked—I am not simply negated but the subject of the negative experience of failing to be myself. This possibility of failure is a necessary boundary condition for any practical and existential identity. The prospects of failing to be myself—of losing my integrity, losing my boat, losing my life by drowning—remind me why it matters that I have integrity and that I lead my life.

The ability to bear a negative self-relation makes it possible for me to *strive* to live up to the demands of a practical and existential identity, even at the expense of great personal suffering. I may persist in being a political activist even though I am beaten, persecuted, and risking my life, thereby demonstrating my spiritual commitment to who I take myself to be. The demands of my practical identity, however, do not come to an end when I am apparently safe and fulfilled in my life as a political activist. As long as I am committed to being a political activist, I will have to strive to live up to the demands of that practical identity and the existential identity to which it belongs. Striving to be who I take myself to be is not a task that can be completed or a goal that can be achieved. Rather, striving to be myself is intrinsic to any form of practical and existential identity. I cannot *have* a practical identity without *continuing to try* to have a practical identity, and I cannot *have* an existential identity without *continuing to try* to have an existential identity. Even in the fullest actuality and flourishing of who I am, *I have to strive to be who I take myself to be*, since *being* someone is essentially a temporal activity. The relation to the negative is therefore intrinsic to personhood and part of its positive constitution.

The third trait of spiritual freedom is the ability to ask myself what to do with my time. Like all living beings, I have a surplus of time, but as a spiritual being my relation to the surplus of time is inseparable from the question of how I *should* spend my time. This is *the* question that underlies all normative considerations, since what I do with my time is what I do with my life. Every question of what I *ought* to do—or ought not to do—is ultimately a question of what I ought to do with my time. For any norm to matter to me, it has to matter to me what I do with my time. Furthermore, what I do with my time can matter to me only because I grasp my life as finite. If I believed that I had an *infinite* time to live, the urgency of doing anything would be unintelligible to me and no normative obligation could have any grip on me.

The philosophical insight here can be elucidated by attending to the colloquial phrase "Life is too short." When I say, "my life is too short not to pursue my dreams," or "my time is too precious to waste on this meaningless job," I make explicit the relation to finitude that is implicit in all my decisions and deliberations. The phrases express an ability to discriminate between what is worth doing and not worth doing. To say that my life is too short is to say not only that I will die but also that I am *anxious* to lead a flourishing life: to bring my time into focus and respond in practice to the question of what makes my life worth living.

My anxiety is not reducible to a psychological condition that can or should be overcome. Rather, anxiety is a condition of intelligibility for leading a free life and being passionately committed. As long as my life matters to me, I must be animated by the anxiety that my time is finite, since otherwise there would be no urgency in trying to be someone and trying to do something. Even if my project is to lead my life without psychological anxiety before death, that project is intelligible only because I am anxious not to waste my life on being anxious before death. Indeed, it is because I am living with the anxiety that my time is finite that I can reject certain occupations or activities as unworthy of who I take myself to be. Even the sense that something lasts *too long*—that it takes too much time—is intelligible only because I hold that my life is too short. If the brevity of my lifetime were not an issue for me, the temporal length of an activity could not be experienced as an imposition.

To be clear, no amount of time can make my life *long enough*. Leading a life is not a project that can be completed but rather a purposive activity that must be sustained. The judgment that my life is too short is constitutive of leading a life, which requires that I postpone the death I bear within myself. The judgment is implicit in taking anything to be urgent ("my life is too short not to pursue X") and in taking anything to be a waste of time ("my life is too short to waste on Y"). The judgment does not have to be explicit but is at work in all forms of practical engagement. In being devoted to someone or something—e.g., spending time with a loved one, playing an instrument with great intent, learning a new profession—I express in practice that the activity is a priority and that other claims on my attention would count as a distraction.

To hold that my life is too short is a normative judgment, since it expresses what I take to be *worth* doing with my time. The judgment is concerned with the *quality* of my lifetime rather than with the mere *quantity* of my lifetime. Hence, to judge that my life is too short is not directly correlated with how long I think my life should last in terms of objective time. I may think that I have a long time left to live in an objective sense and still judge that my time has run out in an *existential* sense, since it is no longer possible to live a life that is worthy of who I take myself to be. For example, if I am severely ill, have lost everyone who matters to me, or suffer from irredeemable boredom, I may choose to end my life even though I have the physical possibility of surviving for years to come.

Far from expressing that I think it is the right time to die, the decision to end my life is tragic. In deciding to end my life, I express a tragic contradiction between the conception of how my life *ought* to be (how my life would be worth living) and how it *is* (how it is possible to lead my life). Without such a contradiction, I would not suffer from my situation, since there would be no discrepancy between how my life is and my conception of how it ought to be. My terminal illness, the loss of all my loved ones, or my irredeemable boredom, would not be intelligible *as* terrible and *as* a reason to end my life. The decision to end my life does not reflect that my life is complete but that I hold my life to be too short in an existential sense, and indeed so short that there is no time left for me to be who I take myself to be. If my continued life seems *too long to bear* in an objective sense, it is because I judge that my life is *too short to live* in an existential sense.

Likewise, if I help someone else to die because her circumstances are unbearable, I do not hold that it is the right time for her to die. Rather, I hold that the objective conditions under which she would survive are unworthy of her dignity and that her life is too short—in an existential sense—to endure senseless suffering. This is a *judgment*, rather than a neutral observation, since I may be wrong in my assessment of the relation between the objective and the existential conditions. That is why decisions regarding euthanasia and suicide are so difficult and contestable. We may be mistaken in thinking that our lives are no longer worth living and others may help us to see that we are wrong.

My point is not to provide criteria for the difficult decisions regarding life and death, but to elucidate why their difficulty is an essential feature of leading a free, spiritual life. Existential anxiety is at work in every form of spiritual life, since it opens us to the question of what we *ought* to do with our time. Moreover, the anxious relation to finitude is not even ideally to be overcome. Instead of trying to achieve a final peace of mind, we should own the existential anxiety of our freedom. If we had no anxiety about what to do with our time, we would not be able to discriminate between which activities are worthy and unworthy of who we take ourselves to be. To lead a spiritual life, I have to hold that "my life is too short." And in caring for the spiritual life of anyone else, I have to hold that "your life is too short."

For the same reason, any form of spiritual life must be dependent on a fragile material body. For my life to be constitutively too short—and for your life to be constitutively too short—our time must be finite in a way that exceeds any attempt to master how long we will live. We can try to prolong our lives by maintaining our vitality—and as long as we lead our lives we are engaged in that activity of self-maintenance—but our bodies must remain fragile beyond our control. Even if the material we are made of were improved and made more durable, our bodies would still have to run the risk of breaking down and ending our lives. Without such a risk, there would be nothing at stake in leading our lives.

The implications of my argument can be seen in light of what the philosopher Sebastian Rödl has called "true materialism." As Rödl underlines in his seminal book *Self-Consciousness*, we cannot understand how we are material beings if we assume a contemplative standpoint. A materialist understanding of ourselves is severely distorting if we reduce it to a set of material properties and functions. This is, for example, the standpoint we take up when we reduce who we are and what we do to material operations in the brain that can be observed from a third-person standpoint. A "true" materialism should instead establish how we have a spontaneous, first-person understanding of ourselves as material beings. The understanding of ourselves as material beings is not something that arises when we take up a second- or third-person standpoint on our own bodies. Rather, the understanding of ourselves as material beings is built into our own first-person standpoint.[10]

Yet the question is *how* to account for the understanding of ourselves as material beings from a first-person standpoint. My life does not continue merely by virtue of the objective persistence of my material body, but is inseparable from the subjective activity of sustaining my life. If there is no subjective activity of sustaining my life—e.g., if I am in a coma—*my* life is not continuing but is at best suspended and at worst already over. My self-consciousness (my first-person standpoint) is inherent in everything I experience and everything I do, rather than something that is added in a second step of reflection. Following Rödl's important argument, to be self-conscious is *not* to observe myself as an object. I am not aware of what I believe through a separate mental act of inspecting my beliefs, but by *being* the believer. Likewise, I am not aware of what I do through a separate mental act of assessing my deeds, but by *being* the actor. When Rödl specifies the activity of self-consciousness, however, he does not bring into view the finitude that is intrinsic to any form of spiritual self-maintenance. Rödl makes clear that I must hold myself to a standard of integrity, but he does not acknowledge the fragility of the integrity itself. To be self-conscious is always to be engaged in the precarious activity of *trying* to lead my life and *trying* to be responsive to what I have done. By the same token, who I am and what I do is always at issue. In *taking* myself to be doing something and believing something, I am necessarily responsive to being *mistaken* about my actions and beliefs. In trying to maintain my integrity, I must hold myself open to self-correction, self-transformation, and breakdown.[11]

Moreover, I must hold myself open not only to the breakdown of a particular self-conception but also to the end of my life. The sense of mortality—which Rödl never addresses—is built into my first-person standpoint and explains how I understand myself as a material being from the beginning. To lead my life—to pursue any form of spiritual self-maintenance—I have to believe that my time is finite. And to believe that my time is finite, I have to take myself to be dependent on a fragile material body, which always runs the risk of disintegration and death. The belief that my time is finite does not have to be explicitly self-conscious; it is rather the practical self-understanding implicit in caring for my own life and the lives of others. In leading my life, I have to hold that my life is too short and needs to be sustained, which is only intelligible because I grasp myself in practice as a finite material being. The conditions of *possibility* for spiritual life are the conditions of the *fragility* of spiritual life.

IV

We can here begin to see the link between spiritual freedom and secular faith. The deepest reason I am spiritually free is that I can engage the question of what I should do with my time *as a question*. If there were a given answer to the question, I would not be spiritually free. Who I ought to be and what I ought to do would already be determined. Neither social norms nor natural instincts, however, can by themselves determine what I do. When I adhere to a norm or follow what I take to be my natural instinct, *I* am the one adhering to the norm or following the instinct and I can hold myself responsible for doing so. Even kinship relations—in which natural instincts and social norms may seem especially powerful—require that *I* maintain them. The mere biological or social fact of fatherhood is not sufficient for me to care for my child (as evidenced by the many fathers who abandon their children). Rather, I have to take myself *as* a father and hold myself to that practical identity. This is a matter of *faith* for two fundamental reasons. First, being a father is not something that can be accomplished once and for all but a practical identity with which I have to *keep faith*. Being a father does not depend on my figuring out a fact about myself but on my continued fidelity to the well-being of my child. Second, my commitment to being a father is not reducible to the *reasons* I have for being a father. On the basis of my commitment I am compelled to give reasons for what I do with my child and understand myself to succeed or fail as a father. Yet the commitment itself cannot be derived or deduced from reason. There is no way I can demonstrate conclusively (to myself or to anyone else) that being a father is the right thing to do with my life. Rather, I find myself already constrained by my existential commitment to being a father. This commitment opens a space of reasons, since it makes me accountable for being a father and for what I do with my child, but the commitment itself is sustained by faith.

Secular faith and secular reason are therefore two sides of the same coin. Secular faith has nothing to do with religious revelation or mystical intuition, but is inherent in the structure of a normative commitment. I must keep faith with my commitment *as* normative—as something to which I am bound—since it only lives in and through me. I can come to question, transform, or betray my commitment, but only in terms of a different commitment with which I keep faith.

For example, I may have a life-defining commitment to being both a father and a political activist. If the two commitments come into conflict—e.g., if my political engagement requires that I sacrifice the care for my child—the question of what I should do cannot be settled merely by considering what is the right thing to do. Should I be faithful to the political cause or to my child? Before any explicit deliberation, what appears to me as the right thing to do is itself expressive of the practical identity I prioritize and the commitment with which I keep faith. I can try to revise my priorities, but I cannot do so from a detached standpoint. The difficulty is not only the test of reason—however demanding that may be—but also the trial of faith. Failing as a father is not necessarily a failure of reason, since I may be justified in sacrificing my parental obligations for the sake of my political obligations. I am nevertheless failing as a father, since I am failing to be faithful to my child. I may have good reasons for what I do and still fail as a father, insofar as my actions betray the demands of fatherhood.

The same precarious dynamic holds for all life-defining commitments. Because it is not given what we should do or who we should be, there is always a question of with whom and with what we should keep faith. These questions—"Who should I be?" "Whom should I love?" "With what should I keep faith?"—concern our spiritual freedom. As I emphasize throughout this book, they can be *living* questions only for a being who understands herself as finite. The questions do not have to be explicitly self-reflective but are already at work in the way I practically care about my life. The questions concern what *matters* to me and there can be no pressure to answer them (whether through direct action or reflective deliberation) unless I understand my time to be finite.

To answer the question of what matters to me is to decide what is urgent in my life and what I should prioritize. If something is important to me, it matters that I do it *sooner* rather than *later*. To do something sooner rather than later, however, is not necessarily to do it right away. What counts as sooner rather than later cannot be measured directly by objective time but depends on my practical commitments and constraints. Thus, acting on my commitment to being a father does not necessarily mean that I try to have a child with my partner here and now. In an existential sense, postponing the possibility of pregnancy can be a way of acting on my commitment sooner rather than later, insofar as I take prudential steps in light of the project of fatherhood. Saving money and getting an education, for example, can be a way of prioritizing my commitment to fatherhood over other commitments on which I could spend my money and time.

Furthermore, the distinction between sooner and later is not absolute but relative and relational. That I want to do something sooner rather than later can mean that I want to do it one year from now rather than ten years from now. It may be important to me to become a father, but *how* important it is to me is revealed by how long I am willing to wait before taking the steps toward its realization and how much it would pain me to fail to take the steps. If I am fine with waiting ten years before acting on my commitment to being a father, it is less important to me than if I am eager to take the first steps within the next year. If it does not matter to me at all *when* I see someone or do something—if there is no time scale on which I take it to matter that I do it sooner rather than later—then the prospect of doing it has no importance to me at all. Inversely, if something matters to me, there has to be an existential time scale on which I take it to matter that I do it sooner rather than later.

To be sure, I do not necessarily act in accordance with what matters the most to me. The mere fact that I am eager to do something does not mean that it is truly important to me; my eagerness can be a matter of frivolous indulgence. Moreover, even when it is of the utmost importance to me that I do something sooner rather than later, I can still fail to do it. Precisely because it is so important to me, I can become paralyzed by anxiety over the stakes and do something else instead. Insofar as I experience that as a failure, however, I am still holding myself to the commitment. The importance of doing something sooner rather than later answers to a *normative* self-conception—e.g., my practical identity as a father—in relation to which I can succeed or fail.

My distinction between "sooner" and "later" should not be conflated with the distinction between "before" and "after" on a time line of events that are seen from a third-person standpoint. The distinction between sooner and later is available only from a first-person standpoint and presupposes that I am engaged in the project of leading my life. It is because I am projecting myself into a future that I can understand what it would mean for something to happen sooner rather than later.

Moreover, it is because I am projecting that *it will be too late*— because I am projecting that my life will end—that I can be responsive to the urgency of doing anything sooner rather than later. In everything I do, I project myself into a future, which is a condition for experience to be possible. To be anyone and do anything is to project myself into possibilities that I must sustain. To be a father, for example, is to project myself into possible ways of being and acting as a father, which depend on what I do. The projection of my death, however, is the unique form of possibility that structures all of my life. My death is not something that I can experience, since any experience of mine presupposes that I am alive. Rather, my death is the projection of an unsurpassable limit of my life, which makes it possible to distinguish between sooner and later in my life.

The projection of my death does *not* mean that I project when I will die. On the contrary, the time of my death is *indefinite*, both in the sense that it can happen at any moment and that it may be postponed. The indefinite time of my death is both what gives me the chance to prolong my life—to live on—and what makes it urgent to decide what I should do with my life.

My death is therefore the necessary *horizon* of my life. In spatial terms, the horizon is a condition of possibility for anything to be visible at all. Everything I see, I see against a horizon, which makes it possible to distinguish between proximity and distance: to distinguish between what is close and what is far away. The horizon allows me to discern spatial relations, but the horizon is not itself located at any point in space. No matter how far I walk, I will never arrive at the horizon, since the horizon moves with me.

In temporal terms, the same holds for my death. No matter how long I live, I will never arrive at my death, since I cannot *be* dead. Nevertheless, any possibility of my life—any possibility of doing something or being someone—can only be grasped *as* a possibility against the horizon of my death. My death is the horizon that renders intelligible all temporal relations of my life. If I actually believed that my life would last forever, I could not make any sense of the distinction between sooner and later in my life. The distinction itself would be *unintelligible* for me, since I would have no sense of a horizon in relation to which anything could be sooner or later. For the same reason, any question of priority would be unintelligible. For anything to be urgent and for anything to be at stake in prioritizing one thing over another, I have to project the horizon of my death.

The horizon of my death is not a psychological projection, since it is not something I can "choose" to project. Rather, the horizon of my death is a condition of intelligibility for my life. In being a person at all, I necessarily project the horizon of my death. As long as I am here, the horizon is there. Just as I cannot "choose" to see a spatial horizon—since it is a condition for anything to be visible—I cannot choose to project the horizon of my death, since it is a condition for any possible projection of my life. The horizon of my death opens the question of what I should do with my finite time and thus makes it possible to lead my life in the first place.

The horizon of my death always exerts a pressure on my life, but it precedes the distinction between negative and positive pressure. The horizon of my death is the condition of possibility for all experiences of joy and release as well as for all experiences of intensity and dedication. Even the psychological experience of being relieved of pressure—of having time to be grateful for my life—is intelligible only because I understand my time to be finite and appreciate the precious quality of my experience as something that cannot be taken for granted.

Yet the horizon of my death does not by itself give a direction to my life. A horizon is the condition both for finding a path and for being lost, since even the experience of being lost presupposes that I am trying to orient myself. The horizon cannot by itself tell me where to go, but makes it possible to look for a direction in the first place. In the same way, the horizon of my death does not by itself give me a reason for acting. My reasons for acting do not come from the prospect of my death but from my practical identities (e.g., being a father). I am a father not because I will die but because I am committed to my child, which makes me answerable for what I do as a father and gives me reasons for acting. My practical identity as a father and my reasons for acting can only matter, however, against the horizon of my death. To have a reason for acting is to have a priority and the urgency of making something a priority in my life requires that I grasp my life as finite. This is why my spiritual freedom—my ability to engage the question of what I should prioritize—depends on the projection of my death. The horizon of my death does not provide an *answer* to the question of what I ought to do with my life but renders intelligible how the *question* can matter to me.

A comparison with the seagull is once again instructive. Like all living beings, the seagull is acting in relation to its own death. Even the most elementary purposive behavior of a living organism (the purpose of maintaining the life of the organism and the species) makes sense only in relation to the prospect of death. Yet the purpose of maintaining the life of the organism and the species is not itself in question for the seagull. The seagull is always acting in light of that purpose and is therefore restricted to a form of natural freedom. For us, on the contrary, the purpose of our lives is itself in question. Even when we are completely devoted to what we do and who we take ourselves to be, our fundamental commitments can come into question. We can wake up in the middle of the night, asking ourselves what we are doing with our lives. What used to be utterly meaningful can lose its grip and what we do can cease to make sense to us. These forms of existential anxiety can be paralyzing (as in boredom or depression), but they can also transform, change, and reinvigorate our commitments. Existential anxiety is a sign of our spiritual freedom. It is because our fundamental commitments are not given that we can bind ourselves to an ideal rather than a natural purpose. Moreover, it is because our fundamental commitments are trembling and may fall apart that we can even engage the question of what to do with our lives.

V

The notion of spiritual freedom allows us to assess the deepest difference between secular and religious faith. In one sense, religious forms of faith are a clear example of spiritual freedom. To organize your life in relation to an invisible higher power—and with the aim of attaining a state beyond anything that is possible for a finite being—requires the ability to call into question existing norms and hold yourself to different requirements. Moreover, religious faith is itself fragile: it always lives in relation to doubt and can cease to make sense to you. Yet the aim of religious faith is to eliminate spiritual freedom in favor of eternal salvation. Rather than hold open the question of what to do with your time, eternal salvation would close down the question completely. Eternal salvation would not allow for any form of spiritual freedom, since it would remove the question of who you should be and what you should do with your time.

Let me recall why. An eternal salvation is either timeless or endless. In a *timeless* state of being, there is no freedom because there is nothing to do and nothing for which to strive. There can be no actions, no intentions, and no aspirations without a surplus of time. An *endless* life may therefore seem more attractive, since it would allow an infinite time for experience. An endless life, however, could never be *your* life. Since your life could never end, you would never be able to ask yourself what to do with your life, and you could never sacrifice your life for something that mattered more to you than your own existence. Most fundamentally, you would have no horizon of death against which you could give any direction to your life.

A prominent scholar of Buddhist thought, Steven Collins, has made a related observation in his systematic study of the notion of nirvana. Collins perceptively points out that eternal salvation (whether conceived as a timeless or an endless existence) is incompatible with any form of personal agency. "I would ask any reader who may think it possible to know *what* eternal happiness might be like: if it is timeless, how are *you* present, and if it is endless, what possible well-being could retain its attraction, indeed its meaning *as* well-being, when infinitely repeated?"[12] Collins elaborates the case against an endless life as follows:

If one—anyone—tries to imagine his or her existence stretching forward not merely 300 years, but 300,000 or 300 million or

300 billion, or whatever (in immortality, "world without end," these lengths of time are but a beginning), it will soon, I contend, become impossible to retain any sense of a recognizable structure of human emotions, reactions, intentions, aspirations, interrelations, etc.[13]

Collins's point can be made more precise in light of my argument that death is the necessary horizon of leading a life. The problem is not that an endless life *eventually* would become impossible to recognize as a life, but that an endless life is unintelligible from the beginning. The duration of your life is indefinite, but you cannot grasp your life as endless. Anyone who is leading her life in any way must project the temporal horizon of her death, just as anyone who is walking in any direction must project a spatial horizon. Without a horizon that delimits your visible space, you could never engage the question of where to go, since you would not be able to make any distinction between what is near and what is far away in relation to where you are. Likewise, without the horizon of your death, you could never engage the question of what to do with your time, since you would not be able to make any distinction between sooner and later in your life.

An endless existence would have no horizon of death and could therefore never be the life of a *person*. The same problem is even more obvious in the case of a timeless eternity. "Even if we can make sense of the idea of a timeless consciousness, such a prospect clearly will not be *me*," Collins writes. He continues:

No action, no thought, no intentions, aspirations, or memories can be possible without time. With no time to remember anything, let alone to have new experiences, it would be impossible to have any sense of personality, any sense of "who one is." For this reason such a prospect, although certainly a possible aim for me now, cannot be said to be a form of *survival*—rather, for me now it is indistinguishable from death.[14]

Buddhism is remarkably honest about this implication of eternal life. Rather than promising that your life will continue, or that you will see your loved ones again, the goal of nirvana is to extinguish your life and your attachments. The aim is not to lead a free life, with the risk of suffering that such a life entails, but to reach the "insight" that personal agency is an illusion and to dissolve in the timelessness of nirvana.

The Buddhist conclusion may seem extreme, but it makes explicit what is implicit in all religious ideas of eternal salvation. An immortal soul is ultimately just as impersonal as the selfless oblivion of nirvana. As Collins recalls:

> I used to worry that I couldn't understand nirvana until I realized that I didn't understand the Christian (or Islamic) heaven or the Hindu idea of absorption into the World Spirit (*brahman*), or indeed any other such conception of *eternal* salvation either; it is a mistake, I think, to assume that the presence in doctrine of a self or a soul, whether individual, as in Christianity, or collective, as in (much of) Hinduism, makes eternity any more comprehensible.[15]

Collins is here on the verge of understanding that eternal salvation is inseparable from death. Yet he backs away from the conclusion that the aspiration for eternal salvation is indistinguishable from an aspiration to end one's life. "I do not mean to denigrate religious aspirations to eternity," he assures us,[16] since he thinks that a critique of such aspirations would not show sufficient empathy for those who hold religious beliefs. "As an attempt at humanistic, empathetic understanding, rather than as a conceptual point, the suggestion that untold millions of our fellow human beings can have simply and explicitly aspired to a 'superior sort of death' as their highest conceivable goal seems rather unsatisfactory."[17] Instead, Collins short-circuits the possibility of calling into question the ideal of eternal salvation. "It is certainly coherent," he asserts, "to hope *that* a resolution of suffering and a fulfillment of human aspiration are possible, without knowing anything about *what* that is or might be."[18]

Collins's argument is the last line of defense for a religious ideal of eternal salvation. Even though he concedes that eternal salvation is incompatible with any sense of leading a life—any sense of personhood—he maintains that it is coherent to hope for eternal salvation as a fulfillment of human aspiration and that such hope should be sheltered from critique by virtue of empathy with the religious. This line of defense is misleading. It is certainly important to show compassion for those whose suffering leads them to subscribe to a religious ideal of salvation. The right form of compassion, however, is not to promote the promise of eternal bliss but to transform the conditions of social suffering in this life. Collins fails to distinguish between the religious ideologies that promise salvation and the "untold millions of our fellow human beings" who are socialized into such ideologies. To argue that eternal salvation is inseparable from death—as I have done throughout this book—is not to say that untold millions of our fellow human beings *actually do* strive for salvation/death as their highest conceivable goal. Rather, I argue that ideals of eternal salvation are self-contradictory and self-undermining. Eternal salvation is not a goal worthy of our aspirations and it cannot even in principle redeem any forms of social injustice, since it would eliminate our freedom and any sense of who we are.

Far from being innocent doctrines, religious ideals of eternal salvation have pernicious practical consequences. Buddhism is once again an instructive example. In Buddhism, the body is regarded with contempt because it is subject to decay and personal agency is held to be an illusion that should ultimately be overcome. These are not merely theoretical ideas but enacted in practice. In his study of Buddhist monastic life, Collins recounts how "the ascetic effort to subdue bodily desires is not merely expressed in the fact of celibacy; all sexual thoughts, even in dreams, are for monks forms of bad *karma*."[19] Thus, in meditating on the body, the monk should begin by reciting textual lists of bodily parts (there are thirty-two) to apprehend that they are foul and repulsive. As Collins explains: "The body is mentally analyzed into its constituent parts, all of which are described as impure and repulsive, largely but not only because they are subject to decay and death."[20] Indeed, because salvation "is conceived as a spiritual state manifested in both mind and body," it requires "the attempt wholly to inhibit all sexual drives and thoughts, and not merely to avoid overt sexual activity."[21] Through such meditation, "the desexualized, and thus in one sense desocialized individual can embody in imagination the immateriality posited in the doctrines of Buddhism."[22]

The ideal of a desexualized, desocialized, and immaterial individual, however, is self-undermining. Even the most advanced Buddhist monk must in practice understand himself as an agent and exercise his spiritual freedom in order to submit to rigorous meditation. Yet the supposed goal of his purposive activity is to be released from all sense of agency and purpose. His life project is to let go of all projects in favor of an empty tranquillity.

My argument is that such an ideal is indeed empty and not worth striving for. Any spiritual life must tremble with the anxiety of freedom, even in the most profound fulfillment of our aspirations. The attempt to eradicate all forms of anxiety—all forms of attachments that expose us to suffering and make us run the risk of bereavement—is thoroughly misguided, since it seeks to eradicate the condition of spiritual life itself. From this perspective, it is no accident that many monks do not actually devote themselves to the aim of eternal salvation but find ways of pursuing a passionate life even within the walls of the monastery. Such behavior is symptomatic of a social institution that is based on a self-contradictory ideal. Of course, a conscientious Buddhist monk may object and assert that he really *does* want to abolish his own agency and repose in timeless peace. My argument leaves him free to make that choice, but invites him to ask himself if the eternal salvation of nirvana actually is an end with which he identifies, and if it is worthy of the sacrifices he makes. While my invitation may be declined, it recalls and opens up the possibility of owning the pursuit of a free life, rather than aiming for the desexualized, desocialized, and immaterial existence posited as an ideal by the doctrines of Buddhism.

To be clear, Buddhist meditation practices can certainly be employed to great effect for secular ends. In particular, there has been success in adapting various forms of meditation techniques for cognitive therapy as well as for practical forms of compassion training.[23] If you learn Buddhist meditation techniques for such therapeutic purposes—or simply for the sake of having more strength and energy—then you are adapting the techniques for a secular project. You engage in meditational practices as a means for the secular end of deepening your ability to care for others and improving the quality of your life. The religious aim of Buddhism, however, is to release you from life itself. According to Buddhism, you should ultimately treat your agency as a means toward the end of relinquishing the attachment to your life. This is the difference between a religious commitment to *salvation* as an end in itself and a secular commitment to *freedom* as an end in itself. The ultimate purpose of a religious practice is the liberation *from* finite life, whereas the ultimate purpose of a secular practice is the liberation *of* finite life.

A religious ideal of salvation is therefore incompatible with a secular ideal of freedom. This is equally clear when we turn to the question of morality. One of the most persistent arguments for our supposed need of religion is that moral responsibility requires religious faith. As I mentioned in the introduction to this book, more than 50 percent of Americans hold that morality depends on religion. The idea is that moral norms can be binding for us only if we believe that the norms are based on a divine command and/or that there will be a divine reward for good behavior. This religious model of morality denigrates our freedom, since it articulates a coercive structure of command and reward. Genuine moral responsibility, on the contrary, requires a secular sense of freedom.

An illuminating example is offered by Phil Zuckerman, who is a leading sociologist of secular life. Zuckerman elucidates the difference between a secular and a religious form of morality with the thought experiment of two children who are both entrusted with looking at an artwork in a room all by themselves.[24] The first child is told that the artwork is deeply valuable and very fragile. The work of art is unique—the only one in existence—but it may easily break and be irreparably damaged. The first child is therefore instructed *not to touch* the artwork, but she is not threatened with punishment or promised a reward for her behavior. Rather, it is explained to her that she should be careful with the artwork because it deserves to be respected in its fragility and because many people would be sad if it were damaged. The second child is also told that the artwork is deeply valuable and very fragile. However, she is told that she should not touch the artwork because the principal of the school will watch her from a small hole in the ceiling. If she touches the artwork the principal will punish her, whereas she will be rewarded if she refrains from touching the artwork.

Both of the children go into the room alone, look at the artwork, and do not touch it. They perform the same action, but their motivations are radically different. The first child chooses to respect the artwork because she understands that something valuable is fragile and depends on her care. This is a secular model of morality, where the child is taught responsibility on the basis of her own freedom and sense of finitude. In contrast, the second child refrains from touching the artwork because she fears punishment and hopes for a reward. This is a religious model of morality, where the child is taught responsibility on the basis of coercion.

The problem with the latter—religious—model of morality is at least threefold. First, if the child is doing the right thing because she believes that a divine authority is keeping score, she is not acting morally but merely obediently and out of fear of punishment. The child who is taught to act morally because she is being watched from above does not learn to do the right thing for its own sake but rather on the basis of subservience to God. This model of morality fails to establish a sense of responsibility in her own self-relation and makes moral behavior contingent on religious faith. If the child were to lose her faith in God, she would have no resources to make sense of moral obligations but would rather believe that everything is permitted. Second, if the child is taught to believe that moral norms are commanded by God, she is deprived of a perspective that enables her to interrogate and transform the norms themselves. She may do what her religion says that she ought to do, but she will be discouraged from asking herself *if she ought to do what she supposedly ought to do*. Her spiritual freedom—and especially her ability progressively to change the norms of her community—will be compromised rather than cultivated. Third, if the child is taught to act morally out of concern for a reward (salvation), her commitment to justice becomes instrumental rather than an end in itself. She will not do the right thing because she is committed to justice but because she wants to be saved. Both her sense of freedom and her sense of justice are at odds with the religious teaching of salvation as the ultimate end.

These problems plague all attempts to ground moral responsibility in religious faith. Once again Buddhism is the most honest religion when it comes to acknowledging the consequences. Buddhism does not posit a God who keeps watch over us, but rather the absolute monitoring system of karma. The impersonal calculation of karma is able to evaluate exactly the moral worth of every deed and enact the precise retribution that is deserved. By virtue of karma, all the injustice in the world is only apparent and actually justified. As Collins explains, in Buddhism all forms of suffering are understood by means of "the ultimate explanatory schema of karma, action and its effects, which operates automatically and impersonally in the universe of conditioning, *samsara*, both within a particular lifetime and across a series of rebirths. In this scheme, there is no injustice, no accident: all distress is in some sense merited, as a form of retribution for previous misdeeds."[25] Buddhist metaphysics thereby eliminates the question of justice in favor of an absolute principle of cause and effect. There is no injustice (since all forms of suffering are adequate forms of retribution for previous misdeeds), so there can be no question of justice. For the same reason, moral action is not motivated by a concern for justice but serves as a vehicle to achieve good karma and ideally attain salvation by being liberated from karma altogether. The ultimate aim is not to act on behalf of justice and lead a free life, but to be released from anything that can cause suffering.

The Buddhist standpoint reveals the implication of all religious ideals of salvation. Even in a religion like Christianity, which places great emphasis on individual freedom, leading a free life is not an end in itself. Rather, our freedom is a means toward the end of serving and being saved by God. The service to God may take the form of caring for the poor and destitute (as in many forms of Christianity), but the goal is not to emancipate the poor so that they can flourish on the basis of their own evolving commitments and lead their free, finite lives as ends in themselves. The goal of religious salvation is not to emancipate our finite lives but to save us from the finitude that is the condition of our freedom. As soon as emancipation becomes the goal, we have moved from a religious to a secular practice of care, in which our aim is freedom and not salvation. We do not seek liberation *from* finite life, but rather the liberation *of* finite life.

5

The Value of Our Finite Time

I

The greatest resources for developing a secular notion of freedom can be found in the writings of Karl Marx. This may be surprising, since Marxism is notorious for having given rise to totalitarian regimes in the twentieth century. Yet, as I will seek to show, there is no support in Marx's thinking for any form of totalitarian state. On the contrary, the premise for all of his work is "the existence of living human individuals"[1] as ends in themselves. This commitment to individual freedom—what Marx describes as "the free development of individualities"[2]—is the foundation for his critique of capitalism and his critique of religion.

The starting point for Marx is what it means that we are *living* beings. The young Marx pursued this question by analyzing both what we have in common with other animals and how we are different from them. As we saw in chapter 4, all living beings are defined by their purposive *activity*. Like other animals, we always have to do something (breathe, eat, metabolize) to stay alive. The need to consume—and therefore to produce means of subsistence—belongs to the realm of necessity. No living being can sustain itself without some process of production and consumption. This realm of necessity in turn provides the condition of possibility for freedom, since the self-maintenance of living beings generates a surplus of time. What Marx calls the realm of freedom is opened up by the capacity of living beings *to generate more lifetime than is required to secure the means of survival*. The seagull, for example, does not have to spend all its time hunting for food but has a surplus of disposable time that it may use to fly around, linger in the air, or play with other seagulls.

As Marx emphasizes, however, human beings are the only animals who can relate to their activity *as* a free activity. Other animals are identical with their life-activity, in the sense that they cannot call into question the purpose of what they are doing. Human beings, on the contrary, can transform the purpose of their life-activity. Rather than treat our own survival and the survival of our species as the given *end* (as the ultimate purpose of our life-activity), we can treat survival as a *means* toward the end of leading a free, spiritual life. For the same reason, the question of what should count as a satisfying, successful form of life is never finally settled for us. Like other animals we have to satisfy our needs and reproduce our life form, but *how* and *why* we should satisfy our needs and reproduce our life form is always at least implicitly at issue. We are not simply consigned to reproduce a given form of life but capable of calling into question and changing our way of living. This is why our life-activity fundamentally is a free activity.

The ability to engage our life-activity as a free activity is what the young Marx calls the "species-being" (*Gattungswesen*) of human beings.[3] The notion of species-being has often been dismissed as a naive appeal to a supposed human nature or human essence, but such a critique is misleading. The species-being of the human is precisely that we have no given nature or essence. To be sure, Marx holds that labor is a necessary feature of human beings, but for Marx labor does not specify any essential content that would define us once and for all. Rather, "labor" is his term for all forms of purposive activity. Ranging from the most instrumental action to the most elevated spiritual pursuits, labor can be individual and collective, artisanal and artistic, political and philosophical. Labor may be driven by physical need, but it can also be motivated by creative aspirations and communal commitments. While Marx is highly critical of all forms of coerced labor—whether slavery, serfdom, or wage labor—emancipation is a matter of not only being free *from* work but also of being free *to* work in light of the ends that matter to us.

In an emancipated society, we would be able to work on the basis of our commitments rather than due to coercion. We would thereby engage in what Marx calls "actual free labor" (*wirklich freie Arbeiten*).[4] He glosses actual free labor in terms of the activity of composing (*komponieren*), which does not refer exclusively to creating music but to any form of purposive activity with which you identify and to which you are freely committed. The activity of composition can express itself in any number of projects—e.g., building a house, taking care of children, producing social goods, putting together and sustaining a study group—but it requires that you treat the activity as an end in itself. The actual free labor of composing is "the most damned seriousness" (*verdammtester Ernst*) and "the most intense effort" (*intensivste Anstrengung*)[5] because you are at stake in what you do. That we are essentially defined by labor, then, does not mean that it is given *who* we are or *what* we should do. On the contrary, it means that we are essentially dependent on historical and social practices that can change. *Who* we are is inseparable from *what* we do and *how* we do it.

Accordingly, I will show that there is no opposition between the appeal to "species-being" in the young Marx and the method of historical materialism in his mature work, which seeks to analyze historically specific conditions of social-economic life. These two strands of his thinking are systematically linked, as indicated by the fact that the notions of life and living individuals remain central in all his writings. The key is to grasp that neither life nor species-being should primarily be understood in biological or anthropological terms. Marx himself tends to invite such a reading, but we can deepen his concepts of life and species-being by grounding them in the distinction between natural and spiritual life that I developed in the previous chapter.

The first thing we need to remember is that life is essentially a self-maintaining form. Anything that is *intelligible* as living must exhibit a self-maintaining form. Even when we dream of forms of life that do not have the biological basis of our lives, these forms must be self-maintaining to be intelligible as dreams of *life*. To be alive is to be engaged in the activity of maintaining a life; otherwise living would have no purpose. By the same token, all dreams of life are dreams of *finite* life. To be self-maintaining is not to be self-sufficient but to pursue an activity that is inherently *fragile*. The activity of self-maintenance makes sense only because your life depends on it. If your life were not fragile—if you could not disintegrate and die—the activity of self-maintenance would make no sense and your life would not be intelligible as *a life*. This is why any living being depends on a body that can die.

The dependence of life on a fragile material body is not a contingent biological fact about life, but a condition for any possible life. As I have argued, even the most elevated form of spiritual life must reckon with its own finitude. To lead a spiritual life, you have to be the subject *of* what you do—rather than merely subjected *to* what you do—which requires that you actively sustain your existential identity. This activity matters because your life is at stake in it. To sustain your existential identity is to lead your life in light of what you value, which is only possible because you understand yourself as finite. Only a finite being can lead a spiritual life, since only for a finite being can it be urgent to do anything and prioritize anything, which is a condition for valuing anything. This link between the sense of finitude and the sense of value should not be understood as a mere anthropological fact about how our lives happen to matter to us. On the contrary, finitude is a minimal condition for anyone to lead a spiritual life and for anything to be intelligible as a value. An infinite being like God cannot value anything and cannot lead a spiritual life, since nothing is urgent and nothing is at stake for an infinite being. For the same reason, there cannot be any form of economy for an infinite being, since an economy is intelligible only for someone who is dependent on others and who is valuing something that he or she can lose.

Analyses of value and economy must therefore be understood in light of the finitude of time. Any economy is ultimately an "economy of time," Marx writes in his *Grundrisse,* since any form of "activity depends on economization of time."[6] This is the argument that I seek to ground on the deepest level. To grasp the stakes and implications of the economy of time, we must proceed from the conditions of intelligibility for spiritual life, which are implicit in Marx's account but that he himself does not explicitly recognize as such.

Marx's analysis of economy can be seen to operate on three levels. These levels allow Marx to analyze historically specific forms of economic life, but I will show that the analytical levels themselves reflect conditions of intelligibility for any economy.

The first level is what Marx calls the level of *appearance.* All economies must appear in some form, and the form of appearance is *price.* In capitalist economies, price has many forms of appearance—wages are the price paid by the capitalist, profit is the price paid by the worker and consumer, rent is the price paid by the leaser of property, and so on. Even a noncapitalist economy, however, must appear through some form of price. An economy is not intelligible unless there is a *cost* of production, which means that there must be a price to pay for both parties in an economic transaction. If it did not cost me *anything* to provide you with something, it would not be intelligible that any price is involved in our transaction. Even when I give you something for free, the mere act of giving it to you must involve a cost for me—if only the cost of the time it takes me to give it to you. My act would not be intelligible as a gift unless giving it entailed a cost for me and just by virtue of recognizing it *as* a gift you become indebted, even if neither one of us insists on the debt.

Under capitalism, the form in which economic relations appear is money, which allows us to measure the price of goods and services. Yet we all know that there is a difference between price and value. Something can be sold for a higher *price* than before and still have less *value* than before (e.g., due to inflation). Prices can fluctuate in accordance with a number of factors on the market, but they are intelligible *as prices* only due to a measure of value. We cannot understand how much something is worth merely by looking at the price, but must understand the price in light of a measure of value.

The measure of value is the second level of Marx's analysis, which he calls the level of *essence*. The measure of value is essential, since it determines *how* we calculate growth in an economy and thereby how we measure the overall wealth in a society. An economy does not grow because there is more money circulating—on the contrary, an economy can be shrinking when there is more money circulating than previously—but because there is an overall increase of value in the economy. The measure of value, then, is the *essence* of any economy. In traditional philosophy, an essence designates a substance that remains the same regardless of historical transformations. For Marx, however, the essence of an economical system—the measure of value—is itself something that can change historically. We can change the essence of our economy (our measure of value) and thereby also change the form in which our economic relations appear. *How* we organize our economy and *how* we measure the value of our time are open to historical transformation.

Nevertheless, we will always have to organize our lives into *some form* of economy of time, since there will always be a question of what we should do with our time—what we should prioritize. The third level of Marx's analysis is therefore concerned with the *transhistorical* conditions for any economy. Transhistorical conditions are not *beyond* history but rather a feature of every historical epoch. *How* we organize our lives into an economy of time is historically specific, but *that* we have to organize our lives into an economy of time is a condition for any form of society. Likewise, *how* we organize our social relations and *how* we relate to our embodiment is historically specific, but *that* we are social beings and *that* we are embodied are general features of spiritual life. In short, *how* we exist is historically specific, but *that* we exist as historical beings—finite, embodied, and social—is a condition for every moment of history. There has never been and there will never be a historical epoch that does not require some form of economy of time, some form of labor, some form of social relations, some mode of producing and reproducing life.

The deepest question, however, is *why* these features are necessary for every form of historical and spiritual life. Marx's own analysis here begins to falter and lapses into biological or anthropological explanations. The transhistorical conditions of economic life, he tells us in *Capital*, are ultimately due to "the ever-lasting Nature-imposed condition of human existence,"[7] which makes us embodied and finite social beings, who have to divide labor among ourselves in order to sustain our lives. Marx thereby makes it seem as though these features of economic life are due to our supposed biological and anthropological nature. Yet the deeper question is what makes life *intelligible* as an economy of time in the first place. For all living beings, life is *valuable* in the sense that they seek to maintain life through their purposive activity. Only a spiritually free being, however, can treat her life as a matter of what she *values*—and thereby as structured by an economy of time that reflects her priorities—since only a spiritually free being can ask herself what is *worth* doing with her time. The question, then, is what makes it possible to understand an economy *as* an economy, a value *as* a value, and a cost *as* a cost.

Answering the question requires a *fourth* level of analysis, which Marx never explicitly pursues but that I provide in depth. The fourth level of analysis concerns the conditions of intelligibility for spiritual life. On this level of analysis, we can establish that all forms of spiritual life must be finite, embodied, and social—not because of imposed biological or anthropological conditions but because life is intelligible *as* spiritual life only in terms of an economy of time. Even for someone who would be made of different materials than us and belong to a different species of spiritual life, leading a life would be possible only in terms of an economy of time. Economical questions—*which* activities you value and *how* you value them—cannot be contained in a specific and supposedly independent sphere of spiritual life (e.g., the market). Rather, economical questions are at the heart of any form of spiritual life. To lead a life, you have to be engaged in some form of practical deliberation regarding what you ought to do and why you ought to do it. Such practical deliberation requires that you can compare the *value* of different activities and ask yourself what is *worth* doing with your time.

The question is intelligible only for someone who believes that her life is too short. It is because the scarcity of your lifetime is an issue for you that you can ask yourself how you *should* spend your time. If the scarcity of your lifetime were *not* an issue for you—if you were not at stake in your actions—you could not have any normative relation to what you do or what happens to you. It would make *no difference* to you how you spend your time or how you are forced to spend your time. You could languish in passivity or be ruthlessly exploited by others and it would not disturb you on any level. Only for someone who is anxious about her life can there be a right or a wrong time for an action, and only for someone who is anxious about her life can there be too much or too little time. Moreover, only someone who is anxious about her life can try to resist exploitation and be determined to lead her life. In leading a life, you are necessarily engaged in the question of how you should spend your time and what you should prioritize, which is fundamentally a question of valuing. All your normative relations to time—even your most fine-grained sensations of something being too fast or too slow, too persistent or too fleeting, a precious gift or a wasted opportunity—depend on you being at stake in what happens and actively valuing your own time.

The originary measure of value is therefore your finite lifetime. That you value your own finite time *renders intelligible the possibility of valuing anything at all*. You can compare the value of two different activities—discriminate between what is worth doing and not worth doing—only because it matters to you what you do with your finite time.

We must pay attention here to the philosophical distinction between *valuing* something and merely *believing that something is valuable*. To value someone or something is not reducible to believing that a person, an object, or a pursuit is valuable.[8] There are many things I believe are *valuable*, but only a few things that I am *valuing* in the sense of making them a priority in my life. For example, I believe that the discipline of medicine is highly valuable, but it is not a priority in my life to be a doctor. By contrast, in valuing the life of my child— even and especially because the life of my child is *invaluable* to me— I am not merely avowing a belief. I am expressing a commitment to which I hold myself and that places demands on me. This is obvious in the case of a child whom I love and who requires my care, but in a minimal form it is true of anything I value. To value someone or something is to put myself *at stake* in what happens to what I value. By virtue of my commitment, I cannot be indifferent but must be responsive to the fate of what I value. Even when I believe that something is valuable without being directly involved with it—e.g., the discipline of medicine—I have to be willing to do *something* on its behalf. Indeed, if the discipline of medicine were threatened, I would be compelled to do what I can to save it. If I am not willing to do or say anything to defend the discipline of medicine, I do not actually believe that it is valuable.

Thus, while the activity of valuing can be distinguished from the belief that something is valuable, the two are ultimately inseparable. Even if I do not make the discipline of medicine a priority in my life, my belief that it is valuable has practical implications. Whether I hold something to be of small, great, or inestimable value, I must be committed to caring for it in some form. Such care may be expressed by advocating, sustaining, nurturing, or striving to realize what I value, but in all cases it is a question of devoting my own lifetime to what I value. To value something, I have to be prepared to give it at least a fraction of my time. This is why finite lifetime is the originary measure of value. The more I value something, the more of my lifetime I am willing to spend on it. If someone or something is invaluable to me, I may even be willing to give up my life—all my lifetime—for its sake.

II

My argument that finite lifetime is the originary measure of value provides the key to Marx's thinking. The key unlocks his understanding of necessity and freedom, his revaluation of the notion of value at the heart of capitalism, and his critique of religion.

The finitude of our lifetime, I argue, opens both the realm of necessity and the realm of freedom. It is because we are finite and self-maintaining that we live in a realm of necessity but also have the chance to lead a free life.

My distinction between the realm of necessity and the realm of freedom hinges on two different relations to the time that is required for an activity. Let me take a simple example. I have to drink water to stay alive. If I am required to walk two hours per day to acquire water from a distant well, my activity is in the realm of necessity, since the time I spend walking to the well is not valuable in itself but merely a means for the end of sustaining my life. If I could reduce the necessary labor time by having running water in my house, I would do so. Inversely, if I enjoy walking two hours per day as an intrinsic part of a fulfilling life, my activity is in the realm of freedom, since the time I spend walking is valuable for its own sake. The activity of walking is not merely a means for getting exercise or acquiring water but an end in itself for me, so even if I could reduce the time I spend walking I would not do so.

What here holds for walking is true of any intentional activity. The activity in question can belong either to the realm of necessity or the realm of freedom, depending on the purposive structure of my activity. If my activity essentially belongs to the purpose of what I am doing—e.g., if I am walking for the sake of being a hiker—my activity is in the realm of freedom, since the time I devote to the activity is valuable in itself. Whereas if my activity does not essentially serve the purpose of what I am doing—e.g., if my walking is an effort to secure the water I need but would prefer to acquire by more efficient means—my activity is in the realm of necessity, since the time I devote to the activity is not valuable in itself.

How we distinguish between the realm of necessity and the realm of freedom is never settled once and for all, but we have to *make* the distinction for there to be a question of freedom in our lives. If I treated all my activities merely as means—if nothing I did counted as valuable in itself for me—I could not lead a life, since my life would have no purpose internal to its own activities. Inversely, if I treated everything I do as valuable in itself, I could not lead a life either, since whatever I do would be an essential part of the purpose of my life and there would be no question of what I *ought* to do with my life.

The realm of freedom and the realm of necessity are thus interdependent. Like two sides of the same coin, they are *inseparable* but *distinguishable*. The two realms are not the same—and we can analyze the distinct formal features of each realm—but one cannot exist without the other.

The distinction between the realm of necessity and the realm of freedom reflects two sides of how finite lifetime is the originary measure of value. When I do something in the realm of necessity, the time I spend on the activity is normatively understood as a "cost" for me. The work I do in the realm of necessity concerns objects that I need—e.g., water—and which require some form of labor on my part. The more time I must spend on my labor in the realm of necessity, the higher is the value I ascribe to the product of my labor. If I have to walk for hours every day to acquire water, each cup of water is more valuable to me than if I merely have to turn on the faucet at home to have enough to drink. If I spill my water after hours of walking home from a distant well, it is a greater loss for me than if I spill my water next to a running faucet, since in the former case it will cost me more of my lifetime to retrieve the water I need.

The correlation between labor time and value holds for all the objects I produce or acquire in the realm of necessity. The time I spend on securing the objects I need is not valuable in itself, so their value is determined by how much lifetime it costs me to generate and maintain them for consumption.

The preferred form of labor in the realm of necessity is therefore what Marx calls "dead labor." Dead labor designates work that is already done and stored up for future use. A bottle of water that I have brought back from the well contains a certain amount of completed ("dead") labor, and its value is determined accordingly. More generally, the practical know-how that I have acquired through repeated practice is a form of objectified, past labor that I can draw on without having to start from the beginning every time I have to do something. Most importantly for Marx, all kinds of material technologies are forms of dead labor, since technologies allow us to get things done more efficiently while reducing the amount of living labor involved in the process. After we have drilled a well in the middle of our village, we can all get the water we need without having to spend more than a fraction of our day on the pursuit.

The rational aim, then, is to reduce the realm of necessity and increase the realm of freedom. The less time we must devote to activities that are merely means to an end, the more time we can devote to activities that for us are ends in themselves. What those activities are is not a given, and part of living in the realm of freedom is having time to develop or transform our conceptions of what makes life worth living. In the realm of freedom my activities are ends in themselves—including the activity of interrogating what should count as an end in itself—since I pursue the activities on the basis of my commitments rather than because of material need or coercion.

The measure of value is thus different in the realm of freedom than in the realm of necessity. The value of an object or an activity in the realm of freedom is not directly correlated with the amount of labor time required to produce or maintain it. Rather, the value of an object or an activity depends on my normative commitments. For example, a chapter of the book I am writing does not become more valuable just because I spend a lot of time working on it. In the realm of freedom, the value of my chapter is determined by the degree to which it answers to what I think the chapter *ought* to be. If I manage to produce a profound argument quickly, it is worth more than a mediocre claim that took me a long time to articulate. Likewise, a love relationship does not become more valuable merely because we spend many years working on it. In the realm of freedom, the value of our relationship is a matter of our commitment to one another and the life we share. For the same reason, the time we spend in the realm of freedom is not normatively understood as a negative "cost" for which we should be compensated. Rather, spending time in the realm of freedom is a value in and for itself. In the realm of freedom, value is not measured by accumulated, dead labor time but by how much time we have to lead our lives. The more free time we have to pursue the activities that matter to us, the wealthier we are.

The negative measure of value in the realm of necessity (the cost of labor time) presupposes the positive measure of value in the realm of freedom (the value of having time to pursue the activities that matter to us). The dead labor that serves as the measure of our wealth in the realm of necessity (i.e., the goods and technologies we have secured for our benefit) is valuable only insofar as it reduces our necessary labor time and frees up more time for us to lead our lives. The reason we are better off with a well in the middle of our village is that it gives us more disposable time for other pursuits.

We can here begin to see why the measure of value in the realm of freedom and the realm of necessity are two sides of the same coin. It is because I positively value my own free time that I can count it as a negative cost when I have to spend time on something that is merely a means to an end. The same is true of you, since otherwise you would be happy to serve as my slave. The reason the division of labor can be an issue between us is that you value your ability to lead your own life, which is inseparable from your ability to decide what you should do with your time. Thus, when we discuss who should walk to the well to retrieve the water we need, we are discussing how we should divide our time between the realm of necessity and the realm of freedom. This discussion—and the economic arrangements that follow from it—is only intelligible because we value our own free time.

Accordingly, when I say that the rational aim is to increase the realm of freedom and decrease the realm of necessity, I am not imposing an external standard of rationality. Anyone who is committed to being an agent is committed to increasing her realm of freedom and decreasing her realm of necessity. Even someone who claims that she wants to devote her life to servitude can do so only by invoking servitude as her free choice and thus defining servitude as belonging to her realm of freedom.

In this fundamental sense, we are all spiritually free just by virtue of leading a life. The distinctive promise that I will trace in the modern idea of freedom, however, is to recognize each one of us as an end in ourselves and thereby to recognize our spiritual freedom as an *unconditional* value. Spiritual freedom is an unconditional value because it makes possible for us to value anything and hold ourselves to any commitment in the first place. Spiritual freedom has always been the *implicit* condition of leading a life, but the modern idea of freedom makes it *explicit*. By the lights of a modern conception of freedom, we should not be defined once and for all by a given social role (family, profession, religion, nationality, ethnicity, gender). Rather, we should be free to transform the normative conception of ourselves and our institutions should reflect that freedom.

The commitment to spiritual freedom as an unconditional value is crucial for all of Marx's thinking. His critique of capitalism makes sense only in light of his commitment to the freedom of social individuals to lead their own lives. This is why his critique of liberal democracy is an *immanent* critique. An immanent critique does not criticize an institution or an ideology in the name of an ideal that is imposed from the outside. Rather, an immanent critique locates a *contradiction* between the avowed ideals of an institution or an ideology and the actual practical form it legislates for itself. Such a contradiction is immanent because it is intrinsic to the institution or the ideology itself.

In the case of liberal democracy, what matters the most to Marx is the avowed ideal that each one of us should be able to lead our own life. While the different forms of liberalism have become ever more various since the time of Marx, a core commitment of all liberal thought is to the *equal* worth of each individual, not in the sense that we are all the same but in the sense that each individual's life is of *ultimate* worth, rather than relative to another life. In short, the core commitment of liberalism is to recognize each one of us as an end in ourselves.

It is worth pausing to consider the remarkable and demanding character of the liberal commitment to individual freedom. Christianity is often credited for the idea that each individual is of equal and ultimate worth, but that is demonstrably a false attribution. In Christianity, our infinite value as individuals depends on the assumption that we have immortal souls and are the objects of God's love. Our value as individuals is not intrinsic to our finite lives but requires the horizon of salvation. Indeed, Christian discourses are full of reminders that our lives would be nothing but worthless, transient dust without the love of God and the salvation of immortality.

The idea that we can be utterly finite and still of ultimate value—an end in ourselves—is unthinkable in Christianity. Yet that is precisely the idea at the heart of liberal thought. The liberal commitment to the ultimate worth of each individual is not dependent on any assumption about the immortality of our souls or the inherent goodness of our nature. Liberalism can acknowledge our finitude, our fallibility, and our corruptibility without regarding these traits as testifying to an original sin or a fallen condition. Rather, our corruptibility and our perfectibility go together. This is why everything is at stake—for better and for worse—in how we lead our lives individually and collectively. Our lives are of ultimate worth *not* because we are immortal or destined to do good, but because we are capable of *leading* our lives, which always comes with the risk of doing harm or failing in our pursuits. These risks cannot and should not be eliminated, since they are part of what it means to lead a free life.

The liberal commitment to individual freedom can be seen as an explicit form of secular faith. The idea that our capacity to lead our own finite lives is of *ultimate* worth cannot be derived either from any empirical fact about the world or from any religious revelation. Rather, the idea expresses a normative commitment to which we hold ourselves and with which we have to *keep faith*. The commitment opens a space of reasons—since it binds us to a set of implications regarding how we ought to treat one another—but the reasons only have binding force insofar as we keep faith with the commitment. As always, secular reason and secular faith are two sides of the same coin. We must keep faith with our commitment to individual freedom *as* normative, since it only lives in and through us.

The decisive question is what is entailed by the commitment to individual freedom. The entailments are not specified by the commitment itself. A first example is the commitment to equality before the law and the protection of constitutional rights. Virtually every liberal thinker has endorsed these principles, but *who* should enjoy equality before the law and constitutional rights remains the subject of ongoing debate. As early as his classic treatise *On Liberty,* John Stuart Mill appeals to liberal principles in order to argue that "wives should have the same rights and should receive the protection of the law in the same manner as all other persons," while noting that "on this subject, the defenders of established injustice do not avail themselves of the plea of liberty but stand forth openly as the champions of power."[9] Mill is here pursuing an immanent critique—a critique of the liberal tradition on its own terms—since he is calling attention to how avowed liberals fail to apply their own principles by denying married women the legal status that is granted to men. The same logic of immanent critique underlies all the extension of rights that we have witnessed in the past 150 years, from the emancipation of women to other excluded groups identified by race, class, and sexual orientation. However partial the work of emancipation remains— and however hypocritical it may be that formally egalitarian societies tolerate so much actual unfreedom—no progress would have been possible without the appeal to individual freedom. The reason that actual unfreedom is even intelligible to us *as* hypocrisy—*as* an opportunity for critique—is our collective commitment to freedom. It is easy to forget that such a commitment is a fragile and unprecedented historical achievement. In previous periods of human history, there was no such commitment but only forms of reigning tribal norms, according to which there are "natural" slaves or "naturally" subordinated groups who have no claims on those in power.

A second form of immanent critique that is characteristic of the liberal tradition concerns the status of rights themselves. Classical liberal theories that are committed merely to a *formal* or *legal* notion of freedom—a mere *right* to freedom—have long been criticized for depriving the idea of freedom of any real content. My legal right to liberty is of little value if I do not have the *means* to lead my life and make use of my freedom. These means include an education that opens me to a range of possible ways of leading my life, as well as sufficient material resources to reduce the time I have to spend on securing my survival and allow me time to engage the question of what I should do with my freedom. As the liberal philosopher Isaiah Berlin points out, the value of freedom depends on "adequate conditions for the use of freedom."[10] Exactly what should count as adequate conditions for the use of freedom is widely debated, but the general commitment to providing adequate conditions is captured by the *effective freedoms principle*, which is a fundamental tenet of liberal egalitarian justice.[11] The principle holds that all citizens have a legitimate claim to a fair share of the resources that enable them to make effective—actual—use of their freedoms. This principle is the foundation for brands of liberalism that go beyond a formal focus on individual liberty, in favor of redistribution of wealth and social democratic reform.

A third—and deeply related—form of immanent critique is focused on the liberal conception of the individual herself. Classical liberal theories are charged with having an "abstract" notion of the individual, which disregards how our individuality is dependent on a social context and the recognition of others. I cannot be anyone or do anything in isolation. Even when I am all alone, my sense of who I can be and what I can do is informed by social norms that shaped me before I had any choice in the matter. This is not to say that I am completely determined by a given social norm (in that case there would be no freedom), but my sense of being an independent individual requires that others recognize and treat me *as* an independent individual. The sense of independence—of leading a free, spiritual life—cannot be achieved independently (e.g., by someone who grew up in the wild with no one to take care of her). The sense of independence depends on being recognized *as* independent by others, as well as on having the material resources that allow for a sufficient degree of independence from the activity of merely securing the means of subsistence for one's life.

Marx pursues all three forms of immanent critique of liberalism and in fact he was one of the first to give them a rigorous formulation. Marx, however, goes much further and deeper in his immanent critique of liberalism than anyone in the liberal tradition. Marx regards the basic social form that provides the framework for all liberal reflections on freedom—capitalism—as itself inimical to the actualization of freedom. Liberal theories may advocate various forms of restrictions on capitalism, but they never call into question the social form of capitalism itself. In contrast, Marx argues that the commitment to freedom is betrayed by the social organization and division of labor that is enforced by capitalism. Most fundamentally—I will show—the measure of *value* and *social wealth* under capitalism directly contradicts the value of free time.

To grasp the stakes of Marx's critique of capitalism, it is helpful to draw on the notion of freedom that is articulated by his most important philosophical predecessor: G. W. F. Hegel. According to Hegel's philosophy of history, all historical peoples have always been free "in themselves" (in their actions), but only in Ancient Greece did the freedom of a historical people become explicit "for themselves" (in their own understanding of their actions). Nevertheless, the Greeks did not achieve what Hegel calls the Idea of freedom, which requires institutional practices that embody the commitment that "all are free." The actual commitment of Ancient Greece was instead that "only some are free," since the free lives of some were dependent on the slave labor of others. The contradictions inherent in this view are on display in Aristotle, who *both* defends the idea that there are "natural" slaves *and* concedes that "since slaves are people and share in rational principle, it seems absurd to say they have no virtue."[12] For Hegel, such an explicit self-contradiction is itself a form of progress, since it enables one to see the denial of freedom through slavery *as* a contestable contradiction rather than as something that is naturally justified. Yet the Idea of freedom ("all are free") was achieved neither in Ancient Greece nor in the Roman Empire nor in medieval feudalism, since all these forms of life maintained the legitimacy of the institution of slavery and/or the notion of "natural" subordination.

Hegel's radical philosophical claim is that the Idea of freedom is inseparable from material and social practices. The Idea of freedom is not abstract but must be embodied in concrete institutional practices in order to be an Idea of freedom. To use Hegel's favorite word, the Idea of freedom must be *wirklich*—actual, real, effective, at work—which requires that we sustain institutions that recognize the freedom of everyone to lead their own lives. For Hegel, the freedom to lead our own lives is *not* a matter of being free to follow our supposedly natural inclinations. Rather, the freedom to lead our own lives is itself a social-historical achievement, which requires that we are *formed* as free subjects by the institutional practices through which we come to understand ourselves and our inclinations in the first place.

As living beings, we seek self-satisfaction, but since we are spiritually living beings it is not naturally given what *counts* as self-satisfaction for us. The fatal philosophical mistake is to conflate the constitutive form of striving for self-satisfaction with the specific content of striving for egoistic enjoyment. When that conflation is made—as it is in our dominant traditions of political and economic theory—the purpose of egoistic enjoyment is treated as the natural cause of our actions, which is antecedent to our social formation. Rather than understand ourselves as originally social beings, we are seen as naturally egoistic creatures who are driven to cooperate and form a state for purely instrumental reasons.

It is question begging, however, to posit what we would be committed to independently of the social form of life in which we find ourselves. There has never been an agent who did not find herself already shaped by the social world through which she makes sense of herself and her actions. As a spiritual being, I can understand myself to *be* someone or *do* something only if I have a practical identity that is recognized by others. For my actions to be taken as an expression of who I am—including the expression of myself as an egoist—what I do must be subject to norms that are socially instituted and in relation to which I can succeed or fail. Being an egoist is not a natural fact but a practical identity that I have to sustain.

Our practical identities are inseparable from the society to which we belong. If we live and work in a society in which the dominant way of relating to one another is to compete for resources, we will understand ourselves primarily as creatures who are competing for resources. Our apparently natural egoism is itself a matter of our social formation. If we see ourselves as atomistic individuals who form an aggregate in society—with each of us driven to pursue an egoistic end—it is not because we are an aggregate of atomistic individuals as a matter of natural fact, but because we are socialized into a world where we treat and acknowledge one another as though we were atomistic individuals who are naturally driven to pursue an egoistic end.

The conflation of the form of self-satisfaction with the content of egoistic enjoyment is a category mistake, with a clear provenance in the religious notion of original sin. The problem is *not* that we are committed to self-satisfaction. All of us deserve to lead satisfying lives. The decisive issue is what counts as self-satisfaction for us. By virtue of our spiritual freedom, what counts as self-satisfaction for us is never given once and for all. To find self-satisfaction in egoistic enjoyment is a particular and limited *content* of self-satisfaction, not the *form* of self-satisfaction in general. For example, finding fulfillment in helping others to flourish is a form of self-satisfaction, but the form of self-satisfaction does not make my helping others a matter of egoistic enjoyment. On the contrary, the form of self-satisfaction makes it possible for the activity of helping others to be something that I find fulfilling rather than alienating, to be an activity with which I identify and in which I recognize my own commitments.

For Hegel, an actual free society is one in which we can recognize our commitment to the common good as the condition of possibility for our own freedom. Rather than seeing the laws of the state as imposed on us and as coercively restricting our self-interest, we should be able to see ourselves as bound to the laws of the state by virtue of our own commitment to lead a free life, which requires that the laws of the state in turn are seen as contestable and transformable by us. This mutual recognition of the state and the individual is the condition for actual freedom. As Hegel emphasizes, "the Idea of freedom is truly present only as *the state*."[13] To grasp the truth of this point, we do not have to accept Hegel's historically specific conception of the state. We only have to grasp the necessity of some form of collective self-legislation for any exercise of individual freedom to be possible. The question is not *if* we should have a state. Participation in a state—in the sense of a collective form of life—is not optional; it is an originary and irreducible condition for all spiritually free beings, who are constituted by socially instituted norms from the beginning. The question is *which* kind of state is required for actual freedom and mutual recognition. For Hegel, mutual recognition is *not* a psychological issue. The point is not to ensure that everyone as a matter of psychological fact identifies with the laws of the state. Rather, mutual recognition is a matter of the rational institutional structures of the state, which must be such that it is possible in principle for everyone to recognize the formation and cultivation of the common good as enabling the formation and cultivation of their own freedom.[14]

For the same reason, the institutional formation of freedom is not a matter of imposing externally motivated laws and rules on subjects in order to make them obedient citizens. On the contrary, it is matter of providing forms of education—and other institutional practices—that enable persons to be citizens who can understand the norms to which they are subjected as ones to which they have bound themselves; to be citizens who are internally motivated in their actions and who can justify what they are doing to themselves as well as to others.

In his *Philosophy of Right,* Hegel seeks to justify the baselines (*Grundlinien*) of the modern state and the market economy by appealing to the historical achievement of the Idea of freedom as "freedom for all." The progress in question does not reflect any form of divine providence that secures our historical freedom. There is no prospective historical necessity in Hegel, only the retrospective recognition that we have achieved a more adequate notion of freedom by progressing from the commitment that "some are free" to the commitment that "all are free."[15] This explicit recognition of our freedom is not simply the observation of a fact about ourselves but is itself transformative of who we can be and what we can do. The commitment to freedom entails a sense of *practical* necessity, in the sense that certain institutional practices can be shown to be necessary for us to be true to our commitment to freedom. This sense of practical necessity must be strictly distinguished from the antiquated sense of a metaphysically necessary progress in history, which is wrongly ascribed to Hegel. The Idea of freedom might never have become actual—it is a contingent historical achievement that depends on the commitments we maintain—and it can always fail to be actual, since the Idea of freedom exists only insofar as we sustain it through our practices.

The question, then, is whether the modern state and the market economy on which it depends are compatible with an "actual" (*wirklich*) free society. This is the critical question that Marx poses to Hegel, but it has to be posed in the right way. Marx's own critique of Hegel is not as powerful as it could be, since he does not grasp Hegel's philosophical logic. Marx assumes that Hegel is imposing an "abstract" Idea of freedom on society in order to justify the state protection of capitalist property rights and the exploitation of wage labor. Marx thereby misses how Hegel's philosophical logic and his Idea of freedom provide crucial resources for the critique of capitalism that Marx himself pursues. To the extent that Hegel justifies capitalism, it is *not* because he imposes an abstract ideal on society, but because he does not follow through on the implications and demands of his own Idea of freedom in his actual analysis.

While Hegel clearly acknowledges that not everything is as it ought to be in his own Prussian state, he holds that the baselines for the Idea of freedom have been achieved with the advent of the modern state, the institution of fundamental rights of freedom, and the basic regulations of a market economy. At the same time, Hegel himself gives us the resources to question this contention in his *Philosophy of Right*, particularly through his treatment of the problem of "the rabble." Hegel's notion of the rabble refers to any social group that cannot recognize the demands of society as their own. Hegel's main example of the rabble are those who are left suffering from poverty by the market economy of civil society. "The poor man feels excluded and mocked by everyone," Hegel writes, "and this necessarily gives rise to an inner indignation. . . . The poor man feels as if he were related to an arbitrary will, to human contingency, and in the last instance what makes him indignant is that he is put into this state of division through an arbitrary will."[16] Importantly, Hegel notes that the disposition of the rabble can arise due to great wealth just as well as due to great poverty. "On the one hand, poverty is the ground of the rabble-mentality, the non-recognition of right. On the other hand, the rabble disposition also appears where there is wealth. The rich man thinks that he can buy anything, because he knows himself as the power of the particularity of self-consciousness. Thus, wealth can lead to the same mockery and shamelessness that we find in the poor rabble. The disposition of the master over the slave is the same as that of the slave. . . . These two sides, poverty and wealth, thus constitute the corruption of civil society."[17] The problem of the rabble is especially acute for Hegel, since his attempt to justify the modern state and the market economy hinges on that each citizen in principle can recognize these institutions as enabling her to lead a free life, a recognition which is precluded for the rabble.

Hence, the critical question is whether a capitalist society can avoid the production of a rabble and embody the commitment to the freedom of all in its institutional rationality. While Hegel's answer is yes, his own analysis of civil society confirms Marx's argument for why the answer is no.

As Hegel makes clear, the institutional rationality of a free society requires that the production of wealth is not an end in itself but for the sake of the well-being of each citizen. "The livelihood and welfare of individuals should be *secured*," Hegel emphasizes, "i.e. *particular welfare* should be *treated as a right* and duly *actualized*."[18] Particular welfare is here not merely a matter of basic sustenance, but of having the social possibilities to lead a free life that can be recognized as dignified by oneself and by those whom one recognizes in turn. The commitment to the welfare and dignity of each citizen is contradicted, however, by the dynamic of wage labor that is the condition for producing social wealth under capitalism. As Hegel points out, the market economy of civil society can provide only two possible solutions to the problem of poverty and unemployment, with both solutions being fundamentally unsatisfactory.[19] On the one hand, the poor can be supported by charity or public welfare provisions, but this is ultimately inadequate, since it does not allow for the social recognition of having a meaningful profession through which one contributes to one's own well-being and to the common good of the society to which one belongs. On the other hand, the livelihood of the poor can be provided by the creation of more paid employment—more wage labor—"which would increase the volume of production" in civil society.[20] Yet, as Hegel perceptively observes, "it is precisely in overproduction and the lack of a proportionate number of consumers who are themselves productive that the evil consists, and this is merely exacerbated by the two expedients in question."[21]

The problem of overproduction arises when the production of commodities exceeds the purchasing power (the wages) of those who produce the commodities. Civil society is led to overproduction by trying to remedy the effects of poverty and unemployment, which in turn generates new forms of poverty and unemployment. Hegel therefore concludes that "despite an *excess of wealth*, civil society is *not wealthy enough*—i.e. its own distinct resources are not sufficient—to prevent an excess of poverty and the formation of a rabble."[22] To resolve the problem of overproduction, civil society is driven "to go beyond its own confines and look for consumers" in other nations.[23] Indeed, Hegel explains that "civil society is driven to establish colo-

nies" due to "the emergence of a mass of people who cannot gain satisfaction for their needs by their work when production exceeds the
needs of consumers."[24] Far from resolving the problem, however, the
international expansion of capitalist markets reproduces the problem
of overproduction and the formation of a rabble on a global scale.

Hegel here points the way to what Marx will analyze as the fundamental contradiction in the capitalist production of wealth. The
problem of overproduction and unemployment that Hegel identifies
is unavoidable as long as the production of social wealth depends
on wage labor. As we will see, the dynamic of wage labor minimally
defines all forms of capitalism and is fatal for any attempt to justify
capitalism as compatible with the institutional rationality of a free
society.

Marx's critique of capitalism is therefore best understood as
motivated by a commitment to making the Idea of freedom actual.[25]
The comparison between wage labor and slavery, which Marx often
invokes, is illuminating here. As Hegel was well aware in his own
time, the professed commitment to the Idea of freedom ("all are
free") did not prevent allegedly democratic states from maintaining
the institution of slavery. The crucial point for Hegel, however, was
that the historical achievement of the Idea of freedom made it possible to recognize slavery as a contradictory and self-undermining
social form, which must be overcome for us to be true to our Idea of
who we are. Likewise, Marx argues that wage labor is a contradictory
and self-undermining social form, which must be overcome for us
to achieve actual freedom and equality. There are many who would
respond by saying that our economic and social life simply could not
function without wage labor. One should remember, however, that
the same argument used to be made with regard to slavery. Even
many prominent thinkers who acknowledged negative and regret-
table aspects of slavery still held the institution of slavery to be a
necessity, without which a free society would fall apart. The idea
that the enslavement of some is necessary for the freedom of others
could only be overcome by disclosing—from within a historical form
of life—other possibilities of living and working together. The same

challenge holds for the critique of wage labor, which must disclose why our commitment to the freedom of everyone calls for a different form of sharing our economic life. Thus, I will seek to show that the Idea of freedom demands that we overcome the social form of wage labor. While the social form of wage labor bears the democratic promise of freedom and equality within itself, the dynamic of wage labor ultimately makes it impossible to achieve and sustain an actual democratic state, which would enable everyone to see themselves in the institutions on which they depend and to which they contribute. Such a state—as well as a global alliance of actual democratic states—is a necessary condition for mutual recognition of our ability to lead free lives.

III

As in the case of liberalism, it is crucial to understand that Marx's critique of capitalism is an immanent critique—a critique of capitalism on its own terms. Marx has no nostalgia for the social forms and material modes of production that preceded capitalism. Moreover, capitalism is the historical condition of possibility for the ideals of equality and freedom to which Marx himself appeals. As Marx emphasizes, the economic relations of capitalism provide "the productive, real basis of all *equality* and *freedom*," since "equality and freedom presuppose relations of production as yet unrealized in the ancient world and in the Middle Ages."[26] While the liberal ideals of equality and freedom can be fulfilled only through the overcoming of capitalism, the historical emergence of the ideals themselves is inseparable from the capitalist mode of production.

Two features of capitalism are of particular importance here. First, in a capitalist society the social order is no longer justified by appeals to religious dogma or aristocratic bloodlines. In previous forms of social life, power hierarchies were justified by a supposed divine or natural right—as though the superiority of one person over another could be established by mere birth. The economic class interests at the root of domination and exploitation were thereby hidden. Under capitalism, by contrast, economic power is explicitly acknowledged as the source of social inequalities. In principle we are all *equal* under capitalism, in the sense that no one has a given right to dominate anyone else. Power hierarchies are established through the relation between buyer and seller, capitalist and worker. But there is no divine or natural order that entitles anyone to occupy (or excludes anyone from occupying) one position rather than another. Each buyer is in principle entitled to property if he or she can afford it, and each seller is entitled to reject or accept a given bid. As Marx explains: "A worker who buys commodities for 3 shillings appears to the seller in the same function, in the same equality—in the form of 3 shillings—as the king who does the same. All distinction between them is extinguished. The seller *as* seller appears only as owner of a commodity of the price of 3s, so that both are completely equal."[27] No bloodline, no caste, no race, no gender, and no sanction of any God can legitimize domination under capitalism. This is not to deny that racism, sexism, and other forms of bias have continued to serve as justifications for exploitation under capitalism, but unlike in previous historical epochs these justifications can in principle be exposed as unjust.

Second, each participant in an economic relation under capitalism is formally recognized as *free*. Unlike the system of slavery in Ancient Greece and Rome, or the system of serfdom in the Middle Ages, no one has the right to own another person's life under capitalism. Of course, as a matter of historical fact, many capitalist societies have nevertheless allowed for various forms of slavery. The system of wage labor, however, makes it possible in principle to recognize each person as "owning" her life. We are not forced to work for someone else, but are "free" to sell our labor-power to whomever we want. Most significantly, what is recognized as our own is the *time* of our lives. I may not own any property, and all the property I own can be transferred to someone else. But what is irreducibly my own—what belongs to me for as long as I live—is the time of my life. When I sell my labor time to someone else for a wage, I am therefore necessarily *selling my own life*. My time cannot be separated from my life, and under capitalism my time is explicitly recognized as *valuable*.

The ideas of equality and freedom that emerge through capitalist economic relations thus open themselves to an immanent critique. While we are formally recognized as equal, we are still unequal from the beginning, since the relation of power between us depends on how much property and capital we have inherited. If I own means of production, I can employ you for a wage and make a profit that in turn increases my capital. Whereas if you do not own means of production, you have no choice but to sell your labor time either to me or to some other capitalist (unless you "choose" not to live at all). While you are formally recognized as free, you are effectively forced to labor for the sake of someone else's profit in order to survive. Instead of religion or nature, economic relations now serve as the justification for the subordination of one person by another.

To see how this works, we first need to have Marx's basic categories in view. Let us therefore return to our village and its water supply. Even before capitalism, a supply of water can be a commodity in Marx's sense, since the acquisition of water costs labor time. We do not have access to water automatically, but must perform some form of labor—if only the labor of gathering water from a stream—in order to acquire it. Anything that costs labor time can be a commodity in Marx's sense. This is why the air we breathe (unlike the water we drink) cannot be a commodity. The air we breathe is available for us without any labor on our part and cannot therefore be a commodity. *Clean air* can become a commodity if we have to do something to clean it, and indeed it may become a highly priced commodity in the future owing to pollution.

The general form of a commodity is not specific to capitalism, but pertains to anything that has both a *use value* and an *exchange value*. The use value of a commodity is the purpose it serves, which means that a commodity can have multiple use values. The use value of a gallon of water, for example, can be to replenish someone who is thirsty, clean someone who is dirty, wash clothes or dishes, grow vegetables, and so on. The exchange value of a gallon of water, however, is not concerned with its specific use value but is determined by a comparison to the value of other commodities.

The question of exchange value is at work whenever we trade one thing for another. If I have two gallons of water when I only need one, I may set out to trade my extra gallon of water for a pair of shoes. By trading one for the other we establish that they have the same *exchange* value, even though their *use* value is entirely different (if I am thirsty a pair of shoes will not help me and if my feet are cold a gallon of water will not help me). The equivalence of exchange value can be expressed in the form of money—as when we say that a pair of shoes costs as much as a gallon of water—but it is important to remember that the money form precedes capitalism and is in turn preceded by more primitive forms of measuring exchange value. Any form of exchanging goods requires the category of exchange value, and thereby a standard of measure that makes it possible to compare the value of different commodities.

The profound question is how to understand the measure of *value* in exchange value. As Marx reminds us in *Capital*, Aristotle was the first to raise this question in a rigorous form. "There can be no exchange," Aristotle points out, "without equality, and no equality without commensurability."[28] To exchange a gallon of water for a pair of shoes we must be able to *compare* their value, even though a gallon of water is *incomparable* to a pair of shoes. Aristotle himself concedes that he cannot see how there can be a real basis for such a comparison. "In reality, it is impossible," he asserts, "that such unlike things can be commensurable," so he reduces the measure of exchange value to "a makeshift for practical purposes."[29] In contrast, Marx emphasizes that there is a real measure of value for exchange value, namely, labor time. The one thing that all commodities have in common—and that makes it possible to compare their value—is that they *cost* labor time to produce. We can compare the value of a gallon of water to the value of a pair of shoes because they both cost labor time. The exchange value of a commodity thus depends on the labor time required to produce it, even though the price of a given commodity can vary in relation to a number of factors.

According to Marx, Aristotle was unable to grasp the measure of value in exchange value because he lived in a society that was founded on slave labor. A commodity produced by a slave is not recognized as having "cost" labor time, since the slave is not granted any ownership of his time. The general value of labor time can be recognized only in a society where each participant in the process of exchange—and each producer of a commodity—is held to be equal. As Marx explains:

> The secret of the expression of value, namely the equality and equivalence of all kinds of labor because and in so far as they are human labor in general, could not be deciphered until the concept of equality had already acquired the permanence of a fixed popular opinion. This however becomes possible only in a society where the commodity-form is the universal form of the product of labor, hence the dominant social relation is the relation between men as possessors of commodities. Aristotle's genius is displayed precisely by his discovery of a relation of equality in the value-expression of commodities. Only the historical limitation inherent in the society in which he lived prevented him from finding out what "in reality" this relation of equality consisted of.[30]

This is one of many passages where Marx makes clear that his own insights would not be possible without the historical emergence of capitalist economic relations and the notion of equality that is intertwined with them. Even before capitalism, labor time was *implicitly* the measure of value in exchange—otherwise it would be impossible to compare the "cost" of two different commodities—but only with the advent of capitalism is labor time *explicitly* the measure of value in exchange. The latter transformation requires not only that each person be recognized as *equal* but also that each person be recognized as *free* to spend her own time. Only the recognition that we have free time—and that our free time is inherently valuable for us—can make our labor intelligible as a cost and bestow value on the products of our labor. This is one of my central arguments, which is merely implied by Marx's analysis but required for it to make sense.

The social form that recognizes the general right to free time under capitalism is wage labor. The institution of wage labor acknowledges that when I work for my subsistence I am operating in a realm of necessity, where my labor counts as a negative "cost" for which I am compensated with a wage. By the same token, it is acknowledged that wage labor is a *means* for the *end* of leading my life in a realm of freedom that opens up beyond my working hours. My wage is literally a means for my subsistence, which is supposed to give me free time to pursue the projects and commitments that matter to me (otherwise there would be no institutional difference between wage labor and slavery). Yet, as Marx maintains, the promise of freedom through wage labor is necessarily betrayed by the social form of wage labor itself. This argument needs to be carefully unpacked, since it illuminates how we are treating the time of our lives under capitalism and why that treatment contradicts our commitment to leading a free life.

The social form of wage labor has the capacity to produce large amounts of *surplus value* in the overall economy. The capacity for such a "growth" of value is the main reason why supporters of capitalism believe it is the best economic system possible. The decisive question, however, is how to account for the growth of value in a capitalist economy. Contrary to a widely held assumption, the source of economic growth cannot be located in the process of circulation (buying and selling). Particular economic actors can make a profit when buying something cheaply and selling it for a higher price, but in the economy as a whole this kind of profit is a zero-sum game, since gain for one actor amounts to loss for another. Accordingly, the process of buying and selling cannot explain why there is an *increase* of value in the economy as a whole. Yet we know that capitalist economies generate such a surplus (e.g., an annual growth of value). From where is the surplus value coming? The explanation resides in the process of production and specifically in the activity of *living labor.*

As I demonstrated in chapter 4, living beings necessarily generate a surplus of time by virtue of their own activity of self-maintenance. Speaking economically, we produce more lifetime than we need to "spend" on keeping ourselves alive. This is why we have free time, but it is also why we can be exploited. A being who would consume all her time merely in order to survive could never be used for any other purpose, since she would die as soon as you forced her to do anything but maintain her own life. Our activity of self-maintenance, however, generates more lifetime than it "costs." The surplus of time makes it possible for us to lead free lives but also to be exploited in the social form of wage labor, which converts our surplus of lifetime into surplus value for the sake of profit and the growth of capital.

We can pursue the details of Marx's argument by following the fate of wage labor and the dynamic of capitalism in our village. As a capitalist, I own the well that is located one hour from the village and is our only available means for producing water in an efficient manner. The demand for water is high—for drinking, cleaning, washing, growing vegetables, etc.—so I have hired five hundred workers to walk and retrieve water from the well for eight hours per day, six days a week.

The value of the commodity I am selling (a gallon of water) is determined by how much time it costs to produce it. More exactly, the value of a gallon of water is determined by the amount of labor time it takes for the average worker in our society to produce a gallon of water (two hours). This is what Marx calls *socially necessary labor time.* The socially necessary labor time depends on the available means of production in a society at a time, which in our case are the available well technologies in the country and the available tools for transporting water. If developments in technology and general work efficiency decrease the socially necessary labor time for producing a gallon of water from two hours to one, the value of a gallon of water will also be cut in half, since the production of a gallon now "costs" only one hour of labor time instead of two.

The value of the labor-power I am buying on the job market (the wage of the worker) is in turn determined by how much it costs to produce the power in question. Marx emphasizes that what I am buying as a capitalist is not the worker himself—in which case he would be a slave—but precisely his "labor-power" (*Arbeitskraft*). However, since labor-power exists only as the capacity of a living individual, the labor-power of a worker cannot be separated from the life of the worker himself. The cost of *producing* labor-power is therefore inseparable from the cost of *reproducing* the life of the worker, granting him enough food, sleep, and other means of subsistence to ensure that he can continue to labor. This is why the rate of wages is essentially related to the average cost for the means of subsistence in a society at a given time. For capitalism to reproduce itself day after day, it must provide the means for workers to reproduce themselves, so that they can generate both their own labor-power for tomorrow and children who can become workers the day after tomorrow. As Marx explains: "The labor-power withdrawn from the market by wear and tear, and by death, must continually be replaced by, at the very least, an equal amount of fresh labor-power. Hence the sum of the means of subsistence necessary for the production of labor-power must include the means necessary for the worker's replacements, i.e., his children."[31]

The investment in labor-power is generally a profitable investment because living beings generate more lifetime—and therefore more labor-power—than it costs to maintain them. This is the origin of the surplus value that is transformed into capital. The value that the average worker can produce in an hour of labor is greater than the cost of maintaining the life of the average worker for an hour of labor. *How* much greater the value is relative to the cost depends on numerous factors, but *that* the value produced by labor is greater than the cost of labor is necessary for there to be an increase of wealth in capitalist economies. Even after all the additional costs of production and retail have been factored in, there must be a surplus value that is generated by the activity of living labor—otherwise there would be no overall profit in the system, no "growth" in the economy. Moreover, the surplus cannot go back to the worker himself but must be reinvested and accumulated as capital by the owner of the means of production.

Yet, while the investment in living labor is *generally* a profitable investment, I cannot be certain that my investment in a *particular* worker will pay off and that my *particular* business will be profitable. Accordingly, as a capitalist employer, I must try to get my workers to labor as hard as possible. When I hire you, I am buying your labor-power for a certain amount of time—in our case: eight hours per day, six days a week—but I cannot know in advance how efficiently you will make use of the time. For this reason I cannot know how much profit you as a particular worker will bring me—or even if you will bring me any profit at all. If it takes you more than one hour to bring back one gallon of water to the village—because you are slow or lazy or for any other reason—the gallon of water does not become more valuable. The particular gallon becomes more expensive *for me* (since I am paying for your time), but the general value of a gallon remains the same and as a consequence my profit margins are negatively affected. The value of a gallon of water is not determined by the quantity of time it takes for you as a particular worker to produce it, but by the quantity of time it takes for the average worker under current societal conditions of production (the socially necessary labor time), which in our case is one hour for one gallon of water. If it takes you more time than the socially necessary labor time to deliver a gallon of water (if you are slower than the average worker), my profit decreases and may even dwindle away altogether. Inversely, if it takes you less time than the socially necessary labor time (if you are faster than the average worker), my profit increases and I can stay in business.

The reason that I am driven—as a capitalist employer—to press more labor out of my workers is therefore not primarily a matter of psychology or individual vice. Before Marx, socialist writers tended to portray capitalists as evil villains who exploit workers out of greed, as though the problem were one of morality. In contrast, Marx shows that the dynamic of exploitation is intrinsic to the social form of capitalism itself and not reducible to individual vice or virtue.[32]

To be sure, the exploitation of wage labor can be more or less violent and Marx was certainly attuned to the particular horrors of labor practices in the nineteenth century, with many workers (including children) driven to death from working both in factories and in the homes of individual employers. Furthermore, Marx's insights should remind us of the terrible labor practices that persist throughout the world today. For example, workers are committing suicide in response to the conditions under which they produce the kind of computer on which I am typing this book. Yet, to reduce the issue to individual choice and character is to disregard how exploitation is *systemic* under capitalism. As an individual consumer, I can choose not to buy certain products, but without a collective transformation of the system of exchange I will continue to participate in capitalist exploitation. Likewise, as a capitalist employer, I will go out of business and find myself consigned to wage labor if I do not extract surplus value from my workers. As a wage laborer, finally, I have no choice but to submit to a capitalist employer if I want to make a living and survive.

In our village, I am a liberal and well-meaning capitalist employer. I have read Mill's *On Liberty* and I endorse his definition of freedom as the right of each one of us to pursue "our own good in our own way, so long as we do not attempt to deprive others of theirs or impede their efforts to obtain it."[33] Moreover, I have studied *A Theory of Justice* by the great liberal philosopher John Rawls and I am committed to his idea that the best form of life should allow everyone to formulate their own personal "life plans,"[34] so that they can articulate what matters to them and set out to accomplish it. I regard wage labor as a means to that end, and I take myself to be doing something good for the community when I hire five hundred workers to walk and retrieve water from the well. My water business alleviates the unemployment in our village, allowing the workers better means to provide for themselves and their families. I am genuinely concerned that the eight hours of labor for six days a week will not leave much time for my workers to articulate life plans that involve anything other than securing their means of survival. But in order to stay competitive with the water businesses in neighboring villages, I have to enforce the same labor practices as they have.

You are one of my workers and I pay you a wage of ten dollars per hour, which amounts to a weekly income of $480. This wage is established in relation to the socially average cost of subsistence for an individual in the village. Like me, you regard wage labor as a means for leading your life, securing free time that you can devote to planning and pursuing your life plan. The wage you receive for your labor—ten dollars per hour—is sufficient for you to sustain your life. The gallon of water you retrieve for my business during one hour of labor, however, I am able to sell for twenty dollars, since water resources are extremely scarce in our country and every gallon is highly priced. Even when I have deducted my other expenses (for rent, tools, retail, overhead, and so on), my remaining profit is five dollars for the gallon of water you procure during one hour of labor. This profit—which stems from your surplus labor time—is converted into my growing capital.

Now, to increase their profits, the water capitalists in neighboring villages begin to push their workers to labor more intensely and for more hours per day. There are no organized labor unions and the workday is extended to ten hours, combined with demands on each worker to walk faster and carry more water on the trail. Through these innovations, the neighboring capitalists can export cheaper water to our village and take over my market for water consumption. Thus, I adopt the same labor practices to save my business and the local jobs. The awareness that I am risking the lives of my workers keeps me up at night, but I stick with it, since otherwise I would lose my business and condemn myself to wage labor. Because of the new labor conditions, my workers do not get enough time to eat, sleep, and recover. Some of them even die from exhaustion on the trail to the well. In protest, the workers organize to form a union. You become the union leader and call attention to the exploitative practices of my business. You demand a shorter workday and higher wages for all workers. After a general strike, I and the other water capitalists in the country give in. The workday is now limited to a maximum of seven hours and the minimum wage is fifteen dollars.

With the new regulations in place, my profit rates are falling and I have to find a new way to make my business viable. Here I turn to improving the available technology. I invest my capital in creating an advanced machine for retrieving water—a kind of hyper-well—within the village itself. Thanks to the new technology, each one of my workers can produce *ten* gallons of water per hour, even though the average production time in the country (the socially necessary labor time) remains one gallon per hour. I am thus able to make what Marx calls *super-profits*. While each gallon now is ten times cheaper for me to produce, I can still price my gallons in accordance with the socially necessary labor time (or better: I sell my gallons for slightly less than the current price, to edge out my competitors). In effect, I am making ten times more profit from selling water in our village and I am also able to export water to the other villages with large profit margins.

Yet the period of super-profits is temporary. The other water capitalists soon acquire the same technology that I have and take back their share of the market. With the limits of the workday established, however, something fundamental has changed. I and the other capitalists cannot increase the amount of *absolute* surplus value we extract from our workers by making them labor for a longer time. Each hour of labor is a unit of surplus value, so when we added hours to the workday we added surplus value in absolute terms (unit by unit). With set restrictions on the length of the workday, extracting more surplus value from our workers depends on what Marx calls *relative* surplus value. Relative surplus value concerns the difference between the wage I have to pay my workers for one hour of labor and the value my workers can produce during one hour of labor. The development of technology is the best way to increase relative surplus value, since with a more efficient technology I can make my workers produce more value in less time *and* keep their wages down at the same time.

Let me explain how. When my workers produce a gallon of water twice as fast thanks to a new technology, the value of a gallon is reduced by half. To produce the same amount of value, my workers are now producing twice as much water during one hour of labor. As a consequence, a gallon of water is cheaper to buy in the village. The average cost of living for my workers is decreased and their wages lowered (or at least limited in their increase) while still allowing them to attain their necessary means of subsistence. The result is an increase in relative surplus value. My workers produce the same amount of value in an hour, but due to the decreased living costs *a smaller percentage* of the value is allocated to their wage and a greater percentage is surplus value for my business.

As a result, the technological race between water capitalists in the country is becoming more and more intense. With every advance in technology, our workers can produce more in less time and the relative surplus value is converted into capital that in turn is invested in the development of even more advanced technologies. The wheels are spinning, but the collateral effects are making themselves felt in our village. Given the more efficient technology, fewer workers are required in the production process and we are faced with growing unemployment. The workers who lose their jobs join an increasing surplus population that has to move between temporary employments and accept lower wages to make a living at all. For me and the other capitalists, this is an advantageous situation, since it allows us to decrease or at least keep down the general level of wages. Moreover, members of the surplus population are now available as cheap labor and we can employ them for minimal costs to perform a range of services for us (housekeeping, gardening, childcare, cooking, washing clothes, and so on).

At the same time, with increased unemployment the possibility of crisis is always looming, since the population must have enough money to buy the commodities we produce. The consensus of our leading economists and politicians is that we must have an annual growth of value of at least 3 percent to avoid economic crises. The annual growth of value requires not only the production of more commodities but also the *consumption* of more commodities, not only selling but also buying. If a commodity is not purchased, its surplus value cannot be converted into capital and it will not contribute to the annual growth of value in the economy.

The contradiction in the capitalist mode of production is now apparent in our village. Capitalism can sustain itself only by extracting more and more relative surplus value, which is why we are committed to an annual growth of value. The extraction of relative surplus value depends on continually reducing the socially necessary labor time, which is accomplished by technological progress. The reduction of the socially necessary labor time *could* lead to more free time for everyone, but under capitalism that is not possible, since surplus time must be converted into surplus value. The reduction of the socially necessary labor time—which could be liberating— instead leads to a fatal contradiction. On the one hand, we must produce more and more commodities, since each commodity contains less of the labor time that generates surplus value for the capitalist. On the other hand, fewer and fewer people are required to produce the commodities. At one and the same time, we thus increase the number of commodities and decrease the number of people with an income to buy the commodities.

The crisis of overproduction—when commodities flood a market that does not have sufficient means to purchase them—is therefore always on the horizon. To stave off the crisis, we must find ways of employing people in wage labor, regardless of whether the work they do is needed and regardless of whether the work is meaningful for those who labor. Moreover, we must get people to consume ever more, regardless of whether they need the goods they consume and regardless of whether consuming the goods is fulfilling for them. We must even produce commodities in view of having them break sooner rather than later, so that consumers are forced to buy the commodity again. Under capitalism, all questions of what we need, what we want, and what is durable, must be subordinated to the question of what is *profitable*.

The privileging of the profit motive is not a moral failure of individuals under capitalism but expresses what we are collectively committed to in being committed to capitalism and its necessary requirement of an annual growth of value.

To find profitable investment opportunities at a rate that generates an annual growth of value, we must commodify ever more of our natural resources and ever more aspects of our lives. The more of our natural resources that are commodified, the more profit they can yield. Likewise, the more of our activities that can be transformed into a matter of selling and buying—e.g., health care, education, public services, domestic chores—the more sources of profit we will have. The expanding commodification of natural resources and life-activities is not optional but necessary for capitalism to sustain itself. If we are committed to capitalism, we are committed to commodifying more and more aspects of our lives. This vicious circle can be broken only through an overcoming of capitalism, which requires a transformation of our conception of value.

IV

The term "capitalism" is often used loosely, but in light of Marx's work we can give it a precise definition. Capitalism is a historical form of life in which wage labor is the foundation of social wealth. The deepest stakes of Marx's critique of capitalism reside in his critique of the measure of value that is entailed by the dependence of society on wage labor. The measure of value is essential, since it determines *how* we calculate growth in our economy and thereby how we measure our social wealth. Under capitalism, the production of wealth depends on living labor time, which is the source of the surplus value that is converted into profit and gives rise to capital growth. What distinguishes the capitalist mode of production is wage labor for the sake of profit, which entails that socially necessary labor time becomes the essential measure of value.

The most fatal mistake in reading Marx—a mistake as prevalent among his followers as among his critics—is to think that he accepts a general labor theory of value, which holds that labor is the necessary source of all social wealth. Such a theory was first formulated by the classical political economists Adam Smith and David Ricardo and supposedly further developed by Marx. For Smith and Ricardo, labor as the essential measure of value is a transhistorical fact. They assume that labor has always been and will always be the source of social wealth. For Marx, by contrast, socially necessary labor time as the measure of value is specific to the commodity form and becomes the essence of value only in the capitalist mode of production. Labor time as the measure of value is not transhistorically necessary but the historically specific essence of capitalism, which is *contradictory* and can be overcome.

Everything in Marx's critique of capitalism stands or falls on his analysis of the concept of value. Yet regarding this issue—the most seminal in all his work—Marxists have generally failed Marx, either by assuming that labor time is the transhistorical essence of value and/or by failing to explain why labor time is the measure of value for commodities, which forms the historically specific essence of value under capitalism. What is required is a rigorous account of why socially necessary labor time is the measure of value under capitalism and why such a measure of value is self-contradictory.

The failure to provide such an account is especially significant since Marx's argument that socially necessary labor time is the measure of value for commodities is widely held to be discredited by neoclassical economics, which began in the late nineteenth century and now holds sway among all leading economists as well as among the general public.[35] What is known as the marginalist revolution of neoclassical economics seeks to explain the value of commodities not in terms of labor time but in terms of supply and demand. The supply and demand theory is the one that every student learns in an introductory course to economics. The theory shapes virtually the entire field and serves as an alibi for dismissing—without ever really engaging—Marx's systematic analysis of capitalism.

According to the supply and demand model of neoclassical economics, the *demand* for a commodity is determined neither by the amount of labor time required to produce the commodity nor by its overall utility, but by the "marginal utility" it has for the person who buys the commodity. A canonical example is the difference in value between water and diamonds. As a matter of overall usefulness—*total* utility as distinct from *marginal* utility—water is more valuable to human beings than diamonds, since we need water to survive but can live our whole lives without diamonds. Nevertheless, a diamond is generally held to be much more valuable than a gallon of water. The explanation is that the *supply* of diamonds is scarce, while the supply of water is abundant. If I only need to turn on the faucet to have all the water I need, the marginal utility of buying an extra gallon is low, since it does not add much to what I already have. By contrast, the marginal utility of a diamond is high, since the supply of diamonds is very limited and many of us do not have any diamonds. The value of the commodity is thus a matter of where supply and demand meet on a curve. If the supply increases there is a decrease in the marginal utility that determines demand, and if there is a decrease in supply there is an increase in the marginal utility.

Far from challenging Marx's insights, the model of supply and demand confirms his argument that socially necessary labor time is the measure of value for commodities. The categories of supply and demand, scarcity and abundance, cannot be understood merely in spatial terms but must be understood in temporal terms. When we say that water is in abundant supply, it means that the average *time* required for acquiring water (the socially necessary labor time) is minimal. The average citizen only has to turn on the faucet to have all the water she needs. Inversely, when we say that the supply of diamonds is scarce, it means that the average *time* required for acquiring diamonds (the socially necessary labor time) is nearly maximal. The average citizen would have to spend a lot of time to find a diamond. If these objective social conditions of production were to change, the value that results from supply and demand would also change. If we were able to transform carbon into diamonds through a simple operation, the marginal utility of diamonds would fall, since the socially necessary labor time for producing diamonds would diminish. Likewise, if we were deprived of our water supplies and had to walk for hours to acquire a gallon of water, the marginal utility of water would rise, since the socially necessary labor time would increase.

The idea that the notion of marginal utility challenges Marx's arguments is thus an illusion, which stems from the failure of neo-classical economists to reflect on the conditions of intelligibility for their own categories. The categories of supply and demand, scarcity and abundance, are intelligible only in terms of the measure of value established by socially necessary labor time. This measure of value is in turn intelligible only in terms of finite lifetime, which makes it possible for anything to be understood *as* a cost or *as* a gain in the first place. Something can be scarce or abundant only for someone who stands to win or lose the time to lead a life that matters to her. The very notion of an *opportunity cost*—which is of central importance in neoclassical economics—is intelligible only for someone who values her own finite lifetime. This is why the marginal utility of water increases dramatically when the objective social conditions for pro-ducing water break down.

For the same reason, the fundamental idea of neoclassical economics—the *subjective* theory of value—is undermined by its own account of the role of scarcity in the dynamic of supply and demand. The value of a commodity cannot be an aggregate of merely *subjective* preferences that are independent of the *objective* social conditions of production. The value you place on water is not simply a subjective preference but essentially related to the scarce or abundant supply of water, which depends on the objective conditions for producing water in the society of which you are a part. You cannot determine the marginal utility of water except in relation to the socially neces-sary labor time, which is a matter of *how much time* it takes on average to produce water in the society to which you belong.

By the same token, we can clarify the distinction between price and value, which all the neoclassical critiques of Marx fail to under-stand. Marx is *not* arguing that the actual price of a commodity is directly correlated with the amount of labor time required to pro-duce it. The *price* of a commodity can vary depending on a number of factors, but its *value* is measured by the cost of socially necessary labor time. Neoclassical economists deny such a distinction between price and value, in spite of the fact that their own account of marginal utility presupposes the measure of value in terms of socially necessary labor time.

An instructive example is the leading light of neoclassical economics, Friedrich Hayek, whom I engage at length in the next chapter. "In a competitive society," Hayek claims, "the *prices* we have to pay for a thing, the rate at which we can get one thing for another, depend on the quantities of other things of which by taking one, we deprive the other members of society."[36] If this were the case, it would be inexplicable how there can be an overall increase of value ("growth") in a capitalist economy. The process of circulation— selling and buying, supply and demand—is a zero-sum game in the economy as a whole, since the gain of one actor from selling at a high price amounts to the loss of another actor from buying at a high price. For there to be an overall growth of capital wealth in the economy, there must rather be a source of surplus value in the process of production. That source—as we have seen—is the labor time of living beings.

As living beings, we produce more lifetime than the amount of time it "costs" to keep ourselves alive. Thus, we have a surplus of time that can be sold in the form of labor-power. If we did not generate a surplus of lifetime we would have no labor-power to sell—since all our time would be consumed by the activity of merely staying alive—and nothing could be gained from employing us. Inversely, because we continually generate a surplus of time, a capitalist employer can in principle extract a surplus value by purchasing our labor-power for a wage. For the surplus value of our labor to be converted into profit, however, we must not only produce but also consume commodities, not only sell our labor-power but also buy the products of labor for more than it cost to produce them. The resulting profit for capitalist employers is the source of capital growth.

The dynamic of wage labor thus defines all forms of capitalism, since wage labor for the sake of profit is the condition of possibility for generating capital wealth. Only the employment of living beings who both produce and consume commodities can give rise to a surplus of value—an overall "growth" of capital wealth—in the economy. This is why living labor time is the *source* of value in a capitalist economy and why socially necessary labor time is the *measure* of value for commodities.

Hayek, by contrast, has no account of the source of surplus value, since he ignores how the social form of wage labor is constitutive of capitalism. In a manner that is typical of neoclassical economists, Hayek describes the determination of price in terms of the *spatial* process of circulation, while failing to consider the *temporal* process of production that makes circulation possible and requires labor time. In Hayek's account, price is determined by the circulation of a quantity of things through selling and buying, supply and demand, which ignores the labor time that is required to produce and sustain the process of circulation itself. By thus ignoring the problem of labor time, Hayek's account fails to render intelligible even the phenomenon of price. If we restrict ourselves to a spatial account of the process of circulation—selling and buying, supply and demand—it is unintelligible why anything has a price at all, since there is no "cost" of labor time involved. If something does not cost any labor time to produce or acquire, it is inconceivable that it has a price at all. This is why any form of price under capitalism—the price of any commodity—is essentially related to the value of labor time.

In light of my analysis, we can see that the measure of value under capitalism (labor time) answers to the measure of value that is operative in the realm of necessity. When we labor in the realm of necessity—when we do something that is merely a *means* to an end—our labor time is normatively understood as a "cost" for us. The more time we spend working in the realm of necessity, the more expensive is our labor and the more value is contained in the commodities we produce. More labor time equals greater cost and thereby greater value. This is why each gallon of water is more "valuable" when it requires two hours of pedestrian labor than when we have running water at home.

Such a measure of value, however, makes no sense on its own.

Labor time is intelligible as a cost only because we value our finite lifetime as *our own free time,* which we in principle could devote to an activity that is meaningful in itself.

Hence, my argument that finite lifetime is the originary measure of value makes it possible to pursue a critique of neoclassical economics on its own terms, while defending Marx's arguments and developing their implications. Marx's account powerfully demonstrates *that* the measure of value under capitalism is contradictory and traces the pernicious practical consequences of the contradiction. To understand *why* the measure of value under capitalism is contradictory, however, requires a level of analysis that Marx does not explicitly provide. That is why I proceed from analyzing the conditions of intelligibility for any economy of spiritual life, which must distinguish between the measure of value in the realm of necessity and in the realm of freedom. The deepest reason capitalism is a contradictory social form is that it treats the *negative* measure of value as though it were the *positive* measure of value and thereby treats the *means* of economic life as though they were the *end* of economic life.

The real measure of value is not how much work we have done or have to do (quantity of labor time) but how much disposable time we have to pursue and explore what matters to us (quality of free time). The measure of social wealth in terms of free time is not an *ideal* that I impose as an *external* alternative to the measure of social wealth in terms of labor time. On the contrary, the value of having time in the realm of freedom—the value of disposable time—is the *real* measure of wealth because it is *internal* to the value and measure of labor time in the realm of necessity. The value of labor time in the realm of necessity (i.e., the *cost* of labor time) can be understood as such only because we are already committed to the value of free time. Likewise, the purpose of accumulating dead labor—in the form of produced goods and technologies that allow us to reduce the amount of living labor required for production—is to enable us to lead our lives rather than merely secure the means of our survival. The value of dead labor is intelligible *as* a value only because it is *for the sake of* liberating time for the living. Having a hyper-well in the middle of our village makes us wealthier not because it cost people a lot of time to build it, but because the well liberates time for all of us to do something else than pump and carry water.

Yet the capitalist measure of social wealth would have us believe otherwise. As long as we live under capitalism, the hyper-well in our village cannot generate any value for us by virtue of its own operation. The only way we can extract value from the well is by extracting surplus value from a person who has to operate the well in order to make a living. This is a direct consequence of measuring value in terms of labor time. If the quantity of labor time determines our wealth, then a machine that reduces the labor time *reduces* our wealth—unless we make up for the decrease in necessary labor time by increasing the amount of surplus labor time for the worker. The exploitation of workers is *necessary* under capitalism, since only the extraction of surplus value can generate any form of social wealth. Even if we developed our technologies to the point where we could provide the necessary means for everyone to lead their lives— with only a small amount of social labor required to operate the technologies—we would still have to exploit wage labor as much as possible, since capitalism recognizes no other source of value.

The very calculation of value under capitalism, then, is inimical to the actualization of freedom. Indeed, the deepest contradiction of capitalism resides *in its own measure of value.* Capitalism employs the measure of value that is operative in the realm of necessity and treats it as though it were a measure of freedom. Capitalism is therefore bound to increase the realm of necessity and decrease the realm of freedom. Even when capitalism *potentially* expands the realm of freedom by reducing the socially necessary labor time, we cannot *actually* recognize the expansion of the realm of freedom under capitalism, since disposable time is not allowed to serve as the measure of social wealth. The form of activity that is only intelligible as a means (necessary labor time) is treated as though it were an end in itself, and the actual end (free time) is not recognized as having any value at all.

As a consequence, even the wealthy cannot convert their capital into free time. If they spend their capital on something that has no value under capitalism—disposable time—they will cease to be wealthy and become part of the proletariat. Of course, individual capitalists may be wealthy enough to "waste" part of their capital on disposable time, but that is beside the point, since the principle of their wealth still requires that they adopt their wealth as an end in itself rather than as a means to leading a free life. The point of wealth under capitalism is to accumulate more wealth, not to use it as a means for a meaningful end. The accumulation of dead labor is what we call value, and the more dead labor we accumulate the wealthier we take ourselves to be. This is why Marx describes the dead labor of capital as a vampire that "lives only by sucking up living labor, and lives more, the more of this it sucks up." Rather than dead labor being in the service of living labor, living labor under capitalism is in the service of accumulating more and more dead labor. The purpose of labor in the realm of necessity is thereby fundamentally distorted and prevented from achieving its own end. Instead of serving as a means for leading a life in the realm of freedom, labor as a means becomes an end in itself.

The most striking example is of course when people in our society are not needed for wage labor and we regard this as a *problem* that needs a solution ("unemployment") rather than as an *opportunity* to be seized. The idea that wage labor—which by definition is a *means*—is required for the sense of purpose and meaningful activity (an end in itself) is entirely specious. If we value freedom, what we need is *time* to figure out who we should be and what matters to us. This requires time to educate ourselves and to deliberate on what should count as meaningful activities for us—both individually and collectively—rather than being prescribed what should count as meaningful activities by what happens to be profitable for a capitalist at the moment. The latter is serfdom and not freedom.

The key to the critique of capitalism is therefore the *revaluation of value*. The foundation of capitalism is the measure of wealth in terms of socially necessary labor time. In contrast, the overcoming of capitalism requires that we measure our wealth in terms of what I call *socially available free time*. As long as our measure of wealth is socially necessary labor time, machine technologies cannot produce any value for us by virtue of their own operations. The technologies that could make us wealthier—that could give us more time to lead our lives— are instead employed to exploit human labor even when such labor is not needed. If we measured our wealth in terms of socially available free time, however, then machines *would* produce value for us by virtue of their own operations. The technological means that make work more efficient would make us wealthier if socially available free time were our measure of value, but because our measure of value is socially necessary labor time the technological means that reduce the need to work are seen as reducing our wealth.

The revaluation of value is an *immanent* critique of capitalism. The revaluation does not propose a new value that is opposed to the capitalist measure of social wealth. Rather, the revaluation demonstrates that the capitalist measure of social wealth makes no sense on its own and presupposes the value of free time that it denies. The problem with capitalism is *not* that it privileges value and social wealth. The problem with capitalism is that it distorts the *meaning* of value and social wealth. The measure of value under capitalism is distorted and self-contradictory, since the means are treated as the end.

The profound distortion at work in the capitalist measure of social wealth can be illustrated by a comparison with the measure of social wealth in smaller unities like the family or a group of friends or lovers who live together. Unless we operate like the families that Marx studied in Manchester (where the children had to labor for their parents to secure their means of survival), the level of social wealth in our household is not measured by how much labor time is required to sustain our life together. If we acquire a dishwasher and a vacuum cleaner—with the result that each member of the household is required to spend less time on cleaning and doing dishes—we do not think that this entails a *decrease* of our level of social wealth that needs to be compensated by surplus labor. There is also no crisis of "unemployment" as a result of the daily chores being less time consuming, so we do not have to invent pointless tasks to keep the members of the household busy. Rather, we can affirm as a feature of our freedom that all the members of the household now have more time to lead their lives: to pursue their education or chosen profession, to connect with people who matter to them, to engage in sports or dancing, to observe nature, to read or paint, to learn new skills, or to engage in some other way with the question of what they *ought* to do with their time. Likewise, we now have more time to deliberate on how we should lead our life together and how we should divide the social labor that remains necessary in the household.

If we were not committed to such an expansion of the realm of freedom—and a corresponding reduction of the realm of necessity—it would have made no sense to acquire the dishwasher and the vacuum cleaner in the first place. To be sure, there may be a member of the household who enjoys the activity of doing dishes for its own sake and for whom the activity accordingly belongs to the realm of freedom rather than the realm of necessity. This is not a problem, since there is nothing that prevents him or her from doing the dishes by hand even though we have a dishwasher. The point of expanding the realm of freedom is not to decide in advance which activities should count as free, or to prescribe that living labor must be replaced by dead labor to the maximum degree possible. On the contrary, the point of expanding the realm of freedom is to enable these questions to be genuine *questions*—the subject of individual and collective deliberation—rather than being determined for us by our material conditions. When we have a dishwasher, doing dishes by hand is not a necessity but a choice.

The aim of the revaluation of value is to transform our conception of social wealth in such a way that it reflects our commitment to free time. The degree of our wealth is the degree to which we have the resources to engage the question of what we ought to do with our lives, which depends on the amount of socially available free time. To be wealthy is to be able to engage the question of what to do on Monday morning, rather than being forced to go to work in order to survive.

Such freedom should *not* be conflated with a freedom from obligations and pressing responsibilities. To live in the realm of freedom is to be bound by the demands of your practical identity—as a parent, a citizen, a doctor, an athlete, a scholar, and so on. The point, however, is that you are bound by your commitments rather than by necessities dictated by your material needs. To be free is not to be free *from* any practical identity, but to be free *to* engage the demands of having a practical identity. Such freedom includes the demanding question of whether you are succeeding or failing in your practical identity and the equally demanding question—a question of your existential identity—which concerns whether you should hold on to a given practical identity or have to let it go. There are no given answers to these questions of our practical and existential identity, which is why the actualization of freedom requires that we have the time and the material resources to engage them *as* the demanding questions that they are. Having the time and the resources cannot *guarantee* that we will engage with the questions in a productive way—there can be no such guarantee precisely because we are free to fail—but the point is that we should collectively enable rather than disable one another to lead a free life. This is the point of the revaluation of value.

The revaluation of value as the foundation for Marx's arguments has generally been overlooked and never fully understood, partly because Marx restricts his own use of the term "value" to the capitalist conception of value as the quantity of labor time. Yet Marx explicitly challenges and seeks to transform the capitalist measure of social wealth, which implicitly commits him to a revaluation of value. A measure of wealth analytically presupposes a measure of value, so in order to transform the measure of wealth one must transform the underlying conception of value.[37]

The key text for the revaluation of value in Marx is the seventh notebook of his *Grundrisse*, written in London in the winter and spring of 1858. During this period Marx's own personal poverty deprived him of free time to work during the day and he had to stay up through the nights to pursue his research, while battling both illness and the stress of trying to support his family. Yet the years when he was writing his *Grundrisse* (1857–58) were some of the most productive and philosophically fertile in Marx's life. *Grundrisse* means "fundamental features" in German and the seventh notebook in particular distills the fundamental features of Marx's thinking. On a few luminous pages, Marx here captures the central contradiction of capital.[38] The contradiction explains why capitalism *potentially* liberates free time for all, but also enables us to see why only the overcoming of capitalism *actually* can convert the value of free time into real social wealth.

The contradiction is the one we have observed between labor time and technological development. Capitalism measures value in terms of socially necessary labor time, but it also "calls to life all the powers of science" in order to *reduce* the socially necessary labor time. This process has rapidly accelerated since the epoch in which Marx lived and the need for living labor has been reduced due to technological efficiency. The reduction of the need for living labor in the process of production is what Marx describes as "one of the civilizing aspects of capital," which generates "conditions that are more advantageous to social relations and to the creation of elements for a new and higher formation [of society] than was the case under the earlier forms of slavery and serfdom."[39] Indeed, Marx underlines that capitalism "creates the material means and the nucleus for relations," which *could* lead to "a higher form of society, with a greater reduction of the overall time devoted to material labor."[40] By demonstrating that we can dramatically reduce socially necessary labor time, the technological advances achieved under capitalism *could* contribute to an expansion of "the true realm of freedom, the development of human abilities as an end in itself."[41] Nevertheless, under capitalism we *cannot* directly devote ourselves to an expansion of the realm of freedom, since there is no other measure of social wealth than the surplus value extracted from living labor. No matter how advanced our technological capacities for production become, capitalism must continue "to use labor time as the measuring rod for the giant social forces thereby created,"[42] since there is no other source for the growth of capital than the surplus time of living labor.

The contradiction in the capitalist mode of production can move in two different directions, and it is here that the revaluation of value becomes crucial.

As long as we measure our social wealth in terms of labor time, technological development is bound to intensify exploitative methods for extracting relative surplus value from workers. Due to increased technological efficiency in the process of production, workers either become unemployed and part of an army of surplus labor whose presence can be used to keep down wages (as tends to happen in the Western world today), or they become subjected to extremely cruel working conditions that are designed to extract as much surplus value as possible from their labor (as tends to happen in the parts of the world where we now locate most of our manufacturing).

At the same time, the contradiction of capital bears an emancipatory potential within itself. The more advanced our technological powers of production become, the more manifest it becomes that labor time is an inadequate measure for social wealth. When the process of production is increasingly automated and the need for living labor reduced, "the human being comes to relate more as a watchman and regulator to the production process itself."[43] This is potentially emancipatory, since it can lead us to develop ourselves as "social individuals." For us to become truly social individuals in Marx's sense, we have to be *the subjects of* production—planning and directing it for our purposes—rather than being *subjected to* production for the sake of capital. "In this transformation," Marx writes, "what appears as the great foundation of production and wealth is neither the immediate labor performed by the worker nor the time that he works, but rather the appropriation (*Aneignung*) of his own general productive power, his understanding of nature and his mastery over it by virtue of his existence as a social body—in a word, the development of the social individual."[44]

Such a transformation requires that we are educated as social individuals who democratically plan the purposes of production. Given such a transformation of the way we reproduce our life together, "necessary labor time will be measured by the needs of the social individual,"[45] which is to say that we will produce in view of what we need *to lead our lives* rather than in view of making a profit. Furthermore, when we can design technology and plan production for our own purposes, "the development of the power of social production will grow so rapidly that, even though production is now calculated for the wealth of all, *disposable* time will grow for all."[46]

Strikingly, Marx uses the English term *disposable time* in italics in the original (rather than the German *verfügbare Zeit*). The social transformation that Marx advocates requires the revaluation of value. "It is no longer," Marx emphasizes, "labor time that is the measure of wealth, but rather *disposable time*."[47] What Marx here describes as disposable time is what I call socially available free time. The revaluation of value discloses that socially available free time— rather than socially necessary labor time—is the real measure of our wealth. Given the revaluation of value, we can strive to "reduce the necessary labor of society to a minimum," instead of "reducing the necessary labor time in order to posit surplus labor"[48] (as we do under capitalism). We can seek to increase the surplus of socially available free time, rather than extract relative surplus value from wage labor. Socially available free time is thus both the means and the end of emancipation, since it allows for "the free development of individualities," which Marx specifies as "the artistic, scientific etc. development of individuals *in the time set free, and with the means created, for all*" (emphasis added).[49]

Marx does not, however, explicitly make clear that such a social transformation requires an active revaluation of value on our part. As he observes, capitalism is "instrumental in creating the means of social disposable time, in order to reduce labor time for the whole society to a diminishing minimum, and thus to free everyone's time for their own development."[50] Capitalism thus creates the material conditions that make it possible to "blow up"[51]—*in die Luft zu sprengen*—its own foundation. Yet, in the *Grundrisse*, Marx elides the question of what is required of us to make use of this explosive power in an enabling rather than disabling way. He merely emphasizes that "*the theft of alien labor time, on which the present wealth is based, appears as a miserable foundation in face of this new one, created* by large-scale industry itself. As soon as labor in its direct form has ceased to be the great source of wealth, labor time ceases and must cease to be its measure."[52]

Everything at stake in Marx's work hinges on the status of the "must" (*muß*) in the above sentence. Thanks to the level of our material technological development, we are potentially in a position to see that the generation of wealth does not depend on exploiting surplus labor for capital gain and that we would be better off devoting our abilities to conceiving more adequate technologies, in view of liberating time for all of us to lead our lives. As Marx emphasizes, "The surplus labor of the mass has ceased to be the condition for the development of general wealth."[53] Labor time *should* therefore cease to be the measure of social wealth, but whether or not it *will* cease to be the measure of wealth depends on whether we pursue a collective transformation of our conception of value. To say that labor time *must* cease to be the measure of wealth can either be read as the statement of an inevitable necessity (i.e., the dynamic of capitalism automatically leads to its own overcoming) or as an *injunction to us*—stating that *we* must revalue our conception of value.

Marx has often been read as advocating the first alternative (the overcoming of capitalism as historically inevitable), but that is a serious mistake. If the overcoming of capitalism is historically inevitable, then Marx's own analysis is unnecessary, since the dynamic of material forces alone will secure the overcoming of capitalism, independently of what we are committed to, what we value, and what we understand about the world in which we live. Inversely, the revaluation of value requires not only a *theoretical* but also a *practical* transformation of the way we reproduce our lives. All the way from our production of goods to our education and other forms of socialization, we must actively promote the value of leading a free life and the challenging responsibility of being spiritually free, rather than subordinated to capital or religion.

Because the revaluation of value concerns the most fundamental ways in which we organize our lives collectively, the revaluation requires an emancipation of the forms of the state. To recall, there can be no spiritual life without some form of the state: some form of institutional organization of our life-activities governed by norms to which we have bound ourselves. As spiritually free beings, we have always lived and will always live in a state. There is not *first* a free individual who is *then* formed by a state. From the beginning, our freedom is formed by some kind of state—some kind of collective self-legislation—since we can make sense of who we are only in terms of socially instituted norms. Because the norms that govern our lives are not naturally given, however, we can challenge and change the forms of the state through revolution. Indeed, many such revolutions have already taken place and shaped our history, with the French Revolution being the most important for Marx.

The *means* required for a revolution depends on the historical situation, and Marx himself emphasizes that a revolution achieved through "peaceful means" of democracy is preferable to a violent one.[54] In either event, the *end*—the purpose—of a revolution that emancipates us from capitalism must be the revaluation of value, which requires new institutional forms. Marx rightly calls for the overcoming of the state as a social form that maintains a capitalist division of classes. However, such a conception of the state is not its defining form (as Marx sometimes tends to assume). Rather, the state as an organ of competing class interests is a *historically specific* conception of the state, which can be overcome through the overcoming of capitalism. For life after capitalism to have any determinate form, we must reinvent rather than abolish the form of the state. As I have argued, the state as an institutional form of our lives—which can comprise a plurality of institutions—is not itself something that can be eliminated, since it is a condition for spiritual freedom to be possible.

As Marx himself points out, "the question then arises: what transformation will the state undergo in communist society? In other words, what social functions will remain in existence that are analogous to present functions of the state?"[55] I choose to describe the post-capitalist state in terms of a novel conception of democratic socialism—rather than communism—in order to underline that the commitment to *democracy* is indispensable for Marx's critique of capitalism. As Marx rightly underlines, "freedom consists in converting the state from an organ superimposed upon society into one completely subordinate to it."[56] To subordinate the state to society is to transform the state into an *actual* democracy. "All forms of states have democracy as their truth," Marx writes, "and therefore they are untrue inasmuch as they are not democracies."[57] Emancipated forms of the state are thus required for what I call democratic socialism. Moreover, since capitalism is global, the overcoming of capitalism ultimately requires a global alliance of democratic socialist states.

As we will see in the next chapter, capitalism is incompatible with actual democracy. Actual democracy requires that our political debates and deliberations—as well as our forms of political representation—are based on competing conceptions of how best to serve the interests of society as a whole, rather than on competing private interests that are put forth in the name of society as a whole. For the same reason, actual democracy requires that our society is organized in such a way that there does not have to be an antagonism between serving our own interests and serving the interests of society as a whole. While the commitment to serve the interests of society as a whole will always be challenging and contestable, it is in principle impossible to sustain such a commitment under capitalism. Because of the social form of wage labor, democratic politics and democratic states necessarily serve as organs for representing class interests that are competing for control. We cannot actually deliberate on how best to serve the interests of society as a whole, since we must prioritize the private interests of capitalists. This prioritization is not optional, since under capitalism there can be no production of social wealth without the profits of privately owned enterprises.

All our democratic decisions regarding the distribution of wealth are thus constrained by the need to facilitate continued profiteering. Moreover, because the wealth itself is produced through unequal relations of production, the formal equality required for democracy is compromised in advance. The interests of capitalists who have the power to generate wealth for society will necessarily count for more than the interests of those who labor for a wage, even prior to any manipulation of the political process. Even the interests of wage laborers themselves are shaped by the interests of the owners of capital, since everyone who works for a wage depends on the continued growth of capital wealth in order to make a living.

For democracy to be true to its own concept of freedom and equality, capitalism must therefore be overcome. My aim is not to provide a blueprint for the institutional forms that will be required, since a blueprint would ignore that the specific forms of institutions must evolve through an ongoing democratic process. Nevertheless, it must be possible to specify the *principles* of democratic socialism, in light of which the specific questions of economic and political organization will have to be negotiated. Without such principles, the idea of democratic socialism is nothing but an abstract utopia with no actual claim on us. Moreover, the principles of democratic socialism cannot simply be posited but must be shown to be implicit in the Idea of freedom that is our historical achievement. Thus, in the following chapter, I derive the three principles of democratic socialism from the commitment to freedom and equality that we already avow. The principles of democratic socialism are not *sufficient* to determine which kinds of states and which kinds of institutions we need. However, the principles are *necessary*, in the sense that any kind of state and any kind of institution must be compatible with the principles in order to be democratic.

6

Democratic Socialism

I

From the beginning to the end of his work, Marx is guided by the commitment to freedom and equality, which come together in *democracy*. "Democracy is the solution to the riddle of every constitution," Marx writes, since only in democracy do "we find the constitution founded on its true ground; real human beings and the real people . . . posited as the people's own creation."[1] Through the institution of democracy, we can achieve the profound secular recognition that *we* are responsible for organizing and legislating the form of our life together. Neither God nor Nature can justify the social order—only *we* can justify the values we promote and the principles to which we hold one another. By the same token, the form of our life together must be open to democratic negotiation. We cannot invoke religious dogma as the final word in a debate or as the founding authority of a law. We are not *subjected to* the law (as in religion) but *subjects of* the law. "In democracy," Marx emphasizes, "human being does not exist for the sake of the law, but the law exists for the sake of human being, it is human existence."[2] In a democracy, we are answerable not to God but *to one another*. We have to give reasons for our conception of the common good and deliberate on the best means to achieve our goals together.

For Marx, the democratic revolution that began in the eighteenth century was an event of world-historical importance, which opened the possibility of real emancipation. Like his liberal counterparts, Marx recognizes civil rights—including the right of everyone to have an equal vote in democratic elections—as a *necessary* condition for a truly free society. For Marx, however, civil rights are not *sufficient* for actual democracy. For political democracy to be actual—for us to *actually* be able to negotiate the form of our life together—the purpose and practice of our economy must itself be a matter of our democratic deliberation. This is why capitalism and actual democracy are incompatible. Under capitalism, the purpose of our economic production is already decided. What matters above all is to generate a "growth" of capital in the economy. This purpose is beyond democratic discussion, since it is built into how we measure our social wealth in the first place. We may discuss democratically how we should distribute our wealth, but how much wealth we have to distribute is determined by the growth of capital we are able to sustain in our economy. If there is a greater growth of capital in our economy, we have more wealth available for taxation and distribution. If there is a smaller growth of capital in our economy, we have less wealth available for taxation and distribution.

Accordingly—as long as we accept the capitalist measure of social wealth—the purpose of our economy will remain beyond any possible democratic deliberation. If our social wealth depends on the growth of capital, we have no choice but to promote the purpose of profit, since our wealth as a society depends on it. We can restrict the possibility of capital growth through various forms of legislation, but by the same token we restrict the possibility of generating a larger amount of wealth available for redistribution.

The critique of capitalism must therefore be aimed at the measure of value itself. This is why my previous chapter analyzed exactly how the capitalist measure of value is self-contradictory and inimical to democracy. Under capitalism, the measure of value does *not* reflect our actual social wealth—our socially available free time—since it does not measure our actual capacity to produce goods and reduce socially necessary labor time. Even when the necessary labor time in our society is reduced thanks to technological innovations, we cannot democratically decide which forms of labor should be available to pursue in our expanded realm of freedom. We cannot create new occupations on the basis of what would be *important* and *meaningful* to do for ourselves and for our society, but must find occupations that are profitable on the market, since only such occupations generate a growth of value in the economy. In effect, our social wealth under capitalism is not measured by actual productivity and surplus time. Rather, we are forced to measure our social wealth in terms of the surplus value we extract from the exploitation of living labor and transform into capital growth. We do not measure our real social wealth, which resides in how fast we *actually can produce* the goods and services we need and how much free time we *actually can have* to lead our lives.

For the same reason, the overcoming of capitalism and the advancement of democratic socialism require a *revaluation of value,* which I articulated in the previous chapter and will continue to develop here.

To begin with, democratic socialism cannot be achieved merely through a redistribution of wealth. As the pathbreaking Marx scholar Moishe Postone has shown, the problem with most forms of Marxism (and related left-wing political projects) is that their critiques are restricted to the capitalist mode of distribution and do not interrogate the measure of value that informs the mode of production itself.[3] The production of value through proletarian-based labor is seen as a given condition, and socialism becomes a matter of distributing the wealth generated by proletarian labor in a more equal way across society. Socialism is thereby reduced to a mode of political administration and economic distribution, which leaves the mode of production and the measure of value intact. This is exactly what happened in the Soviet Union, which managed to betray all of Marx's fundamental insights. The Soviet legislation under Stalin literally changed the formulation of Marx's core principle ("from each according to his ability, to each according to his needs") to the following: "from each according to his ability, to each according to his labor." It is hard to imagine a greater distortion of Marx's thought. As soon as the satisfaction of our needs depends on the contribution of our labor, we are back to the form of coercion that Marx sought to overcome through his critique of wage labor. Under Stalinism, the state effectively becomes one giant capitalist that wields its power over the citizens by forcing them to do proletarian labor in order to survive.

As Postone demonstrates, most forms of Marxism are ill equipped to provide the deepest form of critique of the Soviet Union and other allegedly socialist regimes. The problem with these regimes is not only that they failed to be politically democratic—a massive failure in its own right—but also that they failed to be socialist in their economic mode of production. Most forms of Marxism cannot grasp this point because they assume that the fundamental contradiction of capitalism resides *between* the mode of production and the mode of distribution. The wealth produced by proletarian labor is seen as potentially adequate to satisfy the needs of all members of society, and the critique of capitalism is restricted to a critique of the socio-economic relations that prevent the wealth from being distributed in the right way.

As we have seen, however, the fundamental contradiction of capitalism resides *within* the measure of value that informs the mode of production itself. As long as we accept the measure of value that is based on labor time, the exploitation of proletarian labor will remain necessary for the production of wealth.

It is here instructive to consider the utopian vision of a socialist society proposed by the influential contemporary Marxist Fredric Jameson. In his book *An American Utopia,* Jameson claims to present a vision of life beyond capitalism, but he has no account of what capitalism is, since he never interrogates the measure of value as socially necessary labor time and never analyzes the contradiction in the capitalist mode of production, which is unavoidable as long as wage labor is the foundation of social wealth. Instead of engaging with the fundamental question of value, Jameson's utopian vision retains the social form of wage labor and the concomitant necessity of proletarian labor. Indeed, Jameson advocates a universal conscription in the army, which would provide all of us with a "guaranteed annual minimum wage" and ensure that we all participate in the socially necessary labor that the army tells us needs to be done. Any democratic determination of the purposes of our social labor is absent from Jameson's utopia. That we could conceive the purposes of production democratically—and participate in the socially necessary labor as an expression of our freedom—is not a possibility pursued by Jameson.[4]

For the same reason, Jameson's notion of freedom is impoverished. Symptomatically, there are no *institutions* of freedom in Jameson's utopia. All institutions that would determine the purposes of our social labor (including education) are consigned to the realm of necessity and run on the model of the army. The realm of freedom, by contrast, is for Jameson indeterminate. What counts as socially necessary labor is decided by the army, which rewards our participation with provisions for basic needs, and the rest is left to our arbitrary individual choices after working hours. When we are done with our required hours of labor under the supervision of the army, we are free to do whatever we want.

Such a view fails to grasp the conditions of possibility for leading a free life. The exercise of freedom requires a practical identity that cannot be invented out of nothing by an individual, but is formed by social institutions. To be free is not to be free *from* normative constraints, but to be free *to* negotiate, transform, and challenge the constraints of the practical identities in light of which we lead our lives. The question is not *if* our freedom will be formed by social institutions—there can be no freedom that does not have an institutional form—but *how* and *by which* social institutions our freedom will be formed.

The key to democratic socialism is to have institutions (including educational institutions and forms of political deliberation) that enable individuals to lead their lives in light of recognizing their dependence on others and on collective projects. Moreover, the key to democratic socialism is to have institutions in which we participate because we *recognize ourselves and our freedom* in their form. The participation in social institutions—including the social labor that we recognize as necessary to sustain our society—should not be secured by coercion but be motivated by our active commitment to participation. It should not be the job of the army or any other institution to force us to work. Rather, the task of our democratic society is to be organized in such a way that we are intrinsically motivated to participate in, contribute to, and transform its ongoing life, by virtue of having been educated to exercise our spiritual freedom. The exercise of spiritual freedom must include the possibility of criticizing or rejecting the established forms of participation. Just as the institution of marriage is not an institution of freedom unless it grants the legal possibility of divorce, democratic socialism as an institution of freedom must grant us the practical possibility of refusing to participate in a given form of life—otherwise our participation will not be free but a matter of material need.

In contrast, Jameson has nothing to say about the values or principles that should inform our social institutions of freedom, and he does not even recognize that such institutions are needed. Rather, Jameson describes the realm of freedom as unconstrained by anything except individual, arbitrary choice. In Jameson's utopia, collective projects of self-determination are operative only in the realm of necessity, whereas the realm of freedom is merely the liberation of individuals from constraint.

A more sophisticated version of the problem can be found in Postone. Unlike Jameson, Postone has a profound understanding of the problem of value under capitalism and its relation to the social form of wage labor. Nevertheless, Postone's conception of freedom ultimately remains indeterminate and cannot account for the possibility of achieving a revaluation of value.

As Postone argues, capitalism creates the material conditions for its own overcoming through technological innovations that reduce

the socially necessary labor time. For Postone the key to emancipation is the *dead labor* of technology, since it can liberate us from the
need to expend our living labor on the process of production. Thus,
Postone is able to avoid two classical mistakes in Marxist theories
concerning the status of technology. On the one hand, technology
should *not* be seen as something that alienates us from a natural form
of labor or a primitive communism. All such forms of nostalgia are
misguided and ignore Marx's fundamental insight that the commitment to social freedom for all became possible because of the historical advent of capitalism. There has never been a natural form of labor
for spiritual beings and a primitive communism is neither possible
nor desirable. The labor of spiritual beings is from the beginning a
matter of technology (some form of tools), and the overcoming of
capitalism requires the further development of technology rather
than its rejection. On the other hand, capitalism cannot be overcome through a linear continuation of the same mode of production,
accompanied merely by a redistribution of the wealth generated by
proletarian labor. The aim is not to glorify proletarian labor but to
overcome it. The overcoming of proletarian labor requires a transformation of the mode of production itself, which should be based
on the power of dead labor rather than on the value of living labor.
Technological advances entail that more and more of the *production
time* that is required for our goods can be separated from the *labor
time* of living beings. By thus replacing living labor with dead labor
in the process of production, we can overcome the capitalist measure
of value in terms of labor time.

For Postone, however, such a transformation does not require a
revaluation of value on our part. Postone claims that under socialism
"a new social mode of production will be based upon a new technology,"[5] with the result that *"not only the goal of machine production but the
machines themselves will be different"* (emphasis in the original).[6] Postone
does not acknowledge that such a social transformation requires a
transformation of our *normative* understanding of the purposes of
social production. Material forces of production cannot by them-

selves transform the measure of value that shapes our conception of social wealth. If our machines will be different it is not only because our technological abilities will be different, but because *we will design the machines for a different purpose.* A difference in purpose is a *normative* difference, which cannot be reduced to material conditions, since machines cannot by themselves determine the purpose of their production. The purpose of production is intelligible only in light of a measure of value that cannot be derived from the machines themselves. Thus, our normative purpose necessarily informs *how* we reproduce our material conditions. For example, under capitalism many of our technological devices are designed to break sooner rather than later, since it is more profitable for the producer if we are forced to buy a new device. Our technological know-how is not developed and employed in service of the practical purposes of our lives, but in service of maximizing profit. Under democratic socialism, by contrast, our research into new forms of technology, our designs of actual machines, and our actual process of production will all be different because we are producing *for the sake of* increasing socially available free time rather than for the sake of generating profit.

In Postone's story of the transition from capitalism to socialism, however, historical agents do not have the power to change anything. In Postone's account, historical agents are one-sidedly conditioned by transformations in the material mode of production. He does not address what is required of *us* to overcome capitalism and what *we* will have to do to sustain our emancipation when we have achieved it. Postone rightly emphasizes that the *possibility* of emancipation depends on the resources of material production. But he fails to grasp that the *actuality* of the struggle for emancipation—and the continued striving that will be required even after emancipation has been achieved—depends on the normative commitments of historical agents. As a result, Postone's notion of the realm of freedom is indeterminate. His only concern is that we shall be free *from* submitting our living labor to the process of production, but he offers no account of what we will be free *to* do and why our freedom matters.

The only distinguishing feature of socialism in Postone's account is that the machines will take care of the process of production, so that we will not have to do anything determinate.

Such an indeterminate conception of freedom is incompatible with democratic socialism. The point of leading a free life—both individually and collectively—is not to transcend the realm of necessity but to be able to negotiate its relation to the realm of freedom. No matter how productive dead labor may become, it will always require at least the living labor of our planning the purposes and directing the operations of technology. Furthermore, the value of dead labor itself depends on our normative commitments. It is far from given that we will want to replace living labor with dead labor as much as possible and in all areas of necessary social labor. For example, even if we could design machines to take care of the sick and the elderly, we may hold that there is an intrinsic value in having care provided by other beings who care and who can understand suffering. The principle "from each according to his ability, to each according to his needs" is not the imposition of an anonymous collective will, but the condition of possibility for genuinely democratic deliberations regarding what matters to us and how we should care for one another.

II

The condition of possibility for democratic socialism is the revaluation of the capitalist measure of value. The revaluation of value makes it possible—as I will show in detail—to pursue increased productivity and profound technological advancements *without* being committed to economic growth understood as the accumulation of capital. We are committed to increasing the wealth of our society, but we no longer measure social wealth in terms of capital growth. Rather, our wealth is measured in terms of our actual production of goods and our socially available free time.

The revaluation of value is the most important aspect of the immanent critique of *both* capitalism *and* liberalism. For all their professed faith in our freedom, liberal thinkers have never been able to conceive that we can have a progressive, scientifically and technologically innovative society that is not based on the capitalist measure of social wealth. Yet, as we will see, the major liberal thinkers of political economy—Mill, Rawls, Keynes, and Hayek—unwittingly concede that the capitalist measure of wealth distorts the values to which they themselves are committed.

The basic premise of liberal economic thought is formulated in Mill's *Principles of Political Economy*, which asserts that "the laws and conditions of the production of wealth partake of the character of physical truths. . . . It is not so with the distribution of wealth. That is a matter of human institutions solely."[7] Only the *distribution* of wealth is treated as a political issue that depends on our institutions and historical commitments, whereas the *production* of wealth is seen as obeying a natural law that we cannot change. The fact that our conception of value is a *normative* notion (not a natural given) is thereby ignored. Far from being a neutral standard of measure, our conception of value is a historical commitment that shapes how we plan and pursue production. That we measure our social wealth in terms of capital growth—which entails that the aim of our economy is the increase of capital wealth—is not a natural necessity but a norm to which we hold ourselves. Moreover, the norm is self-contradictory, since the means are treated as the end. Under capitalism, we produce for the sake of production and we accumulate for the sake of accumulation.

In order to resolve the contradiction, liberal thinkers of political economy are led to dream of what Mill called "the stationary state." This would be the moment when we have accumulated enough wealth to let go of pursuing capital growth and instead have time "to cultivate freely the graces of life."[8] Versions of such a dream can be found in Rawls and Keynes (both of whom are heirs to Mill), but they fail to understand that the dynamic of capitalism will never allow such a moment to arrive.

For example, Rawls argues that the prerequisite for a good society is *not* the pursuit of profit and the accumulation of surplus value but rather "meaningful work in free association with others."[9] The phrase is virtually a quotation from Marx's *Capital*, even though Rawls himself does not seem to be aware of it. Marx's key description of an emancipated society in the first volume of *Capital* is "an association of free human beings, working with the means of production held in common," so that the material process of production "becomes production by freely associated human beings, and stands under their conscious and planned control."[10] As Marx goes on to explain in the third volume of *Capital*, the freely associated producers "govern the human metabolism with nature in a rational way, bringing it under their collective control instead of being dominated by it as a blind power."[11] The aim of such collective self-governance, I argue, is to provide more time for the development of our spiritual freedom as an end in itself.

The crucial part of Marx's argument is the democratic ownership of the means of production. Such democratic ownership is decisive for the actual possibility of a society that would privilege meaningful work in free association with others. As long as the means of production are privately owned, the growth of capital—rather than the creation of meaningful forms of labor—will be the aim of the system as a whole, regardless of what our individual intentions may be. Rawls holds that we may arrive at a point when "real saving (net increase in real capital) may no longer be necessary,"[12] but he does not grasp that such a transformation would require a different economic system. When Rawls objects to the principle that "real saving and economic growth are to go on indefinitely, upwards and onwards, with no specified goal in sight,"[13] he is objecting to the very principle of capitalism. Yet Rawls remains committed to maintaining the economic system that is based on the principle he rejects, since he thinks capitalism is necessary to generate the state of wealth.

The same contradiction can be traced in the work of John Maynard Keynes. While Keynes supports capitalism, he openly acknowledges that it is an economic system which leads us to elevate "some of the most distasteful of human qualities into the position of the highest virtues."[14] Indeed, Keynes dreams of the day when "we shall be able to afford to dare to assess the money-motive at its true value":

> The love of money as a possession—as distinguished from the love of money as a means to the enjoyments and realities of life—will be recognized for what it is, a somewhat disgusting morbidity, one of those semi-criminal, semi-pathological propensities which one hands over with a shudder to the specialists in mental disease. All kinds of social customs and economic practices, affecting the distribution of wealth and economic rewards and penalties, which we now maintain at all costs, however distasteful and unjust they may be in themselves, because they are tremendously useful in promoting the accumulation of capital, we shall then be free, at last, to discard.[15]

In spite of acknowledging our economic system as a pathological form of life, Keynes holds that we must refrain from recognizing the capitalist measure of wealth for the distorted form of value that it is, since capitalism will be necessary for at least another century in order to bring us to the level of economic wealth that we need. Even though the capitalist way of life according to Keynes himself is a form of mental disease, which makes us participate in activities that are at least semi-criminal and semi-pathological, we have no choice but to obey for the time being, since only capitalism can deliver the goods that will set us free. "For at least another hundred years *we must pretend to ourselves and to every one that fair is foul and foul is fair,*" Keynes writes, "for foul is useful and fair is not. Avarice and usury and precaution must be our gods for a little longer still. For only they can lead us out of the tunnel of economic necessity into daylight" (emphasis added).[16]

Keynes wrote these words in 1930. We will soon have walked in the tunnel of economic necessity for the additional one hundred years that Keynes envisaged would be required to set us free, but capitalism cannot lead us into the daylight. On the contrary, even though our material wealth is greater than ever before it is also more unevenly distributed than ever before and even those who possess astronomical amounts of capital wealth are still seeking to accumulate even more. This is not an accident but a dynamic that is intrinsic to capitalism. The accumulation of ever more capital wealth as an end in itself—with its necessary exploitation of living labor and its recurrent crises due to overproduction—is not a temporary phase of capitalism but its operating principle.

Keynes, by contrast, does not grasp the contradiction in the capitalist mode of production and the pernicious dynamic it entails. "The course of affairs will simply be," he assures us, "that there will be ever larger and larger classes and groups of people from whom problems of economic necessity have been removed."[17] Such a development *could* indeed be possible, but it would require democratic socialism. A continuously increasing collective liberation from the realm of economic necessity is only possible if we measure our social wealth in terms of our *actual capacity* to produce the goods that we need and our *actual capacity* to reduce the socially necessary labor time. Under capitalism, however, the measure of our wealth is *not* our actual capacity to produce goods and reduce socially necessary labor time. We do not produce goods for the sake of practical purposes but for the sake of generating profit. This is why we can have housing crises and homeless families even when we have produced millions of vacant apartments, which are left empty because they cannot be sold for profit. Likewise, under capitalism we do not reduce the socially necessary labor time in order to increase the socially available free time, but in order to extract more relative surplus value from living labor. This is why the reduction of socially necessary labor time under capitalism does not lead to *solutions* regarding economic poverty but generates the *problem* of unemployment.

Keynes himself identifies the problem of "technological unemployment," which he defines as "unemployment due to our discovery of means of economizing the use of labor outrunning the pace at which we can find new uses for labor."[18] For Keynes, however, the problem of technological unemployment is only due to "a temporary phase of maladjustment,"[19] which will eventually lead us to resolve our economic problems. He does not understand that unemployment is a positive feature of the production of capital wealth. A surplus population of the unemployed is essential to the extraction of relative surplus value, for at least three reasons. First, the reduction of socially necessary labor time through technological innovation necessarily leads to unemployment, since fewer workers are required in the process of production. Second, the unemployed have to accept less pay to find a temporary job and thereby allow capitalists to keep down the general level of wages. Third, the surplus population of the unemployed is highly useful for the irregular rhythms of capitalist production, since the unemployed are available for employment when an increase of production is profitable and can be dispensed with when production needs to be decreased for the sake of capital gain.

The dynamic of capitalism, then, is not oriented toward solving the problem of unemployment, but actively benefits from the existence of unemployment. Moreover, under capitalism we cannot transform the negative value of unemployment into the positive value of free time to lead our lives, since our measure of value is labor time. Keynes's claim—that we must endure capitalism because eventually it will set us free—is untenable. The increase of capital wealth cannot liberate more and more of our lives from the realm of economic necessity, since the exploitation of wage labor is the only source of the surplus value that leads to a "growth" of capital wealth.

Hence, the attempt to achieve social justice through the redistribution of capital wealth is inherently contradictory. The more welfare policies and state regulations that prevent the exploitation of living labor, the more restricted are the possibilities of extracting surplus value, and the less "wealth" is available to distribute in the economy. To take a striking example, when health care, education, and other public services are run by the welfare state, they are not sold as commodities that generate a profit that is reinvested as capital, which means that they do not contribute to the "growth" of our social wealth as measured under capitalism. Inversely, when these public services are privatized and commodified—transformed into a matter of buying and selling for profit—they contribute to the growth of capital wealth. This is the economic rationale for the neoliberal dismantling of the welfare state and deregulation of the job market. As long as we accept the capitalist measure of wealth, social democratic reforms will tend to reduce the wealth that they aim to distribute more equally. For the same reason, social democratic policies will be vulnerable to the neoliberal critique that they cause the economy to shrink and eliminate jobs that are vital for those members of society who are most in need and deserve the chance of social mobility. Simply to put the unemployed on welfare is not a viable long-term solution for anyone. This is *not* to say that we should accept neoliberal reforms and deregulations, but that social democratic reforms must be understood as a means toward the end of democratic socialism.

Accordingly, I make an analytical distinction between any form of *social democracy* and the notion of *democratic socialism* that I will elaborate. I do not define these two terms—social democracy and democratic socialism—in direct correspondence with any of their various historical meanings. Social democracy in my sense is not limited to welfare state politics and my notion of democratic socialism is not reducible to any previous visions of socialism. Rather, my analytical definitions are the following. What I call social democracy comprises any form of socialism or Marxism that limits itself to *redistribution* and does not grapple with the fundamental question of value in the mode of production. Democratic socialism, by contrast, requires a fundamental and practical *revaluation* of the capitalist measure of value.

During the twentieth century, social democracy developed into a "soft" form of capitalism, whose crowning achievement was the welfare state. I myself grew up in one of the most successful welfare states (Sweden), which converted the massive economic growth after 1945 into a distribution of wealth across society. While my grandparents were poor peasants in northern Sweden, my parents could ascend to stable middle-class lives thanks to free public education and a booming economy. When I grew up, everyone in Sweden received free health care and free childcare, and all education including university was free. It was the pinnacle of a development that started in the nineteenth century, when workers began to organize politically and gradually improved everything from labor conditions to voting rights and public services. Social democracy, however, restricts itself to transforming the mode of distribution and remains dependent on the capitalist mode of production.

As a consequence, the fate of the welfare state is bound to the fate of the capitalist economy. During a few decades after World War II, it could seem as if social democracy had found a way to tame capitalism and put it to work for the common good. Yet the crisis in the world economy in the 1970s—and the slow compound growth ever since—clearly recalls that capitalism is in control of the welfare state and not the other way around. The welfare state depends on capitalism (since the social democratic welfare system literally lives *off* the wealth generated by wage labor), but capitalism does not depend on the welfare state. Thus, with less wealth to distribute across society because of economic crises, the neoliberal strategies to generate more compound growth—deregulation of the job market, privatization of public services, and so on—won political assent.

The neoliberal reforms we have witnessed over the past decades are no doubt pernicious. The downfall of the welfare state, however, is due not only to neoliberal ideology but also to the general reliance on the generation of capital wealth, which makes the welfare state hostage to economic crises. To criticize neoliberal ideology merely from the standpoint of the welfare state (or some other form of redistributive justice) is to disregard how *both* social democracy *and* neoliberalism are plagued by the contradiction in the capitalist measure of value and its mode of production.

An illuminating example is the current debate regarding universal basic income (UBI). The idea of a UBI is one of the most widely discussed political issues of our time, largely due to the automation of previously necessary labor and the increasing problem of unemployment. The idea of a UBI has supporters both on the neoliberal right and the social democratic left. For the neoliberals, a UBI is a way to ensure that even the unemployed have sufficient purchasing power to participate in the market economy, while enabling the removal of other forms of welfare support from the state. For the social democrats, by contrast, a UBI should be a supplement to the welfare state (rather than its replacement) and it must be generous enough to give workers the power to stand up against their employers, making it possible to leave an alienating, exploitative job without being thrown into poverty.

Accordingly, many influential figures on the Left have advocated a form of UBI that would give every citizen enough money to maintain a reasonable standard of living. Such a basic income would supposedly release us from the indirect form of coercion that characterizes a capitalist labor market, in which those who do not own capital are formally "free" to do what they want but in fact have to labor for a capitalist in order to survive. As the sociologist David Calnitsky argues in the most thoughtful defense of a universal basic income: "The main reason UBI ought to be a part of a Left normative vision is because it facilitates exit from relations of exploitation and domination."[20] A sufficiently generous UBI gives people not only abstract freedom from direct coercion but also "the material resources to make freedom a lived reality. It gives people the power to say no— to abusive employers, unpleasant work, or patriarchal domination in the home."[21] For example, as part of a very interesting empirical study, Calnitsky shows that a three-year experiment with guaranteed annual income in Canada helped to decrease domestic violence, since it reduced the material dependence of women on their abusive partners and facilitated an exit from destructive relationships. More generally, a UBI "changes the background conditions under which negotiation takes place, both at work and at home,"[22] since "if a stable flow of cash gives you the power to threaten to leave a marriage or a job—that is, if your threat of exit has real credibility—you are in a better position to speak your mind."[23]

A universal basic income can thus have emancipatory effects. Yet it is seriously misleading to describe UBI—as Calnitsky and many others do—as a potential solution to the problem of wage labor that Marx analyzed. Calnitsky rightly underscores that "socialism lost something in the reorientation from a vision defined by the abolition of the wage relation to one that fastens us all to it."[24] Moreover, he avows the normative goal of abolishing wage labor, since "the objective is to free workers not only from a given capitalist, but also from capitalists as a class."[25] Calnitsky fails to grasp, however, that a UBI *cannot even in principle overcome the dependence on wage labor.* On the contrary, any form of universal basic income is altogether dependent on the social form of wage labor, since any form of UBI consists in a redistribution of the capital wealth that is generated by wage labor. Under capitalism, wage labor in the service of profit is the necessary source of social wealth. This dependence on wage labor is perpetuated rather than overcome by a UBI. Calnitsky himself observes that wage labor is required to finance a universal basic income, but he ignores that this contradicts his claim that a UBI can liberate us from the dependence on capitalists as a class. No form of universal basic income can free us from capitalist exploitation, since only wage labor in the service of profit can generate the wealth that is distributed in the form of a UBI.

The basic problem here is not limited to Calnitsky's analysis but symptomatic of the limitations of any social democratic politics. The emancipatory vision is restricted to the redistribution of wealth, while blind to the fundamental question of how wealth is produced under capitalism. Advocates of a universal basic income (or other forms of redistributive justice) never question the *measure* and *production* of value under capitalism but focus only on the *distribution* of wealth across society. For the same reason, they cannot grasp the contradiction in which any progressive reform of capitalism will be caught, whether it seeks to strengthen the welfare state, provide a universal basic income, or combine the two. "We ought to be able to afford," Calnitsky asserts, "both a basic income *and* high quality public goods."[26] Given the capitalist measure of value, however, such a program will always be trapped in a contradiction that makes it liable to degenerate and dissolve. The less our lives are exploited for the sake of profit—i.e., the more we devote our lives to the public goods of the welfare state or to non-profit projects supported by a UBI— the less wealth there is to finance the welfare state and the universal basic income. This practical contradiction in the redistribution of wealth is unavoidable under capitalism, since the measure of value is socially necessary labor time rather than socially available free time. The more we emancipate ourselves from the exploitation of living labor time, the less wealth we have to support our state of freedom.

III

To understand the consequences of the capitalist measure of value for the possibility of democracy, it is instructive to turn to Thomas Piketty's widely celebrated study *Capital in the Twenty-First Century*. Piketty's argument is a paradigmatic example of a social democratic critique of neoliberal capitalism, which is centered on redistribution and does not recognize the question of revaluation. Piketty's goal is not the overcoming of capitalism, but rather a reformed and regulated capitalist system that limits inequality of wealth.

Piketty's most important contention is that "free market" capitalism—if left to its own devices—does *not* promote the distribution of wealth and does *not* protect individual liberties. Through the deployment of innovative statistical techniques that track the relation between wealth and income over long historical periods, Piketty shows that capitalism exhibits a tendency toward the concentration of wealth in the hands of the few rather than the many. The dynamic of capitalist wealth accumulation leads to the formation of family dynasties and oligarchies with the resources to manipulate politics for their own interests rather than the interests of the majority, a dynamic that Piketty rightly describes as "threatening to democratic societies and to the values of social justice on which they are based."[27]

According to Piketty, the mechanism that accounts for why capitalism tends toward a growing inequality of wealth is captured by the formula $r>g$. The rate of return on capital (r) grows faster—or falls slower—than the growth rate (g) of the economy as a whole. Thus, the dynamic of capitalism favors the accumulation of existing wealth over the wealth that is based on income. The growth of inherited and accumulated wealth outruns the growth of income, leading to what Piketty calls a "terrifying"[28] spiral of unequal wealth distribution between those who own capital and those who must subject themselves to wage labor in order to survive.

Nevertheless, Piketty holds that democracy in principle can "regain control of capitalism"[29] through reforms such as increased taxes and job creation by the state. In contrast to those who promote neoliberal deregulation of the market, Piketty advocates a social democratic welfare state that would offer universal health insurance and universal education (including higher education), while restricting inequality and redistributing wealth through a progressive annual tax on global capital.

Piketty's proposed solution to the problem of wealth inequality has often been described as unrealistic in pragmatic terms, but the deeper problem with his analysis is that he does not display any systematic understanding of the structural dynamic of capitalism. For Piketty—as for the advocates of a UBI—the problem of capitalism merely concerns the *distribution* of wealth, whereas the *production* and *measure* of wealth under capitalism are never interrogated. Indeed, Piketty explicitly dismisses Marx's analyses of the inherent contradiction in the capitalist mode of production, while it is clear that he does not understand the logic of Marx's argument. According to Piketty, "Marx totally neglected the possibility of durable technological progress and steadily increasing productivity, which is a force that can to some extent serve as a counterweight to the process of accumulation and concentration of private capital. He no doubt lacked the statistical data to refine his predictions."[30] This is a very misleading claim. Technological progress and increasing productivity are *at the core of* Marx's analysis of the dynamic that drives the process of accumulation and concentration of capital. Furthermore, Marx is not collecting statistical data to make "predictions" about how capitalism functions. Marx analyzes the inner purposiveness of capitalism (producing for the sake of profit rather than consumption) and explicates the constitutive tendencies of such a dynamic.

If Piketty had grasped the logic of Marx's analysis, he would have had the resources to render intelligible the meaning of his own data. While Piketty shows statistically that capital has a tendency to become concentrated in fewer hands, he does not understand the dynamic that accounts for this tendency and its relation to technological productivity, since he ignores the specificity of the capitalist mode of production and treats the measure of social wealth under capitalism as though it were a natural necessity. As a result, Piketty ignores how both unemployment and the tendency toward crises are necessary features of the production of capital wealth. Economic crises cannot be avoided either through regulations of the market (social democracy) or deregulations of the market (neoliberalism), since the tendency toward crises is inherent in the capitalist mode of production itself.

To understand the inherent tendency toward crises in the capitalist mode of production, we must turn to Marx's analysis of "the law of the tendential fall in the rate of profit," which he pursues in the third volume of *Capital*.[31] Marx's analysis of the tendency of the rate of profit to fall is one of his most famous, but also one of his most widely misunderstood. Contrary to what Piketty and many others allege, Marx is *not* offering a prophecy that the rate of profit will fall irreversibly and lead to the self-destruction of capitalism. While such an apocalyptic vision of the fate of capitalism is often ascribed to Marx, it is incompatible with his actual analysis. Marx is not making any empirical predictions. Rather, he is analyzing the "moving contradiction" in the capitalist mode of production. Because the contradiction is dynamic and moving, there can be any number of "counteracting" strategies that manage to sustain the continued life of a capitalist system. The point is *not* to establish that capitalism inevitably will kill itself, but to show that capitalism can keep itself alive only through a pernicious and self-contradictory dynamic, which is inimical to the production of real social wealth.

Let us here return to the example of our village and its water supply, in order to understand why the capitalist mode of production entails that the rate of profit has an inherent tendency to fall. The rate of profit is the relation between *the total amount* of capital I invest in the production of a commodity—e.g., the sum total of the cost of wages, machinery, and raw materials that are required for the production of a gallon of water—and *the amount of surplus value* I am able to extract from the production of the commodity.

Striving to make the rate of profit *rise* is intrinsic to any capitalist enterprise. In order to sustain my water business, I have to keep making a profit from the production and distribution of water. Such profit depends on converting the surplus time of living labor into surplus value for my capitalist enterprise. Given the limits of the workday and legal constraints on labor conditions, however, there are restrictions on how much I can exploit the lifetime of my workers. The major method for making my business profitable and staying competitive is rather to extract relative surplus value from my workers by making the technological means of production more efficient. This is why I built a hyper-well in the middle of our village when I sought to increase the rate of profit for my water business. The hyper-well makes it possible for my workers to produce more water in the same amount of time and thereby increases the relative surplus value I can extract from their labor.

Striving to make the rate of profit rise is thus inseparable from pursuing a technological development that reduces the socially necessary labor time for a given commodity. If I seek to make the production of a commodity more profitable, I seek to make the production of the commodity more efficient, which is to say *less time consuming.*

By the same token, however, I am caught in the contradiction that characterizes the capitalist mode of production. As a capitalist, I can extract surplus value only from living labor time. Yet, in seeking to extract more surplus value from my workers, I am led to develop technologies that increasingly replace *living labor time* (from which I can extract surplus value) with *nonliving production time* (from which I cannot extract any surplus value).

As a result of such technological development, the rate of profit for my water business has an inherent tendency to fall. When my production of water becomes more efficient, there is a shift in what Marx calls "the organic composition of capital."[32] The ratio of living labor time (from which I can make a profit) decreases, while the ratio of nonliving production time (from which I cannot make a profit) increases. Thus, even if the *mass* of surplus value and profit increases due to the efficiency of the hyper-well as a means of production, the *rate* of profit for my water business will tend to fall for the same reason.

Hence, we can specify the dynamic of the contradiction in the capitalist mode of production. On the one hand, in striving to make a profit, I develop ever more efficient technological means of production. On the other hand, the more efficient my technological means of production become, the more my rate of profit tends to fall.

To sustain a rate of profit, the capitalist mode of production must inhibit its own drive toward increased technological productivity. If the proportion of nonliving production time is allowed to increase indefinitely, the proportion of living labor time will decrease indefinitely and the possibility of making a profit will diminish. When I have perfected my hyper-well to such a degree that it barely requires any living labor time to operate, I am left with almost nothing from which I can extract surplus value in order to make a profit.

The law of the tendential fall in the rate of profit is *not* a prediction but a *structural dynamic* that renders intelligible the counteracting tendencies under capitalism. It is because the rate of profit tends to fall that capitalist employers must intensify the exploitation of living labor and/or export the production facilities to locations where labor is cheaper to buy. Given the reduction of socially necessary labor time, the only way to increase the extraction of relative surplus value—on which profit depends—is to intensify the exploitation of workers by lowering the relative value of their wages. Unemployment and the exportation of jobs are not something that can be removed under capitalism, but a necessary condition for the production of capital wealth. Lowering the relative value of wages and sustaining a rate of profit depends on a surplus population of the unemployed who are willing to work for less, either domestically or in poorer countries to which production is moved.

Most importantly, the law of the tendential fall in the rate of profit renders intelligible the tendency toward crises under capitalism. A continuously increasing technological productivity leads to crises under capitalism, since the replacement of living labor time with nonliving production time makes the rate of profit fall. The falling rate of profit can be counteracted through numerous strategies, but ultimately it requires the destruction of large amounts of capital, either through crises of devaluation or through full-on destruction of existing capital in war or through other means. Only such a "bust" in the economy can lead to a new "boom." When large amounts of machinery and other forms of productive capital are destroyed, the capacity for nonliving production decreases while the need for living labor increases. This is why the destruction of war can lead to a boom in capitalist economies. The destruction removes large parts of nonliving production capacities and the process of rebuilding requires large amounts of living labor time, from which we can extract surplus value that is converted into the "growth" of capital wealth in the economy.

Hence, it is a grave mistake to think that the tendency toward crises heralds the end of capitalism. Crises are essential to cycles of capitalist accumulation and necessary for the continued production of capital wealth. For the rate of profit to rise again, the ratio of living labor time must increase relative to nonliving production time, which requires the devaluation or destruction of productive capital. Far from being a threat to capitalism, such crises are a condition of possibility for capitalism as a system to reproduce itself. Individual capitalists (and entire capitalist societies) can of course be vanquished in a crisis, but all that is needed for capitalism as a system to be maintained is that a new cycle of growth can begin again.

Nevertheless, many avowed Marxists continue to hinge their critique of capitalism on the prediction of a "terminal crisis." Such a critique of capitalism is deeply misguided. The problem with capitalism is not that it will collapse, but that it can sustain itself only through a self-contradictory dynamic that has pernicious social consequences. Given the capitalist measure of social wealth, the free time we gain thanks to technological efficiency cannot be recognized as a value in itself. Increased technological productivity *could* give everyone more free time to lead their lives, *if* we pursued technological innovation for the sake of emancipation rather than for the sake of profit. As long as we produce for the sake of profit, however, the reduction of socially necessary labor time through technological innovation is caught in a vicious contradiction. We cannot pursue the reduction of socially necessary labor time as an end in itself, but only as a means for extracting surplus value from workers, which leads to unemployment, exploitation, and crises rather than emancipation.

A rigorous critique of capitalism should not prophesy an apocalyptic end of the system. Rather, a rigorous critique should articulate why the measure of value under capitalism is self-contradictory and requires a collective revaluation of value. The revaluation of value can be achieved only through a political transformation of the economy, which would allow us to recognize socially available free time as an end in itself. Such a transformation of the economy is at the center of what I am calling democratic socialism.

IV

To elaborate the stakes of democratic socialism, it is helpful to engage the most powerful and philosophically sophisticated critic of socialism: the Austrian economist and philosopher Friedrich Hayek. Hayek received the Nobel Memorial Prize in Economic Sciences in 1974 and he was the leading figure in the formation of the so-called Chicago School, which has strongly shaped the reigning neoliberal ideas of the virtues of "the free market."

Hayek's critique of socialism hinges on the assumption that all forms of socialism require a form of central planning that is structured in a top-down, undemocratic fashion. As Hayek points out, "most planners who have seriously considered the practical aspects of their task have little doubt that a directed economy must be run on more or less dictatorial lines," since "the complex system of inter-related activities, if it is to be consciously directed at all, must be directed by a single staff of experts," where "ultimate responsibility and power must rest in the hands of a commander-in-chief whose actions must not be fettered by democratic procedure."[33] Socialism would then require a separation between political democracy and economic life. A central planning authority would dictate the form of our economic life, whereas we would be free to lead our lives in other respects. "Such assurances," Hayek writes, "are usually accompanied by the suggestion that, by giving up freedom in what are, or ought to be, the less important aspects of our lives, we shall obtain greater freedom in the pursuit of higher values. On this ground people who abhor the idea of a political dictatorship often clamor for a dictator in the economic field."[34]

In contrast, Hayek pursues an important argument regarding the inseparability of economic, political, and existential freedom. As Hayek rightly emphasizes, it is a mistake to believe that "there are purely economic ends separate from the other ends of life."[35] Rather, there is a constitutive "economic problem" at the heart of freedom, since "all our ends compete for the same means"[36] and we have to decide which ends to prioritize in light of our limited means. This is why the question of who controls the economy is of such vital importance. "Economic control is not merely control of a section of human life which can be separated from the rest; it is the control of the means for all our ends."[37] Accordingly, "whoever has sole control of the means must also determine which ends are to be served, which values are to be rated higher and which lower—in short, what men should believe and strive for."[38]

Hayek here comes close to seeing the intrinsic link between eco-nomic life and spiritual freedom, which I have developed in depth through my reading of Marx. Nevertheless, Hayek falls short of his own potential insight, since he still conceives of economic organiza-tion in strictly instrumental terms—as a mere *means* for the pursuit of individual ends. Questions of economic organization, however, are not reducible to the means with which we pursue our ends. Rather, how we organize the economy of our lives is itself an expression of how we posit the relation between means and ends. Economical questions are at the heart of any form of spiritual life, since they concern our *order of priorities*. How we organize the economy of our lives is ultimately a matter of how we understand the *value* of different activities and what we take to be *worth* doing with our time. Our economical self-organization shapes not only our means but also our ends.

The way we organize and plan our economy is thus formative for all aspects of our lives. As Hayek himself recognizes, economic planning is constitutive of any economy. Hayek defines economic planning as "the complex interrelated decisions about the allocation of our available resources"[39] and he emphasizes that "all economic activity is in this sense planning."[40] There has to be some form of planning for any economy to be operative, so the question is not *if* there will be planning but rather *who* is to do the planning. "This is not a dispute about whether planning is to be done or not," Hayek maintains, "it is a dispute as to whether planning is to be done centrally, by one authority for the whole economic system, or is to be divided among many individuals."[41]

The crucial question for any form of economic planning is the relation between part and whole. Central planning misconstrues the relation between whole and part as a top-down relation, since it seeks to impose a "direction of the whole economic system according to one unified plan."[42] Thereby, central planning is bound to be out of sync with the needs and demands of individual parts of the economy. What is required is rather a form of economic planning that allows for "the utilization of knowledge which is not given to anyone in its totality."[43] All the variables of economic planning can never be given either to an individual agent or a central planning authority, since the economy essentially depends on forms of practical activity that cannot be predicted in advance. Economic planning must be receptive to a form of practical knowledge that is not reducible to a set of general rules or given statistical data—namely, "the knowledge of the particular circumstances of time and place."[44] As Hayek puts it, every individual possesses "unique information of which beneficial use might be made only if the decisions depending on it are left to him or are made with his active cooperation."[45]

Hayek thus conceives of the relation between part and whole as a technical problem of coordinating individual needs and desires (the demand of buyers) with the available resources (the supply of sellers). He locates the solution to the problem in the price system, since the price of a commodity reflects the relation between supply and demand. In a free market, the price of a commodity supposedly communicates the level of scarcity (to the buyer) and the level of demand (to the seller). The price system would then hold the key to "a rational economic order," since it would allow for the right form of practical knowledge and relevant information to be transmitted among the different members of the economy, in a reciprocal determination between supply and demand. For Hayek, the ideal relation between part and whole is achieved by "the spontaneously formed order of the market,"[46] which gives rise to a "more efficient allocation of resources than any design could achieve."[47]

The problem with Hayek's analysis, however, is that he never asks himself how value is produced in a capitalist market economy. Like other liberal thinkers, he treats the capitalist market economy as the optimal instrument for the *distribution* of wealth, rather than as a unique social form for the *production* of wealth. Hayek is certainly right that one of the central issues for a rational economic order should be "how to secure the best use of resources known to any of the members of society, for ends whose relative importance only these individuals know."[48] Hayek fails to see, however, that a capitalist market economy cannot be a rational economic order. As an individual capitalist, I am not concerned with the best use of available resources but with the most efficient way to make a profit. Moreover, as a capitalist society, we are not collectively committed to producing for the sake of consumption. Rather, we are committed to producing for the sake of extracting surplus value that can be converted into the growth of capital.

For the same reason, the capitalist price system cannot function as a neutral medium for relaying information regarding actual relations of scarcity and need, supply and demand. The "marvel" of the price system, according to Hayek, is that it provides "a mechanism for communicating information"[49] in a way that "will make the individuals do the desirable things without anyone having to tell them what to do."[50] In Hayek's account, the price system enables real relations of scarcity and need to be communicated across society, so that "without an order being issued, without more than perhaps a handful of people knowing the cause, tens of thousands of people whose identity could not be ascertained by months of investigation, are made to use the material or its products more sparingly."[51] Yet it is precisely these features of the price system that make it such an effective tool for manipulating both supply and demand under capitalism. As a capitalist, I do not price my commodities in an attempt to "communicate" how efficiently I actually can produce the commodity in question. If it is more profitable to restrain my production capacities and create an artificial scarcity, I will do that instead. Likewise, as a capitalist, I am not trying to obtain the right kind of "information" about the actual needs of the population, so that my supply can meet the relevant demands. My aim is rather to manipulate both supply and demand for the sake of maximal gain, regardless of the social consequences.

The manipulation of supply and demand for the sake of profit is not a moral failure of individual capitalists, but an effect of the principle of production to which we are collectively committed in sustaining capitalism. To be committed to capitalism is to hold that the purpose of production ought to be profit rather than consumption. Hence, it is no accident that supply and demand come apart under capitalism—both through the *overproduction* of commodities we do not need or cannot afford and the *underproduction* of goods we do need but cannot purchase. These divergences follow from a principle of production that privileges the accumulation of profit over the satisfaction of needs and the provision of resources for spiritual development.

The critique that Hayek levels against central planning can thus also be leveled against the capitalist free market that he himself defends. "The control of the production of wealth," Hayek maintains, "is the control of human life itself."[52] This is why Hayek takes issue with any form of undemocratic central planning, which would deprive us of our economic freedom to decide "what is more, and what is less, important for us."[53] Such economic freedom cannot be separated from our political and existential freedom. As Hayek rightly emphasizes, it is a mistake to think that something which "affects only our economic interests cannot seriously interfere with the more basic values of life."[54] On the contrary, the loss of our economic freedom "would not affect merely those of our marginal needs that we have in mind when we speak contemptuously about the merely economic. It would, in effect, mean that we as individuals should no longer be allowed to decide what we regard as marginal."[55]

Nevertheless, Hayek ignores the undemocratic control of the production of wealth under capitalism. Far from safeguarding our economic freedom, capitalism deprives us of the ability to decide our economic priorities and democratically deliberate on the form of our economic life. The priority of our economy is already determined for us—to labor for the sake of profit—since it is built into the capitalist definition of social wealth.

Hayek cannot see the problem in question, since he reduces *freedom* to *liberty*.[56] As long as we are not directly coerced to act in one way rather than another—i.e., as long as we have formal liberty—we are free in the relevant sense for Hayek. For the same reason, Hayek in effect reduces *decision* to *choice*. As long as we can make a choice without anyone forcing us or telling us what to do, we are free.

Such a formal conception of freedom, however, is utterly impoverished. To lead a free life it is not sufficient that we are exempt from direct coercion and allowed to make choices. To lead a free life we must be able *to recognize ourselves in what we do,* to see our practical activities as expressions of our own commitments. This requires that we are able to engage not only in *choices* but also in fundamental *decisions* regarding the purposes that determine our range of choices

and for the sake of which we lead our lives. Freedom requires the
ability to participate in decisions regarding the form of life we are
leading and not just the liberty to make choices. Moreover, since all
forms of choices and decisions are social, we must be able to recognize the commitment to our freedom in the institutional forms of
life in which we participate. This is why capitalism is an inherently
alienating social institution. To lead our lives *for the sake of* profit is
self-contradictory and alienating, since the purpose of profit treats
our lives as means rather than as ends in themselves.

Under capitalism we are all in practice committed to a purpose
in which we cannot recognize ourselves, which inevitably leads to
alienated forms of social life. The actual needs and abilities we have
are secondary; what matters first of all is whether capitalists can
profit from our needs and exploit our abilities in wage labor. The
market decides which abilities we should harness, while our needs
are transformed in view of what we can buy. Many of the abilities
that we could develop—if we had the time to lead our lives—are
discarded because they are not deemed to be profitable, and many
needs are engineered to make us purchase more commodities rather
than to provide satisfaction.

To be clear, my point is *not* that we have a pristine set of needs and
abilities that should be sheltered from social transformation. On the
contrary, who we are—i.e., what we do and what we value—is from
the beginning a matter of our social praxis and any form of progress requires that we change our practices for the better. The point,
however, is that the sustenance or transformation of our practices
should be determined by our democratic participation rather than
be dictated to us by the dynamic of capital. We should be the *subjects of* what we do and what we value, rather than being *subjected to*
what we supposedly need to do and what we supposedly value. How
such a revolution of our lives is possible—and what it requires of
us—is specified by the principles of democratic socialism that I will
articulate.

The challenge of democratic socialism is to develop forms of participating in and contributing to our shared economic life, without

relying on either undemocratic central planning or the capitalist purpose of profit. To grasp the status of the principles involved, it is important to distinguish the general from the abstract and the concrete from the particular. The principles of democratic socialism do not appeal to an *abstract* utopia that will resolve our economic questions once and for all. Rather, they specify the *general* principles in light of which any democracy must form and maintain itself in order to be democratic. Likewise, the principles do not impose a *particular* blueprint for how to organize our economy. Rather, they specify the *concrete* transformations of the economy that must be enabled rather than disabled by any democratic state and any democratic institution.

The general and concrete principles of democratic socialism cannot be posited as an ideal that is *external* to our historical form of life, since in that case they would have no claim on us. The principles must be *internally* derived from the Idea of freedom through which we already seek to justify liberal democracy and capitalism. As I have emphasized throughout, the critique of liberalism and capitalism must be an immanent critique, which locates the resources for emancipation within the commitments we already avow. The assumed justification of liberal democracy is that it should allow each one of us to lead a free life, and the assumed justification of capitalism is that it should progressively increase our social wealth. The capitalist measure of value, however, contradicts and betrays these promises of emancipation. To make it possible for us to lead *actual* free lives and progressively increase our actual social wealth, we must pursue a practical revaluation of the measure of value that shapes our economy and our material production. The principles of such revaluation are the principles of democratic socialism.

V

The first principle of democratic socialism is that we measure our wealth—both individual and collective—in terms of socially available free time. Our free time depends on social and institutional forms because it does not concern a mere *quantity* of time. Rather, our quantity of free time is inseparable from the *quality* of our free time, which requires institutions that allow us to shape, cultivate, and transform the commitments in light of which we lead our lives. For the same reason, free time is not necessarily leisure time but any time we devote to activities that for us count as ends in themselves. For example, the time I devote to writing this book counts as free time, since having time to think through and articulate fundamental philosophical ideas is an end in itself for me. To pursue philosophical ideas and write books is not something I can do on my own, however, since the activity requires institutional forms that render intelligible what I am doing (both to myself and to others). The realm of freedom—our socially available free time—thus depends on our institutional forms of life and on how we maintain or change those institutions. Our social institutions are not necessarily explicit but always implicit in what we do and in all forms of practical identities (e.g., being a philosopher or being a parent). All the activities we regard as essential parts of a practical identity—as essential parts of a vocation with which we identify—belong to the realm of freedom, and the time we devote to them counts as free time. Even activities that may seem to be means rather than ends—e.g., going through a demanding education—belong to the realm of freedom insofar as the education is an essential part of what it means to be committed to the vocation. Likewise, many tasks that may seem to be mere practical necessities—e.g., changing diapers on our children—belong to the realm of freedom insofar as such childcare is recognized as an essential part of the practical identity of being a parent.

We must here carefully distinguish between practical identities and mere social roles. All practical identities (e.g., parent, philosopher, political activist) are social roles, but not all social roles we take on count as practical identities for us. Only the social roles with which we identify as ends in themselves are practical identities for us, whereas other social roles merely serve as means to an end. To be clear, even a mere social role has normative criteria that we can seek to fulfill or transform in light of an end to which we are committed, as when we participate in sanitation work for the sake of the common good. However, to the extent that sanitation work is understood as a means to an end—rather than as an end in itself—we are also committed to reducing the socially necessary labor time it requires.

To grasp the relation between the realm of freedom and the realm of necessity, the distinction between practical identities and mere social roles is crucial. The realm of freedom is defined by our practical identities—and their internal relations of priority in the form of our respective existential identities—which are expressed by the activities we pursue for their own sake. To expand the realm of freedom, we must increase the quantity and improve the quality of our socially available free time (the time available to pursue, question, and transform our practical identities). The realm of necessity, by contrast, is defined by the mere social roles we have to fulfill to meet the needs of our society at the current stage of its development. To reduce the realm of necessity, we must therefore decrease the quantity and improve the quality of our socially necessary labor time (the time required to meet our needs).

In light of the first principle of democratic socialism—the measure of our wealth in terms of socially available free time—we are committed to reducing our socially necessary labor time through technological innovation. For example, the living labor time required for street cleaning can be dramatically reduced by a machine that only requires the push of a button to operate. Even if the machine is not more efficient than a human being but requires the same amount of time to clean the street (say thirty minutes), a clean street now contains only one minute of socially necessary labor time (to get the machine started) and twenty-nine minutes of nonliving production time through which no one is exploited. If someone enjoys cleaning a street as an end in itself, he or she is of course free to do so, but the labor is no longer socially necessary. Moreover, since we have overcome the capitalist measure of value, the reduction of socially necessary labor time is directly converted into socially available free time, which we can use to engage the question of what we should do with our lives and pursue the activities that matter to us. The more time we can spend on what we count as ends in themselves—and the less time we have to spend on what we count as socially necessary labor—the wealthier we are as individuals and the better off we are as a society.

To be sure, what should count as belonging to the realm of necessity (socially necessary labor time) and what should count as belonging to the realm of freedom (socially available free time) is not given and demands an ongoing democratic conversation. The point, however, is that we are in a position to pursue such a conversation only if our measure of wealth reflects a commitment to socially available free time (democratic socialism) rather than a commitment to exploiting socially necessary labor time (capitalism). Only the revaluation of value can allow us to own our collective commitment to increasing the realm of freedom and decreasing the realm of necessity. The first principle of democratic socialism is therefore required for us to build and maintain a free society.

The second principle of democratic socialism is that the means of production are collectively owned and cannot be used for the sake of profit. The second principle is entailed by the first, since collective ownership of the means of production is the material condition of possibility for recognizing socially available free time as the measure of our wealth. As long as the means of production are privately owned and used for the sake of profit, the measure of our wealth is the amount of surplus value derived from the exploitation of living labor. Efficient technologies of nonliving production cannot generate any value for us by virtue of their own operations. Only if we produce for the sake of socially available free time can we acknowledge the value generated by operations of nonliving technology. This practical revaluation requires collective ownership of the means of production. Because we own the means of production collectively, we can engineer technologies with the aim of generating as much surplus time as possible for everyone. We are not forced to convert surplus time into the surplus value of capital, but can freely pursue the reduction of the need for living labor in the process of production. Increased efficiency of production is not a problem that we have to try to "solve" by finding new ways of exploiting surplus labor. Rather, increased efficiency of production is an opportunity to liberate more time for all members of society to lead their individual lives.

Collective ownership of the means of production does *not* mean that we are prevented from having private property in a concrete sense. We can have our own houses, our own computers, our own books, and so on, in the sense that we can use them for our own ends and no one has the right to take them away from us against our will. While we can have private property in a concrete sense, however, we cannot have private property in the abstract sense that transforms property into a commodity that can be bought and sold for profit. The recognition of your property *as* your property is not based on your right to its abstract value as a commodity (or as a means for producing commodities), but on your right to its concrete specificity as valuable *to* you and as useful for you in leading *your* life.

For the same reason, collective ownership of the means of production does not commit us to a top-down model of central planning. On the contrary, collective ownership of the means of production is a necessary condition for the reciprocal determination of part and whole in the economy, which Hayek mistakenly thinks can be achieved under free-market capitalism. An instructive example is Internet service. Under democratic socialism, everyone would have Internet access at the maximal speed enabled by our currently available technology, with a collective commitment to create technology that makes Internet access even faster and possible to maintain with even less socially necessary labor. While our democratic state provides the Internet service, the actual use and applications of the Internet are not restricted by the dictates of a central planning committee. Rather, we have both the material resources and the socially available free time to develop applications that resolve problems which emerge in "the particular circumstances of time and place"—to recall Hayek's language—allowing for "the utilization of knowledge which is not given to anyone in its totality" and drawing on "unique information of which beneficial use might be made only if the decisions depending on it are left to [the individual] or are made with his active cooperation."

Such concrete utilization of knowledge is facilitated under democratic socialism, since the incentive to create or distribute an application is not to make a profit. Rather, the recognition of a problem *as* a problem and a need *as* a need are themselves the incentive to provide an application that can resolve a problem and satisfy a need. Moreover, since technological applications are not proprietary under democratic socialism, they are taken up and become socially general to the extent that they prove helpful beyond the contexts in which they emerged, thus demonstrating their social worth by virtue of their concrete use value rather than their abstract exchange value.

In a capitalist free market, by contrast, Internet service will always be provided by regional monopolies that operate for profit. Contrary to what Hayek assumes, monopolies tend to form naturally in a free market, since private ownership of the required technological infrastructure makes it harder and harder to compete with the company that has built the dominant network. Given the profit motive, a company has no inherent interest in offering us general Internet access at the maximal speed possible. Slower and partial access will be preferred if that is more profitable. Likewise, given the profit motive, the development of technological applications is not primarily guided by the attempt to resolve actual problems and satisfy actual needs. The capitalist mode of production is conducive neither to the efficient allocation of our available resources nor to the progressive development of our technological possibilities. Only by removing the profit motive can we have a reciprocal determination of our evolving resources (the whole) and our evolving demands (the part).

Collective ownership of the means of production, then, does not mean that we are subjected to an undemocratic control of our economic life. Collective ownership of the means of production is rather the material condition of possibility for actual economic democracy. Because we own the means of production collectively, we can decide through democratic processes how and what we produce, based on which abilities we seek to cultivate and which needs we have to satisfy.

Such a collective determination of which abilities we cultivate and which needs we satisfy is already at work under capitalism. The difference, however, is that under capitalism the process of collective self-determination is profoundly *undemocratic*. The purpose of our collective social production is already decided: to generate profit for corporations and a "growth" of capital in the economy, despite the exploitation, unemployment, and crises of overproduction that follow from such an alienated conception of value. Given that the value in question is not the value of our time and our lives but the value of accumulated profit, we cannot see ourselves in the social whole of which we are a part. Rather, we come to see ourselves as essentially self-interested, atomically constituted individuals, who have no inherent motivation to care for the common good.

Under democratic socialism, by contrast, our technological innovations, our political debates, our evolving legislation, and our elections can actually be concerned with the purposes of our economic life and the collectively held values that we seek to sustain. How to define our ends and how to achieve them are the political questions that can be continually engaged under democratic socialism. Because we own the means of production collectively we can develop these means—technology in a broad sense—with the aim of *both* producing the goods that we take ourselves to need *and* increasing the amount of socially available free time for everyone to explore their abilities.

Hence, the third principle of democratic socialism is the one formulated by Marx: "From each according to his ability, to each according to his needs."[57] Marx does not develop the meaning of the principle, but in light of the first two principles of democratic socialism we can elaborate the implications. The aim of democratic socialism is to allow us not only to *live* our lives by satisfying our needs but also to *lead* our lives by cultivating our abilities. We are collectively committed to producing the necessary means of subsistence, as well as the means and institutions for each one to pursue the activities that matter to him or her (painting, writing, music, athletics, theater, and so on).

The key feature here is that democratic socialism enables us to live our lives in the realm of necessity *in light of* the way we lead our lives in the realm of freedom. The realm of necessity and the realm of freedom cannot be *separated*, but everything hinges on *distinguishing* between them in the right way. In the realm of necessity, we have to produce the social goods that are required to satisfy our needs: water, food, clothes, houses, and so on. Thus, in the realm of necessity, we are primarily concerned with the *quantity* of labor time that is socially necessary to sustain our lives. Under democratic socialism, we are committed to *sharing* the socially necessary labor time, but also to *reducing* it as much as possible through technological innovation.

Based on our different abilities, we participate in the social labor that we recognize as necessary for the common good (food production, construction, health care, childcare, education, science, political deliberation, and so on). Yet under democratic socialism no one is *forced* to participate in social labor, since each one is provided for in accordance with his or her needs just by virtue of being part of society. The idea, however, is that we will be intrinsically motivated to participate in social labor when we can recognize that the social production is *for the sake of* the common good and our own freedom to lead a life. Capitalist wage labor is inherently alienating, since we are not part of deciding the purpose of what we are producing and our work is conceived for the sake of a profit that is posited as an end in itself rather than as a means to our freedom. Democratic social labor, by contrast, is inherently free, since we are working on the basis of our commitment to leading a life and for the sake of a form of life that we can recognize as committed to our freedom. Even tedious work we do in the realm of necessity—e.g., participating in the garbage removal in our neighborhood on a weekly basis—can be seen in light of the realm of freedom, since the work is geared toward reducing socially necessary labor time and increasing socially available free time. Unlike under capitalism, we can *make sense* of why we are doing what we are doing, through education and democratic deliberation regarding the form of life we are sustaining.

Those who object that we will not be motivated to work unless we have to secure our survival—or have the chance to make a monetary profit—should consider their lack of faith in our spiritual freedom. Their argument assumes that we need to be commanded by a single *ought* of survival or profit in order to work and cannot be allowed to engage the *double ought* of our spiritual freedom. A single *ought* of survival or profit alienates us from our spiritual freedom, since it commands us to work on the basis of a perceived necessity rather than in light of a responsibility to which we have bound ourselves. Only if we are granted the material, social, and institutional resources to exercise our spiritual freedom can we actually identify with what we are doing as *our own activity*. To make an activity or an identity our own, it cannot be imposed as a necessity. We must be free to ask ourselves if we ought to do what we do and if we ought to be who we take ourselves to be. This requires the resources that allow us to work for the sake of something other than our own survival and the free time that allows us to adopt a different purpose than profit. In short: we must be able to see how the way we *lead* our lives in the realm of freedom determines how we *live* our lives in the realm of necessity.

We can thus further specify how to understand the relation between the realm of necessity and the realm of freedom under democratic socialism. In the realm of freedom, we have socially available free time to engage the question of who we are, which cannot be answered once and for all. Who we are is inseparable from the practical identities we sustain and their order of priority in our life (our existential identity). In the realm of necessity, by contrast, we share the socially necessary labor time that is required to sustain the material life that is inseparable from our spiritual life and the material conditions that are inseparable from our spiritual activities. Because we are fragile, embodied beings, we need shelter, nourishment, and health care not only to survive but also to maintain our spiritual commitments. Likewise, we need tools and various forms of infrastructure to pursue our spiritual projects. The strength of our bodies is finite and needs to be regenerated, while our tools and our infrastructures are worn down by use and have to be replaced or repaired. All these necessary material conditions cost labor time to sustain. How much labor time they cost, however, is a matter of our technological development and the way we organize our labor.

Under democratic socialism, we have three ways of reducing and qualitatively transforming socially necessary labor time.

First, large parts of our socially necessary labor can be done in the realm of freedom, insofar as it is performed by persons who are committed to the occupation as an end in itself and thus take up the required social role as a practical identity in light of which they lead their lives. For example, architecture is a socially necessary form of labor, since we cannot live our lives without inhabiting spaces that are conducive to our activities. Yet if the work of planning buildings is valuable in itself for the architect, the time she devotes to architecture does not count as a negative cost of socially necessary labor time but as a positive access to socially available free time. Her socially necessary labor as an architect is being done in the realm of freedom rather than in the realm of necessity.

Second, the socially necessary labor that no one wants to do for its own sake (that everyone counts as a negative cost of necessary labor time) is not being done as alienated labor by persons who need money to survive and cannot identify with the social purpose of what they are doing. Rather, the socially necessary labor time is qualitatively transformed in being shared by members of society on the basis of their abilities and commitments, with the explicit purpose of contributing to a common good that everyone can recognize as devoted to improving their own possibilities of leading a free life. Moreover, if you cannot recognize yourself in the conception of the common good—if you are a dissenter or conscientious objector to the work that is being done—no one is forcing you to participate in the socially necessary labor, but there are multiple resources available for you to find a way to make a meaningful contribution that makes sense in light of your commitments and for you to help transform the practices to which you object.

Third, through technological development and innovative solutions, we are collectively committed to reducing the labor time that is socially necessary to maintain our lives and increasing the free time that is socially available to lead our lives. Reducing socially necessary labor time does not necessarily mean that we spend less time on socially necessary labor, but that the time we spend on such labor is to a greater degree a matter of socially available free time. Technological improvements are a quantitative means that can contribute to such a qualitative transformation of our labor time, both in the relation among different occupations and within a given occupation. For example, if I am an architect and the time required for my computer to process my design plans is reduced thanks to a technological innovation, the material conditions for my practice are transformed in such a way that I have to spend less time waiting for my program to process data. Instead I have more socially available free time to engage with my design plans on the computer or pursue other aspects of my life. The point of such a transformation is not necessarily to maximize my efficiency, since there is no given imperative that I should be maximally efficient or that I should spend all my time working on my design plans. The point is rather to make my labor time less constrained by the given material conditions (e.g., the operating speed of my computer) and more a matter of my free commitment to the amount of time I want to devote to my work.

The difference between socially available free time and socially necessary labor time is not a difference between being unconstrained and being constrained, but a difference between being subjected to constraints that are recognized as essential rather than inessential for the practice to which we are devoted. For example, there are practices in which the established degree of the instrument's material resistance is taken to be essential to the practice itself, rather than as something to be reduced. Many kinds of musical practices could here serve as illuminating examples. Such examples, however, do not gainsay that we are committed to decreasing socially necessary labor time and increasing socially available free time. Rather, in such cases, the time we are required to devote to the practice by virtue of the instrument's degree of material resistance—e.g., the amount of effort required of us by virtue of a saxophone's constitutive constraints—is itself recognized as socially available free time rather than socially necessary labor time, since the degree of material resistance is recognized as an essential part of the practice to which we are committed. In pursuing architecture or music—as in pursuing any practical activity—we will always be dependent on material instruments that both enable and constrain what we can do. The dependence on some form of material instruments is an essential constraint of the practice, but we can still seek to reduce material constraints that we take to be inessential for the practice, as part of our project to decrease socially necessary labor time and increase socially available free time.

The project of *reducing* socially necessary labor time, however, should not be conflated with an aspiration to *eliminate* socially necessary labor time. It is neither possible nor desirable to eliminate socially necessary labor time altogether. Our lives will always require some form of maintenance and the question of how to maintain our material lives is an intrinsic part of our spiritual freedom. Eliminating socially necessary labor time is not even an intelligible goal for a free life, since the question of where to draw the distinction between necessity and freedom must itself remain a living question for anyone who leads a free life.

How we distinguish between social roles and practical identities is an expression of how we distinguish between the realm of necessity and the realm of freedom. Under democratic socialism, the question of how to negotiate these distinctions is at the center of political deliberation. We identify the realm of necessity in terms of the labor that is needed to sustain our shared life and the social roles that are required for such labor. We aim to decrease the realm of necessity by reducing the socially necessary labor time and making it possible to transform the required social roles in light of our ends. By the same token, we identify the realm of freedom in terms of the socially available free time that we aim to increase and the social roles to which we are committed as ends in themselves (our practical identities). Since it is a matter of freedom, nothing can or should guarantee that everyone has the same set of practical identities. What counts as a practical identity for me may be a mere social role for you and vice versa. Moreover, for each one of us, what counts as our practical identities and their order of priority (our existential identity) must remain at issue and possible to change.

To be sure, the project of democratic socialism depends on the social role of citizen counting as a practical identity for us. Such an active identification of ourselves as citizens, however, cannot be imposed from above but must emerge and be sustained by virtue of our social practices. Precisely because the practical identity of being a citizen—of participating in the project of democratic socialism—is pursued as an end in itself, the meaning of such a commitment must itself be open to question. Under democratic socialism, we are committed to providing not only socially available free time for everyone to engage the question of who they are trying to be, but also socially available institutions for pursuing the question concretely through various forms of creative activity and education, which themselves are open to revision.

What you discover about your abilities and your commitments through education will in turn inform the kinds of work you do in contributing to society—e.g., treating patients, designing houses, taking care of children, inventing new forms of medicine, building better machine technology. The practical identities in question (being a doctor, an architect, a nursery teacher, a scientist, an engineer) entail a sense of what you *ought* to do, but under democratic socialism there is no inherent demand that you have to choose only one vocation for your whole life. Since you are not required to work for your survival, you have the spiritual freedom to ask yourself *if you ought to* sustain a given practical identity and if you ought to transform or abandon the practice. The question of what you should do with your life—the question of your existential identity—is recognized as an irreducible question, which must be allowed to remain explicitly at issue in any vital spiritual life.

The fundamental questions of economy—the questions of what

we prioritize, what we value, what is worth doing with our time—
are thus recognized as being at the heart of our spiritual lives. How
we organize our economy is inseparable from how we live together
(how we make our shared home, our *oikos*), since the way we organize our economy is ultimately how we express our priorities and
our conception of value. The aim of democratic socialism is not to
answer our economic questions once and for all, but to enable us to
"own" the questions as the most important questions of our shared
lives. The three principles of democratic socialism therefore express
the recognition of the inseparability of economic and spiritual life.
To lead emancipated lives, we have to measure our wealth in terms
of socially available free time, own our means of production collectively, and pursue our labor from each according to her ability, to
each according to her needs.

VI

The stakes of my arguments in this book come together in the principles of democratic socialism. Democratic socialism seeks to provide the institutional, political, and material conditions for spiritual
freedom. The project of democratic socialism thus depends on the
cultivation of *secular* faith, since it requires that we avow and in
practice acknowledge the commitment to our shared, finite lives as
ends in themselves. Under democratic socialism we can "own" the
question of what to do with our time, which does not mean that our
time belongs to us as our possession. On the contrary, in owning the
time of our lives we put ourselves at stake in what we do and recognize that we are vulnerable to the loss of time. In accordance with
the dynamic of secular faith, the recognition of the fragility of our
lives is an intrinsic part of what animates our fidelity to the project
of democratic socialism. The project is not something that can be
completed once and for all but depends on our continued engagement
as citizens. The aim of democratic socialism is not to overcome finitude but to enable us to own the question—both individually and
collectively—of how to lead our finite lives.

Accordingly, the idea of democratic socialism must be dissociated from any form of utopianism that conflates the overcoming of capitalism with the overcoming of finitude. An influential example of such utopianism is the work of the philosopher Theodor W. Adorno. As a leading member of the Frankfurt School of critical theory, Adorno is the most sophisticated of the many Marxists who fail to think of the secular faith and spiritual freedom that is required for democratic socialism. While Adorno is committed to emancipation, we will see that he ultimately conflates a secular notion of freedom (the liberation *of* finite life) with a religious notion of salvation (the liberation *from* finite life). As a result, his own valuable insights into freedom and the possibility of emancipation are compromised.

The most instructive example is Adorno's late essay "Free Time," in which he comes closest to grasping the relation between freedom and time that is at the center of democratic socialism. In his essay, Adorno rightly proceeds from the premise that freedom is inseparable from having the material and social resources "to seek out and arrange"[58] one's work according to one's own intentions. To be free is to be devoted to one's activities as ends in themselves, which is why freedom requires that people are "able to make their own decisions about themselves and their lives."[59] The crucial task of emancipation is how "to help free time turn into freedom."[60] This requires free time not only for leisure but also for exploring one's commitments through education and other forms of institutional activity. Freedom cannot be reduced to an individual achievement, since both how much free time we have and what we are able to do with our free time depends on how we organize our society. Or as Adorno puts it: "free time depends on the totality of societal conditions."[61]

If we develop the implications of Adorno's compressed formula, we can say that both the *quantity* and the *quality* of our free time depend on how we organize the time of our lives collectively. As Adorno notes, free time in a quantitative sense has "already expanded exorbitantly" thanks to technological inventions that automate production and by virtue of which "free time should increase enormously."[62] Adorno does not, however, link this problem to the measure of value under capitalism and the need for a revaluation of our conception of value. As I have shown, under capitalism neither the quantity nor the quality of free time can be recognized as having any value in itself, since the measure of value is labor time and only activities that are commodified can contribute to our economic "growth." While the measure of value that determines our notion of economic growth is treated as natural, we need to recognize that it is a collective normative commitment that is inimical to the actualization of our freedom. As far as the capitalist system is concerned, it does not matter if what we do is intrinsically meaningful for us, as long as we spend our free time consuming commodities that contribute to the growth of capital in the economy. This is why I have emphasized that capitalism is a historically specific form of organizing the time of our lives, which is inseparable from how we *valorize* the time of our lives. The social form of capitalism recognizes each one of us as "owning" a lifetime that is inherently valuable (in contrast to societies that keep slaves who are systematically denied ownership of their time), but our lifetime is treated as a means for the end of accumulating surplus value in the form of capital.

The contradictory relation between means and ends under capitalism is clearly visible in the opposition between work and free time that is due to the social form of wage labor. In receiving a wage, our labor is normatively recognized as a negative "cost" for which we ought to be compensated. Our wage labor is a *means* for the *end* of leading our lives in a realm of freedom that opens up beyond our working hours. Our free time outside of work, however, itself becomes a means for the end of restoring our strength and ability to work, since the measure of value under capitalism is socially necessary labor time. As Adorno himself observes, given the form of wage labor, "the time free from labor is supposed to generate labor power."[63] As a consequence, "free time should in no way whatsoever suggest work, presumably so that one can work that much more effectively afterward," and "the time bereft of labor—precisely because it is merely an appendage to labor—is separated from the latter with puritanical fervor."[64]

Free time is thus reduced to leisure time. Rather than being the form in which we engage the question of who we are and what matters to us, our free time is commodified for the sake of profit and reduced to "a selection of *hobbies* that matches the supply offered by the leisure industry."[65]

In contrast, Adorno holds that freedom requires that we overcome the opposition between work and free time. In a striking move, Adorno takes his own life as an example. As a famous philosopher, he is regularly asked in interviews about his "hobbies." Rather than answer the question, he underscores that the question itself testifies to a separation between work and free time that is fatally misleading:

> I am startled by the question whenever I meet with it. I have no *hobby*. Not that I'm a workaholic who wouldn't know how to do anything else but get down to business and do what has to be done. But rather I take the activities with which I occupy myself beyond the bounds of my official profession, without exception, so seriously that I would be shocked by the idea that they had anything to do with *hobbies*—that is, activities I'm mindlessly infatuated with only in order to kill time. . . . Making music, listening to music, reading with concentration, constitute an integral element of my existence; the word *hobby* would be a mockery of them. And conversely, my work, the production of philosophical and sociological studies and university teaching, so far has been so pleasant to me that I am unable to express it within the opposition to free time that the current razor-sharp classification demands from people.[66]

Adorno is well aware that he is speaking as someone who has had the privilege of both personal wealth and an outstanding education, which have allowed him to discover and cultivate his passions. Adorno was not only a successful philosopher and sociologist but also a classically trained pianist who studied composition with the prominent composer Alban Berg and wrote his own music. For such a person, it is easy to see that there does not have to be an opposition between work and free time. The work you do as your official profession (e.g., being a philosopher at a university) is meaningful in itself and expresses your own commitments, so even when it is demanding and difficult the time you devote to your work can count as free time. Likewise, the activities you pursue in your spare time (e.g., composing music) are not mere "hobbies" designed to kill time but meaningful in themselves and expressive of who you are. While the work you do as your official profession can be seen as free time, the free time that does not belong to your official profession can itself be a form of dedicated work. This is Adorno's model of freedom. "If free time would really finally become that state of affairs in which everyone would enjoy what once was the prerogative of the few," he writes, "then I would imagine the situation along the lines of the model I observe in myself, although under altered conditions this model would change as well."[67]

Adorno does not say anything about what the altered conditions would be, but in light of the principles of democratic socialism we can clarify what is at stake in overcoming the opposition between work and free time.

Let me first make clear that neither your official professions nor your other activities have to belong to so-called high culture in order to count as free. As we have seen, when Marx speaks of the activity of composing as "actual free labor" he is not primarily thinking of the composition of music or philosophy. The free activity of composition can express itself in any number of social projects, ranging from cooking, harvesting, and building to child rearing, athletics, and study groups, while including music and philosophy as well. The activities in question can be pursued either as your chosen professions or in your spare time. The difference between what you do as your chosen professions and what you do in your spare time is not a matter of wage labor but of the nature of your commitment. If you commit to being a doctor as an official profession, you are bound by a different set of obligations than if you commit to participating in a study group in your spare time. In both cases there are constraints to which you bind yourself, but their weight and significance is different. Actual free labor is not a matter of being free from constraints, but of being able to identify with the constraints to which you subject yourself.

Accordingly, the key term in Marx's discussions of alienated versus free labor is *aneignen*,[68] which is a German verb for "making something your own." Capitalism alienates labor and makes the sense of owning your life abstract by aligning it with the ownership of private property for the sake of profit. The concrete sense of owning your life that Marx affirms is, on the contrary, a matter of being able to make your life your own by putting yourself at stake in what you do.

An illuminating example is the production and consumption of artworks. Under capitalism, "owning" a work of art means having the abstract property right to a work of art rather than having the concrete ability to appreciate and understand the object in question. Under capitalism, we can be "owners" of artworks while having a merely abstract relation to the objects in question. We can hang a Cézanne on our wall as a token of social prestige without having either the time to appreciate it or the education to grasp its significance. Furthermore, artists under capitalism have the abstract property right to their works of art, but concretely they have to sell their artworks for profit in order to make a living. Under democratic socialism, by contrast, artworks cannot be commodities that are bought and sold for profit, but artists have the concrete property right to their work—in the sense that no one can take it away from them against their will—by virtue of having created it. Given that artworks are created to be seen and appreciated by others, however, there will be an intrinsic motivation for artists to donate their works to galleries, households, libraries, offices, or public museums and make a case for why they deserve a place among the collections. For the same reason, the only ones who will "own" artworks under democratic socialism are the ones who make it a priority to engage with artworks. The artworks themselves will in principle be available for all in public museums, or on display in other venues hosted by the artists themselves or by supporters of their work. In practice, however, the artworks will be accessible only to those who devote time to attend the exhibits, receive education concerning the history of art, and participate in committed conversations regarding what art ought to be. Concretely "owning" a work of art requires taking *time* to engage with the work of art, learn how to understand it, and put yourself at stake in an attempt to grapple with its meaning.

The point is not that everyone ought to be art lovers, but that everyone ought to have the socially available free time to explore the questions of what they love and to which activities they are committed. This requires the material and social resources to engage, cultivate, and transform your own senses, in order to explore what matters to you. As Marx emphasizes, our senses are themselves formed by the kinds of labor we do and the conditions under which we live. If you are worn out after a day of alienated labor, your ability to engage with other aspects of your life will itself be diminished and your free time will become a means to restore your labor-power rather than the form in which you lead your life. Actual free labor, by contrast, requires the socially available free time that allows you to own the question of what to do with your life.

Actual free labor does not mean that you can do anything you want. Which occupations you can take up as your official professions and what you can do in your spare time will depend on your concrete abilities. For example, under democratic socialism everyone has access to free education and can apply to medical school, but which of us will actually become doctors is a matter of how able we turn out to be. Likewise, everyone has the chance to learn to play an instrument—if we are collectively committed to having music in our lives—but which of us will be able to take it up as a vocation or even be good enough to play meaningfully in our spare time is a matter of talent and dedication. Actual freedom does not mean guaranteed success, but the freedom to explore who you can be and to fail by virtue of your own limitations rather than by virtue of systemic injustice. As Marx points out in a brilliant passage, when you cannot buy love, art, and influence over other people for money, then being a lover, an art connoisseur, or an influential person will depend on who you actually are, rather than on the purchasing power you have:

Then you can exchange love only for love, trust for trust, and so on. If you want to enjoy art, you must be an artistically cultivated person; if you want to exercise influence over other people, you must be a person with a stimulating and encouraging effect on other people. Every one of your relations to human beings and to nature must be a *specific expression,* corresponding to the object of your will, of your *real individual* life. If you love without evoking love in return—that is, if your loving as loving does not produce reciprocal love; if through a *living expression* of yourself as a loving person you do not make yourself a loved person, then your love is impotent—a misfortune.[69]

Democratic socialism is in no way designed to insure us against such misfortune. To lead a free life is to be defined by what you do and how you are received—what Marx here calls the specific and living expressions of your real individual life. Precisely because you are defined by what you do and how you are received, leading your life must include the risk of failing to be who you are trying to be. You are entitled to the resources that enable you to *try* to be a lovable person, an artistically cultivated person, or a politically influential person. But nothing can—or should—guarantee that you *succeed* in being a lovable person, an artistically cultivated person, or a politically influential person. Because you are essentially a social being, your successes and failures must themselves be a matter of the social recognition of your deeds. Of course, you can be misunderstood and contest the given social recognition of your deeds, but there is no space outside the social in which these concerns can be adjudicated. To own your life is to own that who you are is essentially a social achievement, which always comes with the risk of failure.

For the same reason, your own actual freedom depends on the freedom of others. For you to be genuinely recognized as having achieved a social status by virtue of your own deeds—e.g., being lovable or a great composer—others must have socially available free time to engage with who you are and what you do. Such engagement requires that they have the material and spiritual resources to assess the meaning of your deeds. If their time is consumed by alienated labor or if they are forced to recognize you as lovable or as a great composer because you wield your purchasing power over them, then you will at best have a compelled assent to your supposed achievements but no genuine recognition. Because everything we do and everything that matters to us is a form of social activity, to will our own freedom we must will the freedom of others. For any one of us to be recognized as free, others must have their own free time to confirm or challenge our self-conception. Inversely, to the extent that others are alienated from exercising their freedom, we too are alienated from our own freedom. Our freedom is inseparable from the freedom of others to acknowledge or contest our claim to be who we are trying to be and to do what we are trying to do. It is impossible for any one of us to be in the realm of freedom alone, since who we are and what we do is unintelligible without the recognition of others.

Hence, the requirement that we share and increase our socially available free time is *both* a commitment to true equality of opportunity *and* a condition for our own freedom as social individuals. If to be free is to be able to see what I do in light of my commitments, such freedom must include the ability to recognize my commitment to freedom in the institutions I sustain and that sustain me. This is why neither Adorno nor I nor anyone else can fully actualize our freedom under capitalism, even if we get to devote our lives to what we love in teaching philosophy, writing books, and composing music. If the institutions on which we depend exploit the labor time of others even as they give us free time to lead our lives, then we ourselves fall short of actual freedom.

Democratic socialism therefore requires that we develop practices which allow us to grasp explicitly that our material and spiritual lives are two sides of the same coin. If the time we spend in the realm of necessity—e.g., doing some form of labor that is necessary to sustain our life together—can be seen as socially shared and as contributing to the expansion of our collective realm of freedom, then even tedious forms of labor become expressive of our commitment to lead a free life. For example, my spending an hour per day mopping classroom floors and running the dishwashers in the cafeteria could itself be expressive of my commitment to being a university professor, if our lives were organized in such a way that we shared the socially necessary forms of labor. There would still be a distinction between the time I spend in the realm of freedom (teaching my classes) and the time I spend in the realm of necessity (mopping classroom floors). The time I spend teaching is valuable in itself and not to be reduced (insofar as there are people who want to devote the time to my classes), whereas the time I spend mopping the floors is not valuable in itself and can happily be reduced through advanced technology. The crucial point, however, is that the distinction between the realm of freedom and the realm of necessity does not have to be a distinction between free and alienated labor. The time spent in the realm of necessity is not alienated labor if it is not being exploited for the sake of profit but is being done for the sake of a recognizable common good, which moreover embodies our collective commitment to reducing the socially necessary labor time for all.

Accordingly, the actual freedom of labor must include that we share the burden of the material production and reproduction of life. Contrary to what many influential philosophers have claimed (from Hannah Arendt to Michel Henry),[70] freedom for Marx does *not* consist in a liberation from labor and necessity. Overcoming capitalism will not lead us to a state of "overabundance" in which all our needs are automatically fulfilled and we do not have to make any effort to sustain our material lives. Such a state of overabundance is not only impossible to attain but also undesirable, since there cannot be a realm of freedom that is not bound to a realm of necessity. If we did not have to sustain our lives, there would be no question of how we should lead our lives. Thus, I have argued at length that spiritual life cannot be separated from material life. How we *lead* our lives in the realm of freedom is inseparable from how we *sustain* our lives in the realm of necessity, since any form of spiritual life depends on a fragile material body that must be maintained.

Moreover, in leading any form of free life we must reckon with the possible loss of time, both through the risk of illness or disability that follows from being embodied and the risk of "wasting" our time that follows from leading a spiritual life that can fail in its integrity or turn out to be based on principles that themselves are misguided. As a spiritually free being, I can fail by not living up to the demands of a given practical identity, but I can also come to see the very aspiration to live up to that practical identity as itself a failure. The question that is always *implicit* in my life (the question of what is *worth* doing with my time) then becomes *explicit*. In a full-blown crisis, the very life I was trying to lead—the order of priorities that defined my existential identity—can come to be seen as a waste of my time.

At stake here is my ability to judge that my time is being wasted and that I myself am wasting my time. The ability to make such judgments—and the concomitant risk of existential crisis—is inseparable from the exercise of my spiritual freedom. If I could not judge that my time is being wasted, I could not see myself as alienated and I could not struggle for any form of emancipation. Moreover, if I could not judge that I myself am wasting my time, I could not deliberate— whether implicitly or explicitly—on what I ought to do with my life.

Under democratic socialism our time will not be wasted on generating surplus value, but we will still run the risk of wasting our surplus time, since such a risk is intrinsic to leading a free life. To be emancipated is *not* to be released from the question of what to do with our finite time and the concomitant risk of wasting our time. Rather, the point of emancipation is to enable us to own the risk by owning the question of our priorities—the question of what we ought to strive for and what we ought to forsake—as the vital question of our lives.

The overcoming of capitalism, then, should in no way be conflated with the overcoming of finitude. Yet this is precisely the mistake made by Adorno and many other utopian Marxists. "I believe," Adorno maintains, "that without the notion of an unfettered life, freed from death, the idea of utopia, the idea of *the* utopia, *cannot* even be thought at all."[71] Adorno places great emphasis on this overcoming of temporal finitude. "The elimination of death is indeed the crucial point,"[72] he underlines, since the idea of utopia "cannot be conceived at all without the elimination of death; this is inherent in the very thought."[73] Following the same line of argument, Adorno holds that "the possibility of a completely unshackled reality remains valid."[74] He specifies that such a completely unshackled reality would be "a world in which senseless suffering has ceased to exist"[75] and in which even "the smallest trace of senseless suffering"[76] has been removed.

Given Adorno's demands regarding how our lives *ought* to be—freed from death and suffering—it is hardly surprising that he cannot form any positive conception of his utopia. Adorno repeatedly emphasizes that there must be a "ban on images" of utopia, which can be posited only as a negative absence.[77] Yet, while Adorno cannot picture a life freed from death and suffering, he is convinced that it is desirable and would give us the fulfillment that we seek.

Adorno's understanding of our finitude is thus essentially "religious" in my sense of the term. Even if Adorno does not believe that we can attain an eternal life, he regards our finitude as a negative restriction and assumes that we fundamentally suffer from the lack of a utopian life that would be exempt from death. For the same reason, Adorno fails to understand that finitude is a condition of possibility for freedom. Only someone who is finite can be free, since only someone who is finite can engage the question of what is worth doing with her time and grasp her own life as being at stake in how she leads her life. An infinite being could never lead a free life, since her own life could never be at stake in her activities. Indeed, an infinite being would have no life to live at all, since her life would not depend on self-maintenance. The problem with Adorno's utopian life is not that it is unattainable but that it is undesirable and incompatible with the fragile possibility of freedom. The fragility of freedom cannot be eliminated but is intrinsic to freedom itself. The reason we cannot conceive of leading a life that is exempt from death is not because of cognitive or historical limitations but because such a conception of life is unintelligible.

For his part, Adorno never addresses the conditions of intelligibility for life and freedom, but persistently conflates such conditions with historically specific conditions. In the "Free Time" essay, the conflation is manifest in Adorno's treatment of the problem of boredom. Adorno argues that the problem of boredom can be seen as "a function of life under the compulsion to work and under the rigorous division of labor."[78] Our labor time is haunted by boredom because it is compulsory rather than expressive of a free commitment, while our leisure time is haunted by boredom because it requires "superficial distraction" in order "to summon up the energy for work."[79] If we understand these observations as pertaining to a historically specific form of boredom, Adorno is here making an important point. Capitalist labor conditions qualitatively transform the problem of boredom, formally acknowledging our free time but making our lives much more tedious than they could be if our material and social conditions enabled us to own the question of what to do with our time. In a characteristic move, however, Adorno conflates the historically specific problem of boredom under capitalist labor conditions with the existential category of boredom per se. "Boredom need not necessarily exist," Adorno asserts, since "if people were able to make their own decisions about themselves and their lives, if they were not harnessed to the eternal sameness, then they would not have to be bored. Boredom is the reflex reaction to objective dullness."[80]

If Adorno were right, then leading a free life would mean that one could never be bored with what one is doing. In Adorno's account, boredom is reducible to the fact that there is something objectively wrong ("dull") with the world and our boredom is merely an automatic reaction (a "reflex") to the objective dullness. By claiming that boredom ought to be eliminated, Adorno thus commits himself to the vision of a utopia in which we could never judge the world to be dull and would always be completely absorbed by what we do. Far from allowing us to be free, however, such a utopia would eliminate the question of both objective and subjective freedom. There would be no question of objective freedom, since we could never discern any deficiency (dullness) in the world to which we belong. Rather, we would take the world to be exactly what it ought to be and not call for any transformation of our objective social conditions. Likewise, there would be no question of subjective freedom, since we could never discern any deficiency (dullness) in how we lead our own lives. Rather, we would take ourselves to be exactly who we ought to be and find everything we do to be absolutely interesting. For Adorno, any sense of "negativity"—any sense that there is something *wrong* with ourselves or the world—is operative only insofar as we fall short of utopian life. If we were granted utopian life, we would never suffer from anything, never be bored by anything, never die from anything.

Adorno does not grasp that the relation to the negative—suffering, boredom, and death—is intrinsic to the positive possibility of freedom. Suffering, boredom, and anxiety before death are *not* reducible to psychological states—or historically specific pathologies—but rather necessary conditions for leading a free life. The relation to suffering, boredom, and death renders intelligible how leading our lives can matter to us in the first place. If nothing could count as suffering for us, we would never have a reason to object to anything that happens to us and no reason to change or improve our condition. Likewise, if we could not take ourselves to be bored *by* anything or bored *with* our own activities, we would never have a reason to try to transform how we conduct our lives.[81] Finally, if we could not grasp ourselves as finite and as anxious before death, we would not be able to understand the urgency of pursuing any project or any activity, since we would not be able to distinguish between sooner and later in our lives. The relation to suffering, boredom, and death is a necessary condition for spiritual freedom. If we could not suffer, could not be bored, and could not die, there would be no distinction for us between success and failure, engagement and indifference, life and death. By the same token, we could never be committed to doing anything, since nothing that we do would make a difference for us.

Hence, it is deeply revealing that Adorno's visions of utopian life keep returning to the idea of a state in which we would not have to do anything. "The animal phase in which one does nothing at all cannot be retrieved," Adorno says with an almost audible sigh of lament.[82] One wonders which kind of animal he could possibly be thinking of, since being an animal—indeed *being alive in any way at all*—means that one *always has to do something* to stay alive. Not heeding any such questions, Adorno affirms that "none of the abstract concepts come closer to fulfilled utopia than that of eternal peace."[83] He tries to give concreteness to such an abstract idea of fulfilled utopia by imagining a state of "doing nothing like an animal, lying on water and looking peacefully at the sky, 'being, nothing else, without any further definition and fulfillment.' "[84]

Now, it can certainly make sense to take time to float on water and look at the sky. For the activity to be something that matters to me and that expresses my freedom, however, it must be something *that I am doing*. Even when I am "doing nothing" I am doing something (e.g., taking a break, appreciating a precious day in my life, absorbing the gentle movement of the water, beholding the beauty of the cloud formations). If I were truly doing nothing—if it were an experience of "pure being" or "eternal peace"—it would not be an experience at all and *I* would not be there. There would be a corpse floating on the water and not a person, since there would not be anyone for whom anything matters. No one would suffer from anything while floating on the water, no one would become bored with the activity of looking at the sky, and no one would ask herself what to do with her life in light of death, but only because no one would be alive. This is why visions of eternal peace are indistinguishable from eternal indifference and why Adorno's notion of utopian "life" makes no sense. Pure being is nothing.[85]

Accordingly, we must carefully distinguish the two levels of analysis that Adorno conflates. On the one hand, there are historically and socially specific forms of suffering that we should seek to overcome. We do not have to suffer from the injustices of capitalism, we do not have to be subjected to the opposition between worktime and leisure time that makes a certain form of boredom pervasive, and we do not have to die from many of the causes that currently wreck our lives. We can and should do better. On the other hand, if we conflate historically or socially specific forms of suffering, boredom, and death with the existential categories of suffering, boredom, and death per se, we deprive ourselves of the ability to identify the actual forms of suffering that we are committed to overcoming. Instead of engaging the problem of how to identify and transform the pernicious ways in which we are leading our finite lives, the problem is conflated with the fact that we are leading a finite life at all. We are thus led to the dead end of religious despair over finite life itself and saddled with the religious longing for a redemption from the condition of finitude.

Such is the dead end to which Adorno leads us. In the finale to his *Minima Moralia,* he declares: "The only philosophy which can be responsibly practiced in the face of despair is the attempt to contemplate all things as they would present themselves from the standpoint of redemption."[86] From such a contemplative standpoint of redemption, the world would appear "as indigent and distorted as it will appear one day in the messianic light."[87] Adorno concedes that it is "utterly impossible" for us to occupy such a perspective on the world, since it "presupposes a standpoint removed, even though by a hair's breadth, from the scope of existence."[88] Yet Adorno laments the impossibility of such a standpoint and thinks that it testifies to a negative inability on our part. If only we were able to overcome the conditional in favor of "the unconditional,"[89] we would be able to occupy the contemplative standpoint of redemption that is removed from existence and let the world be illuminated by messianic light.

Adorno thereby betrays the most fundamental insights regarding emancipation in Marx. For Marx, a contemplative standpoint that is removed from existence is not only utterly impossible but also utterly undesirable and a truly incoherent idea, since the world can matter only to someone who is engaged in the fragile activity of leading a life. Rather than turn us toward an unintelligible promise of redemption, Marx seeks to make us recognize that everything depends on what we do with our finite time and our shared lives. This is why Marx's critique of capitalism from the beginning is intertwined with his critique of religion and why one cannot understand one without the other. "The critique of religion," Marx writes, "is the premise of all critique."[90]

Capitalism and religion have proved to be highly compatible, which from Marx's perspective is no accident. He keeps returning to how both capitalism and religion are forms of self-alienation. Both capitalism and religion prevent us from recognizing in practice that *our own lives*—our only lives—are taken away from us when our time is taken away from us. While capitalism alienates us from our own time by subordinating it to the purpose of profit, religions offer the consolation that our time ultimately is insignificant and will be redeemed by eternity. While capitalism makes poverty perennial and distorts the meaning of wealth, religions promote poverty as a virtue and as a path to salvation. While capitalism disables our capacity to lead free lives, religion teaches us that submission leads to liberation. In short, both capitalism and religion make us *disown* our lives, rather than enabling us to *own* the question of what we ought to do with our finite time.

Accordingly, Marx famously argues that religion is "the *opium* of the people."[91] The suffering caused by social injustice is alleviated by the promise of a religious redemption. Religions serve as a form of "opium" *both* by diminishing the pain of our not being able to lead flourishing lives *and* by pacifying us, making us dream of an impossible bliss rather than waking up and taking action to transform the conditions of our only life. As Marx emphasizes, "the abolition of religion as the *illusory* happiness of human beings" must therefore be understood as "a demand for their *real* happiness. The call to abandon their illusions about their conditions is a *call to abandon a condition which requires illusions*."[92] If we merely criticized religious beliefs as illusions—without being committed to overcoming the forms of social injustice that motivate these illusions—the critique of religion would be empty and patronizing. The task is rather to transform our social conditions in such a way that people no longer need to have recourse to the opium of religion and can affirmatively recognize the irreplaceable value of their own lives. As Marx explains in one of his most beautiful and important formulations, his critique of religion "has plucked the imaginary flowers from the chain, not in order that human beings shall bear the chain without caprice or consolation but so that they shall cast off the chain and pluck the living flower."[93]

The "living flower" can here be read as a figure for the time of our lives. Like all living organisms, we generate a surplus of time by virtue of our own activity of self-maintenance. What distinguishes us as spiritual beings, however, is that we can seize ("pluck") our surplus of time *as* free time to lead our lives. By the same token, we can also exploit and alienate ourselves (put ourselves in chains). Under capitalism, our chains consist in that we have to convert the surplus time of our lives into surplus value. We are thereby dominated by a purpose (profit) that is inimical to the actualization of our own freedom. Even our technological means for nonliving production—which should serve our ends as living beings—are employed for the sake of exploitation rather than emancipation.

In contrast, the purpose of democratic socialism is to transform the surplus time of our lives into socially available free time. This transformation is achieved by founding and sustaining institutions that promote our spiritual freedom, as well as by developing the means of nonliving production in order to decrease our socially necessary labor time and increase our surplus of lifetime. While capitalism and religion make it seem as if we depend on a transcendent principle (whether profit or God), we must grasp the democratic truth that only we can put ourselves in chains and only we can set ourselves free. The power of our lives is inseparable from what we do—inseparable from the power of the people. To cast off our chains and seize our time we must grasp that all we have—who we are—is inseparable from the material and social practices through which we reproduce and transform our lives.

Such democratic emancipation requires that we remove "the imaginary flowers" which make our current chains seem bearable. Whether the imaginary flowers are the promises of the free market or the religious promises of eternal life, they serve to make us accept or forget the injustices of *this life*. As Marx recalls, the fact that many people have recourse to the opium of religion can be seen as "an *expression* of real suffering and a *protest* against real suffering."[94] Yet the religious understanding of finitude makes us misrecognize the suffering we seek to overcome. What we are missing is not eternal life but social and institutional forms of being together that enable us to lead flourishing lives.

The flourishing of an emancipated life—the living flower that is actively cultivated—is itself finite and will require our continued care even in its fullest actuality. But when we remove the imaginary flower of eternity—when we recognize that eternal life would be death, would not be a form of life at all—we can see that our finitude is not in itself a restriction. Rather, the finitude of flourishing is an essential part of why we are devoted to making flourishing actual and keeping it alive.

The critique of religion—like the critique of capitalism—must therefore be an immanent critique. We must locate the resources for overcoming the religious understanding of finitude *within* the practice of faith and its commitment to a shared social life. The practice of religious faith has often served—and still serves for many—as an important communal expression of solidarity. Likewise, religious organizations often provide services for those who are poor and in need. Most importantly, religious discourses have often been mobilized in concrete struggles against injustice. None of these social commitments, however, requires religious faith or a religious form of organization. For these commitments to fulfill their promise of emancipation, religious faith must be converted into secular faith and be devoted to social justice as an end in itself. If we are committed to abolishing poverty rather than promising salvation for the poor, the faith we embody in practice is secular rather than religious, since we acknowledge our life together as our ultimate purpose. This argument—which brings together secular faith and spiritual freedom in the pursuit of actual emancipation—leads us to the concluding movement of this book.

Conclusion: Our Only Life

I

On April 3, 1968, Martin Luther King, Jr., landed at the airport in Memphis, Tennessee. It was raining, and there were warnings of an upcoming storm. After a disrupted public protest march the week before, King had returned to Memphis to support the ongoing strike of the black sanitation workers in the city. By evening a tornado was sweeping through western Tennessee, leaving twelve people dead, and the civil defense sirens rang out across Memphis, with lightning and thunder rolling through the city.

King was exhausted from traveling on behalf of his Poor People's Campaign. Owing to a fever and a sore throat, he wanted to cancel his speaking engagement, but at the last minute he was persuaded to keep his promise to the local union. King drove through the storm and made it to the meeting at the Mason Temple. Despite the forbidding weather that prevented many from attending, more than two thousand union members and strike supporters had come to listen to King, who delivered what would turn out to be his last public speech. He addressed the assembled crowd at 9:30 p.m., without notes but carried forward by the committed response of his audience. No one could have known that King had less than twenty-four hours left to live, but there had been persistent rumors about an impending attempt on his life. The plane that carried King and his associates from Atlanta had been held at the gate because of a bomb threat. When King arrived in Memphis, there were further reports of threats to his life but no reliable information. Such rumors were a commonplace by then and it could have been just another day in King's political campaign for social justice.

Threats to his life had been frequent ever since King emerged as a leader of the Montgomery bus boycott in 1955 and 1956. In Montgomery his house was bombed by white segregationists, nearly killing his wife, Coretta, and daughter Yolanda. At mass meetings in Birmingham and Selma, he was beaten and punched in the face. On a march through an all-white neighborhood in Chicago, he was hit by a rock. Local authorities arrested him at least eighteen times and those close to King knew that he lived constantly with the imminent risk of being killed for his political work.

Yet the last year of King's life had seen an unprecedented level of hostility against him. The liberal establishment—which supported King when he focused on acquiring formal civil rights for African Americans—became increasingly antagonistic to King as he turned his attention to the systematic forms of *economic* injustice underpinning and informing the racial forms of injustice. With King publicly declaring his strong opposition to the Vietnam War and highlighting what he called "the hard-core economic issues" of the United States, both the media and the Johnson administration turned against him. FBI director J. Edgar Hoover (who had been wiretapping King since 1961) created a new "racial intelligence" section, with a mission to "publicize King as a traitor to his country and race."[1] Through infiltration, violent disruptions of protest marches, and dissemination of compromising claims, the racial intelligence section of the FBI planned ways to sabotage the Poor People's Campaign headed by King. President Johnson, the attorney general, the Pentagon, and the Secret Service—as well as prominent members of the media—continuously received FBI memos with the title: "Martin Luther King, Jr.—Security Matter—Communist."[2]

At the same time, both the New Left and the emerging Black Power movement tended to dismiss King as outdated. Especially in the wake of the riots that began in the mid-sixties, King's nonviolent methods and his coalition politics were derided as inadequate to the demands of the time. While the establishment regarded King as too radical, the avant-garde regarded him as not radical enough and criticized him for being essentially a middle-class preacher who pursued middle-class goals.

The view of King as a mere reformist, however, is deeply misleading. King himself distinguished between two phases of the civil rights movement, with the second phase requiring increasingly radical measures. The first phase lasted from the Montgomery boycott in 1955 until the passage of the Voting Rights Act on August 6, 1965. The main aim of this phase was to secure basic rights and forms of liberty for the black population in the South. As King pointed out, the cost of these reforms was negligible for the political establishment and involved no direct economic demands. "The practical cost of change for the nation up to this point has been cheap," King wrote in *Where Do We Go from Here* (1967).[3] "The limited reforms have been obtained at bargain rates. There are no expenses, and no taxes are required, for Negroes to share lunch counters, libraries, parks, hotels, and other facilities with whites."[4] Moreover, "even the more significant changes involved in voter registration required neither large monetary nor psychological sacrifice. Spectacular and turbulent events that dramatized the demand created an erroneous impression that a heavy burden was involved."[5] We can add—as Marxist historians have done—that there were structural and economic incentives for the political establishment to support desegregation in the South. The maintenance of dual labor markets (black and white) is economically irrational under capitalism, since it creates an artificial barrier to labor recruitment and prevents each unit from being treated as abstractly equivalent for the sake of efficiency. A simple but illuminating example (which I borrow from Adolph Reed, Jr.) is the economic wastefulness of having to maintain two different sets of toilets—for blacks and whites respectively—in the plants.[6]

More generally, the violent instability of the segregationist South was itself inefficient and an obstacle that needed to be removed for capitalist enterprise to expand.

After the civil rights victories culminating in 1965, King knew that the most difficult challenges were still to come. "The real cost lies ahead. The stiffening of white resistance is a recognition of that fact," he wrote in *Where Do We Go from Here.* "The discount education given Negroes will in the future have to be purchased at full price if quality education is to be realized. Jobs are harder and costlier to create than voting rolls. The eradication of slums housing millions is complex far beyond integrating buses and lunch counters."[7] These questions of substantial economic justice were for King at the center of the second phase of the civil rights movement.

Following King, we can date the beginning of the second phase to August 11, 1965, only five days after Lyndon B. Johnson signed the Voting Rights Act into law. On August 11, riots broke out in the Watts neighborhood and spread rapidly through South-Central Los Angeles. Such riots were to continue for the remaining years of King's life, and he grasped directly that the urban ghettos were the new frontier of the civil rights movement. "The flames of Watts illuminated more than the Western sky," King maintained only days after the riots, "they cast light on the imperfections of the civil rights movement and the tragic shallowness of white racial policy in the explosive ghettos."[8] The militant but nonviolent struggle for emancipation must now, King concluded, expand from the South to the North and resolutely cut across class divisions. As King recognized, "the civil rights movement has too often been middle-class oriented" and it needed to move toward "the grassroots levels of our communities,"[9] with the aim of ending poverty, preventing labor exploitation, and creating economic justice.

True to form, King moved with his family to a West Side ghetto in Chicago. King's goal was not simply to speak *for* the ghettos but to mobilize and organize the urban poor for self-liberating action. In contrast to those who thought the alienated citizens of the slums were capable only of violence, King pursued a remarkable campaign that included the recruitment of gang members, with whom he engaged on the streets of Chicago and invited into his own home to debate pressing social issues as well as the politics of nonviolence. As King made clear, nonviolent action is not passive and submissive but militant and coercive. "Nonviolence must be adapted to urban conditions and urban moods," King avowed. "We must fashion the new tactics which do not count on government goodwill, but instead serve to compel unwilling authorities to yield to the mandates of justice."[10] Moreover, King emphasized that forms of mass protest and civil disobedience should be used to attack not only unequal rights but also economic inequality. To this end, King argued that "militant non-violence" was not only morally but also pragmatically and politically superior to violent riots. "To dislocate the functioning of a city without destroying it can be more effective than a riot because it can be longer-lasting, costly to the larger society, but not wantonly destructive."[11] King rightly predicted that riots would only strengthen the right-wing demonization of the black population and facilitate repressive measures on the part of the governing authorities. By contrast, politically articulated forms of mass civil disobedience—which highlight actual forms of racial and economic inequality—exhibit moral authority in practice and are "more difficult for the government to quell by superior force."[12]

While King's organizing efforts were fraught with difficulties, he successfully mobilized a wide range of citizens in the ghettos, including gang members from the Vice Lords, the Roman Saints, and the Blackstone Rangers, in both the 1966 Mississippi Freedom March and open-housing marches in Chicago that same summer. As Brandon M. Terry has shown in an important study, King's work in the ghettos was a form of practical and critical engagement with the contentions of the Black Power movement.[13] Like many of the representatives of Black Power, King regarded the crimes committed by rioters to be "derivative crimes," the roots of which were social and economic injustice (what King called "the crimes of white society"). Yet King's conception of what needed to be done was profoundly different from the advocates of Black Power. While leaders of the Black Power movement laid claim to the riots as part of an emancipatory project, King pointed out that they had no actual control over the unfolding of the riots and therefore no actual authority with regard to the expressive meaning of the actions undertaken by the rioters. Only organized political action could lay claim to such authority. Moreover, King clearly saw any form of black nationalism or separatism as a dead end, since it ignored the issues of class and economic justice that cut across racial boundaries. There is no "separate black road to power and fulfillment," King repeatedly emphasized.[14] Instead, he articulated the need for a cross-racial labor movement and engaged in depth with labor activists, while combating persistent forms of racism within labor unions themselves.

King was thus led to launch the Poor People's Campaign, which he was in the midst of organizing when he was assassinated in Memphis in 1968. The Poor People's Campaign was supposed to be a "genuine class movement" transcending racial and ethnic lines to include Native Americans and Hispanics, as well as the white working poor and the unemployed, who had been left behind by deindustrialization in the cities or by automation in the countryside.[15] This "non-violent army" would engage in massive forms of civil disobedience in order to bring fundamental economic issues into focus. As part of this mobilization King also began to collaborate with the National Welfare Rights Association, through which black women had organized militant protests. At the time of his death King was planning a new march on Washington, D.C., which would lead to an occupation of the capital and display an interracial alliance of the poor. As he told a reporter in Memphis shortly before his assassination: "You could say we are engaged in the class struggle, yes."[16]

King was well aware of the opposition he would meet from those in power, but it did not prevent him from radicalizing his public stance. "Something is wrong with the economic system of our nation," King emphasized more and more often in the last years of his life. "Something is wrong with capitalism."[17] These were not abstract claims but directly linked to the concrete problems regarding housing, education, and welfare that he encountered while working in the ghettos of the North, as well as with the urban and rural poor in the South. "For years I labored with the idea of reforming the existing institutions of the society, a little change here, a little change there," King said in an interview in 1967. "Now I feel quite differently, I think you've got to have a reconstruction of the entire society, a revolution of values."[18] King knew that his radical agenda would make his political work all the more difficult and that the "class issues" he was now engaging would be countered with much greater violence than his campaign to end legal discrimination. At a retreat for the Southern Christian Leadership Conference (SCLC) in November 1966, King made clear that the demand for real economic justice meant "getting on dangerous ground because you are messing with folk then. You are messing with Wall Street. You are messing with captains of industry."[19]

The following year—at the SCLC convention in August 1967—King emphasized that "we've got to begin to ask questions about the whole society" and "to question the capitalistic economy."[20] King had studied Marx already in his early twenties and throughout his life he expressed his appreciation of Marx's economic analysis of systemic injustice. "We are called upon to help the discouraged beggars in life's market place," King reminded his audience at the convention, "but one day we must come to see that an edifice which produces beggars needs restructuring. . . . When you deal with this, you begin to ask the question: 'Who owns the oil?' You begin to ask the question: 'Who owns the iron ore?' "[21] Thus, King's quest for freedom and his commitment to ending poverty led him to question capitalism. As he persistently argued: "The problem of racism, the problem of economic exploitation, and the problem of war are all tied together."[22]

Today King's radical legacy is largely forgotten. He is the most celebrated American political figure of the twentieth century, but the celebration has come at the cost of domestication. "Dead men make / such convenient heroes," the black poet Carl Wendell Hines once wrote. "They / cannot rise / To challenge the images we would fashion from their lives / And besides, it is easier to build monuments / than to make a better world."[23] Since King's death many

monuments have been built in his honor. In Washington, D.C., the
Capitol Rotunda holds a bust of King (the first black person to be
given the honor) and the National Mall exhibits a massive sculpture
of King looking out over the city. Perhaps most strikingly, Martin
Luther King Jr. Day is the only federal holiday commemorating an
individual American civilian. Apart from Columbus Day, it is the
only holiday named after an individual at all.

These forms of ritual celebration, however, do not ensure that
we are keeping King's legacy alive. On the contrary, his legacy has
increasingly been reduced to a message of peace and consensus, at
the expense of what he actually said and fought to accomplish. While
King is often enrolled in a conciliatory narrative regarding achieved
civil rights and formal racial equality, he was emphatically clear that
the most important challenges for achieving actual reconciliation and
equality still lay ahead. Moreover, these challenges still lie ahead for
us today. As Hosea Williams—who worked closely with King in the
civil rights movement—has observed: "There is a definite effort on
the part of America to change Martin Luther King, Jr., from what he
really was all about—to make him the Uncle Tom of the century. In
my mind, he was the militant of the century."[24]

Yet we only have to listen to the speech King gave on the steps
of the Lincoln Memorial—the famous "I Have a Dream" delivered
on August 28, 1963—to be led down the radical path he came to follow. King here proceeds from the commitment to freedom, which
is inscribed in "the magnificent words of the Constitution and the
Declaration of Independence."[25] In producing these documents, the
Founding Fathers were "signing a promissory note to which every
American was to fall heir," namely, that each person "would be
guaranteed the unalienable rights of life, liberty, and the pursuit of
happiness."[26] By virtue of the historical achievement of such a commitment to freedom, we can criticize the Founding Fathers for failing
to live up to the principles they avowed—e.g., by keeping slaves and
subordinating women—as well as criticize our contemporary society
for failing in its commitment to freedom. "It is obvious today," King
declares in the speech, "that America has defaulted on this promis-

sory note in so far as her citizens of color are concerned."[27] King's appeal to the Constitution and the Declaration of Independence is not an appeal to stay true to who we already are. Rather, it is a transformative appeal to become who we have never been but *ought* to be in light of our own commitment to freedom and equality. As early as in *Stride Toward Freedom* (1958), King had made clear that freedom and equality are "inseparable" from economic justice.[28] At the Lincoln Memorial in 1963, he makes the point by speaking of freedom in terms of economy from the beginning. "America has given the Negro people a bad check," King underscores, "a check which has come back marked 'insufficient funds.' We refuse to believe that there are insufficient funds in the great vaults of opportunity of this nation. And so we've come to cash this check, a check that will give us upon demand the riches of freedom and the security of justice."[29]

The economic dimension of King's argument became more and more pronounced as he progressed into the second phase of the civil rights movement. When he returns to the promissory note of the Founding Fathers in a 1968 speech, he makes explicit that liberty and the pursuit of happiness require the economic resources to lead one's life. "It is a cruel jest," King underscores, "to say to a bootless man that he should lift himself up by his own bootstraps."[30] He gives the example of African Americans being granted formal freedom (freedom from slavery) while not being granted any resources to pursue and cultivate their freedom. When African Americans were released from the bondage of physical slavery in 1863, they were not given land, money, or access to educational institutions that would enable them to lead their lives. "It was something like keeping a man in prison for many, many years," King points out, "and suddenly discovering that he is not guilty of the crime for which he was imprisoned. And then you just go up to him and say, 'Now, you're free.' But you don't give him any bus fare to get to town. You don't give him any money to get some clothes to put on his back. You don't give him anything to get started in life again. . . . We were left illiterate, penniless, just told, 'you're free.'"[31] In the same period of U.S. history, King recalls, Congress was giving away millions of acres of land to white peasants from Europe, for whom the state "built land-grant colleges to teach them how to farm, provided county agents to further expertise in farming, and then later provided low interest rates so that they could mechanize their farms."[32]

The division of privilege is perpetuated today in terms of what King calls "the two Americas," where there is "socialism for the rich" and "rugged individualism for the poor."[33] In one America, there are "millions of people who have food and material necessities for their bodies, culture and education for their minds, freedom and human dignity for their spirits."[34] In the other America, by contrast, "millions of people find themselves forced to live in inadequate, substandard, and often dilapidated housing conditions," while their children "are forced to attend inadequate, substandard, inferior, quality-less schools," which are "so overcrowded, so devoid of quality, so segregated, if you will, that the best in these minds can never come out."[35]

As I myself work in New Haven, Connecticut, I am reminded every day that the two Americas in King's analysis still persist. On the one hand, there is Yale University where I teach, which is one of the richest educational institutions in the world. On the other hand, only a few blocks away from the university, there is severe and widespread urban poverty, with a population that is predominantly African American. Even within Yale the legacy of slavery in America is manifest, with a majority of white faculty and a majority of black service personnel. Compared with the sixties, there is now a greater institutional commitment to represent ethnic and gender diversity on the faculty. As King was well aware, however, such a solution can never address the root of the problem, which is fundamentally economic. A society that seeks to promote true equality of opportunity cannot limit itself to having a few representatives of an ethnically defined group in positions of power, while the mechanisms of economic marginalization continue to be operative for the majority. Rather, facilitating true equality of opportunity requires that every citizen have adequate resources for material well-being, education, and social recognition.

King's official proposals for achieving such an end mainly concern the *redistribution* of wealth. He advocates for a guaranteed annual income that would eliminate poverty, supplemented by job creation by the state, programs for housing assistance, free health care, and the invigoration of a public school system. These reforms are in line with what I analyzed as "social democracy" in chapter 6 and they resonate with the leading proposals on the progressive Left today, where a universal basic income or other forms of redistribution are seen as the solution to the problems of economic injustice under capitalism. Yet King also senses that there is a deeper problem of *value* under capitalism, which cannot be resolved through the redistribution of wealth.

As we have seen, the problem of value becomes especially manifest in the replacement of living labor time with nonliving, automated production time. In his speeches and books, King keeps returning to automation as a double-edged phenomenon. The automation of previously necessary labor should be emancipatory, since it liberates us from the need to expend our lifetime on tedious forms of work. Yet, under capitalism, automation does not lead to the emancipation of workers but rather to their unemployment, which makes them available for further exploitation in temporary jobs and with lower wages. "As machines replace men, we must again question whether the depth of our social thinking matches the growth of our technological creativity," King emphasizes in a speech to the Workers Union of America in 1962.[36] "We cannot create machines which revolutionize industry unless we simultaneously create ideas commensurate with social and economic reorganization, which harness the power of such machines for the benefit of man. The new age will not be an era of hope but of fear and emptiness unless we master this problem."[37]

The social and economic reorganization that King envisions would require what I have called the *revaluation* of the capitalist measure of value. Under capitalism, technology is not developed for the benefit of our life together but for the sake of profit. Such profit depends on converting the surplus time of our lives into surplus value. Only the extraction of surplus value from living labor time can generate profit and lead to the accumulation of capital wealth. This is why the production of value under capitalism—as we have seen—is measured in terms of socially necessary labor time. No matter how efficient a machine becomes, we cannot extract any surplus value from its own operation but only by exploiting the lifetime of someone who is operating the machine. The purpose of capital gain—the generation and accumulation of capital wealth—thus requires the exploitation of socially necessary labor time. The purpose of capital gain shapes not only the use of machines but also the conception and construction of the relevant technology in the first place.

Hence, the exploitation of the lifetime of workers is necessary under capitalism. For the power of technology to serve emancipation rather than exploitation, we must transform our measure of value from socially necessary labor time to socially available free time. As I argued in chapters 5 and 6, such revaluation demands not only a *theoretical* but also a *practical* transformation of the way we reproduce our lives through technology, education, and labor. Rather than private ownership of the means of production, which exploits socially necessary labor time for the sake of generating capital wealth, we must own the means of production collectively, developing our technologies and producing our goods for the sake of increasing socially available free time.

To recall, socially available free time is not merely leisure time but time devoted to activities that we count as meaningful in themselves. These activities can range from participation in forms of labor that we recognize as necessary for the common good, all the way to the pursuit of individual projects that challenge the given norms of what may be a meaningful activity. For socially available free time to be recognized as a value, we must develop democratic institutional forms of acknowledging one another as social individuals who are ends in ourselves. These institutional forms of democratic life must enable us both to discuss collectively what needs to be done in our community and to engage individually the question of what to do— what is worth doing—with the socially available free time that is produced by the reduction of the socially necessary labor time. The problem with life under capitalism is not only that we are subjected to wage labor but also that we do not have adequate institutional forms for recognizing and cultivating the value of socially available free time. While the decrease of socially necessary labor time under capitalism leads to the problem of unemployment and the loss of a sense of purpose in existence, the increase of socially available free time under democratic socialism leads to the possibility of exploring our priorities and what matters to us, through different kinds of education, forms of work for the sake of the common good, shared projects, leisure activities, and individual pursuits.

The reformation of capitalism through the redistribution of wealth can never achieve such a transformation of society, since the wealth to be distributed is produced by the social relations of capitalist exploitation and commodification. The more we restrict exploitation and commodification, the less wealth we have to distribute. This practical contradiction in any progressive attempt to redistribute wealth is unavoidable as long as we live under capitalism. If we are to understand the concrete challenges that will face all redistributive reforms, we need to recognize the practical contradiction and take it into account in pursuing our political strategies as well as in articulating our priorities.

Let me recall, however, that the practical contradiction does *not* entail that redistributive reforms are meaningless and should be abandoned. As Rosa Luxemburg argued at the beginning of the twentieth century, "the daily struggle for reforms, for the amelioration of the condition of the workers within the framework of the existing social order, and for democratic institutions"[38]—such reform work is absolutely indispensable. Yet, as Luxemburg went on to emphasize, reforms should be understood as means toward the end of a "social revolution,"[39] which requires the overcoming of wage labor. This is why I have argued that social democratic reforms—whether in terms of a universal basic income or a stronger welfare state—should not be conflated with a solution to the basic problem of value under capitalism. Rather, social democratic reforms should be explicitly conceived

and developed as means toward the end of a fundamental transformation of our economic system in terms of democratic socialism, which
requires revaluation rather than redistribution.

In the last years of his life, King can be seen to be on his way
toward such an insight. Rather than limit himself to advocating
reforms, he repeatedly calls for "a radical revolution of values,"[40]
which he links to a notion of "democratic socialism." In Montgomery
in 1955, King had already declared: "We must oppose all exploitation,
we want no classes and castes, we want to set everybody free."[41] Moving into the sixties, King avows his commitment to forge "episodic
social protest into the hammer of social revolution."[42] He urges his
followers not to "think of our movement as one that seeks to inte-
grate the Negro into the existing values of American society,"[43] and
he emphasizes with explicit reference to capitalism that "we are not
interested in being integrated into *this* value structure."[44]

King does not explain at length what he means by "a radical revolution of values," but he makes clear that it hinges on a "shift from a
thing-oriented society to a person-oriented society,"[45] which targets
the purpose of profit in favor of recognizing one another as ends in
ourselves. Moreover, there are indications that King's vision of social
revolution was more radical than his official pronouncements made
it seem. At a staff meeting for his Poor People's Campaign in January
1968, King asked for the tape recorder to be turned off before addressing his idea of democratic socialism. "He talked about the fact that
he didn't believe that capitalism as it was constructed could meet the
needs of poor people, and that what we might need to look at was
a kind of socialism, but a democratic form of socialism," we learn
from an eyewitness report. "I can't say this publicly," King told the
staff members, "and if you say I said it I'm not gonna admit to it."[46]

Only three months later King was shot dead in Memphis. Neither
his notion of a radical revolution of values nor his vision of democratic socialism was ever elaborated. The task of such an elaboration
is ours.

To this end, I have provided a philosophical, economical, and
political account of why the capitalist measure of social wealth is

self-contradictory and calls for a revaluation of value. Furthermore, I have specified the three principles of democratic socialism: the measure of wealth in terms of socially available free time, collective ownership of the means of production, and the pursuit of labor from each according to her ability, to each according to her need. These principles express what the revaluation of value demands in practice. The principles of democratic socialism are not posited as an ideal that is external to the lives we lead. Rather, the principles make explicit what is implicit in the commitment to equality and freedom through which we are already trying to justify our liberal democracy and our capitalist economy. The commitment to equality demands that we pursue our labor from each according to her ability, to each according to her need; the commitment to freedom demands that we measure our wealth in terms of socially available free time; and both of these demands can be met in practice only if we own the means of production collectively, employing and developing them for the benefit of our shared lives rather than for the sake of profit.

To be sure, a set of principles does not by itself entail an effective transformation of our society. Given the power relations of capitalism under which we live, the achievement of democratic socialism can only be the result of a sustained and difficult political struggle. An indispensable part of the struggle, however, is to clarify to ourselves what is wrong with our current form of life and where we are committed to going. I am under no illusion that my account of democratic socialism is *sufficient* to secure that it will be achieved, but I hold the account to be *necessary* to orient our struggle for freedom and grasp the meaning of a truly emancipatory social revolution. The *probability* of change is not a given fact of the world that can be observed from a neutral standpoint; the probability of change is itself something that is transformed by an account that discloses the *possibility* of change in a new light.

For the same reason, I do not regard my philosophical account as external to the struggle for social revolution but as itself being part of such revolution. A philosophical account of what is entailed by our commitment to leading a free life—the kind of account I have sought to provide in this book—is not detached and observational but is itself expressive of a practical commitment to transform our sense of who we are and who we can be. Indeed, there can be no detached standpoint from which we merely observe ourselves or the world. All activities are practical—including the activity of observation— and like all practical activities, philosophy cannot leave the world unchanged but necessarily transforms the terrain it explores. Marx's famous claim ("the philosophers have only *interpreted* the world, in various ways; the point, however, is to *change* it")[47] is therefore misleading. Strictly speaking, any interpretation of the world already changes the world, if only by recognizing or misrecognizing where we find ourselves and who we are trying to be. Many philosophers have certainly *taken themselves* to be merely interpreting the world, but in doing so they were *mistaken*. The point is that philosophy changes the world.

The question, then, is not *if* philosophy changes the world, but *how* it changes the world. As Marx makes clear in one of his most important declarations of intent (the public letter to his friend Arnold Ruge), "we do not attempt dogmatically to prefigure the future, but want to find the new world only through criticism of the old."[48] Such a critique proceeds "by taking any form of theoretical and practical consciousness and developing from the *unique* forms of existing reality the true reality as its norm and final end."[49] The true reality in question is not an abstract ideal but derives from the historical achievement of our commitment to freedom and equality, which is why Marx maintains that "we develop new principles to the world out of its own principles."[50] This critical practice undertakes what Marx calls "the reform of consciousness," which consists in "enabling the world to clarify its consciousness, in waking it from its dream about itself."[51] The task is to "show the world what it is fighting for" by pursuing "the work of our time to clarify to itself (critical philosophy) the meaning of its own struggle and its own desires."[52]

The two forms of consciousness that Marx identifies as the main subjects of critique are religious and political. Our religious and political self-understanding are the main subjects of critique for

Marx—as they are for me in the chapters of *This Life*—since religion and politics are the dominant forms in which we express our understanding of what we struggle for, what we are dreaming of, and what we desire. To transform our understanding of our struggles, our dreams, and our desires, we must therefore transform the practice of religion and politics. As Marx explains in the letter to Ruge:

> Our whole aim can consist only in bringing religious and political questions into self-conscious human form. . . . Our motto must therefore be: Reform of consciousness not through dogmas, but through analyzing the mystical consciousness, which is unclear to itself, whether it appears in religious or political form. Then it will be shown that the world has long been dreaming of something that it actually can make its own, if only it becomes conscious of it. It will be shown that it is not a matter of drawing a great dividing line between past and future, but of *carrying out* the thoughts of the past. And finally, it will be shown that mankind begins no *new* work, but consciously accomplishes its old work.[53]

This is Marx's version of King's "I Have a Dream." The commitment to freedom and equality is a promise that was made in the past but never fulfilled, a dream bequeathed to us by previous generations who were not able to make it a reality, a work that was begun but remains to be done and that we have to carry out as we turn toward the future. As Marx emphasizes, the key to waking up—the key to making the dream an actual reality—is the form of self-consciousness: the recognition that it is *our* dream and that we have to make it our *own* through our practical activity. Making the dream come true is a matter of our work because it is a secular dream of *freedom* (the liberation *of* finite life) rather than a religious dream of *salvation* (the liberation *from* finite life). The lives we lead, the form of society we sustain, will always depend on *us* and on what *we* do with our time.

II

The difference between the secular and the religious may seem to be a decisive difference between Marx and King. In his Christian writings, King himself draws a sharp line between his own religious faith and Marx's secular commitments. While King expresses sympathy with Marx's passion for economic justice, he believes that Marx is a material determinist who denies the "spiritual" aspects of life. Moreover, from his religious standpoint, King takes issue with what he calls "the grand illusion that man, unaided by any divine power, can save himself and usher in a new society."[54] In contrast, King affirms his Christian faith that "at the heart of reality is a Heart, a loving Father who works through history for the salvation of his children. Man cannot save himself, for man is not the measure of all things and humanity is not God. Bound by the chains of his own sin and finiteness, man needs a Savior."[55]

As we shall see, however, such a notion of God plays no role in King's political speeches. His religious sermons avow the existence of "a wise and loving God" who ensures that "this universe is not a tragic expression of meaningless chaos but a marvelous display of orderly cosmos"[56] and will lead us "through death's dark night into the bright daybreak of eternal life."[57] Yet there are no such invocations of supernatural agency and otherworldly redemption when King addresses the struggle for emancipation and the possibility of social change. On the contrary, I will show that the apparently religious rhetoric of King's political speeches is better understood in terms of secular faith. What matters is that *we* can overcome our alienation and be emancipated in *this life*. By the same token, we will see in practice how our spiritual freedom is inseparable from our dependence on material conditions and a fragile form of social recognition. Our finitude is not a chain from which we need to be released by an eternal Savior but the condition of possibility for our freedom and our care for one another.

My secular reading of King draws on the insights of a philosopher whose work we first encountered in chapter 5. In addition, he is the philosopher whom both Marx and King acknowledged as their most important influence: Georg Wilhelm Friedrich Hegel. In an interview during the bus boycott in 1956, King told the *Montgomery Advertiser* that Hegel was his favorite philosopher[58] and references to Hegel recur throughout his work. Already as an undergraduate at Crozer Theological Seminary, King had read Hegel, and while pursuing his doctorate at Boston University he studied Hegel's *Phenomenology of Spirit* as well as his *Philosophy of History* and *Philosophy of Right*. Indeed, the philosophical discussion group that King hosted in his Boston apartment was called "the dialectical society," named after the dialectical method of philosophy that Hegel articulated and that Marx sought to develop in his own way.

From the beginning to the end of his work, Hegel is concerned with grasping the conditions of our freedom as social individuals. Hegel lived in Europe during a historical period (1770–1831) characterized by great political revolutions and profound transformations in the understanding of what it means to be free, stretching from the American Revolution in the 1770s to the beginnings of the Industrial Revolution and economic globalization in the first decades of the 1800s. For Hegel, the two most important events were the publication of Immanuel Kant's revolutionary philosophical trilogy— *Critique of Pure Reason* (1781), *Critique of Practical Reason* (1788), *Critique of Judgment* (1790)—and the French Revolution that began in 1789. Both of these events disclosed the stakes of a modern, secular conception of freedom that Hegel pursued throughout his philosophical trajectory. [59]

Kant's revolutionary move is to argue that the question of authority cannot be settled by appeals to religion, tradition, or the given laws of the state. For a given law to be binding, *we* must hold ourselves to be bound by it. A given law cannot have authority automatically and by itself—it must be taken as authoritative *by* us to have authority *over* us. For the same reason, a given law can lose its hold over us or be called into question by us, which was dramatically demonstrated by the French Revolution and more generally by the transition from monarchy to democracy.

Such dramatic transformations illuminate that we are always acting "under the idea of freedom," as Kant famously puts it. As practical agents we have always been free implicitly, but the Enlightenment commitment to freedom (which Kant memorably describes as our emergence from "self-imposed immaturity")[60] makes our freedom explicit. In articulating the philosophical ground for our freedom, Kant is not trying to *prove* from a third-person standpoint that we have free will. Rather, he is trying to show us that we necessarily understand ourselves to be free from our first-person standpoint. Our freedom cannot be refuted by theoretical doubt, since it is presupposed by the first-person standpoint of anyone who is engaged in the practical activity of leading her life.[61] Being free is not a matter of being unconstrained but of being confronted with the question of what you ought to do and what you ought to believe. From your first-person standpoint, such a question is always at work, if only implicitly. In doing anything—and you are always doing something—you are engaged in the process of responding to the question of what you ought to do and what you ought to believe. If there were no such question involved—if it were immediately given what to do, without any possible hesitation, deliberation, or alteration on your part—you could not understand yourself as an agent, since there would be nothing for *you* to do; it would all be automatic.

Our freedom is therefore inseparable from our *self-consciousness* as actors in the world. Our self-consciousness does not have to be explicit but is inherent in everything we do as practical agents. Following the pathbreaking Hegel scholar Robert Pippin, we can see how Kant's insight regarding self-consciousness is deepened and radicalized by Hegel.[62] As Hegel makes clear, that we are self-conscious does not mean that we can retreat to a detached reflection on ourselves and on the world. We are never merely aware of the world but necessarily *self-aware* as being engaged in the world and committed to a practical activity. For the same reason, the notion of self-consciousness or self-awareness should not be understood in terms of an inner self that is available through introspection or observation. That we are self-conscious does not mean that we are transparent to ourselves, but that we always act on a conception of ourselves and of the world, a conception that may be self-deceived and may need to be revised or called into question.

To take a simple example, if I perceive the color blue, I am not merely perceiving blue; I *take myself* to be perceiving blue. This self-awareness is built into the form of the perception itself, rather than added to the perception in a second step of reflection. Likewise, if I perform an act of friendship, I am not merely doing something; I *take myself* to be acting as a friend and this self-understanding is built into the act itself. That I take myself to be doing something does not mean that I can be certain that my color perception is correct or that my self-understanding as a friend is adequate. On the contrary, it is by virtue of the form of self-consciousness that I can be receptive to being corrected regarding my color perception or challenged regarding my self-understanding as a friend. If my perception of blue was immediate—if no form of self-consciousness was involved in the act of perception—it would be inconceivable to me that my perception could be mistaken, since I would not understand that any activity of my own was involved in the perception. Likewise, if my act of friendship was immediate—if no form of self-consciousness was involved in my being a friend—it would be inconceivable to me that my act could fail to be an act of friendship, since I would not understand that I am answerable for what I do. The form of self-consciousness is therefore the condition for being beholden to others, as well as for the possibility of self-correction and self-transformation. It is because I take myself to be perceiving blue that I can hold myself open to being *mistaken* about the color of what I perceive; and it is because I take myself to be a friend that I can hold myself open to being *mistaken* about what the friendship requires.

Who I am, then, depends on what I actually do, as well as on how my actions and perceptions are recognized by others. To see the color blue it is not enough that I take myself to be seeing the color blue, and to be a friend it is not enough that I take myself to be a friend. In trying to see something, I have to take myself to be seeing something (blue), but I can be mistaken about what I am seeing. Likewise, in trying to be someone, I have to take myself to be someone (a friend), but I can be mistaken about who I am and fail to be a friend.

The possibility of such mistakes and failures is what Hegel calls the "negativity" of self-consciousness. Every act of self-consciousness (even the most immediate perception) has the form of a commitment that may be contested, revised, or negated in some other way. This negativity characterizes even our deepest self-relation. Being a person is not something that can be achieved once and for all, but a purposive activity that must be sustained and is vulnerable to breaking down. As Hegel emphasizes, however, such "negativity" should not be understood as simply negative, since it is equally a positive and indispensable part of what it means to be someone for whom something matters. If there were no fragility built into your self-consciousness—if it were simply given who you are and what you see—there would be nothing at stake for you in doing anything.

Hegel's insight regarding the form of self-consciousness can thus be understood in terms of secular faith. The fundamental form of self-consciousness ("I think") should not be conceived on the model of possessing theoretical, contemplative knowledge but on the model of sustaining a practical commitment ("I believe"). To hold a belief—all the way from a belief about what I perceive to a belief about who I am—is not reducible to being in a state of mind. Rather, to hold a belief is to make a commitment with which I have to keep faith. By the same token, I have to hold myself open to the possible contestation of my beliefs and the fragility of my self-conception. Who I am cannot be immediately given or finally established, but must be embodied in my practices and depends on the recognition of others, who may challenge my conception of what I have done and who I am.

In his *Phenomenology of Spirit*, Hegel explicitly connects his notion of self-consciousness with a new understanding of the relation between the Enlightenment and Faith (his umbrella term for various forms of religious faith).[63] On the one hand, Hegel agrees with the general Enlightenment critique of religious faith, which maintains that there is no God—or any other form of infinite agent—in the universe. Our notions of what is good and just (our norms) are neither legislated by any God nor by properties of the universe itself. Rather, our norms are instituted through our practices and do not exist independently of us. On the other hand, Hegel argues against a notion of the Enlightenment that reduces the status of norms to subjective attitudes and the pursuit of particular interests. While our norms are not given by God or Nature, their authority is not merely subjective, since our own attitudes and interests are formed by socially shared practices from the beginning. For us to have any sense of what counts as good and just in the first place, these norms must be enacted in how we are treated as persons (how we are recognized by others) and how we hold one another accountable for what we do.

In traditions of religious faith, Hegel sees an implicit acknowledgment of the primacy of practice. Through congregational worship, edifying instruction, and social services, a religious community institutes a governing set of norms—a shared understanding of what counts as good and just—while bestowing a sense of dignity on its individual members. An instructive example is the African American Christian tradition out of which King emerged, which places great emphasis on building a community of mutual respect, support, and interaction. By going to church regularly and participating in congregational expressions of devotion (singing, praying, praising) a sense of community is created, which in turn serves as a platform for social organizing.

Such a community can be a source of strength and positive social recognition, but it can also be debilitating and repressive. Already in King's lifetime, there were important critiques of the religious roots of the civil rights movement. Ella Baker and other feminist activists in the movement took issue with the tradition of authoritarian leadership, the subordination of women, and the conservative notions of the nuclear family, which were part of the Southern religious tradition that King inherited.[64] The capacity to criticize and transform such legacies proceeds from the secular recognition that *we* are responsible for the norms that we sustain through our practices.

We never start from the beginning—we always inherit a tradition that tells us what we ought to do—but it is not given how we should take up the tradition in question. We do not merely have a sense of what we *ought* to do (a given norm); we also have the capacity to ask ourselves *if we ought to do what we supposedly ought to do*. This *double ought* structure is at the heart of what I have called our spiritual freedom. In Hegel's terms, we are not simply conscious of what we do but self-conscious of being answerable for what we do and thereby capable of questioning the principles of our practices.

For Hegel, the important task is to build institutional practices that acknowledge and enable us to cultivate our spiritual freedom. The problem with religious forms of faith, then, is that they ultimately disown our spiritual freedom. In order to engage the question of who we should be and what we should do, we must recognize that we ourselves produce the communal norms that we seek to defend, critique, or transform. Religious forms of faith, by contrast, restrict our ability to own the responsibility for the form of life that we institute through our practices. In the last instance, the responsibility for what counts as good and just is disowned, since it is delegated to an independently existing God.

In Hegel's account, the self-understanding of religious believers is therefore at odds with their own practical activity. The actual object of devotion in the practice of faith is the community itself. The Christian Trinity is not an independently existing reality but a pictorial representation of the structure of the community of believers. "God" is a name for the self-legislated communal norms (the principles to which the congregation holds itself); "Christ" is a name for the social actors who sustain the norms through their embodied practices; and "the Holy Spirit" is a name for the institutional relations of the Church through which the norms are actualized. By going to church and worshipping together, the members of the congregation bring into being a form of spiritual life: they hold one another responsible, treat one another as committed, and acknowledge one another's personal dignity.

Such mutual dependence is at the heart of any form of spiritual life, which must be developed and sustained through social practices of recognition that are materially embodied. The religious community, however, does not understand its own activity to be an end in itself. Rather, the individual members take the religious community to be a means for the end of serving an independently existing God and earning a salvation that transcends the fragility of the shared congregational life. The object of religious faith—whether God or any other form of infinite being—is ultimately regarded as *separable* from the practice of faith, since it does not depend on any form of finite life.

In contrast, Hegel's understanding of faith is secular in my sense of the term. He seeks to make us recognize that the object of our faith is *inseparable* from the practice of faith. The end to which we are devoted is our life together—our only life—and not any other-worldly beyond.

We can thus understand why Hegel gives such importance to the Christian notion of the incarnation. The conclusion to the *Phenomenology of Spirit* hinges on the difference between Hegel's philosophical concept of the incarnation and what he describes as the religious understanding.[65] Through the incarnation, the object of faith—God—is recognized as materially embodied and fragile. Yet, from a religious standpoint, the incarnation of God in mortal life is a secondary historical event. God himself in his Trinity is eternal and immutable. At one point in time he becomes a human being in the form of Jesus, but that incarnate form is temporary in relation to his eternal being as Christ. When he exists as Jesus on earth, he is subject to hunger, thirst, fatigue, pain, anxiety, and death, but no such limitations afflict Christ in the eternal Trinity.

For Hegel, by contrast, fragile material embodment is an originary and necessary condition for any form of spiritual life. What the incarnation means is not that God becomes man at a moment in historical time, but that every form of spiritual life must be born and is subject to death. The life-defining norms to which we hold ourselves (God) can exist only by being embodied in our practices as individual social actors (Christ), who can live on and be recognized for who we are only through the institutional relations that we share (the Holy Spirit).

The tripartite structure is the key to Hegel's secular reading of the birth, death, and resurrection of Jesus. What Hegel calls spirit (*Geist*) is not something separate from its material conditions but comes into being as a form of life that can die. A spiritual life is never eternal and can live on only through the social practices that sustain it. For the same reason, resurrection is not an event of salvation, but the form in which we live on as individuals through the spiritual life that we share. The religious understanding of Jesus pictures the resurrection as a historical event that leads to the overcoming of finitude and the salvation of eternal life. For Hegel, on the contrary, the only form of resurrection is the way an individual is recognized and commemorated by a community. A community can enable an individual to live on in memory, but the community itself is fragile and depends on the commitments we maintain.

Accordingly, Hegel argues that the defining feature of spiritual life is the burial of the dead. By commemorating an individual through the act of burial, we recognize in practice that material and spiritual life are *inseparable* but *distinguishable*. On the one hand, the act of burial acknowledges that the spiritual life of a person is absolutely lost with the loss of her material life. The one who was leading her life is irredeemably gone and that is why we mourn. To understand that she is dead—that she no longer exists *for herself*—is to understand that spiritual life is inseparable from material life. On the other hand, the act of burial acknowledges that the spiritual life of a person is distinguishable from her material life. As Hegel puts it, to commemorate someone through the act of burial is to express a commitment that "the individual's ultimate being shall not belong solely to Nature."[66] Even though the "particular material elements"[67] of the deceased body are disintegrating, we can still remember and honor the dead person as the unique individual she was. We do not merely acquiesce to death as a natural event, but maintain our spiritual fidelity to the dead person. Rather than simply register that she *is* dead, we affirm that she *ought* to live on in our memory and that we *ought* to suffer the pain of mourning her death.

Through the act of burial we recognize the normative standing of the deceased as a member of our community and affirm that she is an end in herself, who deserves our devotion even when she no longer can contribute to our life together. In Hegel's language, the act of burial confirms "the right of subjectivity" to be recognized. In burying the dead, we acknowledge that our society is not an independent whole but composed of singular social individuals, whose lives are irreplaceable and unrepeatable. By explicitly marking and commemorating the absence of the dead, we avow that we are not self-sufficient but essentially related to those who have come before us and those who will come after us. Our spiritual life together depends on the projection of the past into the future, which will always remain precarious. The past can live on through our commitments and our social practices, but the movement of living on itself depends on the material support of spiritual life.

The act of burial is a *retrospective* recognition of material and spiritual life as distinguishable but inseparable. The same recognition, however, is at work *prospectively* for anyone who understands herself as an individual agent. To lead my life, my spiritual commitments must be distinguishable from my material life. If I merely followed the requirements of my material life, I would not be intelligible as an individual person with commitments of my own. For my life to be recognized as *mine*, the question of what is *worth* doing with my life must be at issue for me. I must be able to risk my life and ask myself if I ought to prioritize my survival. If my life were not at risk, I could not value my life, since my life would simply be given and not subject to loss. My ability to affirm that my life is worth living—as well as my ability to affirm that something is worth more than my life—presupposes that my life is something that I can risk for the sake of something that I value.

The ability to risk my life is therefore a condition of possibility for my agency. To value anything and express a commitment of my own, I cannot simply follow the demands of my material life but must be able to put my life at stake and engage the question of what is worth prioritizing. In this precise sense, my spiritual freedom is *distinguishable* from my material life. For the same reason, however, my spiritual freedom is *inseparable* from my material life. In risking my life, I cannot be indifferent to my material life and I cannot treat it as inessential to who I am. On the contrary, it is because I value my material life as essential to who I am—because I understand that my spiritual life is inseparable from my material life—that the risk of my life is intelligible *as* a risk. Religious martyrs cannot actually sacrifice their lives from the standpoint of their faith, since they believe that their material death will lead to their eternal life. Only from the standpoint of secular faith—only from the standpoint of holding ourselves to be essentially mortal and inherently valuable as mortal beings—can we sacrifice our lives for the sake of something that matters more to us than our own survival.

By the same token, it is only from the standpoint of secular faith that we can recognize "the right of subjectivity" that belongs to each one of us. To recognize anything as rightfully belonging to you—to recognize anything as being *your own*—I must grasp that you are not self-sufficient and that you depend on a material life. Likewise, for any one of us to make anything our own, we must recognize that our lives are at stake in what we do and that we will lose everything (including ourselves) in death.

The prospect of our own death is a matter of what Hegel calls "absolute fear."[68] The fear of our own death is "absolute" because it is not fear of a specific object or subject but fear of losing the very ability to experience any objects or subjects—the fear of losing our own subjectivity. In absolute fear, the subject and the object of fear are identical, since we fear that our own being will cease to be. As Hegel puts it in a striking passage, it is only because we are "infected all the way through" and "shaken to the core"[69] by absolute fear that we can have any sense of our own individuality and be engaged in the project of trying to make our lives our own.

Hegel's notion of absolute fear can thus be understood in terms of what I have analyzed as anxiety before death. As I argued at length in chapter 4, anxiety before death is not reducible to a psychological, anthropological, or biological phenomenon. Rather, anxiety before death is a condition of intelligibility for spiritual freedom. Only through the anxiety of being finite can someone ask herself what is worth doing with her life—what is worth prioritizing—and thereby make something her own.

Accordingly, Hegel maintains that spiritual life can be what it is only in and through its relation to death. "Death," Hegel writes, "is the most worthy of fear, and holding onto the dead requires the greatest force."[70] Yet only by facing death—and holding on to the dead through the movement of living on—can the life of spirit come into its own:

> The life of spirit is not a life that shrinks from death and keeps itself untouched by devastation, but rather the life that endures devastation and maintains itself in it. Spirit wins its truth only by finding itself in absolute dismemberment. Spirit is this power not as the positive which looks away from the negative, as when we say of something that it is nothing or false, and then—being done with it—move on to something else. Rather, spirit is this power only by looking the negative in the face and tarrying with it.[71]

To lead a spiritual life is always to live in relation to the possibility of devastation and death. We can become ill or disabled. Our loved ones may leave us or be taken away from us. Projects to which we devote our lives can fail, and we ourselves may break the integrity to which we hold ourselves. Moreover, the standard of integrity to which we hold ourselves can be called into question—either by ourselves or by others—and the lives we have tried to lead can come to be seen as a waste of our time. In short, who we take ourselves to be and anything to which we are committed can be *negated*, leaving us devastated and—in the last instance—dead. As Hegel makes clear, such "negativity" (the ever-present possibility of negation and loss) cannot be dismissed as inessential but must be recognized as an essential

part of any form of spiritual life. The risk of "absolute dismember-
ment" is intrinsic to why it matters that we keep anything together.
Without the possibility of failure the very notion of success would
be unintelligible and without the possibility of death the very form
of life—the form of self-maintenance—would have no purpose.

The common denominator for what I have called "religious"
ideals is the goal of being absolved from negativity, absolved from
the pain of loss. In the *Phenomenology of Spirit*, Hegel presents three
paradigmatic forms of trying to achieve such religious absolution:
Stoicism, Skepticism, and what Hegel calls the Unhappy Consciousness.[72] What they have in common is that they seek to overcome
secular faith—to be released from the commitment to a finite form
of life—in order to achieve peace of mind. In Stoicism the ideal peace
of mind is posited as a state of apathy (*apatheia*), and in Skepticism
it is posited as a state of being undisturbed by anything (*ataraxia*).
For the Unhappy Consciousness, the ideal peace of mind cannot be
achieved in this life but only in the eternal bliss of an otherworldly
beyond.

Following his characteristic philosophical method, Hegel does not
criticize Stoicism, Skepticism, and the Unhappy Consciousness from
an external standpoint. Rather, he seeks to show that these religious
forms of life cannot resolve their own contradictions and require a
transformation of their own self-understanding.

The point of departure for Hegel is Stoicism (as it was for me
in chapters 1 and 2), since Stoicism is the most fundamental form
of denying the commitment to a finite form of life. Stoicism is still
influential today as a popular form of practical wisdom, with clear
affinities to Buddhism. The Stoic acknowledges that his body is frail
and that all his social relations—all forms of his dependence on other
people—are precarious. Yet the Stoic holds that his own virtue can
be invulnerable to anything that happens to his body or his social
standing in the world. The key to achieving such invulnerability is
to renounce the *beliefs*—the practical commitments—that make us
suffer. If I believe that my physical well-being is important, I will
suffer from being sick, since I am practically committed to sustain-

ing my health. Likewise, if I believe that it is important that I have the material and social resources to lead a free life, I will suffer from being enslaved, since I am practically committed to my emancipation. The Stoic, however, will try to teach me that it does not matter that I am sick or that I live my life in chains. Stoic virtue is a matter of letting go of such concerns and contemplating the rational order of the cosmos, thereby attaining what the Stoic philosopher Spinoza famously describes as "intellectual love of God." The intellectual love of God is independent of any judgment I may have regarding my physical condition or my social standing. According to Spinoza, all our suffering is caused by the "false beliefs" that consist in our practical commitments, which distinguish between what we count as good and evil, success and failure, right and wrong. Such "false beliefs" prevent us from attaining what Spinoza calls the "blessedness" of having "complete peace of mind." Attaining complete peace of mind is for Spinoza the true religious salvation, which makes us accept everything that happens to us as necessary rather than as something that we can change.

The problem with such peace of mind, as Hegel points out, is that it is completely empty. The Stoic says that he is committed to "the true," "the good," and "the just," but he cannot provide any determinate content to these concepts. For truth, goodness, and justice to have any determinate content, we must hold something to be true, good, and just. Moreover, we must distinguish between what we hold to be true and false, good and evil, just and unjust. *How* we make such distinctions is contestable and revisable, but *making* them is necessary for any form of responsibility. To determine anything as true, good, and just requires a practical commitment that binds us to suffer from and revolt against what we count as false, evil, and unjust. Yet the supposed wisdom of the Stoic is to withdraw from such commitments, since they make him liable to agonize over the state of the world and leave him vulnerable to contestation. The Stoic is thus caught in a self-contradiction. Stoicism is supposed to be a way of life that makes us virtuous citizens, but all it can do is point us to an empty peace of mind that dissolves any determinate conception of the true, the good, and the just. In Hegel's apt phrase, the goal of Stoic apathy is a "lifelessness" that "consistently *withdraws* from the movement of existence, *withdraws* from actual doing as well as from suffering,"[73] and in effect renounces any commitment to anything.

The "truth" of Stoicism is therefore Skepticism, in the sense that Skepticism makes explicit the denial of all forms of commitment, which is merely implicit in Stoicism. Like Stoicism, Skepticism was founded as a school of thought in Ancient Greece, with the mission of educating its pupils into a way of life that is absolved from all forms of painful disturbance. Unlike the Stoic, the Skeptic has no pretense that such absolution is compatible with a commitment to truth, goodness, or justice. On the contrary, the Skeptic recognizes that an apathetic peace of mind can be achieved only by negating the determinate content of any thought or action. To this end, the Skeptic learns a method of negating the validity of any belief that anyone may hold—including any belief regarding truth, goodness, or justice—with the aim of being released from all forms of practical commitments and attaining the peace of mind he calls *ataraxia*.

By the same token, however, the Skeptic is caught in a contradiction of his own. Skepticism promotes itself as a therapeutic way of life by promising that its method of negating all beliefs will lead to peace of mind. In practice, however, the Skeptic has to spend all his time refuting beliefs he holds to be false. As long as the Skeptic is doing anything, there will always be at least one belief that he has to refute—namely, the belief that what he is doing matters. Moreover, the Skeptic has no way of justifying his own commitment to *ataraxia*. Why is it better to have peace of mind than to be passionately engaged? Why is it better to be undisturbed than to be moved and deeply affected by what happens to you? The Skeptic denies that anything ultimately matters while holding that *ataraxia* ultimately matters, and he denies being committed to anything, while being committed to not being committed to anything. The Skeptic claims to be indifferent, but he is far from indifferent to the fact that he and others fail to be indifferent.[74]

The "truth" of Skepticism, then, is the Unhappy Consciousness.

Both the Stoic and the Skeptic seek to achieve religious absolution—complete peace of mind—by virtue of their own activity. They are therefore bound to be dissatisfied and unreconciled ("unhappy") with themselves, since their own activity is marked by the condition of finitude that they aspire to leave behind. The unavoidable dissatisfaction is merely implicit in Stoicism and Skepticism, but it becomes explicit in the Unhappy Consciousness. In Hegel's *Phenomenology* the Unhappy Consciousness refers primarily to various forms of Christian faith, but it should also be understood more broadly as any standpoint that regards our finitude as a negative restriction, which prevents us from achieving the salvation we supposedly desire. The Unhappy Consciousness acknowledges that there can be no absolution from finitude in this life, but it treats our dependence on material support and on the fragile recognition of others as a lamentable condition, which falls short of how our lives ideally should be. This is the standpoint that Hegel seeks to overcome and help us leave behind.

The aim of Hegel's *Phenomenology* can thus be seen as a secular "reconciliation" with our finitude, in the sense of grasping that our finitude is not a limitation that blocks us from attaining the absolute. Rather, grasping finitude as the condition of intelligibility for any form of spiritual life is what Hegel calls the "absolute knowing" of "absolute spirit." Hegel's use of these terms has led to centuries of misunderstanding, whereby Hegel is read as promoting some form of theology of a Cosmic Spirit or Absolute God who actualizes himself in human history. Nothing could be further from the truth. The absolute knowing of absolute spirit is not the act of a divine mind, but our philosophical grasp of the conditions of spiritual life. This philosophical grasp makes clear that there can be no life without death, no spirit without matter, no success without failure. Such finitude is "absolute" in the sense that it does not fall short of an eternal life, but is the condition of possibility for any form of life.

We can thus grasp the full stakes of Hegel's secular reading of the incarnation and my secular reading of the crucifixion in chapter 3. For the Unhappy Consciousness of Christian faith, we suffer from a lack of eternal life and need to be redeemed from our finitude. The birth and death of Jesus are supposed to accomplish such redemption. Through a movement that the Bible calls *kenosis*, God descends into the mortal body of Jesus. God thereby becomes susceptible to suffering and death, culminating in the excruciating crucifixion of Jesus. The crucifixion is the lowest point in the descending movement of *kenosis*, but in the end God does not succumb to its gravity. On the contrary, from a religious perspective, the resurrection of Jesus and his ascent to heaven paves the way for salvation by showing that even the most painful form of devastation and death can be transcended.

In Luther's German translation of the Bible—which was important for Hegel—*kenosis* is translated by the term *Entäusserung*, which designates the activity of God emptying himself into the world at the moment of creation and into the body of Jesus at the moment of the incarnation. By becoming mortal, God empties himself of his divine attributes; he renounces omnipotence, omnipresence, and omniscience. Luther's translation makes it possible to hear this act of self-emptying as an expression of devotion, as if God gave himself over to the world wholeheartedly, avowing his belonging to mortal life without reserve. Yet, from the standpoint of Christian faith and the Unhappy Consciousness, we cannot be devoted wholeheartedly to *this life*. The descent of God into a mortal body is merely an intermediary step that is followed by the ascent to heaven. The mortal body of Jesus—subject to need, dissolution, and irrevocable death—is ultimately *separated* from the "glorious" body of resurrection that is immortal. As Luther puts it, the historical Jesus who lived on earth "is really dead as a man," but as the divinity of Christ "he has remained always alive, for life could and cannot die."[75] In the same way, the Unhappy Consciousness separates the notion of its own salvation from the fate of the mortal body to which it is bound on earth. Our mortality is conceived as a descent (a "fall") from which we need to be saved by an ascent to eternal life.

For Hegel, on the contrary, the mortality of Jesus should lead us to recognize fragile material embodiment as *inseparable* from any form of spiritual life. Spiritual life does not descend or "fall" into finitude. Rather, spiritual life is from the beginning subject to—and the subject of—a finite form of life. We can see how Hegel makes this point by converting Luther's religious conception of *Entäusserung* as divine love into a secular notion of spiritual commitment. The term *Entäusserung* is used frequently both in Hegel's *Phenomenology of Spirit* and his *Science of Logic*, but it becomes particularly significant in the concluding sections of the *Phenomenology*, where Hegel employs it on every page.[76]

At stake here are the conditions of possibility for leading a spiritual life, both individually and collectively. Leading a spiritual life requires a conception of who we *ought* to be as individuals and as a community, what Hegel calls an "Idea" of who we are. Following Hegel's secular notion of the incarnation, the Idea of who we are is not something that can exist in a separate realm; it must be materially embodied in our practices. Moreover, the Idea of who we are is not contemplative. We cannot discover who we are through introspection, but only by emptying ourselves out in the sense of being wholeheartedly engaged—being at stake, being at risk—in what we do and how we are recognized by others. The Idea of who we are is not an abstract ideal that is external to our form of life; it is the principle of intelligibility in light of which we can succeed or fail to be who we are striving to be.

For example, the Idea of being Martin is striving to maintain my existential identity: the order of priority among my practical identities that gives me a sense of *what* matters in my life and *when* it matters, what must be done sooner and later. If I had no Idea of what it means to be Martin, I could not strive to be anyone or do anything, since I would not be able to discriminate between what is important and unimportant in my life. Nothing would show up either as urgent or tedious, central or peripheral, since the question of priority would be unintelligible to me. Likewise, the Idea of the United States of America is striving to hold ourselves to the principles with which we identify as citizens. If we had no Idea of the United States of America, we could not strive to be Americans or do anything that we take to be American. No form of legislation or political practice could show up as consistent or inconsistent with our commitment to the United States of America, since we would have no Idea of who we are supposed to be.

The Idea of a form of life is therefore the condition of intelligibility for both any form of fidelity and any form of betrayal. It is because I have an Idea of what it means to be Martin that I can betray myself as a person, and it is because we have an Idea of the United States of America that we can betray ourselves as a nation. Being Martin is not something that happens automatically; I have to strive to be Martin and I can fail to be who I take myself to be. Likewise, being the United States of America does not happen automatically; we have to strive to be the United States of America and we can fail to be who we take ourselves to be. Moreover, striving to be Martin is not a task that can be completed and striving to be the United States of America is not a mission that can be accomplished. Rather, striving to be Martin is intrinsic to being Martin, just as striving to be the United States of America is intrinsic to being the United States of America.

For the same reason, the Idea of who we ought to be is itself something that can be challenged and transformed. Because any Idea—whether of an individual or a collective—must be embodied in practice, the Idea of who we ought to be can always be taken up in a different way, called into question, and be the subject of a revolution. This is the radical implication of Hegel's notion of *Entäusserung.* There is not *first* an inner Idea that is *then* subjected to an external fate in the world, and there is not *first* an inner self that is *then* dependent on the recognition of others. Rather, any Idea and any sense of self must from the beginning be externalized in the material practices they sustain. We cannot even try to be anyone or do anything without putting ourselves at stake—pouring ourselves forth, emptying ourselves out—in the activities to which we are committed and which may demand a profound transformation of who we take ourselves to be. This finitude is both the promise and the peril of spiritual life.

We can thus clarify the stakes of a secular reconciliation with finitude and draw together the threads of *This Life*. The Unhappy Consciousness of religious faith cannot reconcile itself with being *alive*, in the sense of being vulnerable to pain, loss, and death. As we have seen, any form of life must strive to maintain itself—to sustain a fragile material body—in order to be what it is. Even in the most fulfilled form of spiritual life, striving to be ourselves is essential to being ourselves. The Unhappy Consciousness, however, thinks that we are striving to put an end to striving and long to rest in peace. Religious reconciliation is therefore always deferred to an unattainable future, when we will be absolved from the finitude of life. A secular reconciliation, by contrast, recognizes that "there is nothing degrading about being alive" (as Hegel puts it in a poignant phrase).[77] Being vulnerable to pain, loss, and death is not a fallen condition but inseparable from being someone for whom something can matter.

The point is *not* that we should embrace pain, loss, and death. The idea of such an embrace is just another version of the religious ideal of being absolved from vulnerability. If we embraced pain we would not suffer, if we embraced loss we would not mourn, and if we embraced death we would not be anxious about our lives. Far from advocating such invulnerability, a secular reconciliation with finitude acknowledges that *we must be vulnerable*—we must be marked by the suffering of pain, the mourning of loss, the anxiety before death—in order to lead our lives and care about one another. Only through such an acknowledgment can we turn away from the religious promise of absolution and turn toward our time together. Only through such an acknowledgment can we understand the urgency of changing our lives. We are reconciled with being alive, but for that very reason we are *not* reconciled to living unworthy lives. We demand a better society and we know that it depends on us. In taking action, we are not waiting for a timeless future but grasp in practice that our time is all we have.

III

We are now ready to return to Memphis in 1968. On February 12—
the birthday of Abraham Lincoln—nearly thirteen hundred black
sanitation workers in Memphis went on strike. Their labor conditions were intolerable and symptomatic of the economic forms of
exploitation that plagued the black community even after the legal
victories of the civil rights movement. Despite working full-time,
the sanitation workers lived in poverty and did not earn enough to
provide for their families. They had no insurance and regularly suffered severe injuries in the physically demanding work of handling
garbage tubs and packer trucks. They worked all day in filth, but the
city of Memphis did not provide them with gloves, uniforms, or even
a place to shower. The equipment at their disposal was outdated,
but the city refused to spend money on updating it. Moreover, the
sanitation workers were not allowed to form a union and the black
employees were addressed as "boys" by their white bosses, with clear
echoes of the epoch of slavery.[78]

The precariousness of the labor situation had been highlighted
on February 1, when two black workers—Echol Cole and Robert
Walker—were crushed to death in a packer truck, owing to a defec-
tive mechanism that the city had neglected to replace. Less than two
weeks later the strike began, with the sanitation workers demanding
union rights and improved labor conditions. They were met with
fierce resistance from the white mayor and the city council. The
police attacked the strikers and their supporters with mace, while
their demands for basic rights were vilified by the media. Yet the
black community of Memphis came together in support of the sanitation workers. There were nightly meetings in the churches to organize and mobilize the community in daily actions. Ministers joined
workers, students, housewives, and other citizens in picket lines,
protest marches, and a boycott of downtown stores. As the movement grew, leading national union organizers such as William Lucy,
Jesse Epps, and Joe Paisley were sent to Memphis to help the strikers. The city officials responded by stepping up police intimidation,

threats of violence, and sanctions. Memphis was on the verge of a major confrontation between workers and the owners of capital.

At this time, King was traveling across the country to gather support for his Poor People's Campaign. His radical initiative was being met in many areas by large-scale resistance and skepticism, even among those it was meant to emancipate. King was deeply discouraged and his own staff members questioned his vision of building a genuine class movement proceeding from the poorest members of the population. News of the Memphis strike thus emerged as a possible new front line for King's initiative. The sanitation workers had managed to unite almost the entire black community in Memphis across class lines and thereby pursued a version of King's vision on the ground. When he was asked to come to demonstrate his support for the strike, King did not hesitate and flew to Memphis against the advice of his staff.

King first arrived in Memphis on March 18, at a crucial moment of the strike. On the evening when King was scheduled to speak, more than fifteen thousand strike activists were gathering in the Mason Temple Church of God in Christ. It was the largest indoor meeting in the entire history of the civil rights movement and it restored King's faith in the power of the people. "I've never seen a community as together as Memphis," King testified, "you are all doing in Memphis what I hope to do with the Poor People's Campaign."[79]

In the Mason Temple, a space designated for religious worship was transformed into a place for the celebration and reinvigoration of a shared secular commitment to emancipation. The congregation sang old hymns that had been converted into anthems for the labor movement in the 1930s and 1940s, as well as for the civil rights movement in the 1960s. These hymns direct our devotion not to a transcendent God but to what we can achieve if we stand together and keep faith with our commitment to spiritual freedom. On March 18, the congregation sang "We Shall Not Be Moved," followed by "I Woke Up This Morning with My Mind Stayed on Freedom," and then the most famous of the hymns: "We Shall Overcome." The latter hymn has become so iconic that its powerful resonance tends to

be lost for us today, but it is crucial to hear the resolute expression
of secular faith at its core. What we believe deep in our hearts—the
hymn avows—is not that God will save us but that *we* shall overcome our subordination through collective action. The hymn had
first been adopted as a labor movement anthem by black women on
strike in Charleston, South Carolina, in 1946, and it had become an
integral part of the civil rights movement under King. While people
sang, donations were collected for the sanitation workers on strike.
Participants testified to the unworthy labor conditions they were
combating and spoke on behalf of the two workers who had suffered
terrible deaths on February 1. In characteristic fashion, a back-and-
forth developed between the speakers and their audience, in a mutual
recognition and reaffirmation of the struggle for freedom. The whole
evening was a powerful demonstration of what came to be known
as "the spirit of Memphis"—the resolve of a people to change its
conditions—and it gave King new hope. "Martin was visibly shaken
by all this," James Lawson later recalled, "for this kind of support
was unprecedented in the movement. No one had ever been able to
get these numbers out before."[80]

The mass meetings in the Mason Temple—and the two speeches
that King gave there—can be seen as profound manifestations of
secular faith. To engage their implications, we must here make
explicit the final aspect of secular faith. The object of secular faith
is always a *spiritual cause,* which moves us to act and determines what
is important to us.[81] Spiritual causes are those for the sake of which
we lead our lives and try to respond to the demands of our practical
identities. For example, a spiritual cause can be the parental love that
focuses our attention, the artistic vocation that gives direction to
our aspirations, or—as was the case for King and many of the other
activists in Memphis—the political cause for the sake of which we
are willing to risk our lives.

The causes can vary, but any form of spiritual life has a spiritual
cause. The question of who we are and what we do—as well as the
question of whether we are succeeding or failing in our efforts—is
inseparable from the spiritual causes for the sake of which we act.

These are *spiritual* causes—as distinct from *natural* causes—since their efficacy is dependent on the commitments we sustain. A natural cause (e.g., gravity as the natural cause of falling bodies) operates independently of anything we do and desire. A spiritual cause, by contrast, only exists *as* a cause insofar as we believe in it.

The belief in a spiritual cause does not necessarily become explicit and it precedes consciously held beliefs, since it gives us a sense of who we are and what matters to us in the first place. Moreover, there is no neutral standpoint from which we are free to choose our spiritual causes. Before we can decide anything, we are already constrained by the spiritual causes we inherit from the social world into which we are born. Nevertheless, *we* are responsible for sustaining, contesting, or changing the spiritual causes that determine the stakes of our actions. For there to *be* demands of parenthood, artistic vocations, and political causes, we must hold ourselves to those demands and thereby believe that they matter.

When we *own* our secular faith, we acknowledge that the object of our faith—our spiritual cause—is *dependent* on our practice of faith. The practice of faith is our practical identity (e.g., political activist) and the object of faith is our spiritual cause (e.g., our political cause).

Secular faith is a condition of intelligibility for all forms of care, but there is always a question of the degree to which we own or disown our secular faith—the degree to which we acknowledge that our own being is at stake in our actions and that our spiritual cause depends on our commitments. Throughout this book, I have sought to show the emancipatory and transformative possibilities that are opened up when we *own* our secular faith, both individually and collectively.

Inversely, what I call religious faith *disowns* our secular faith. Religious faith takes the object of faith to be a god—or some other form of infinite being—that is *independent* of our practice of faith. Our spiritual cause is treated as though it were a being that commands and has power over us without being dependent on us. This is the type of faith that King espouses in his religious sermons. In his role as a Christian preacher, King claims that "the universe is guided by a benign Intelligence whose infinite love embraces all mankind," namely, "the one eternal God" who has "strength to protect us" with his "unlimited resources"[82] and on whose grace we depend. From this religious perspective, we cannot save ourselves through collective action. Rather, we must have faith in an eternal Savior who is beyond our comprehension, since "his will is too perfect and his purposes are too extensive to be contained in the limited receptacle of time and the narrow walls of earth."[83]

For the same reason, however, the supposed relation between God and our emancipation becomes incomprehensible. What we take to be evil and unjust can be part of God's "plan" or his unfathomable "purposes," which purportedly redeem what happens to us beyond anything we can understand. Moreover, if God is beyond our comprehension, his notion of goodness and justice can be completely at odds with our own. As King avows in one of his religious sermons, "I do not pretend to understand all of the ways of God or his particular timetable for grappling with evil. Perhaps if God dealt with evil in the overbearing way that we wish, he would defeat his ultimate purpose."[84] Given this acquiescence of religious faith, the very idea of an "ultimate purpose" (a spiritual cause) becomes empty and unintelligible. The purpose of God's "infinite love" is anything and nothing, since it has no determinate content. Any determinate content is what *we* sustain—what we hold to be good, just, and true—and only we can be responsible for the spiritual cause to which we devote ourselves. To own our secular faith is to acknowledge this responsibility and make ourselves answerable to others for the commitments we maintain.

In contrast, the Unhappy Consciousness of religious faith—the notion that we are sinful, fatally limited creatures who must defer to an incomprehensible God—cannot prevent itself from reverting back into Skepticism and Stoicism. If what we take to be evil can be good in the eyes of God, we can deny any authority to our moral judgments (Skepticism); and if what we take to be injustice can be part of God's plan for justice, we can be enjoined to accept anything that happens to us with equanimity (Stoicism). As King explicitly affirms in one of his religious sermons, we do not need "an earthly fallout shelter" since "God is our eternal fallout shelter" and we should therefore "face the fear that the atomic bomb has aroused with the faith that we can never travel beyond the arms of the Divine."[85]

Such a religious notion of God cannot account for the way King uses the term in his political speeches. When King says that "God" has commanded us to help the poor to emancipate themselves—and that he is doing "God's will" in pursuing social freedom as an end in itself—King cannot be referring to the religious notion of an eternal God, since by his own admission he cannot determine the will of such a God. The command or the will of God only makes sense if we understand the term in a Hegelian way. "God" is a name for the communal norms that we have legislated to ourselves and to which we hold ourselves. When King invokes the will and the command of God in his political speeches, he is reminding us of what we are committed to in being committed to social freedom for all. The commitment to mutual social freedom as an end in itself—as a spiritual cause that commands us to act—is our secular achievement and not due to any religious revelation. Freedom as an end in itself is not promoted by any of the world religions or by any of its founding figures. Neither Jesus nor Buddha nor Muhammad has anything to say about freedom as an end in itself. That is not an accident but consistent with their teachings. What ultimately matters from a religious perspective is not freedom but salvation; what ultimately matters is not to lead a life but to be saved from being alive.

When King pursues the struggle for social freedom as an end in itself, he is therefore committed to a secular rather than a religious cause. In King's own account, he chose the ministry because of "an inescapable urge to serve society" rather than because of any religious revelation: "My call to the ministry was not a miraculous or supernatural something; on the contrary, it was an inner urge calling me to serve humanity."[86] Indeed, according to his biographer David J. Garrow, already as a young man King was dissatisfied with how "many ministers preached only about the afterlife, rather than about what role the church could play in improving present-day society."[87]

The turn toward secular freedom rather than religious salvation is brought to a head in King's final speech on April 3, 1968, the night before he was killed. While the storm was rattling the windows of the Mason Temple, King laid down the promise of his legacy:

> It's all right to talk about "long white robes over yonder," in all of its symbolism. But ultimately people want some suits and dresses and shoes to wear down here. It's all right to talk about "streets flowing with milk and honey," but God has commanded us to be concerned about the slums down here, and his children who can't eat three square meals a day. It's all right to talk about the new Jerusalem, but one day, God's preacher must talk about the new New York, the new Atlanta, the new Philadelphia, the new Los Angeles, the new Memphis, Tennessee. This is what we have to do.[88]

To speak of the new Memphis—rather than the new Jerusalem—is to avow that we can achieve our collective emancipation in this life. The new Memphis is the object of a secular faith, a spiritual cause that moves us to take action and fight to establish the social conditions for mutual recognition of our freedom. The commitment to the new Memphis must therefore be distinguished from a commitment to Christian charity. Christian charity does not seek to abolish poverty in this life but rather maintains the poor in an asymmetrical position of dependence on those who offer them charity, leaving them waiting for redemption in an eternal life (the new Jerusalem). To be committed to the new Memphis is, on the contrary, to be committed to the actual emancipation from poverty in this life. No one should depend on charity, since everyone should be part of a society in which we are committed to give from each of us according to our ability, to each of us according to our need. This is the core of democratic socialism.

The spiritual cause of democratic socialism can be sustained only through secular faith. The new Memphis only exists insofar as we strive to achieve it. Even in being achieved, it will always remain fragile, always depend on what we do and how we recognize one another. Whether in striving to achieve or to sustain the new Memphis, it will always be necessary to make the double movement of secular faith. We must acknowledge the utter fragility of what holds our lives together—our institutions, our shared labor, our love, our mourning—and yet keep faith with what offers no final guarantee. This is the double movement of secular faith. What we believe in requires our devotion because it can be lost and cease to be if we do not act on its behalf. It is because our spiritual cause is fragile—because what sustains us can break apart or be shattered—that it matters what we do and how we treat one another.

When King turns toward the new Memphis at the end of his last speech, his words reverberate with a profound secular transformation of the religious notion of the promised land. King spoke without notes, and the gravity of the moment pervades the final sentences. Acutely aware that his own lifetime may be coming to an end—that he is risking his life for the sake of a spiritual cause—his words bear the weight of a future in which everything is at stake. He holds forth the promised land not as a personal afterlife but as the possibility of a different society for those who will live on after him:

> Like anybody, I would like to live a long life. Longevity has its place. But I'm not concerned about that now. I just want to do God's will. And He's allowed me to go up to the mountain. And I've looked over and I've seen the promised land. I may not get there with you. But I want you to know tonight, that we as a people will get to the promised land.[89]

King's vision of the promised land is not a vision of eternal life—not a vision of the new Jerusalem—but a vision of what we the people can achieve, a vision of the new Memphis. Because it is a vision of collective emancipation that can become a reality only through our generational efforts, it does not project a timeless eternity where we will all come together as one. Rather, King's vision of the new Memphis is committed to a temporal future that we ourselves may not live to see. Like King, we may not get there. Yet we can act on behalf of the new Memphis, we can own it as our spiritual cause, we can make it our creed through our deeds.

At the first mass meeting in the Mason Temple—the one on March 18—King had promised to turn the creed into a revolutionary deed. Encouraged by his interaction with the fifteen thousand strike activists in congregation, King concluded his speech by calling for a general strike in Memphis. The momentous response can be heard right before the tape recording of King's speech breaks off. As the labor historian Michael K. Honey recounts the event, the Mason Temple erupted in a "thunderous ovation from the crowd" as "people stood, cheering and yelling, clapping, dancing, singing, celebrating the very audacity of the idea. . . . Black workers in alliance with the community could shut down all of Memphis."[90] As Honey reminds us, no one had ever proposed a general strike of the black population during the civil rights movement and general strikes are rare in American labor history. For King, it was a watershed moment. His call for a general strike embodied the shift from the struggle for civil rights to the struggle for economic justice, which was at the heart of the Poor People's Campaign he was in the midst of launching.

More than any other form of collective action, a general strike makes explicit the social division of labor that sustains our lives. A general strike in Memphis would have brought home in the most concrete way that the city could not function without the labor of the black population who were working full-time but nevertheless living in poverty. As Honey argues in his study of the Memphis strike, "nonviolent direct action on such a scale would have marked a turning point in the trajectory of the black freedom struggles of the 1960s,"[91] which could have led to a further radicalization of the movement led by King.

Yet the general strike in Memphis never came to be. King was planning to return to Memphis on March 22 to lead the initiative of the general strike. The spiritual cause of the movement, however, was disrupted by an unexpected natural cause. A massive snowstorm— the second-largest in the entire history of Memphis—descended upon an otherwise warm early spring. Instead of a general strike shutting down the city, more than sixteen inches of snow prevented anyone from going to work.

At least nine people died from the violent weather and the impact of the snowstorm on the emancipatory movement in Memphis turned out to be severe. King was prevented from returning to the city until March 28, when he led a mass protest march through downtown. The delay due to the snowstorm had broken the momentum toward an imminent general strike and gave the police as well as the FBI time to plan how to infiltrate the mass protest. Planted participants began smashing windows during the march led by King, giving the police an excuse to attack. More than seven hundred people were taken to the hospital as a result of the violent confrontations, and an unarmed black sixteen-year-old—Larry Payne—was killed by the police. The FBI disseminated secret memos blaming the events on King and the national news media adhered to the narrative, indicting the strike movement as well as King's leadership.

The backlash was intense. Not only the strike in Memphis but also King's planned march on Washington with the Poor People's Campaign was in jeopardy. Nevertheless, King returned to Memphis on April 3 to plan another protest march and to attend the meeting in the Mason Temple at which he gave his last speech. The day after—in the early evening of April 4, 1968—he was shot to death outside his motel room. He was thirty-nine years old.

IV

There is no way to assess all the consequences of King's death, or to estimate what he could have accomplished. What can be said is that the murder of King belongs to a number of murders of socialist organizers in the 1960s, along with other forms of violent repression that gradually weakened the struggle for freedom. The sanitation workers in Memphis did win their strike, and their labor conditions were improved, but the larger project to which the strike belonged for King (the Poor People's Campaign) was defeated shortly after his death. The march on Washington took place in May and June 1968, without King but carrying forth his memory, with thousands of poor people setting up a camp called "Resurrection City" in the capital. There were resilient demonstrations and articulated demands, but in June the Washington police tore down Resurrection City, attacking the poor with teargas and batons.

I relate these events because it should never be forgotten that the historical defeats of socialist movements are not merely a matter of having an insufficient analysis or an insufficient strategy. The defeats are also deeply linked to the asymmetry of capitalist power relations and the all too real violence exercised to suppress attempts to organize for the sake of a different vision of society.

As the political-economical framework of the 1970s, the 1980s, and the 1990s gradually shifted toward neoliberal capitalism, the very idea of "freedom" predominantly became part of a right-wing discourse, where the freedom of the market to operate for the sake of profit explicitly took precedence over the freedom of we the people to recognize ourselves—to recognize our commitments—in the institutions we maintain. As I have argued, however, it is not enough to criticize neoliberal forms of capitalism in order to reclaim the idea of freedom for an emancipatory agenda and pursue a commitment to democratic socialism. Rather, we must grasp how the very conception of *value* under capitalism—how value is produced and measured in a capitalist society—is inimical to the actualization of our freedom, the care for our material conditions, and our lifetime.

We can thus return to the issue with which I began this book and which is arguably the most pressing global issue of our time: climate change. Our ecological crisis is a stark reminder that our lives depend not only on the fragile self-maintenance of our material bodies but also on the fragile material self-maintenance of the global ecosystem to which we belong. Moreover, the insight that our way of life is destroying the ecosystem on which we depend has reanimated questions regarding the viability of "capitalism" even in mainstream political debates. Yet the systematic understanding of capitalism that is needed to grasp the fundamental issues involved is strikingly absent and calls for the revaluation of value that I have articulated.

A telling example is Naomi Klein's influential book *This Changes Everything: Capitalism vs. the Climate*. Klein rightly emphasizes that the problem of climate change cannot primarily be addressed on an individual level but must be understood in terms of the economic system under which we live. Drawing on a wide body of research, Klein shows that our economic priorities—the generation of profit and the "growth" of capital—are the main reasons we are not able to implement the measures that are needed to prevent an ecological disaster. When it comes to organizing for the sake of profit, governments are able to cooperate globally and effectively (as in the creation of the World Trade Organization), but when it comes to organizing for the sake of the ecosystem on which our survival depends there is no such cooperation or efficiency, since it is not profitable. Likewise, when it comes to averting economic crises in the "growth" of capital, we are made to endure sacrifices of our collective social good in the name of "austerity." In contrast, when it comes to averting ecological crises there are no major government initiatives to restrict our consumption of commodities, since doing so would have a negative impact on the rate of profit. We continue to exploit ever more of our natural resources for the sake of profit, even when it is clear that doing so is destroying our own environmental conditions. Moreover, as Klein reminds us, we know all too well how our current economic system "will deal with the reality of serial climate-related disasters: with profiteering, and escalating barbarism to segregate the losers from the winners."[92]

The large-scale questions raised by the problem of climate change should therefore be understood as "a civilizational wake-up call. A powerful message—spoken in the language of fires, floods, droughts, and extinctions—telling us that we need an entirely new economic model and a new way of sharing this planet."[93] Rising to the challenges posed by climate change will require "reinventing the very idea of the collective, the communal, the commons, the civil, and the civic,"[94] which is why we must engage politically with the question of what "we collectively value more than economic growth and corporate profits."[95] As Klein repeatedly emphasizes, "we are left with a stark choice: allow climate disruption to change everything about our world, or change pretty much everything about our economy to avoid that fate."[96]

Despite her calls for a fundamental economic transformation, however, Klein never interrogates the production of wealth under capitalism and the measure of value that informs it. Her subtitle identifies capitalism as the root of the problem, but there is no definition of capitalism in Klein's book. When she defines what she means, it turns out that she is not talking about capitalism as an economic system but merely about what she calls "deregulated capitalism" (i.e., neoliberalism), the evils of which she blames on "an elite minority that has a stranglehold over our economy, our political process, and most of our major media outlets."[97] To be sure, the corporate stranglehold over our political economy is pernicious and in need of urgent critique, but to treat it as the *cause* of the structural contradictions of capitalism is to deprive ourselves of the ability to understand the economic system of which we are a part. That we prioritize profit is not reducible to the manipulations of a corporate elite, since the priority of profit is built into how we measure our social wealth from the beginning. For the same reason, that we collectively value the "growth" of capital as the final purpose of our economy is not reducible to the reigning ideology of neoliberal capitalism. Rather, the purpose of our economy is beyond democratic deliberation under any form of capitalism, since the defining purpose of capital accumulation is built into how we produce our social wealth in the first place. Moreover, as I have shown in depth, the capitalist measure of value is inimical to the production of real social wealth, since it valorizes socially necessary labor time rather than socially available free time, requires unemployment as a structural feature, and has an inherent tendency toward destructive crises.

For Klein, all these features of the capitalist mode of production are out of view, since she assumes that the decisive issue is the distribution rather than the production of wealth. As she approvingly quotes Frantz Fanon: "What matters today, the issue which blocks the horizon, is the need for a redistribution of wealth."[98] Klein—like

Fanon—thereby falls short of an analysis and critique of capitalism. To criticize the given distribution of capital wealth—and advocate for its redistribution—is *not* a critique of capitalism.

The shortcoming here is not particular to Klein but characteristic—as we saw in chapter 6—of much of contemporary left-wing thinking. It does not make sense to argue that the problem is capitalism and at the same time argue that the solution is the redistribution of capital wealth. Yet this argument is routinely made on the Left today. The form of the argument is a contradiction in terms: it asserts that the problem is capitalism and that the solution is capitalism. The contradictory form of the argument is covered over by a sleight of hand, whereby capitalism is tacitly defined as neoliberalism and redistribution is tacitly defined as an alternative to capitalism. These conflations are persistently made but never justified. Inequality, exploitation, and commodification are regularly denounced, but their relation to the capitalist mode of production is not taken into account and the critical injunction is reduced to calls for redistribution. Redistributive reforms can certainly be a helpful *means* for political change under capitalism. But even in order to understand the substantial challenges that our redistributive reforms will encounter—and to conceive our political strategies in relation to those challenges—we need to grasp the contradictions that are inherent in the capitalist production of wealth. Moreover, if we are committed to overcoming the economic injustice of capitalism, then redistribution cannot be our *end*. Inequality, exploitation, and commodification cannot even in principle be overcome through the redistribution of capital wealth, since the wealth itself is produced by unequal relations of production, exploitation, and commodification.

What we are missing, then, are not indictments of capitalism, but a rigorous definition and analysis of capitalism, as well as the principles for an economic form of life beyond capitalism (the principles of democratic socialism). This is what I have provided.

Hence, let me rehearse what I demonstrated in systematic detail in chapter 5: there is only one fundamental definition of capitalism. Capitalism is a historical form of life in which wage labor is the foun-

dation of social wealth. We live in a global capitalist world because all
of us depend for our survival on the social wealth generated by wage
labor. In order to generate wealth through the social form of the wage
relation, we must exploit labor time and consume commodities that
are made for profit. The production of all our goods and services is
mediated by the social form of wage labor, since even how much free
time we have to produce goods or services for nonprofit depends on
the wage we receive or the capital we have. Moreover, the production of the capital wealth that is distributed in the form of wages
requires that there is a "growth" of value in the economy, which is
possible only if we continue to exploit and commodify our lives for
the sake of profit. Under capitalism our collective spiritual cause—
that for the sake of which we labor—is profit. This is why a falling
rate of profit shows up as a form of "crisis" for us and why we have to
take measures to generate new possibilities of profiteering. That our
spiritual cause under capitalism is profit is *not* reducible to an ideological worldview, a conscious belief, or a psychological disposition.
Profit is our spiritual cause not because of what we have to *think* but
because of what we have to *do* under capitalism. We cannot maintain
ourselves—cannot reproduce our lives—without the surplus value
that is transformed into profit and accumulated in the form of capital
that is distributed as wealth. The more we exploit and commodify
our lives as well as our environment, the more wealth we have to
distribute; the less we exploit and commodify our lives as well as our
environment, the less wealth we have to distribute.

Let me emphasize here that capitalism is a *historical* form of life
and that profit is a *spiritual* cause of what we do, rather than a *natural*
cause. The point is that capitalism does not reflect an original state
of nature and does not finally determine who we can be. As living
beings, we seek self-satisfaction—and there is nothing degrading
about being alive, nothing sinful about seeking self-satisfaction—but
since we are spiritually living beings it is not naturally given what
counts as self-satisfaction for us.

Crucially, what counts as self-satisfaction for us depends on the
spiritual causes that determine what matters in our society and move

us to act. If our spiritual cause is profit, then fulfilling the demands of the practical identities that serve the purpose of profit (e.g., being a ruthless capitalist) will count as satisfying, even if it requires that we ignore the consequences of our actions for others and for the environment. Moreover, if our collective spiritual cause is profit, all of us will tend to understand ourselves as individuals who have no intrinsic motivation to care for the common good, since we cannot see ourselves in the collective purpose of our society. Indeed, no one can see herself in the purpose of profit, since it treats our lives as means rather than as ends in themselves. This is why capitalism is an inherently alienating form of social life.

Since profit is our *collective* spiritual cause under capitalism, which determines how we *materially* reproduce our lives, we cannot overcome its power through mere individual will or a change of the official worldview of our society. Rather, we must practically transform how we sustain our lives all the way down to the production of the social goods that we need. The means of production must be collectively owned and employed for the sake of the democratically determined common good, rather than privately owned and employed for the sake of profit.

The principle of collective ownership specifies the material condition of possibility for the other two principles of democratic socialism: the measure of wealth in terms of socially available free time and the pursuit of labor from each according to her ability, to each according to her need. As long as the means of production are privately owned, we can generate wealth only by converting the surplus time of our lives into surplus value. The increase of free time in our society thanks to improved technologies of nonliving production is not *worth* anything in itself under capitalism, since value can be generated only through the exploitation of living labor time. We cannot affirm the general reduction of socially necessary labor time as intrinsically valuable, but must find new ways of exploiting the time of our lives and commodifying the products of our labor.

If we own the means of production collectively, by contrast, we can pursue technological development for the sake of producing social goods for all of us and increasing the socially available free time for each one of us. We can employ nonliving production capacities for the sake of our emancipation—giving ourselves time to lead our lives—rather than for the sake of exploiting our lifetime. We can thus acknowledge in practice that socially available free time is the positive measure of value that renders intelligible socially necessary labor time as the negative measure of value. We can generate wealth by decreasing the socially necessary labor time for all, converting the surplus time of our lives into socially available free time.

By the same token, we can give ourselves time to engage democratically with the question of what it means to be devoted to the common good: from each of us according to our ability, to each of us according to our need. The cultivation of socially available free time requires evolving democratic institutions of education, material organization of labor, political deliberation, artistic creation, physical recreation, and so on. By participating in these institutional forms of life, we can engage the questions of what should count as our abilities and what should count as our needs. We can discover our individual abilities through activities of teaching, learning, and leisure, as well as come to understand our collective needs by sharing the socially necessary forms of labor.

We are thus given time to explore what we are capable of and what we value. We can actively negotiate which activities we take to be necessary and which activities we take to be expressions of our freedom, which pursuits we identify with as ends in themselves and which social roles we are committed to as our practical identities. Neither the practical identities through which we pursue our abilities nor the social conditions that shape our needs are given once and for all. We participate in institutional life on the basis of our commitments and are therefore also part of the possible transformation of our institutions. The point of democratic socialism is not to impose a general consensus regarding what matters, but to sustain a form of life that makes it possible for us to *own* the question of what is worth doing with our lives—what we value individually as well as collectively—*as* an irreducible question of our lives.

For the same reason, democratic socialism does not presume that we will all magically cooperate without antagonisms and that we will be absolved from the fragility of social bonds. The question of how we should live together will always be at issue and run the risk of breaking apart what binds us together. The point is not to have a society that *secures* that we cooperate in mutual recognition of the freedom of one another. To secure mutual recognition is neither possible nor desirable, since such security would eliminate our freedom. The point is rather to have a society that *enables* our cooperation in mutual recognition of the freedom of one another. Nothing can secure the actual exercise of mutual recognition, but mutual recognition can be enabled or disabled depending on the principles to which we strive to hold ourselves, depending on the spiritual cause that moves our actions in social space and time. For our mutual recognition to be enabled rather than disabled, the purposive principles of our society must be possible to grasp in practice as being *for the sake of* both the common good and our individual ability to lead a life. To be emancipated rather than alienated we must be able to see ourselves—to recognize our own commitment to social freedom—in the purposive principles of our society. These principles must do justice to the inseparability of our material and spiritual life, to how economic questions of priority are at the heart of our exercise of freedom both individually and collectively. The principles of democratic socialism designate what those principles of a free society must be.

Under democratic socialism, then, we will be able to own the responsibility of being the source of the authority of our norms. We will acknowledge that the norms to which we hold ourselves are prescribed neither by God nor by Nature, but that we are answerable *to one another* for the commitments we espouse and the actions we undertake.

Accordingly, we will be able to own and actively transform our ceremonies of communal recognition, which previously have been alienated in the form of religious rituals. Under democratic socialism, we will not be baptized in the name of God, but it will make sense to have ceremonies that acknowledge and celebrate the newborn as unique, fragile individuals to whose well-being we are committed: from each according to her ability, to each according to her need. Likewise, the institution of marriage will no longer be mediated by religious faith or capitalist property rights, and there will be multiple forms of institutionalizing partnerships. For these very reasons, however, the partnerships in question will be explicitly recognized as ends in themselves. Thus, it will make all the more sense to have ceremonies that acknowledge and celebrate those who are willing to take the risk of making a life-defining commitment to another person. Finally—recalling the issue I pursued in chapter 1—our funeral ceremonies will be able to honor and avow the devastating loss of an irreplaceable person. Rather than disown our mourning through the supposed consolation of eternal life, we will be able to own our pain as something that we *ought* to feel in the face of death. Moreover, we will be able to affirm expressions of mourning as a practical avowal of our shared commitment to the members of our community, on whom we bestow dignity in recognition of their finitude and for whom we take responsibility even when they no longer exist.

Such secular ceremonies are not "substitutes" or "replacements" for their religious analogues. On the contrary, only from the standpoint of secular faith can we understand the actual significance of baptisms, marriages, and funerals, as expressions of historical commitments that matter because *we* have to sustain them. The Hegelian insight regarding religious practices—that "God" is a name for the communal norms that we have legislated to ourselves—is therefore necessary but not sufficient. To complete our emancipation, we ought to remove all remaining forms of political theology by removing any appeal to "God" in favor of the explicit democratic recognition that what ultimately matters is our relations to one another.

The basic premise of political theology has always been that we the people cannot ultimately own the responsibility for our life together. At the end of the day all forms of political theology are antidemocratic, since they assume that we must defer to a higher authority than we the people in order to hold together as a community. The movement toward democratic socialism is thus inseparable from the overcoming of political theology and the withering away of religious faith. We will recognize that our finitude is inseparable from our dignity and our care for one another. We will acknowledge that everything depends on we the people.

Needless to say, there is no guarantee that we will succeed in achieving democratic socialism. Even if we do succeed, it may take more generations than we would like to imagine. What I have sought to show is that we *can* get there—that we can recognize the principles of democratic socialism as our own commitments, that we can make sense of life beyond capitalism—and that there is never time to wait. To make our emancipation actual will require both our political mobilizations and our rational arguments; it will require our general strikes and our systematic reflections, our labor and our love, our anxiety and our passion. We only have a chance to achieve democratic socialism if we grasp that everything is at stake in what we do with our finite time together. We only have a chance to make it a reality if we help one another to own our only life. This is how we overcome and how we move forward—not toward the new Jerusalem but toward the new Memphis, the new Los Angeles, the new Chicago, the new New Haven, and the new New York.

Notes

Bibliography

Acknowledgments

Index

Notes

INTRODUCTION

1. I quote the article from Steven Collins, *Nirvana: Concept, Imagery, Narrative*, p. 21. In chapter 4, I engage with Collins's analysis of different religious conceptions of eternal life.
2. William James, *The Varieties of Religious Experience*, p. 517.
3. Dalai Lama, "Samtal med Dalai Lama" ["Conversation with the Dalai Lama"], interview by Peter Berglund, Swedish Television (SVT), April 10, 1989.
4. I owe the notion of acting "in light of" norms to the seminal work on freedom by the philosopher Robert Pippin. As Pippin rightly emphasizes, we can never act automatically or purely passively in conformity with given norms; following norms is always something that we must actively do and sustain, however constrained and minimal the activity in question may be. See, for example, chapter 15 in Pippin, *Idealism as Modernism: Hegelian Variations*, as well as Pippin, *Hegel's Practical Philosophy*.
5. See Peter E. Gordon, "Critical Theory Between the Sacred and the Profane." See also Gordon's insightful review essay, "The Place of the Sacred in the Absence of God: Charles Taylor's *A Secular Age*."
6. Max Weber, "Science as a Vocation," pp. 12–13, 30.
7. For Weber's claim that democracy entails the "de-souling" (*Entseelung*) and "spiritual proletarianization" (*geistige Proletarisierung*) of society, as well his claim that we need a *Führer* to lead us, see, for example, Weber, *Gesammelte politische Schriften*, p. 544.
8. Weber, "Science as a Vocation," p. 30.
9. For a pathbreaking account of how the prospect of future generations is a condition of possibility for the value and meaning of many of our own present activities, see Samuel Scheffler, *Death and the Afterlife*. Scheffler's notion of "the afterlife" is secular in my sense of the term, since it seeks to capture our

commitment to future generations of human, temporal life, rather than an eternal afterlife in any religious sense.

10. Bruce Robbins, "Enchantment? No, Thank You!," p. 81.

11. Ibid., p. 90.

12. Ibid., p. 81.

13. Quoted from Nina Björk, *Drömmen om det röda: Rosa Luxemburg, socialism, språk och kärlek*, p. 23. I am indebted to Björk's deeply insightful book on Rosa Luxemburg and the socialist-labor movements in which she participated. See also the important reflections on the relation between freedom and lifetime in Björk's incisive book *Lyckliga i alla sina dagar*.

14. Luxemburg, *The Russian Revolution*, p. 222.

15. Ibid.

16. Ibid., p. 221.

17. Marx, *Economic and Philosophic Manuscripts of 1844*, p. 86.

18. Thompson, *Life and Action*, p. 12; Marx, "Discovering Hegel," p. 7.

19. The most important sources for my thinking regarding freedom, finitude, and temporality are Hegel's *Phenomenology of Spirit* (as well as his *Science of Logic*) and Heidegger's *Being and Time*—in my view the three most insightful works in the entire history of philosophy. I hold that if we pursue the core insights of Hegel and Heidegger in the right way, we will grasp why their notions of freedom are mutually required. Moreover, such a perspective makes it possible to develop a new conception of personhood and agency, which is elaborated in my book in progress, *Being a Person: The Fundamental Ontology of Time and Agency*, where I engage in depth with Heidegger's *Being and Time*.

I. FAITH

1. C. S. Lewis, *A Grief Observed*, p. 36.

2. Ibid., p. 56.

3. Ibid., p. 26.

4. Ibid., p. 66.

5. Ibid., pp. 26–27.

6. Ibid., pp. 24–25.

7. Ibid., p. 68.

8. See Miroslav Volf, "Time, Eternity, and the Prospects for Care." Volf's essay focuses on the arguments regarding time and eternity that I have articulated in my previous work and especially in my book *Dying for Time*. The arguments in question are deepened, improved upon, and further developed in the present work.

9. Aristotle, *Rhetoric*, 1382b31–32. The Greek verb that I translate as "to believe" (*oiomenoi*) has a very rich and instructive range of meanings: "to think," "to suppose," "to expect," "to credit," and so on.

10. See, for example, Epictetus, *The Discourses*; Seneca, *Dialogues and Essays*; and Marcus Aurelius, *Meditations*. For an important and profound study of the Stoics on passion, commitment, and belief, see Martha Nussbaum, *The Therapy of Desire*, in particular her incisive analysis of Chrysippus's notion of judgment in chapter 10.

11. See Spinoza, *The Ethics*, book 5, pp. 244–265.

12. Spinoza, "A Portrait of the Philosopher as a Young Man," pp. 4–5.

13. For an insightful analysis of Nietzsche's revaluation of values, see Bernard Reginster, *The Affirmation of Life*.

14. Nietzsche, *Ecce Homo*, p. 258. See also Nietzsche's claim further on in *Ecce Homo:* "I myself have never suffered from all this; what is *necessary* does not hurt me; *amor fati* is my inmost nature" (p. 324). Thus Nietzsche falls back into the Stoic denial of suffering that he elsewhere subjects to critique. Nietzsche comes closest to the right form of critique of Stoicism in *The Gay Science*, when he argues against the Stoic detachment from suffering on the grounds that the capacity for suffering is inseparable from the capacity for joy. As Nietzsche puts it: "Pleasure and displeasure are so intertwined that whoever wants as much as possible of one *must* also have as much as possible of the other— that whoever wants to learn how to 'jubilate up to the heavens' must also be prepared for 'grief unto death'" (p. 38). As a consequence, "If you want to decrease and diminish people's susceptibility to pain, you also have to decrease and diminish their *capacity for joy*" (p. 38). As Nietzsche points out, the constitutive interrelation of joy and pain is evident from the reasoning of the Stoics themselves: "The Stoics believed that this is how things are and they were consistent when they also desired as little pleasure as possible in order to derive as little pain as possible from life" (ibid.). In Nietzsche's diagnosis, Stoic detachment is nihilistic, since it seeks to withdraw from life in favor of apathy. As Nietzsche wittily makes the point farther on in *The Gay Science:* "Is our life really so painful and burdensome that it would be advantageous for us to trade it for a fossilized Stoic way of life? Things are *not bad enough* for us that they have to be bad for us in the Stoic style!" (p. 182). Nietzsche's critique of Stoicism, however, remains limited to psychological categories and quantitative relations of pleasure/pain, rather than addressing the conditions of intelligibility for leading a life. Hegel's critique of Stoicism in the *Phenomenology of Spirit*—a critique that I develop in the conclusion to this book—is much more powerful, since it seeks to demonstrate the fundamental incoherence of Stoicism, not merely in terms of psychology but in terms of the conditions of intelligibility for being a person at all. Unlike Nietzsche, Hegel also seeks to understand the temptation of Stoicism not in terms of the failure of individual character but in terms of oppressive social and historical conditions. As Hegel puts it, Stoicism as an authoritative spiritual ideal "can only come on the scene during a time of universal fear and servitude" (*Phenomenology of Spirit*, pp. 118–119). That various forms of Stoicism continue to enjoy the status of supposed spiritual "wisdom" in our own historical epoch (in everything from advanced philosophy to self-help books) should remind us of how far we are from having achieved an emancipated society.

15. Taylor, *A Secular Age*, p. 3.

16. Dennett, *Breaking the Spell*, p. 221.

17. Taylor, *A Secular Age*, pp. 4–5.

18. Ibid., p. 16.

19. Ibid., pp. 638, 639.
20. See Taylor, *A Secular Age*, pp. 16–17.
21. Ibid., pp. 720–721.
22. Ibid., p. 723.
23. Ibid.
24. Ibid., p. 720.
25. Ibid., p. 57.
26. Ibid.
27. Ibid.
28. Taylor seeks to justify his analogy between our "gathering" of time and the eternity of God by appealing to Augustine's phenomenology of time in book II of the *Confessions*. According to Taylor, Augustine's notion of the distension of time (*distentio*) designates how we are "cut off from our past and out of touch with our future" (*A Secular Age*, p. 57, cf. p. 56). Taylor contrasts the *distentio* of time to Augustine's account of how we "gather" time when we sing a melody and retain the notes we have sung while anticipating the ones that will follow. Contrary to Taylor's claim, however, there is no contrast between the *distentio* of time and the gathering of time in Augustine's melody example. Augustine's example is explicitly meant to show that the *distentio* of time is the *form* of any experience of time, which requires that we hold on to the past and project ourselves into the future. The form of *distentio* is *not* something that befalls us when we are psychologically cut off from our past and our future. Rather, the *distentio* of time is the only form in which anyone can be related to her past and her future. Thus, Augustine underlines the *disanalogy* between the way we retain our past in relation to the future and the way God reposes in his eternal presence: "A person singing or listening to a song he knows well suffers a distension in feeling and in sense-perception from the expectation of future sounds and the memory of past sound. With you [God] it is otherwise. You are unchangeably eternal. . . . Just as you knew heaven and earth in the beginning without that bringing any variation into your knowing, so you made heaven and earth in the beginning without that meaning a tension between past and future in your activity" (Augustine, *Confessions*, Book II, chapter 31). In retaining the past and projecting into the future, we do *not* overcome the loss of the past and our vulnerability before the future. On the contrary, to gather time is to bear witness to the irreducible divergence between past and future, which is a condition of intelligibility for any experience of time. Inversely, the divergence between past and future is unintelligible in the eternal presence of God. I analyze Augustine's phenomenology of time—and its potentially secular implications—in chapter 2.
29. Ibid., p. 720.
30. Ibid., p. 721.
31. Ibid., pp. 721–722.
32. Quoted from Stork, *The Life of Martin Luther and the Reformation in Germany*, p. 80.
33. Luther spoke these words next to Magdalena's coffin; see ibid.

34. Luther in a letter to Jonas dated September 23, 1542; see *The Letters of Martin Luther*, p. 238.
35. Luther in a letter to Osiander dated June 3, 1545; see ibid., p. 456.
36. C. S. Lewis, *A Grief Observed*, pp. 69–70.
37. Ibid., p. 75.
38. Ibid., p. 61.
39. Ibid., p. 76.
40. Dante, *The Divine Comedy*, Canto 33, p. 481.
41. For a reading of the end of *The Divine Comedy* that reaches a similar conclusion, see the perceptive analysis in Dreyfus and Kelly, *All Things Shining*, pp. 131–132.
42. C. S. Lewis, *A Grief Observed*, p. 15.

2. LOVE

1. Augustine, *Confessions*, 11:15. All citations of the *Confessions* are given by book and chapter number respectively.
2. Ibid., 11:14.
3. Augustine, *Enarrationes in Psalmos*, 121.6. I quote the English translation by Andrea Nightingale in her excellent book *Once Out of Nature: Augustine on Time and the Body*, p. 59.
4. Augustine, *In Ioannis Evangelicum tractatus*, 38.10, English translation by Nightingale in *Once Out of Nature*, pp. 86–87.
5. Augustine, *Eighty-three Different Questions*, p. 62.
6. Augustine, *On Faith in Things Unseen*, p. 453.
7. Ibid.
8. Ibid., pp. 454–456.
9. See Augustine, *Eighty-three Different Questions*, p. 83.
10. See Paul Tillich, *Dynamics of Faith*, pp. 71–73.
11. Ibid., p. 120.
12. Ibid., p. 130. See also Tillich's claim that "the human heart seeks the infinite because that is where the finite wants to rest. In the infinite it sees its own fulfillment" (p. 15). This assertion—that we essentially long to overcome our finitude in favor of infinite rest—is repeated by Tillich throughout *Dynamics of Faith*.
13. For a good discussion of this aspect of Augustine's logic of faith, see Hannah Arendt, *Love and Saint Augustine*, p. 32.
14. See, for example, Augustine, *On Free Choice of the Will*, 1:4.
15. For Augustine's critique of the Stoics, see, for example, *The City of God*, book 14. For an insightful analysis of the difference between Augustine and the Stoics, see Nussbaum, *Upheavals of Thought*, pp. 527–556.
16. Augustine, *Commentaries on the Psalms* 90, 1:8. English translation in Arendt, *Love and Saint Augustine*, p. 17.
17. For a lucid reading of Augustine's distinction between *frui* and *uti* love, as well as his distinction between *cupiditas* and *caritas*, see Anders Nygren's seminal book, *Agape and Eros*.

18. Augustine, *Confessions,* 1:1.
19. For a study of the Buddhist notion of nirvana that is both systematic and grounded in careful textual analyses, see Collins, *Nirvana: Concept, Imagery, Narrative.*
20. Augustine, *Confessions,* 4:4.
21. Ibid.
22. Ibid., 4:8.
23. Ibid., 4:4.
24. Ibid., 1:20.
25. Ibid., 4:10.
26. Ibid., 10:34.
27. Ibid.
28. Ibid., 4:10.
29. Ibid., 4:11.
30. Ibid., 10:13.
31. Ibid., 4:11.
32. Augustine, *Sermones,* no. 163, 28–30. English translation by Nightingale in *Once Out of Nature,* p. 51.
33. Augustine, *Confessions,* 4:10.
34. Ibid., 10:16.
35. Ibid., 10:13.
36. See ibid.
37. Ibid., 10:17.
38. Ibid.
39. Ibid.
40. Ibid., 10:27.
41. Ibid., 11:29.
42. Knausgaard, *My Struggle: Book Two,* p. 67.
43. Knausgaard, *Min kamp: Sjette bok,* p. 365.
44. Augustine, *Confessions,* 10:30.
45. Ibid., 11:1.
46. Knausgaard, *Min kamp: Sjette bok,* pp. 610, 611.
47. Ibid., p. 610.
48. Ibid., p. 409.
49. Augustine, *Confessions,* 10:17.
50. Ibid., 10:3.
51. Knausgaard, *My Struggle: Book One,* p. 25.
52. Ibid., p. 28.
53. Knausgaard, *Min kamp: Sjette bok,* p. 227.
54. Knausgaard, *My Struggle: Book Three,* p. 172.
55. Ibid., p. 178.
56. Ibid., pp. 186–187.
57. Ibid., p. 182.
58. Knausgaard, *My Struggle: Book One,* pp. 164–165.
59. Ibid., p. 29.

60. Proust, *Finding Time Again*, p. 208.

61. Ibid., p. 204.

62. Ibid., p. 459.

63. Proust, *Sodom and Gomorrah*, p. 371.

64. Knausgaard, *Min kamp: Sjette bok*, pp. 1116, 1117.

65. Knausgaard, *My Struggle: Book One*, pp. 25–26.

66. Proust, *Finding Time Again*, pp. 345–346.

67. Ibid., p. 345.

68. Ibid., p. 357.

69. Knausgaard, *My Struggle: Book One*, pp. 3–4.

70. Ibid., *Book Three*, p. 8.

71. Knausgaard, *Min kamp: Sjette bok*, p. 596.

72. Ibid., *Book Two*, p. 98.

73. Ibid., *Book One*, p. 441.

74. Ibid., p. 350.

75. Ibid.

76. Epictetus, *The Discourses*, p. 215.

77. Knausgaard, *Min kamp: Sjette bok*, pp. 916–917.

3. RESPONSIBILITY

1. Gen. 12:2. The cited translations from the Bible generally follow *The New Oxford Annotated Bible*, edited by Michael D. Coogan.

2. Gen. 22:12.

3. Gen. 22:16–17.

4. See Joakim Garff, *Søren Kierkegaard: A Biography*, p. 251.

5. Luther, in *Luther's Catechetical Writings*, vol. 1, p. 203.

6. Kierkegaard, *Fear and Trembling*, p. 20.

7. Ibid., p. 52.

8. Kierkegaard, *Concluding Unscientific Postscript*, vol. 1, p. 204.

9. Kierkegaard, "On the Occasion of a Wedding," p. 58.

10. Ibid., p. 44.

11. Ibid., p. 50.

12. Ibid., p. 62.

13. Ibid.

14. Ibid., pp. 52–53.

15. Kierkegaard, "At a Graveside," p. 83.

16. Kierkegaard, *Eighteen Upbuilding Discourses*, p. 23.

17. Ibid., p. 24.

18. Kierkegaard, *Fear and Trembling*, p. 31.

19. Kierkegaard, *The Sickness unto Death*, p. 25.

20. Ibid., p. 22.

21. Ibid., pp. 14 and 49.

22. Kierkegaard, *The Concept of Anxiety*, p. 189.

23. Kierkegaard, *Eighteen Upbuilding Discourses*, pp. 23–24.

24. Kierkegaard, *The Concept of Anxiety*, p. 190.

25. Kierkegaard, *The Sickness unto Death*, p. 38.

26. Ibid., pp. 39–40.

27. Ibid., pp. 38–39.

28. Kierkegaard, *Fear and Trembling*, p. 36.

29. Kierkegaard, *Concluding Unscientific Postscript*, vol. 1, p. 391.

30. Ibid., p. 393.

31. Ibid., p. 410.

32. Ibid., pp. 410–411.

33. Ibid., p. 412.

34. Kierkegaard, *Christian Discourses*, p. 284.

35. Ibid.

36. Ibid.

37. Ibid., p. 285.

38. Kierkegaard, *Concluding Unscientific Postscript*, vol. 1, p. 386.

39. Ibid., p. 410.

40. Ibid., p. 405.

41. Kierkegaard, *Fear and Trembling*, p. 46. See also the discussion of Religiousness A in *Concluding Unscientific Postscript*, in particular pp. 556–557. For a systematic account of the notion of religious faith in Kierkegaard's major works, see Merold Westphal, *Kierkegaard's Concept of Faith*. As Westphal rightly argues, Religiousness A is "the genus of which Christianity is a species. When Climacus [the pseudonymous author of Kierkegaard's *Postscript*] says that one must first be in Religiousness A in order to actually be in Religiousness B, he is not doing developmental psychology. The meaning is the same as when we say that an animal must first be a dog in order to be a collie. The priority is logical or conceptual, not temporal" (pp. 208–209).

42. Kierkegaard, *Concluding Unscientific Postscript*, vol. 1, p. 393.

43. Kierkegaard, *Fear and Trembling*, p. 45.

44. Ibid.

45. John Davenport has analyzed this Kierkegaardian notion of faith in terms of "eschatological trust"; see Davenport's series of interrelated essays: "Faith as Eschatological Trust in *Fear and Trembling*"; "Kierkegaard's *Postscript* in Light of *Fear and Trembling*"; "Eschatological Faith and Repetition."

46. Kierkegaard, *Fear and Trembling*, p. 20.

47. Ibid., p. 50.

48. Ibid.

49. Ibid., p. 40.

50. See, for example, Dreyfus and Rubin, "Kierkegaard, Division II, and the Later Heidegger"; Dreyfus, "Kierkegaard on the Self"; Lippitt, *Kierkegaard and "Fear and Trembling"*; Mooney, *Knights of Faith and Resignation: Reading Kierkegaard's "Fear and Trembling"*; Krishek, "The Existential Dimension of Faith." In contrast, see J. M. Bernstein's incisive essay "Remembering Isaac," which beautifully articulates what it means to remember the standpoint of Isaac (especially through an extraordinary reading of Caravaggio) and shows how *Fear and Trembling* is predicated on the forgetting of Isaac.

51. Kierkegaard, *Fear and Trembling*, p. 36.
52. Ibid., p. 12.
53. Ibid., p. 14.
54. Ibid., p. 37.
55. Ibid., p. 22.
56. Ibid., p. 39.
57. Ibid.
58. Ibid., p. 41.
59. Ibid., p. 42.
60. Ibid., p. 46.
61. Ibid., p. 44.
62. Ibid., pp. 44–45.
63. Ibid., p. 44.
64. Ibid., p. 49.
65. Ibid., pp. 43–44.
66. Ibid., p. 48.
67. Ibid., pp. 46–47.
68. Ibid., p. 48.
69. Ibid., p. 50.
70. Ibid., p. 40.
71. Ibid., pp. 40–41.
72. Ibid., p. 39.
73. Ibid., pp. 39–40.
74. Ibid., p. 40.
75. Ibid., p. 34.
76. Ibid., p. 40.
77. Kierkegaard, *The Sickness unto Death*, p. 15.
78. Kierkegaard, in *Søren Kierkegaard's Journals and Papers*, vol. 1, p. 10.
79. See Kierkegaard, *Christian Discourses*, pp. 7–22.
80. Ibid., p. 14.
81. Ibid., pp. 15–16.
82. Kierkegaard, *Eighteen Upbuilding Discourses*, p. 307.
83. Meister Eckhart, "Detachment," p. 91.
84. Omri Boehm, *The Binding of Isaac*, p. 23.
85. Kierkegaard, *Fear and Trembling*, p. 22.
86. Ibid.
87. My argument in this paragraph is indebted to the reading of the Gospel of John in Henry Staten's important book, *Eros in Mourning*, chapter 3.

4. NATURAL AND SPIRITUAL FREEDOM

1. The insight that not only human beings but also other living animals are capable of rudimentary forms of practical classification and discrimination—taking food *as* food, distinguishing in practice between what counts as nourishment (essence) and what merely seems to be nourishing (appearance)—is

suggested by Hegel in his *Phenomenology of Spirit*, §109; see also his *Science of Logic*, p. 684. Hegel's argument has been developed with great lucidity by Robert Brandom in "The Structure of Desire and Recognition: Self-Consciousness and Self-Constitution," pp. 132–134. See also the insightful further development of Hegel's and Brandom's argument by J. M. Bernstein in "To Be Is to Live, to Be Is to Be Recognized," pp. 180–198.

2. For a detailed overview of Neurath's various formulations of the boat model throughout his career, see Thomas E. Uebel, *Otto Neurath: Philosophy Between Science and Politics*, pp. 89–166. For an influential philosophical account of Neurath's boat as a model for grasping the problem of objective knowledge, see W. V. Quine, *Word and Object*. For an important deployment of Neurath's boat that goes beyond questions of epistemology to ethical questions of character and virtue, see John McDowell, *Mind, Value, and Reality*, chapters 2, 3 and 9, as well as McDowell, *The Engaged Intellect*, chapter 2. McDowell does not, however, analyze the inherent finitude and fragility of leading a life, which I will argue is crucial for understanding what is at stake in Neurath's boat. McDowell notes that "Neurath's sailor may need to tinker with the boat" (*The Engaged Intellect*, p. 35), but he treats the necessity of maintaining the boat as episodic rather than as constitutive. In contrast, I will show how any form of life is constitutively self-maintaining by virtue of its inherent finitude—the boat must *always* be maintained in order to hold together and it can *always* fall apart—which in turn accounts for the primacy of practical self-consciousness in any form of spiritual life.

3. Privileging the notion of "life" in a logical sense does not entail any kind of vitalism. As I will show, the logic of self-maintenance makes clear that the living necessarily depends on the existence of nonliving matter, while nonliving matter does not necessarily depend on the existence of the living. For the same reason, privileging the notion of "life" in a logical sense is compatible with a modern evolutionary account of life. In the evolution of the empirical universe, there was nonliving matter before there were any living beings, and there was no prospective necessity of the advent of life. Evolution did not require any reason or final purpose to get going as a causal process, and it did not have to be intelligible to anyone in order to proceed. However, in order for evolution to be intelligible *as* evolution—and indeed for anything to be intelligible *as* anything—the *contingent* existence of living beings is *necessary*. Only living beings are able to take anything *as* anything—to practically distinguish between quantity and quality, appearance and essence, the nonliving and the living, and so on—all the way up to our ability to give an evolutionary account of our own existence and a philosophical account of the conditions of intelligibility for our own activities. For an insightful analysis of Hegel's *Logic* along these lines, see Jensen Suther, "Hegel's Logic of Freedom." My general emphasis on conditions of intelligibility is indebted to Robert Pippin's groundbreaking work on the *Science of Logic*; see Pippin, "Hegel on Logic as Metaphysics," "Hegel's Logic of Essence," and "The Many Modalities of *Wirklichkeit* in Hegel's *Wissenschaft der Logik*."

4. I here draw on and transform the notion of "formally distinctive" ways of being alive, which John McDowell formulates in his analysis of the concept of life in Aristotle and Hegel (see McDowell, "Why Does It Matter to Hegel that Geist Has a History?"). Strikingly, the *mortality* of the living plays no role in McDowell's account of what it means that we are living beings. McDowell's admirable philosophical project (pursued in his essays on Aristotle and Hegel as well as in *Mind and World*) is to insist that even our highest rational and spiritual capacities depend on our status as essentially *living* beings. The stakes of our status as living beings, however, are diluted as long as we do not explicitly grasp and spell out the implications of mortality as constitutive of any form of natural life as well as any form of spiritual life. This is what I seek to do on every level of *This Life*. To that end, I have deduced the necessity of (1) finitude, (2) fragile material embodiment, and (3) asymmetrical dependence on inanimate matter, as conditions of intelligibility for the activity of self-maintenance—the activity of the living—as such. I will proceed to give an account of how the mortality of life is actualized in two different ways in natural and spiritual life respectively.

5. My argument seeks to develop Hegel's claim that all living beings are characterized by the ability to bear a negative self-relation: to be in pain and yet stay alive, to break apart and yet hold together (see his *Science of Logic*, pp. 682–685 and *Philosophy of Nature*, pp. 429–441). The negativity of pain—of breaking apart—is intrinsic to any living being as such, since it is a necessary part of what animates the activity of striving to hold together and stay alive. Hegel's radical claim is that it is neither possible nor desirable to overcome negativity. When Hegel describes the form of a living being in terms of the negation of the negation (*Science of Logic*, p. 685), he does *not* mean that a living being can overcome its negative relation to pain, loss, and death. On the contrary, he means that the relation to the negative does not simply negate the existence of a living being but belongs to its positive constitution. A life that was absolved from pain, loss, and death would not be a life at all. Moreover, even though a living being can maintain itself in the pain of loss, it cannot finally master the negativity it bears within itself and cannot immunize itself against its own irrevocable death. Rather, any living being is mortal in the sense that it will be absolutely negated in death. Unlike the *pain* of a living being, the *death* of a living being is not compatible with the living being maintaining itself.

6. Hegel makes a similar distinction in analyzing how certain animals—as distinct from plants—have a capacity for "self-enjoyment," which is expressed through what Hegel calls "the artistic impulse" that is one aspect of "the constructive instinct" of animals (*Philosophy of Nature*, pp. 406–409). Most suggestively, Hegel argues that birdsong expresses a capacity for self-enjoyment that is distinguishable from the activity of mere self-preservation. Birdsong is a "distinterested" activity, *not* in the sense of being contemplative but in the sense of being an end in itself for the bird—enjoyed for its own sake (*Philosophy of Nature*, p. 409).

7. See Korsgaard, *Self-Constitution: Agency, Identity, and Integrity*, pp. 57–58. See also the remarks on "the principle of balancing" in Korsgaard's *The Constitution of Agency: Essays on Practical Reason and Moral Psychology*, p. 92n22.

8. Korsgaard, *The Sources of Normativity*, p. 102.

9. Ibid., p. 101.

10. See Rödl, *Self-Consciousness*, Chapter 4.

11. My argument here is further developed in the Conclusion to this book, where I address Hegel's notion of self-consciousness.

12. Collins, *Nirvana*, pp. 25–26.

13. Ibid., pp. 21–22.

14. Ibid., p. 25.

15. Ibid.

16. Ibid.

17. Ibid., p. 27.

18. Ibid., p. 25.

19. Collins, "What Are Buddhists *Doing* When They Deny the Self?," p. 75.

20. Ibid.

21. Ibid.

22. Ibid.

23. See, for example, the ReSource project led by Tania Singer, director of the Social Neuroscience Department at the Max Planck Institute for Human Cognitive and Brain Sciences in Leipzig, Germany. For two overviews of the research results of ReSource project—which seeks to adapt meditational practices for secular therapeutic purposes—see Singer and Klimecki, "Empathy and Compassion," as well as Singer, "What Type of Meditation Is Best for You?".

24. See Phil Zuckerman, *Living the Secular Life*, pp. 17–20.

25. Collins, *Nirvana*, p. 17.

5. THE VALUE OF OUR FINITE TIME

1. Marx and Engels, *The German Ideology*, p. 149.

2. Marx, *Grundrisse*, p. 706.

3. See Marx, *Economic and Philosophic Manuscripts of 1844*, in particular pp. 74–78.

4. Marx, *Grundrisse*, p. 611.

5. Ibid.

6. Marx, *Grundrisse*, p. 173.

7. Marx, *Capital*, vol. 1, p. 290.

8. For an insightful discussion of the philosophical distinction between valuing something and merely believing that something is valuable, see Samuel Scheffler, "Valuing," in *Equality and Tradition*, pp. 15–39. As I argue below, however, the two aspects of valuing must ultimately be understood as *inseparable* in the activity of valuing anything, even though they are *distinguishable* in important ways. The *degree* to which I value something—rather than merely believe that

it is valuable—is decisive, but the two aspects of valuing cannot ultimately be separated.

9. John Stuart Mill, *On Liberty*, p. 103.

10. Isaiah Berlin, "Two Concepts of Liberty," p. 171.

11. For a discussion of the effective freedoms principle, see, for example, John Rawls, "The Idea of Public Reason Revisited," in *The Law of Peoples*.

12. Aristotle, *Politics*, 1259b.

13. Hegel, *Philosophy of Right*, §57, p. 88.

14. This is what Robert Pippin has called Hegel's notion of "institutional rationality"; see chapter 9 in Pippin's *Hegel's Practical Philosophy*. The importance of Pippin's argument regarding institutional rationality was first brought to my attention by Jensen Suther, who is developing a new appreciation and immanent critique of Hegel/Pippin on institutional rationality in his dissertation *Spirit Disfigured: The Persistence of Freedom in Modernist Literature and Philosophy*. I am indebted to conversations with Suther on this subject.

15. For an excellent and admirably lucid account of Hegel's historical conception of freedom, see Terry Pinkard, *Does History Make Sense?: Hegel and the Historical Shapes of Justice*, in particular chapter 5.

16. Hegel, *Philosophy of Right*, remark from his lectures on the *Philosophy of Right* from 1819–1820, quoted in the English edition on p. 453.

17. Ibid., p. 454.

18. Ibid., §230, p. 260.

19. See Hegel, *Philosophy of Right*, §244–245.

20. Ibid., §245, p. 267.

21. Ibid., §245, p. 267.

22. Ibid., §245, p. 267.

23. Ibid., §246, p. 267.

24. Ibid., §248, p. 269. In his important book *Foundations of Hegel's Social Theory*, Frederick Neuhouser has highlighted the contradiction in Hegel's account of civil society from a different angle, focusing on the problem of colonialism (see pp. 173–174). Despite his careful and insightful analysis, however, Neuhouser does not address the problem of the formation of a rabble, which arguably reveals the deepest structural defect in the market economy of civil society and contradicts the possibility of an actual institutional rationality on either a national or an international level. Furthermore, Neuhouser does not link the contradiction that Hegel reveals in the production of social wealth to Marx's analysis of the dynamic of capitalist wage labor. As I argue, the implications of §245 in the *Philosophy of Right* should be the starting point for an immanent Marxian critique of Hegel's political philosophy. Marx himself fails to see the resources for an immanent critique in Hegel's account of civil society, since Marx's *Critique of Hegel's Philosophy of Right* is restricted to a commentary on Hegel's analysis of the state in §261–313 of the *Philosophy of Right*. Marx thereby disregards how Hegel himself discovers the contradiction in the capitalist production of wealth in the preceding section on civil society and especially in

§245. Indeed, Marx's entire critique of capitalism can be seen as the systematic elaboration of the implications of §245 of Hegel's *Philosophy of Right*.

25. Yanis Varoufakis is thus right on target when he underlines that Marx should be read as pursuing the implications of "Hegel's fantastic idea that no one is free as long as one is in chains." See Varoufakis, "Introduction," in *The Communist Manifesto*, p. xxvii.

26. Marx, *Grundrisse*, p. 245.

27. Ibid.

28. Aristotle, *Nicomachean Ethics*, book 5, chapter 5.

29. Ibid. Marx quotes these passages in *Capital*, vol. 1, p. 151.

30. Marx, *Capital*, vol. 1, p. 152.

31. Ibid., p. 275.

32. For an excellent analysis of the difference between Marx and earlier socialist writers on this point, see William Roberts, *Marx's Inferno: The Political Theory of* Capital. Roberts's deeply insightful reading of *Capital* appeared toward the end of my work on this book, but I hope to engage it on another occasion.

33. Mill, *On Liberty*, p. 12.

34. See Rawls, *A Theory of Justice*, pp. 358–365.

35. The two most influential works for the marginalist revolution of neoclassical economics are William Stanley Jevons's *The Theory of Political Economy* and Carl Menger's *Principles of Economics*. Both Jevons and Menger take issue with the labor theory of value, which they assume is also the theory held by Marx. The neoclassical critique of Marx's supposed labor theory of value and his alleged "price theory" is developed by Eugen Böhm-Bawerk in his classic essay, "Karl Marx and the Close of His System."

36. Hayek, *The Road to Serfdom*, p. 128.

37. Moishe Postone is the one who has come closest to the right analysis of the question of value in Marx, and my own work is indebted to Postone's seminal book *Time, Labor, and Social Domination*. Yet, while Postone rightly emphasizes that the measure of value under capitalism is historically specific, he conflates the historically specific measure of value under capitalism with the category of "value" per se. According to Postone, the overcoming of capitalism requires the *abolition* of value rather than a *revaluation* of value. Thus, Postone does not reach what I call the fourth level of the analysis of the economy. It makes no sense to call for the abolition of the category of value per se, since the category of value is a condition of intelligibility for any form of economic and spiritual life. To explain why the measure of value under capitalism is *self-contradictory*, we must explain why capitalism entails that we treat the *negative* measure of value as though it were the *positive* measure of value. Such an explanation is possible only if we proceed from the fourth level of the analysis of economy, which allows us to grasp the conditions for a value to be intelligible *as* a value (the positive measure of value) and a cost to be intelligible *as* a cost (the negative measure of value).

38. See Marx, *Grundrisse*, pp. 704–709. The significance of these pages in the *Grundrisse* was first highlighted by Postone in his important essay "Necessity, Labor,

and Time." I address the stakes of the difference between my account and Postone's in chapter 6. The development of my argument has benefited from conversations with Jensen Suther, who first brought my attention to the question of "free time" in Marx and Postone.

39. Marx, *Capital*, vol. 3, p. 958.
40. Ibid.
41. Ibid., p. 959.
42. Marx, *Grundrisse*, p. 706.
43. Ibid., p. 705.
44. Ibid.
45. Ibid., p. 708.
46. Ibid.
47. Ibid.
48. Ibid., p. 706.
49. Ibid.
50. Ibid., p. 708.
51. Ibid., p. 706.
52. Ibid., p. 705.
53. Ibid.
54. See Marx, "The Possibility of Non-Violent Revolution," p. 523.
55. Marx, *Critique of the Gotha Program*, p. 532.
56. Ibid., p. 537.
57. Marx, *Critique of Hegel's Philosophy of Right*, p. 35.

6. DEMOCRATIC SOCIALISM

1. Marx, *Critique of Hegel's Doctrine of the State*, p. 87.
2. Ibid., p. 88.
3. See Postone, "Necessity, Labor, and Time: A Reinterpretation of the Marxian Critique of Capitalism," as well as Postone, *Time, Labor, and Social Domination*.
4. See Jameson, *An American Utopia: Dual Power and the Universal Army*.
5. Postone, "Necessity, Labor, and Time," p. 779.
6. Ibid., p. 778.
7. Mill, *Principles of Political Economy*, pp. 5–6.
8. Ibid., p. 128.
9. Rawls, *A Theory of Justice*, p. 257.
10. Marx, *Capital*, vol. 1, p. 173.
11. Ibid., vol. 3, p. 959.
12. Rawls, *The Law of People*, p. 107n33.
13. Ibid.
14. Keynes, "Economic Possibilities of Our Grandchildren," p. 199.
15. Ibid.
16. Ibid., p. 201.
17. Ibid.
18. Ibid., p. 196.

19. Ibid.
20. Calnitsky, "Debating Basic Income," p. 3.
21. Ibid.
22. Ibid.
23. Ibid., p. 4.
24. Ibid., p. 18.
25. Ibid.
26. Ibid., p. 6.
27. Piketty, *Capital in the Twenty-First Century*, p. 571.
28. Ibid.
29. Ibid., p. 570.
30. Ibid., p. 10.
31. See Marx, *Capital*, vol. 3, chaps. 13–15, pp. 317–375.
32. Ibid., pp. 318–320.
33. Hayek, *The Road to Serfdom*, p. 124.
34. Ibid.
35. Ibid., p. 125.
36. Ibid., p. 130.
37. Ibid., p. 127.
38. Ibid.
39. Ibid., p. 124.
40. Hayek, "The Use of Knowledge in Society," p. 78.
41. Ibid., p. 79.
42. Ibid.
43. Ibid., p. 78.
44. Ibid., p. 80.
45. Ibid.
46. Hayek, *New Studies in Philosophy, Politics, Economics, and the History of Ideas*, p. 10.
47. Ibid., p. 63. For an excellent critical analysis of Hayek's notion of the sponta-
    neously formed order of the market, see Bernard E. Harcourt, *The Illusion of
    Free Markets*.
48. Ibid., p. 78.
49. Ibid., p. 86.
50. Ibid., p. 88.
51. Ibid., p. 87.
52. Hayek, *The Road to Serfdom*, p. 124.
53. Ibid., p. 126.
54. Ibid.
55. Ibid.
56. For Hayek's most comprehensive philosophical articulation of freedom in
    terms of liberty, see his book *The Constitution of Liberty*.
57. Marx, *Critique of the Gotha Program*, p. 615.
58. Adorno, "Free Time," 169.
59. Ibid., 171.
60. Ibid., 175.

61. Ibid., 168.

62. Ibid.

63. Ibid., 169.

64. Ibid.

65. Ibid., 170.

66. Ibid., 168.

67. Ibid., 169.

68. See, for example, Marx's *Economic and Philosophic Manuscripts of 1844* and his *Grundrisse*, p. 705.

69. Marx, *Economic and Philosophic Manuscripts of 1844*, p. 105.

70. See Hannah Arendt, *The Human Condition*, pp. 79–174; and Michel Henry, *Marx: A Philosophy of Human Reality*. The term "overabundance" is coined by Henry (pp. 198, 298, 305).

71. Adorno, "Something's Missing: A Discussion between Ernst Bloch and Theodor W. Adorno on the Contradictions of Utopian Longing," p. 10.

72. Ibid., p. 8.

73. Ibid., p. 10.

74. Adorno, in Adorno and Horkheimer, "Towards a New Manifesto?," p. 36.

75. Ibid.

76. Adorno, *Negative Dialectics*, p. 203.

77. See, for example, ibid., p. 207.

78. Adorno, "Free Time," p. 171.

79. Ibid., p. 172.

80. Ibid., p. 171.

81. My account of boredom is indebted to Heidegger's phenomenological analysis of boredom in *The Fundamental Concepts of Metaphysics: World, Finitude, Solitude*. In a forthcoming work, I will show that the three forms of boredom that Heidegger elucidates are constitutive conditions for being a person and leading a free life.

82. Adorno, in Adorno and Horkheimer, "Towards a New Manifesto?," p. 35.

83. Adorno, *Minima Moralia*, p. 157.

84. Ibid.

85. The insight that pure being is nothing—that pure light would be pure darkness, that pure life would be pure death—is one of the fundamental lessons of Hegel's logic. The reason we cannot grasp light without darkness—or life without death—is not because of any cognitive limitation on our part but because the idea of pure light or pure life is unintelligible. There cannot even in principle be light without darkness (or life without death). Only in "light determined through darkness"—only in "illuminated darkness"—can we see anything and make sense of anything (Hegel, *Science of Logic*, p. 69). While Adorno often addresses Hegel's philosophy, he denies the implications of Hegel's dialectical logic. According to Adorno, "dialectics is the ontology of the wrong state of things. The right state of things would be free of it" (*Negative Dialectics*, p. 11). This claim is an instructive example of how Adorno conflates conditions of intelligibility with historically specific conditions. If dialectical logic merely

reflects "the wrong state of things," then Adorno is committed to the view that the impossibility of pure being, pure light, and pure life is a lamentable restriction—the "wrong" condition to which we unfortunately are subjected—rather than a condition of intelligibility. Conversely, if "the right state of things" is defined as being "free" from dialectical conditions of intelligibility, then the right state of things for Adorno would be pure being: light without darkness and life without death. This is what I call Adorno's "religious" understanding of finitude as a negative limitation that blocks us from the absolute. As we will see, Hegel diagnoses this religious understanding of finitude as "the unhappy consciousness," which is an apt description of the pathos of Adorno's philosophy.

86. Ibid., p. 247.
87. Ibid.
88. Ibid.
89. Ibid.
90. Marx, "Contribution to the Critique of Hegel's *Philosophy of Right:* Introduction," p. 53.
91. Ibid., p. 54.
92. Ibid., p. 53.
93. Ibid.
94. Ibid.

CONCLUSION: OUR ONLY LIFE

1. See Michael K. Honey, *Going Down Jericho Road: The Memphis Strike, Martin Luther King's Last Campaign*, p. 288. See also David J. Garrow, *The FBI and Martin Luther King, Jr.: From "Solo" to Memphis.*
2. See Honey, *Going Down Jericho Road*, p. 289.
3. King, *Where Do We Go from Here: Chaos or Community?*, p. 5.
4. Ibid.
5. Ibid., pp. 5–6.
6. See Reed, "Black Particularity Reconsidered," p. 77.
7. King, *Where Do We Go from Here*, p. 6.
8. King, "Next Stop: The North," p. 189.
9. King, quoted in David J. Garrow, *Bearing the Cross: Martin Luther King, Jr. and the Southern Christian Leadership Conference*, p. 540.
10. King, "A New Sense of Direction," transcript available at www.carnegiecouncil .org/publications/articles_papers_reports/4960.
11. King, *The Trumpet of Conscience*, p. 16.
12. Ibid.
13. See Terry, "Requiem for a Dream: The Problem-Space of Black Power," pp. 290–324. See also King's own account of his organizing work in Chicago in *The Trumpet of Conscience*, pp. 55–61.
14. See Terry, "Requiem for a Dream: The Problem-Space of Black Power."
15. For analyses of King's Poor People's Campaign as a class movement, see Honey, *Going Down Jericho Road*; Douglas Sturm, "Martin Luther King, Jr. as Demo-

cratic Socialist"; and Stephen B. Oates, *Let the Trumpet Sound: The Life of Martin Luther King, Jr.*

16. King, quoted in Adam Fairclough, "Was Martin Luther King a Marxist?"

17. King, quoted in Garrow, *Bearing the Cross*, p. 537.

18. Ibid., p. 562.

19. King, quoted in Fairclough, "Was Martin Luther King a Marxist?," p. 120.

20. King, *Where Do We Go from Here?*, p. 250.

21. Ibid.

22. Ibid., p. 250.

23. Carl Wendell Hines, quoted in Vincent Gordon Harding, "Beyond Amnesia: Martin Luther King, Jr., and the Future of America."

24. Hosea Williams, quoted in Garrow, *Bearing the Cross*, p. 625.

25. King, "I Have a Dream," p. 217.

26. Ibid. For a lucid and valuable account of how King sought to radicalize the established historical conceptions of freedom that he inherited, see Richard H. King, *Civil Rights and the Idea of Freedom*, chapters 4 and 5.

27. King, "I Have a Dream," p. 217.

28. King, *Stride Toward Freedom*, p. 77.

29. King, "I Have a Dream," p. 217.

30. King, "The Other America," p. 164.

31. Ibid., pp. 164–165.

32. Ibid., p. 165.

33. Ibid., p. 157.

34. Ibid., p. 156.

35. Ibid., pp. 156–157.

36. King, "I am in one of those houses of labor to which I come not to criticize, but to praise," p. 51.

37. Ibid.

38. Luxemburg, *Reform or Revolution*, p. 3.

39. Ibid.

40. King, "A Time to Break Silence," p. 240.

41. King, quoted in Garrow, *Bearing the Cross*, p. 71.

42. King, "Hammer on Civil Rights," p. 169.

43. King, *Where Do We Go from Here*, p. 142.

44. King, quoted in Fairclough, "Was Martin Luther King a Marxist?," p. 123.

45. King, "A Time to Break Silence," p. 240.

46. The episode with the tape recorder is documented in Garrow, *Bearing the Cross*, pp. 591–592.

47. Marx, "Theses on Feuerbach," p. 145.

48. Marx, "For a Ruthless Criticism of Everything Existing," p. 13.

49. Ibid., p. 14.

50. Ibid.

51. Ibid., p. 15.

52. Ibid.

53. Ibid.

54. King, *Strength to Love*, p. 100.
55. Ibid., p. 101.
56. Ibid., p. 128.
57. Ibid., p. 129.
58. See John J. Ansbro, *Martin Luther King, Jr.: Nonviolent Strategies and Tactics for Social Change*, p. 122.
59. For a superb account of Hegel's life and the historical context of his work, see Terry Pinkard, *Hegel: A Biography*.
60. Kant, "What Is Enlightenment?," p. 54.
61. For the best account of how Kant's practical philosophy fundamentally transforms the philosophical problem of freedom by proceeding from a first-person standpoint, see Korsgaard, *The Sources of Normativity*, chapters 3 and 4, as well as chapter 13 of Korsgaard's *Creating the Kingdom of Ends*.
62. In his *Science of Logic*, Hegel makes clear that Kant's notion of self-consciousness ("apperception") is of crucial importance for his own thinking (see in particular *Science of Logic*, p. 515). This claim is at the center of Pippin's systematic reconstruction of Hegel's thinking, which was pioneered in Pippin's *Hegel's Idealism*. The most radical and important articulation of Pippin's argument regarding self-consciousness can be found in his *Hegel on Self-Consciousness*.
63. For Hegel's account of the relation between Enlightenment and Faith, see §§526–595 of his *Phenomenology of Spirit*. I am indebted to Robert Brandom's profound analysis of these parts of the *Phenomenology*; see Brandom, *A Spirit of Trust*, part 5, pp. 78–109.
64. For an illuminating account of Ella Baker and the feminist branches of the civil rights movement, see Barbara Ransby, *Ella Baker and the Black Freedom Movement: A Radical Democratic Vision*. For a nuanced and incisive analysis of King's gender politics, see Shatema Threadcraft and Brandon M. Terry, "Gender Trouble: Manhood, Inclusion, and Justice."
65. For Hegel's reading of the incarnation, see §§748–787 of his *Phenomenology of Spirit*, as well as the concluding chapter on "Absolute Knowing" (§§788–808). See also the concluding remarks on the Crucifixion in Hegel's early text *Faith and Knowledge*, pp. 190–191.
66. Hegel, *Phenomenology of Spirit*, §451.
67. Ibid.
68. See ibid., §196.
69. See ibid.
70. Ibid., §32.
71. Ibid.
72. Ibid., §§197–230.
73. Ibid., §199. For Hegel's critique of Spinoza, see also in particular his *Science of Logic*, pp. 465–505 and §151 of his *Encyclopedia Logic*.
74. For a related argument, see Martha Nussbaum's brilliant critical analysis of ancient Skepticism in *The Therapy of Desire*, chapter 8. While Nussbaum does not mention Hegel, her insights have deep affinities with his.
75. Luther, in *Martin Luthers Werke: Kritische Gesamtausgabe*, vol. 10.I, p. 208.

76. See Hegel, *Phenomenology of Spirit*, §§788–808.
77. Hegel, *Philosophy of Right*, §123A. The full sentence reads: "There is nothing degrading about being alive, and we do not have the alternative of existing in a higher spirituality." Hegel's subordinate clause is potentially misleading, since it can give the impression that he is holding out the possibility of a "higher spirituality" that is inaccessible for us but which in and for itself would not be subject to the conditions of life. As Hegel makes clear elsewhere, however, life is an essential condition for any form of freedom and spiritual existence. The lesson of Hegel's famous master-slave dialectic is that "self-consciousness learns that life is as essential to it as is pure self-consciousness" (*Phenomenology of Spirit*, §189; see also his *Berlin Phenomenology*, §432). The inseparability of the conditions of life from any conception of "the good" is established on the highest level in Hegel's system in the final book of his *Science of Logic*.
78. For a detailed account of the Memphis strike and its historical context, see Honey's indispensable book, *Going Down Jericho Road*.
79. King, quoted in Garrow, *Bearing the Cross*, p. 606.
80. Lawson, quoted in Honey, *Going Down Jericho Road*, p. 296.
81. The term "spiritual cause" was coined by Jensen Suther in the context of rethinking Hegel's notion of causality; see Suther, "Hegel's Materialism." My own development of the notion in relation to secular faith is part of our ongoing philosophical dialogue.
82. King, *Strength to Love*, pp. 128–129.
83. Ibid., p. 129.
84. Ibid., p. 83.
85. Ibid., p. 129.
86. King, quoted in Garrow, *Bearing the Cross*, p. 39.
87. Ibid., p. 37.
88. King, "I See the Promised Land," p. 282.
89. Ibid., p. 286.
90. Honey, *Going Down Jericho Road*, pp. 303–304.
91. Honey, in King, *"All Labor Has Dignity,"* edited and introduced by Michael K. Honey, p. 170.
92. Klein, *This Changes Everything: Capitalism vs. the Climate*, p. 450.
93. Ibid., p. 25.
94. Ibid., p. 460.
95. Ibid., p. 461.
96. Ibid., p. 22.
97. Ibid., p. 18.
98. Fanon, *The Wretched of the Earth*, p. 55; quoted in ibid., p. 459.

Bibliography

In some cases, I have modified or altered the existing English translations of Augustine's Latin, Hegel's and Marx's German, Kierkegaard's Danish, Proust's French, and Knausgaard's Norwegian. I list here the original editions of their work on which I have relied, along with the English translations that I cite in the text.

Adorno, Theodor W. "Free Time" In Adorno, *Critical Models,* translated by Henry Pickford. New York: Columbia University Press, 2005.
———. *Negative Dialectics.* Translated by E. B. Ashton. New York: Continuum, 1973.
———. *Minima Moralia.* Translated by E. F. N. Jephcott. London: Verso, 2005.
———. "Something's Missing: A Discussion between Ernst Bloch and Theodor W. Adorno on the Contradictions of Utopian Longing." In Bloch, *The Utopian Function of Art and Literature,* translated by Jack Zipes and Frank Mecklenburg. Cambridge, MA: MIT Press, 1989.
Adorno, Theodor W., and Max Horkheimer. "Towards a New Manifesto?" *New Left Review* 65 (2010), pp. 34–61.
Ansbro, John J. *Martin Luther King, Jr.: Nonviolent Strategies and Tactics for Social Change.* New York: Madison Books, 2000.
Arendt, Hannah. *The Human Condition.* Chicago: University of Chicago Press, 1998.
———. *Love and Saint Augustine.* Edited by Joanna Vecchiarelli Scott and Judith Chelius Stark. Chicago: University of Chicago Press, 1996.
Aristotle. *Nicomachean Ethics.* Translated by Terence Irwin. Bloomington, IN: Hackett, 1999.
———. *The Art of Rhetoric.* Edited and translated by Hugh Lawson-Tancred. New York: Penguin Classics, 1992.
———. *Politics.* Translated by Ernest Barker. Oxford: Oxford University Press, 2009.

————. *De Anima*. Translated by Hugh Lawson-Tancred. New York: Penguin Classics, 1987.

Augustine. *Confessiones*. Cambridge, MA: Harvard University Press, 1912.

————. *Confessions*. Translated by Rex Warner. New York: New American Library, 1963.

————. *Eighty-three Different Questions*. Translated by David L. Mosher. Washington, DC: Catholic University of America Press, 1982.

————. *On Faith in Things Unseen*. Translated by Roy J. Deferrari and Mary Francis McDonald. New York: Fathers of the Church, Christian Heritage, Inc., 1947.

————. *On Free Choice of the Will*. Translated by Thomas Williams. Bloomington, IN: Hackett, 1993.

————. *The City of God*. Translated by Henry Bettenson. New York: Penguin Classics, 2003.

Berlin, Isaiah. "Two Concepts of Liberty." In Berlin, *Liberty*, edited by Henry Hardy. Oxford: Oxford University Press, 2002.

Bernstein, J. M. "To Be Is to Live, to Be Is to Be Recognized." In *Torture and Dignity: An Essay on Moral Injury*. Chicago: University of Chicago Press, 2015, pp. 175–217.

————. "Remembering Isaac: On the Impossibility and Immorality of Faith." In *The Insistence of Art: Aesthetic Politics After Early Modernity*. Edited by Paul Kottman. New York: Fordham University Press, 2017, pp. 257–288.

Björk, Nina. *Drömmen om det röda: Rosa Luxemburg, socialism, språk och kärlek* [*The Dream of the Red: Rosa Luxemburg, Socialism, Language, and Love*]. Stockholm: Wahlström & Widstrand, 2016.

————. *Lyckliga i alla sina dagar: Om pengars och människors värde* [*Living Happily Ever After: On the Value of Money and Human Beings*]. Stockholm: Wahlström & Widstrand, 2012.

Böhm-Bawerk, Eugen. *Karl Marx and the Close of His System*. Edited by Paul Sweezy. Clifton, NJ: Kelley, 1975.

Brandom, Robert. "The Structure of Desire and Recognition: Self-Consciousness and Self-Constitution." In *Philosophy and Social Criticism*, Vol 33, no. 1: 127–150.

————. *A Spirit of Trust*. http://www.pitt.edu/~brandom/spirit_of_trust_2014.html.

Calnitsky, David. "Debating Basic Income." *Catalyst* 1, no. 3: (2017).

Collins, Steven. *Nirvana: Concept, Imagery, Narrative*. Cambridge: Cambridge University Press, 2010.

————. "What Are Buddhists *Doing* When They Deny the Self?" In Collins, *Religion and Practical Reason: New Essays in the Comparative Philosophy of Religions*. Albany: State University of New York Press, 1994, pp. 59–86.

Coogan, Michael D. *The New Oxford Annotated Bible*. Oxford: Oxford University Press, 1989.

Dante. *The Divine Comedy*. Edited and translated by Robin Kirkpatrick. New York: Penguin, 2012.

Davenport, John. "Faith as Eschatological Trust in *Fear and Trembling*." In *Ethics, Faith, and Love in Kierkegaard*, edited by Edward Mooney. Bloomington: Indiana University Press, 2008, pp. 196–233.

————. "Kierkegaard's Postscript in Light of Fear and Trembling." *Revista Portuguesa de Filosofia* 64, nos. 1–2 (Dec. 2008), pp. 879–908.

————. "Eschatological Faith and Repetition: Kierkegaard's Abraham and Job." In *Kierkegaard's* Fear and Trembling: *A Critical Guide*, edited by Daniel Conway. Cambridge: Cambridge University Press, 2015, pp. 97–105.

Dennett, Daniel. *Breaking the Spell: Religion as a Natural Phenomenon*. New York: Penguin, 2006.

Dreyfus, Hubert. "Kierkegaard on the Self." In *Ethics, Faith, and Love in Kierkegaard*, edited by Edward Mooney. Bloomington: Indiana University Press, 2008, pp. 11–23.

Dreyfus, Hubert, and Sean Dorrance Kelly. *All Things Shining: Reading the Western Classics to Find Meaning in a Secular Age*. New York: Free Press, 2011.

Dreyfus, Hubert, and Jane Rubin. "Kierkegaard, Division II, and the Later Heidegger." In Dreyfus, *Being-in-the-World*. Cambridge, MA: MIT Press, 1991, pp. 293–340.

Epictetus. *The Discourses*. Edited by Christopher Gill. Translated by Robin Hard. London: Everyman Library, 1995.

Fairclough, Adam. "Was Martin Luther King a Marxist?" *History Workshop Journal* 15, no. 1 (1983): 117–125.

Fanon, Frantz. *The Wretched of the Earth*. Translated by Richard Philcox. New York: Grove Press, 2004.

Garff, Joakim. *Søren Kierkegaard: A Biography*. Translated by Bruce H. Kirmmse. Princeton, NJ: Princeton University Press, 2005.

Garrow, David J. *The FBI and Martin Luther King, Jr.: From "Solo" to Memphis*. New York: Penguin Books, 1983.

————. *Bearing the Cross: Martin Luther King, Jr. and the Southern Christian Leadership Conference*. New York: William Morrow, 1986.

Gordon, Peter E. "Critical Theory Between the Sacred and the Profane." *Constellations* 23, no. 4 (2016): 466–481.

————. "The Place of the Sacred in the Absence of God: Charles Taylor's *A Secular Age*." *Journal of the History of Ideas*, 69, no. 4 (2008): 647–673.

Hägglund, Martin. *Dying for Time: Proust, Woolf, Nabokov*. Cambridge, MA: Harvard University Press, 2012.

Harcourt, Bernard E. *The Illusion of Free Markets: Punishment and the Myth of Natural Order*. Cambridge, MA: Harvard University Press, 2011.

Harding, Vincent Gordon. "Beyond Amnesia: Martin Luther King, Jr., and the Future of America." *Journal of American History* 74, no. 2 (1987): 468–476.

Hayek, Friedrich. *The Road to Serfdom*. Edited by Bruce Caldwell. Chicago: University of Chicago Press, 2007.

————. "The Use of Knowledge in Society." In *Individualism and Economic Order*. Chicago: University of Chicago Press, 1948.

————. *The Constitution of Liberty*. Edited by Ronald Hamowy. Chicago: University of Chicago Press, 2011.

————. *New Studies in Philosophy, Politics, Economics, and the History of Ideas*. Chicago: University of Chicago Press, 1978.

Hegel, G. W. F. *The Berlin Phenomenology.* Translated by Michael Petry. Dordrecht, Netherlands: Reidel, 1981.

―――. *Elements of the Philosophy of Right.* Edited by Allen Wood. Translated by H. B. Nisbet. Cambridge: Cambridge University Press, 1991.

―――. *Faith and Knowledge.* Translated by Walter Cerf and H. S. Harris. Albany: State University of New York Press, 1977.

―――. *Philosophy of Nature.* Translated by A.V. Findlay. Oxford: Oxford University Press, 2004.

―――. *The Encyclopedia Logic.* Translated by H. S. Harris. Bloomington, IN: Hackett, 1991.

―――. *The Phenomenology of Spirit.* Translated by Terry Pinkard. Cambridge: Cambridge University Press, 2018.

―――. *The Science of Logic.* Translated by George di Giovanni. Cambridge: Cambridge University Press, 2010.

―――. *Die Phänomenologie des Geistes.* Hamburg: Felix Meiner, 1999.

―――. *Wissenschaft der Logik.* 2 vols. Hamburg: Felix Meiner, 1969.

Heidegger, Martin. *Being and Time.* Translated by John Macquarrie and Edward Robinson. New York: Harper & Row, 1962.

―――. *The Fundamental Concepts of Metaphysics: World, Finitude, Solitude.* Translated by William McNeill and Nicholas Walker. Bloomington: Indiana University Press, 1995.

―――. *Sein und Zeit.* Tübingen, Germany: Niemeyer, 1972.

Henry, Michel. *Marx: A Philosophy of Human Reality.* Translated by Kathleen MacLaughlin. Bloomington: Indiana University Press, 1983.

Honey, Michael K. *Going Down Jericho Road: The Memphis Strike, Martin Luther King's Last Campaign.* New York: W. W. Norton, 2007.

James, William. *The Varieties of Religious Experience.* New York: Penguin Classics, 1982.

Jameson, Fredric. *An American Utopia: Dual Power and the Universal Army.* London: Verso, 2016.

Jevons, William Stanley. *The Theory of Political Economy.* New York: Macmillan, 1931.

Kant, Immanuel. *Critique of Pure Reason.* Translated by Paul Guyer and Allen Wood. Cambridge: Cambridge University Press, 1999.

―――. *Critique of Practical Reason.* Translated by Mary Gregor. Cambridge: Cambridge University Press, 2015.

―――. *Critique of Judgment.* Translated by Werner S. Pluhar. Bloomington, IN: Hackett Classics, 1987.

―――. "What Is Enlightenment?." In Kant, *Political Writings,* edited by H. S. Reiss. Cambridge: Cambridge University Press, 1991.

Keynes, John Maynard. "Economic Possibilities for Our Grandchildren." In *The Essential Keynes.* Edited by Robert Skidelsky. New York: Penguin Classics, 2016, pp. 560–585.

Kierkegaard, Søren. *Samlede Vaerker.* 20 vols. Copenhagen: Gyldendal, 1962–1964.

―――. *Christian Discourses.* Edited and translated by Howard V. Hong and Edna H. Hong. Princeton, NJ: Princeton University Press, 1997.

————. *Concluding Unscientific Postscript.* 2 vols. Edited and translated by Howard V. Hong and Edna H. Hong. Princeton, NJ: Princeton University Press, 1992.

————. *Eighteen Upbuilding Discourses.* Edited and translated by Howard V. Hong and Edna H. Hong. Princeton, NJ: Princeton University Press, 1990.

————. *Fear and Trembling.* Edited and translated by Howard V. Hong and Edna H. Hong. Princeton, NJ: Princeton University Press, 1983.

————. *The Concept of Anxiety.* Translated by Alastair Hannay. New York: W. W. Norton, 2014.

————. *The Sickness unto Death.* Edited and translated by Howard V. Hong and Edna H. Hong. Princeton, NJ: Princeton University Press, 1980.

————. *Søren Kierkegaard's Journals and Papers.* Vol. 1. Edited and translated by Howard V. Hong and Edna H. Hong. Bloomington: Indiana University Press, 1967.

————. "At a Graveside." In *Three Discourses on Imagined Occasions,* edited and translated by Howard V. Hong and Edna H. Hong. Princeton, NJ: Princeton University Press, 1993, pp. 71–102.

————. "On the Occasion of a Wedding." In *Three Discourses on Imagined Occasions,* edited and translated by Howard V. Hong and Edna H. Hong. Princeton, NJ: Princeton University Press, 1993, pp. 43–68.

King, Martin Luther, Jr. *Stride Toward Freedom: The Montgomery Story.* Boston: Beacon Press, 2010.

————. *Strength to Love.* Minneapolis: Fortress Press, 2010.

————. *Where Do We Go from Here: Chaos or Community?.* Boston: Beacon Press, 2010.

————. *The Trumpet of Conscience.* Boston: Beacon Press, 2010.

————. "I Have a Dream." In *A Testament of Hope: The Essential Writings and Speeches of Martin Luther King, Jr.* Edited by James M. Washington. New York: HarperCollins, 1986, pp. 217–220.

————. "Next Stop: The North." In *A Testament of Hope,* pp. 189–194.

————. "Where Do We Go from Here?." In *A Testament of Hope,* pp. 245–252.

————. "A Time to Break Silence." In *A Testament of Hope,* pp. 231–244.

————. "Hammer on Civil Rights." In *A Testament of Hope,* pp. 169–175.

————. "I See the Promised Land." In *A Testament of Hope,* pp. 279–286.

————. "The Other America." In *"All Labor Has Dignity,"* edited by Michael K. Honey. Boston: Beacon Press, 2011, pp. 155–166.

————. "I am in one of those houses of labor to which I come not to criticize, but to praise." In *"All Labor Has Dignity,"* pp. 49–54.

————. "A New Sense of Direction." Transcript available at www.carnegiecouncil.org/publications/articles_.papers_reports/4960.

King, Richard H. *Civil Rights and the Idea of Freedom.* Athens: University of Georgia Press, 1992.

Klein, Naomi. *This Changes Everything: Capitalism vs. the Climate.* New York: Simon & Schuster, 2014.

Knausgaard, Karl Ove. *Min kamp: Sjette bok.* Oslo: Forlaget Oktober, 2012.

————. *My Struggle: Book One.* Translated by Don Bartlett. New York: Farrar, Straus & Giroux, 2013.

————. *My Struggle: Book Two.* Translated by Don Bartlett. New York: Farrar, Straus & Giroux, 2014.

————. *My Struggle: Book Three.* Translated by Don Bartlett. New York: Farrar, Straus & Giroux, 2015.

Korsgaard, Christine. *The Sources of Normativity.* Cambridge: Cambridge University Press, 1996.

————. *Creating the Kingdom of Ends.* Cambridge: Cambridge University Press, 1996.

————. *The Constitution of Agency: Essays on Practical Reason and Moral Psychology.* Oxford: Oxford University Press, 2008

————. *Self-Constitution: Agency, Identity, and Integrity.* Oxford: Oxford University Press, 2009.

Krishek, Sharon. "The Existential Dimension of Faith," in *Kierkegaard's* "Fear and Trembling": *A Critical Guide.* Edited by Daniel Conway. Cambridge: Cambridge University Press, 2015.

Lewis, C.S. *A Grief Observed.* San Francisco: HarperCollins, 1996.

Lippitt, John. *Kierkegaard and* "Fear and Trembling." London: Routledge, 2003.

Luther, Martin. *The Letters of Martin Luther.* Selected and Translated by Margaret A. Currie. London: Macmillan, 1908.

————. *Luther's Catechetical Writings,* 2 volumes. Translated by J. N. Lenker. Minneapolis: Luther Press, 1907.

————. *Martin Luthers Werke: Kritische Gesamtausgabe.* Weimar: 1883–2009.

Luxemburg, Rosa. *Reform or Revolution.* In *Reform or Revolution and Other Writings.* New York: Dover, 2006.

————. *The Russian Revolution,* in *Reform or Revolution and Other Writings.* New York: Dover, 2006.

Marcus Aurelius. *Meditations.* Edited and translated by Gregory Hays. New York: Modern Library, 2002.

Marx, Karl. *Marx-Engels Werke.* Vols. 1–42. Berlin: Karl Dietz Verlag, 1956–1981.

————. *Economic and Philosophic Manuscripts of 1844.* In *The Marx Reader,* translated by Martin Milligan, edited by Robert C. Tucker. New York: W. W. Norton, 1978, pp. 67–125.

————. "Discovering Hegel." In *The Marx Reader,* pp. 7–8.

————. "The German Ideology." In *The Marx Reader,* pp. 147–200.

————. "Contribution to the Critique of Hegel's *Philosophy of Right:* Introduction." In *The Marx Reader,* pp. 16–25.

————. "Theses on Feuerbach." In *The Marx Reader,* pp. 143–145.

————. "For a Ruthless Criticism of Everything Existing." In *The Marx Reader,* pp. 12–15.

————. *Critique of the Gotha Program.* In *Karl Marx: Selected Writings,* edited by David McLellan. Oxford: Oxford University Press, 2000, pp. 525–541.

————. *Critique of Hegel's Doctrine of the State.* Translated by Rodney Livingston and Gregor Benton. New York: Vintage, 1975.

————. *Grundrisse.* Translated by Martin Nicolaus. New York: Penguin Classics, 1973.

————. *Capital*. Vol. 1. Translated by Ben Fowkes. New York: Penguin Classics, 1980.

————. *Capital*. Vol. 2. Translated by David Fernbach. New York: Penguin Classics, 1992.

————. *Capital*. Vol. 3. Translated by David Fernbach. New York: Penguin Classics, 1991.

McDowell, John. *Mind and World*. Cambridge, MA: Harvard University Press, 1996.

————. *Mind, Value, and Reality*. Cambridge, MA: Harvard University Press, 2001.

————. *The Engaged Intellect*. Cambridge, MA: Harvard University Press, 2013.

————. "Why Does It Matter to Hegel that Geist Has a History?" In *Hegel on Philosophy in History*, edited by James Kreines and Rachel Zuckert. Cambridge, Cambridge University Press, 2017, pp. 15–32.

Meister Eckhart. "Detachment." In *The Best of Meister Eckhart*, edited by H. Backhouse. New York: Crossroad, 1993.

Menger, Carl. *Principles of Economics*. New York: New York University Press, 1981.

Mill, John Stuart. *On Liberty*. Edited by Elizabeth Rapaport. Bloomington, IN: Hackett, 1978.

————. *Principles of Political Economy*. Oxford: Oxford University Press, 1994.

Mooney, Edward. *Knights of Faith and Resignation: Reading Kierkegaard's "Fear and Trembling."* Albany: State University of New York Press, 1991.

Neuhouser, Frederick. *Foundations of Hegel's Social Theory: Actualizing Freedom*. Cambridge, MA: Harvard University Press, 2003.

Nietzsche, Friedrich. *The Gay Science*. Edited by Bernard Williams. Translated by Josefine Nauckhoff. Cambridge: Cambridge University Press, 2001.

————. *Ecce Homo*. In *On the Genealogy of Morals and Ecce Homo*, edited and translated by Walter Kaufmann. New York: Vintage, 1989, pp. 217–338.

Nightingale, Andrea. *Once Out of Nature: Augustine on Time and the Body*. Chicago: University of Chicago Press, 2011.

Nussbaum, Martha. *The Therapy of Desire: Theory and Practice in Hellenistic Ethics*. Princeton, NJ: Princeton University Press, 1994.

————. *Upheavals of Thought: The Intelligence of Emotions*. Cambridge: Cambridge University Press, 2001.

Nygren, Anders. *Agape and Eros*. Translated by Philip S. Watson. New York: Harper & Row, 1953.

Oates, Stephen B. *Let the Trumpet Sound: The Life of Martin Luther King, Jr.* New York: HarperPerennial, 2013.

Piketty, Thomas. *Capital in the Twenty-First Century*. Cambridge, MA: Harvard University Press, 2014.

Pinkard, Terry. *Hegel: A Biography*. Cambridge: Cambridge University Press, 2000.

————. *Does History Make Sense? Hegel on the Historical Shapes of Justice*. Cambridge: Cambridge University Press, 2017.

Pippin, Robert. *Hegel's Idealism*. Cambridge: Cambridge University Press, 1989.

————. *Idealism as Modernism: Hegelian Variations*. Cambridge: Cambridge University Press, 1997.

———. *Hegel's Practical Philosophy.* Cambridge: Cambridge University Press, 2008.

———. *Hegel on Self-Consciousness.* Princeton, NJ: Princeton University Press, 2011.

———. "Hegel's Logic of Essence." In *Schelling-Studien*, Bd. 1, 2013, pp. 73–96.

———. "The Many Modalities of *Wirklichkeit* in Hegel's Science of Logic." In *Hegel: Une pensée de l'objectivité*, edited by J. Seba and G. Lejeune. Paris: Éditions Kimé, 2017, pp. 13–32.

———. "Hegel on Logic as Metaphysics." In *The Oxford Handbook to Hegel*. Edited by Dean Moyar. Oxford: Oxford University Press, 2017, pp. 199–218.

Postone, Moishe. "Necessity, Labor, and Time: A Reinterpretation of the Marxian Critique of Capitalism." *Social Research* 45, no. 4 (1978): 739–788.

———. *Time, Labor, and Social Domination: A Reinterpretation of Marx's Critical Theory.* Cambridge: Cambridge University Press, 1993.

Proust, Marcel. *À la recherche du temps perdu.* Vol. 3. Edited by J-Y Tadié. Paris: Gallimard, 1988.

———. *À la recherche du temps perdu.* Vol. 4. Edited by J-Y Tadié. Paris: Gallimard, 1988.

———. *Sodom and Gomorrah.* Translated by John Sturrock. New York: Penguin, 2002.

———. *Finding Time Again.* Translated by Ian Patterson. New York: Penguin, 2003.

Quine, Willard Van Orman. *Word and Object.* Cambridge, MA: MIT Press, 2013.

Ransby, Barbara. *Ella Baker and the Black Freedom Movement: A Radical Democratic Vision.* Chapel Hill: University of North Carolina Press, 2005.

Rawls. John. *A Theory of Justice.* Rev. ed. Cambridge, MA: Harvard University Press, 1999.

———. *The Law of Peoples.* Cambridge, MA: Harvard University Press, 1999.

Reed, Adolph, Jr. "Black Particularity Reconsidered." *Telos*, no. 39 (1979): 71–93.

Reginster, Bernard. *The Affirmation of Life: Nietzsche on Overcoming Nihilism.* Cambridge, MA: Harvard University Press, 2006.

Robbins, Bruce. "Enchantment? No, Thank You!" In *The Joy of Secularism: 11 Essays for How We Live Now*, edited by George Levine. Princeton, NJ: Princeton University Press, 2012, pp. 74–94.

Roberts, William. *Marx's Inferno: The Political Theory of Capital.* Princeton, NJ: Princeton University Press, 2017.

Rödl, Sebastian. *Self-Consciousness.* Cambridge, MA: Harvard University Press, 2007.

Scheffler, Samuel. *Death and the Afterlife.* Oxford: Oxford University Press, 2013.

———. *Equality and Tradition: Questions of Value in Moral and Political Theory.* Oxford: Oxford University Press, 2010.

Seneca. *Dialogues and Essays.* Translated by John Davie. Oxford: Oxford University Press, 2007.

Singer, Tania: "Empathy and Compassion." In *Current Biology*, vol. 25, no. 18, pp. 1–4.

———. "What Type of Meditation Is Best for You?" In *Greater Good Magazine*, July 2, 2018.

Spinoza. "A Portrait of the Philosopher as a Young Man" In *The Spinoza Reader: The*

Ethics and Other Works, edited and translated by Edwin Curley. Princeton, NJ: Princeton University Press, 1994, pp. 3–6.

———. *The Ethics.* In *The Spinoza Reader,* pp. 85–265.

Staten, Henry. *Eros in Mourning.* Baltimore: Johns Hopkins University Press, 1995.

Stork, Theophilus, ed. *The Life of Martin Luther and the Reformation in Germany.* New York: Wenthworth Press, 2016.

Sturm, Douglas. "Martin Luther King, Jr. as Democratic Socialist." *Journal of Religious Ethics* 18, no. 2 (1990): 79–105.

Suther, Jensen. "Hegel's Logic of Freedom." Manuscript under review.

———. "Hegel's Materialism." Manuscript under review.

———. *Spirit Disfigured: The Persistence of Freedom in Modernist Literature and Philosophy.* Dissertation, Department of Comparative Literature, Yale University, 2019.

Taylor, Charles. *A Secular Age.* Cambridge, MA: Harvard University Press, 2007.

Terry, Brandon M. "Requiem for a Dream: The Problem-Space of Black Power." In *To Shape a New World: Essays on the Political Philosophy of Martin Luther King, Jr.,* edited by Tommie Shelby and Brandon M. Terry. Cambridge, MA: Harvard University Press, 2018, pp. 290–324.

Thompson, Michael. *Life and Action: Elementary Structures of Practice and Practical Thought.* Cambridge, MA: Harvard University Press, 2008.

Threadcract, Shatema, and Brandon M. Terry. "Gender Trouble: Manhood, Inclusion, and Justice." In *To Shape a New World,* pp. 205–235.

Tillich, Paul. *Dynamics of Faith.* New York: Harper One, 2009.

Uebel, Thomas. E. *Otto Neurath: Philosophy Between Science and Politics.* Cambridge: Cambridge University Press, 2008.

Varoufakis, Yanis. "Introduction." In Marx and Engels, *The Communist Manifesto.* London: Vintage, 2018, pp. vii–xxix.

Volf, Miroslav. "Time, Eternity, and the Prospects for Care." *Evangelische Theologie* 76, no. 5 (2013): 345–354.

Weber, Max. "Science as a Vocation." In *The Vocation Lectures,* edited by David Owen and Tracy B. Strong, translated by Rodney Livingstone. Bloomington, IN: Hackett, 2004.

———. *Gesammelte politische Schriften [Collected Political Writings].* Edited by Johannes Winckelmann. Stuttgart: UTB, 1988.

Westphal, Merold. *Kierkegaard's Concept of Faith.* Cambridge: Eerdmans Publishing Company, 2014.

Zuckerman, Phil. *Living the Secular Life: New Answers to Old Questions.* New York: Penguin, 2014.

Acknowledgments

During the six years of working on this book, I have had the good fortune of being a part of Yale University, which allows me to spend my life doing what I love: writing, reading, and teaching in the humanities. I want to thank my students, from whom I continue to learn and who inspire me to try to be the best person I can be.

Dudley Andrew and Howard Bloch led the search committee that brought me to Yale, where the gift of tenure made possible the range and ambition of this book, and where the freedom I have been granted means that all failures or shortcomings are genuinely my own. Much of the writing was done during two periods of research leave and I want to thank Tamar Gendler, Amy Hungerford, and Emily Bakemeier for their great leadership in the Faculty of Arts and Sciences. Among my many outstanding colleagues, I extend my deepest gratitude to Bryan Garsten, David Grewal, Sam Moyn, and David Bromwich—all of whom participated in a day-long workshop on a complete draft of the manuscript. Their incisive feedback greatly improved the final version of the book and I am truly blessed to have such brilliant and generous colleagues. David Grewal also deserves a second mention for being a great friend for almost a decade and for so generously hosting me, together with Daniela Cammack, in their beautiful home in New Haven, now further illuminated by the arrival of their amazing daughter, Artemis.

Numerous friends outside of Yale also helped along the way. Jonathan Culler, Elaine Scarry, Bill Todd, Richard Klein, and Derek Attridge have provided invaluable support of my career for many years now and I cannot thank them enough for the path they have made possible for me, as well as for the inspiration they have provided through their own work. Since 2015, I have been sharing dinners with Taylor Carman in New York on a regular basis. As it should be in any true philosophical friendship, both our agreements and our disagreements have been profoundly illuminating and I thank Taylor for bringing much joy into my life as well as for making this a better book through our vigorous arguments. Klas Molde in turn read drafts of all the chapters of the book with great acumen and I am thankful for our stimulating personal as well as intellectual conversations.

At an early stage of my study of Hegel, many discussions with Rocío Zambrana were important and I am grateful for the philosophical friendship we shared. A very rigorous reading group on *Fear and Trembling* with Noreen Khawaja launched my chapter on Kierkegaard, while conversations with Ben Lerner in the summers of 2016 and 2017 encouraged me to pursue my arguments regarding Marx all the way. Since 2016, Philip Huff has been a dear friend in New York and I am indebted to his feedback on the chapters of the book. I have also benefitted from exchanges and conversations with David Quint, Tony Kronman, Rob Lehman, Audrey Wasser, Thomas Khurana, Andy Werner, Uri Rosenshine, Hans Ruin, Sam Haddad, Miroslav Volf, Michael Clune, Sara Heinämaa, and Paul Kottman. While Noah Feldman has not read this manuscript, I hope he will recognize how my arguments respond to a remarkable set of conversations we had in 2011.

The writing of the book was generously supported both by a Guggenheim Fellowship and a Bogliasco Fellowship. At the stunning Bogliasco Foundation in Italy, I was given free time to write under optimal circumstances, thanks to the gracious leadership of Laura Harrison, Ivana Folle, Alessandra Natale, and Valeria Soave, as well as all the staff members. I also benefitted from many conversations with my excellent co-fellows and especially from discussions with Eric Moe and Tania Singer. At the Yale Divinity School, chapters from *This Life* have been assigned for the annual syllabus of the "Life Worth Living" course and it has been an honor for me to visit the class to discuss my work. I have also had the privilege of presenting parts of the book at Harvard University, Cornell University, Dartmouth College, Fordham University, Duquesne University, South Stockholm University, the New School for Social Research, and the Yale Law School. At all these institutions, I learned a lot from engaged audiences and interlocutors. A very special thank you is due to Damian Stocking and Sydney Mitsunaga-Whitten for an extraordinary seminar on my work at Occidental College in Los Angeles. I also want to thank Sydney for many insightful philosophical and literary conversations over the years.

This book could not have found a better editor than Gerry Howard, who has both given me the freedom to pursue my ideas and reigned me in when necessary. I have learned a tremendous amount from working with Gerry, whose editorial insights and impeccable sense of style has made this a better book than it otherwise would have been. From the beginning, my brilliant agent Kim Witherspoon has understood the kind of book this wants to be and she has always been ready to offer sage advice when needed.

As always, the love of my parents, Hans-Lennart and Margareta, and my sisters, Maria and Karin, has supported me in more ways than I can express. I am also grateful to Jing Tsu for what we shared during several years and I thank her for reading drafts of the first two chapters.

Four persons have meant the most for the genesis and the completion of this book. Ever since I first arrived in the United States in 2002, the presence of David E. Johnson in my life has sustained me in more ways than I can say. Even though we now live far away from each other, the joy, trust, love, and shared philosophical passion of our friendship is always only a phone call away. David has read every page of this book with exacting care. Both my life and my writing are better thanks to him.

My friendship with Adam Kelly is for me a continuous experience of secular grace: something that cannot be expected or asked for but which transforms one's life. To spend time with Adam is to be recalled to why literature and philosophy speaks to the most important questions of our lives. His faith in what this book can be has meant the world to me and his detailed, precise comments improved the entire manuscript, while also pushing me to develop further several of the central arguments.

In terms of philosophical insight, no one has contributed more to this book than Jensen Suther. While I have technically been his teacher and dissertation advisor, I have learned more about the philosophical and political notion of freedom from Jensen than from any other person in my life. Together we have studied Hegel's *Phenomenology* and *Science of Logic*—including many memorable hours discussing the logical status of pain in Hegel's *Begriffslogik*—as well as seminal works by Kant, Heidegger, Marx, Korsgaard, Pippin, Brandom, McDowell, and many others. *This Life* simply would not be what it is without Jensen and our ongoing conversation.

The easiest sentence to write in this book was the dedication to Niklas Brismar Pålsson, who has been my best friend since we met as teenagers in Sweden. While being separated by the Atlantic for most of the year, we are close in every aspect of our lives. Our philosophical and existential dialogue (in my afternoon and his evening, in my late night and his early morning) has been my greatest treasure as well as my most important lifeline during the writing of this book. When trying to explain my friendship with Niklas, I can only translate Montaigne into the present tense: "Because it is him, because it is me."

At the final stages of writing, Alisa Zhulina came into my life and transformed everything in my world from reality to actuality. Her questions about my vision of democratic socialism led me to expand my arguments and her own work as both a playwright and scholar remains an inspiration. First and last, our life together recalls me to the heart of this book, since being with Alisa is a daily reminder that a shared, finite life is infinitely precious.

Index